CUBAN LANDSCAPES

CUBAN LANDSCAPES

Heritage, Memory, and Place

Joseph L. Scarpaci
Armando H. Portela

THE GUILFORD PRESS
New York   London

Para Michael Joseph,
para que conozcas parte de tu herencia cultural
—J. L. S.

Para Leví Marrero
—A. H. P.

© 2009 The Guilford Press
A Division of Guilford Publications, Inc.
72 Spring Street, New York, NY 10012
www.guilford.com

Printed in the United States of America

This book is printed on acid-free paper.

Last digit is print number: 9   8   7   6   5   4   3   2   1

Library of Congress Cataloging-in-Publication Data
Scarpaci, Joseph L.
  Cuban landscapes : heritage, memory, and place / by Joseph L. Scarpaci,
Armando H. Portela.
     p. cm.–(Texts in regional geography)
  Includes bibliographical references and index.
  ISBN 978-1-60623-323-8 (pbk.)–ISBN 978-1-60623-324-5 (hardcover)
  1. Cuba—Geography.   2. Landscape—Cuba.   3. Landscape—Social
aspects—Cuba.   4. National identity, Cuban.   I. Portela, Armando.   II. Title.
  F1760.9.S33 2009
  917.291′02—dc22
                                                              2009011223

PREFACE

Studying landscapes is messy going. Landscapes have multiple meanings that require individual interpretation: Each observer of landscape brings his or her life experiences and subjectivity to bear on extracting meaning. In this regard, landscapes can be thought of (conceptualized) as a sort of text that can be read and deciphered, encoded and decoded. Accordingly, our landscape-as-text approach means that we serve as writers who bring our own backgrounds, experiences inside and outside Cuba, to give meaning for the readers of our book. We approach Cuban landscapes by enlisting in the seven chapters of this book a human–environmental approach that reflects our backgrounds as a human geographer (J. L. S.) and a physical geographer (A. H. P.). We draw on selected literatures that, we hope, will help the reader. Perhaps the Cuban scholar Fernando Ortíz said it best when he described Cuban culture as a wonderful *ajiaco* (stew).

Our belief is that landscapes are useful mirrors to understand what has transpired and what contributed to the visible consequences that give a place or a region its discernible features, or, in the case at hand, what constitutes the essence of Cuba: *cubanidad*.

Acknowledgments

Both of us would like to thank Kristal Hawkins and Seymour Weingarten of The Guilford Press for their patience, encouragement, and support. Jim Newman at Syracuse University's Department of Geography was enthusiastic about the project from the outset, and his feedback sustained much of this writing. Richard Phillips of the Latin American Collection at the University of Florida helped an alumnus way more than was necessary.

Joseph L. Scarpaci would like to thank Orestes del Castillo Jr., Orestes del Castillo Sr., Mario Coyula, Roberto Segre, Tim Brothers, Antonin Kapcia, Mabel Matamoros Tuma, Patricio de Real, Korine Kolivras, Victor Marín, David Robinson, Cristina Scarpaci, Jorge Pérez-López, Phil Peters, Nicolás Quintana, and the Museo Nacional de Bellas Artes in Havana, among others.

Armando H. Portela wishes to thank Joseph L. Scarpaci for his initiative and bravery and for his infinite patience and willingness to pursue the idea of this book; Leví Marrero for his trust and stimulus during the last year of his life; and many Cuban colleagues for their silent support as they wait for a different geography of this magic island. Thanks also to Elena for her push and support, which have definitely been not so silent.

CONTENTS

CHAPTER 1

ON CUBAN LANDSCAPES

[Islands are] the loci of imagination, desire, hopes and fears,
the goal of dreamers and mystics and misfits, multiplying,
drifting, disappearing and reappearing: malleable moulds
into which cosmographers and cartographers could pour both
art and science, material spaces which the merchant venturer,
pirate, colonist, and governor could penetrate and exploit.
—DENNIS COSGROVE (2005, 302)

Cuba is at once a poetic place steeped in history and culture, and a tenacious vestige of land when contrasted with nearby continents. Seen offshore of the Sierra de los Organos in the west, the Escambray Mountains in the south, or the Sierra Maestras in the east, Cuba's green-peaked ridges evoke a wind-whipped emerald sea. Henry Dana (1815–1882) observed in 1859 while approaching Cuba that the "fertile, undulating land comes to the sea, and rises into high hills as it recedes" (Dana 1996, ix). Cuba, not unlike the rest of the Greater Antilles (Haiti, Dominican Republic, Puerto Rico, Jamaica, Cayman Islands), affords land observers a glimpse of its mountains and hills from almost any point on the many plains and flatlands interspersed between higher elevations (Richardson 2002, 15).

But how to approach a tangible and conceptual place we call the Cuban landscape? Indeed, the term "Cuban landscape" carries multiple meanings. Its usage spans the disciplines of architecture, art and art history, cultural geography, literature, poetry, and urban design over the past century or so. There are copious first-impression descriptions about this crescent-shaped island such as those often given by explorers and conquerors. Christopher Columbus—Cuba's first European discoverer—reportedly claimed it was

1

the "most beautiful land [his] eyes [had] ever seen," though many Bahamians, Haitians, Dominicans, and Puerto Ricans claim that the Italian mariner made the same remark about their islands. Baron von Humboldt, known as Cuba's "second discoverer" for systematically studying the island's ecology and social organization, characterized it as "an island of sugar and slaves." And the 20th-century Cuban anthropologist and ethnomusicologist Fernando Ortíz, known as the "third discoverer of Cuba" for reconstructing indigenous and African contributions to the island's rich tapestry, claimed that Cuba was positively enriched by the contributions of Afro-Cuban culture. The island did not need to be rescued by outsiders. Understanding the Africanization of the island (Ortiz coined the term "Afro-Cuban") meant understanding the material culture (plant names, toponyms, farming practices) and nonmaterial contributions (syncretism, language, music, street humor or *choteo*, folklore, botany) to the island's heritage (Mañach 1969). He argued that the Africans' contribution to Cuba stemmed from their long history of survival and knowledge of the land.

Many of the themes promulgated by these three discoverers appear elsewhere. Gonzálo de Quesada (1868–1915), a Columbia University–trained Cuban lawyer who worked in New York for Cuban independence, waxed eloquently:

> Cuba! Beautiful "Queen of the Antilles," the land of the cocoa and the palm—of the golden banana and the luscious orange—well may the hearts of thy sons and the dark, lustrous eyes of thy maidens glow and glisten with pride at the praises of thy sunny Isle! How few Americans there are who have formed any correct conception of "Life in the Tropics"! To the generality of us, Cuba suggests the idea of heat and yellow fever, of venomous reptiles and insects, slaves and sugar, oranges and ever-blooming flowers—an idea in a great degree erroneous. (Hazard 1871, 18)

Like the three discoverers noted earlier, Hazard also captures a defining feature of Cuba and the Caribbean at large: a tragic chapter in human history (slavery) juxtaposed against Garden-of-Eden-like prose, all of which is (often) defined by outsiders (North Americans and Europeans) who have historically felt a need to rescue these islands. Indeed, as analysts of Caribbean landscapes have long argued, the Caribbean is a cultural mosaic made up of incredible diversity and understated intricacy that has been conditioned by its colonial past (Lowenthal 1985, 2007).

To continental dwellers in North America and Europe, islands in general—and Cuba in particular—may offer some respite from the perennial booming of traffic, perhaps to be replaced by the constant booming of surf. Nicolson (2007, 153) argues that an island is like an idea that begins, glows, and expands in the mind like a beam of possibilities.

> The island looks like the place where that mixture of heaviness and insignificance might somehow evaporate, leaving life pure and rich. An island, in other words, concentrates the dreams of Arcadia with which civilization has always been haunted. It is a place defined by otherness, thriving on nothing more than its distance and difference from the mainland, to which it is opposed.

This holds true for Cuba. One is constantly reminded that Cuba is just 90 miles from the United States, though in fact the island is 90 miles from Key West, which is the end of an archipelago extending 120 miles from the soggy bottom of "mainland" south Florida.

Baldacchino (2007) conceptualizes islands as novelty sites. They are cast in the humanities and the natural and social sciences as quintessential places for experimentation (Gillis 2007; Gillis and Lowenthal 2007). A kind of mythical island geography, argue some, has helped Fidel Castro sustain a revolution for nearly 50 years, in essence making the nation an "island of communism" surrounded by a "sea of capitalism." This island experiment in communism builds on the intoxicating fascination that islands are *tabulae rasae*, where anything is possible. Perhaps the relatively small size of islands makes them more malleable to grand designs than continental projects. In 1992, the Soviet Union dissolved but Cuba's experiment continues. Cuban socialism may be small, remote, insular, and peripheral, but Cuba's being an island on the "edge" of mainstream international (and continental) events has exposed the weaknesses of mainstream orthodoxies (e.g., Soviet communism), and has allowed Cuba to foment alternatives to the status quo because, as Baldacchino (2007, 167) suggests, "islands tend toward clairvoyance. They act as advance indicators for what will occur in the future, or as extreme renditions of what exists elsewhere in less exceptional form."

Cubans make the best of a difficult situation imposed by a trade embargo that since 1962 has deprived the island of importing merchandise directly from the United States, or of securing goods from ships that might stop in nearby Miami or Fort Lauderdale. As citizens of a "quintessential site for experimentation," Cubans have learned to innovate and make due with less-than-ideal conditions. Reconfigured Soviet washing machine motors turn grinding wheels, help cobblers mold tire treads into soles, or function as fans. Old American cars made in Detroit now run with motors adapted from Soviet-made Ladas. An extensive tool and dye industry, most of it informally operated, gives credence to Baldacchino's notion that islands spark innovation.

CUBA AS LANDSCAPE

The study of landscapes is an eclectic discipline, requiring us to cast a necessarily broad net to capture the many nuances of Cuba and *cubanidad* ("Cubanness"). Some of the earliest noncartographic representations of the island of Cuba come to us in the form of landscape paintings. This genre departed from 18th-century European treatments of oil portraits, rooms, objects (flowers, vases, and quotidian features), gardens, and other smaller spaces. European landscape painters were particularly inspired by the island's beauty, which was originally communicated by travelers' diaries, journalistic accounts, and personal correspondences. The German naturalist Baron Alexander von Humboldt's detailed account of his short visit to the island triggered considerable interest in Europe once his 1801–1802 descriptions were published in French in 1835 and then in English in 1856 (Humboldt 2001). Thus, it was no small accolade that perhaps the greatest explorer and scientist of the 19th century remarked upon his arrival on December 18, 1800, in Havana's harbor that it was "one of the most picturesque and pleasing on the northern equinoctial shores of America" (Humboldt 2001, 4). Although his writings were not published for nearly 35 years, they served to fuel U.S. annexation of Cuba and in the 1890s to justify U.S. imperialism; it was used by the U.S. subsequently and erroneously to justify the Monroe Doctrine (1823). Cuba became "desirable," in no small measure attributable to the German's keen eye. His acuity and penmanship form a cornerstone of what is now the burgeoning field of Atlantic Studies, or what John Gillis (2004) calls the creation of "islands of the mind." For Spain and other envious nations, Cuban landscapes would be more than silver specks in the Caribbean.

Cuba surely epitomized the changes brought on by industrialization and rising international trade. However, the industrial revolution in the first half of the 19th century meant replacing animal- or slave-driven sugar cane grinding mills (*trapiches*) with steam-powered ones (*centrales*). Commercial agriculture accelerated quickly during the first half of the 19th century. This expansion was ignited by the Haitian revolution of 1791, which sent sugar growers to Cuba and New Orleans in search of new acreage (Marrero 1972). Cuban coffee production, much "gentler" on the land than sugar, jumped in production from 1.25 million pounds in 1804 to 44 million pounds two decades later. Cuban sugar mills doubled, from about 500 in the year of the Haitian slave revolt to 1,000, by 1827 (Martínez-Fernández 2001, 7). Accordingly, landscape paintings captured, if not in unduly romantic fashion, fragments of a changing look of the land and a dying way of life.

Cuba's meteoric rise as a world sugar producer between 1800 and 1850 was dealt a severe blow by the Independence Wars (1868–1898) (Marrero 1950, 341), especially the Ten Years' War (1868–1878). This war came between two improvements in sugar production: The first was a revolution driven by rail and steam, which took hold in the early 19th century. A second occurred after the decade-long war and responded to mounting sugar beet production in Europe and the United States. The arrival of what would become "agribusiness" separated the small plots for small-farmer use and an indentured farmer system from the *latifundia* (plantation) system. Corporate farming teased out the traditional *ingenio* (simple sugar mill) from the plantation, replacing the *latifundia* sugar system with a single industrialized central system (hence the Spanish term, *centrales*). The plantation system continued to work, in that tenant farmers (*colonos*) could contract with the modern sugar mills. Despite this economic and technological restructuring, economic hardship brought on by war seemed to engender a special appreciation for what the land could offer. José Martí captures this sentiment in his essay "Memories of the War: Conversations with a Soldier," penned in November 1893. His description of the ragged colonial army, especially the common soldiers (*mambises*), highlights how these soldiers (mostly former peasants) foraged and gathered whatever the land could offer them:

> In came the officers, nearly every one of them naked, one using his hat as a fig leaf, the other, two tanned *jutia* [rodent] skins, one north, one south. Barefooted, or in cowhide sandals. They had made themselves hats of yarey, or *yuruy-guana* [yuraguano], which is more pliable, or a cap of *cataure* [catauro]; their machete belts were twisted vine, or a strip of cowhide.... When we were drilling we were sometimes so hungry that I have had men faint on me, unable to stand up from hunger. Food? Sometimes it was very good and sometimes very bad.... The fact of the matter is that after a long march or a hard skirmish, or a retreat over the savannah, there's nothing like a piece of fresh cane or a nice ripe mango. The mango is a great fellow; when they were in season we ate them every way you can think of, raw, baked, boiled, fried ... [and] one day a fellow was in bad shape, with pains and stomach ache, from eating too many *piñas* [pineapples]. "I'll never touch *piña* again." "Yes you will," I said to him. "Yes you will. *Piña* is the only thing that's like a woman." It was a banquet when we sat down to roast *jutia*.... And for coffee, we had either "monkey tail," which was orange leaves steeped in water, or *cuba-libre*, which was honey water. Only the bees must be native, and not from a Spanish hive, because the Spanish bee stings. Ours is noisy like the Cubans themselves, but it's considerate, and does you no harm. The Spanish bees, when they sting, die, and their guts pull out with the stinger. (Martí 1968, 304–305)

Martí's description not only underscores both the travesty and resourcefulness that war imposes, but shows a deeper connection to the land in ways that tens of thousands of *mambises* might have never known.

Nineteenth-century Cuba was also a time when the colony—in addition to struggling for independence—forged a strong sense of nationalism that centered on human–environment relationships. Louis A. Pérez Jr. (2001b) cogently documents the rise of nationalism on the basis of how Cubans supported each other before, during, and after hurricanes. Specifically, his aim was "to insert the phenomenon of mid-19th-century hurricanes into the larger circumstances of the Cuban condition as one more variable in the formation of nation." His environmental history studied how the catastrophic storms of the 1840s molded socioeconomic developments in 19th-century Cuba. He shows how the powerless (peasants, slaves, common folks) and powerful (the Spanish colonial authorities) reached compromise in preparing for tropical storms, surviving them, and rebuilding in the wake of the storms. In this way, then, Cuban respect and admiration for the forces of nature take firm hold well before Independence (1898) and the socialist government (1959–), while also cutting across class lines.

Although it is true that the hurricane (also noted as *huracán, hunrakán, yuracns,* and *yorocán* by indigenous Caribbean people[1]) and cyclone (*ciclón*) leave undeniable marks on the geographical, economic, political, social, and moral fabric of all Caribbeaners, Cubans have always judged themselves and their governments on their comportment when facing these natural disasters. Pérez argues that

> so much in the character of economic conditions, social relationships, and cultural forms bear the distinctive imprint of the hurricane. The very notion of nationality, no less than the idea of nation, evolved from the experience and the encounter and contributed [in] decisive ways to the people Cubans have become. (2001b, 155)

Hurricanes also reshape the physical landscape: Shorelines, 1,600 keys and islands, river courses, and landslides often change dramatically after hurricanes (Iñiguez-Rojas 1989). In this way, Cuba's insularity and vulnerability to hurricanes have been a defining feature of Cuba's physical, political, and social fabric.

LANDSCAPE PAINTING IN 19TH-CENTURY CUBA

In the United States, the Hudson River School of landscape painting developed in the 19th century in response to modernity and industrialization, reflecting a romantic clinging to the nation's older established eastern seaboard. While America's frontier moved ever westward, the Hudson River painters found an enthusiastic American public that increasingly appreciated the older settlements. Many of their paintings were forcefully theatrical, often depicting moral or literary themes. In both the United States and Europe, this new school of painting was partly a response to the rise of industrialization and was surely recognition that mechanization was capable of transforming the look of the land in unprecedented ways. Industrial production, driven by smoky steam engines in factories, mills, and railroads, left sooty plumes across cityscapes and countryside alike (Burtner 2002). Cuba was also responsive to this new genre of painting, which altered the initial European influences on its culture.

A few landscape painters stand out in 19th-century Cuba. Esteban Chartrand's 1877 work *Marine Landscape* (*Paisaje Marino*) and Valentín Sanz Carta's *The Malangas* (*Las Malangas*) capture the pristine countryside of colonial Cuba. Chartrand (c. 1824–c. 1889), the son of French immigrants who resided in Matanzas, about 100 kilometers east of Havana, is widely acclaimed for bringing a subtlety and accuracy to his landscape portraits of a nation not yet widely marked by sugar cane planting and great urbanization. He crafted nostalgic, romanticized, and idealized landscapes that were often washed in twilight. Unlike the European painters, gazing at the island through continental lenses, he included the common peasant (*guajiro*) as opposed to the trappings of the economic elite (Figure 1.1). Elements in his paintings emphasized *lo cubano* (Cubanness) and highlighted such cultural elements as *bohíos* (small and simple farmhouses), *ingenios* (simple sugar mills) and *palmas* (the *palma real*, in Spanish—or royal palm, *Roystonea regia*—is the national tree). His massive ceiba trees appear majestic and his palm trees are always svelte. Sanz Carta, a Cuban who hailed from the Canary Islands (called an *isleño* in Cuba), depicted the Cuban countryside more realistically and often bathed his works with strong doses of tropical sunlight (Museo de Bellas Artes 2001).

Although our purpose here is not to digress into the subtleties of Cuban art history, these landscapes, as representations of place, are important because they present an image to the rest of the world depicting the allures the island held for curious travelers. Both Chartrand and Sanz Carta flourished at a time when there was a growing appreciation for local aesthetics and beauty as well as a turn away from elitist and Spanish-based views of local life. This trend in painting rose in tandem with the independence wars and helped to establish certain iconic elements of *cubanidad*—ranging from depictions of huts, wild-growing fruit, palm trees, castles and fortresses, and other natural and cultural elements—that might at one time have been considered too plebian to paint.

FIGURE 1.1. The painting *Landscape* (1880), by Esteban Chartrand (1840–1883), focuses attention on key elements of the natural land-scape; at right, detail of Cuban *bohío* and *guajiro* on horse. Courtesy Museo Nacional de Cuba.

Travel literature and its icons are wellsprings for geographical knowledge and form a key part of the new cultural geography (Duncan and Gregory 1999). Although iconic attractions and writings about Cuba (bucolic tropical landscapes, sandy beaches and blue water, cigar-filled rum saloons, Spanish castles, "fiery" mulattas) would change over time, they rightly or wrongly became symbols in the island's tourist industry over the next century (Schwartz 1997). Curious (and affluent) Americans and Europeans would come to the island in search of these landscape elements. Pen-and-pencil sketchings could be electrotyped inexpensively and then printed in American and European newspapers and magazines. Samuel Hazard's drawings of daily life in Cuba were especially popular beyond the island, as he captured romanticized and pristine versions of Cuba's subtropical forests at about the time the Ten Years' War (1868–1878) began (Figure 1.2).

Consumer items sold in the United States in the 19th and early 20th centuries, such as the five-cent Cuban cigar, "were among the most sought after in the western hemisphere," with their "classical graphic idioms to reflect a real or mythical heritage ... [and whose themes included] a requisite number of pastoral vistas, female personas, and waving flags" (Levi and Heller 2002, 86). These eye-catching embossed chromolithographs became collectible artworks (Figure 1.3). Indirectly, they fired the imagination and aesthetics among a growing middle class in Europe and North America who were increasingly pursuing leisure and travel.

LANDSCAPES AT LARGE

Landscape is a concept tied to the study of places in disciplines as diverse as geography, biology, landscape architecture, urban planning, and the fine arts. "Landscape" refers to the arrangement of the land and how humans have modified it. The concept includes many elements that express themselves as visual representation. Landscape's essence, however, is not limited to the lofty confines of academe. In fact, its rise as a popular medium for describing places can be traced back to the Renaissance and merchant capitalism of 15th-century Flanders and Venice (Aubu-Lughod 1984; Morris 1981). Painters played a key role in bringing exciting, if not romanticized and somewhat distorted, images of faraway places to the elite of their era. These images, in turn, found their way to the masses in reproductions and popular media.

Cuba's sugar potential in the late 18th century evoked much interest in the European elite because of the possible profits (Scarpaci and Portela

FIGURE 1.2. The Falls of the Rosario (also known as Soroa Falls) captured in the late 1860s by Samuel Hazard. "Rosario" refers to the Sierra Rosario in Pinar del Río Province. From Hazard (1871, frontispiece).

FIGURE 1.3. Carmen Flor Fina cigar label, 1900. A pastiche of exotic, pastoral, and tropical themes beautified the individual cigar and boxes of 25. This ancillary form of artwork prospered soon after lithographic printing began in Havana in 1822. Few globally consumed items did as much to disseminate a representation of the island of Cuba as did the Cuban cigar ring, box, and packaging in the 19th and 20th centuries. From Levi and Heller (2002, 92).

2005) and a certain exoticism; Cuba was American *criollo* (creole), but it was also imbued with more than three centuries of Spanish rule. Unlike the ornate and abundant religious architecture of Mexico and Peru, the only highbrow architecture the colony could boast was of a military nature: fortresses, castles, bulwarks, and ramparts, all of which had become obsolete by the middle of the 19th century. Havana in the early 19th century was a busy port, the gateway to an industrious and prosperous island (Figure 1.4).

In a prephotographic age, landscape portraits and their subsequent dissemination through lithographs became important media in casting the essence of places and territories (Burtner 2002). Cuban landscape paintings embraced Western notions of land, art, and nature (Figure 1.5). Some art historians argue that 19th-century landscape paintings everywhere enlisted a simple dichotomy of culture versus nature, the mundane and contaminated versus the pristine. However, Narciso G. Menocal (1996) has carefully shown how depicting the landscape and common folks characterized a key part of the colonial independence project. Cuban art was not a mere extension of European trends and themes. Rather, it established "national imagery through a search for the characteristic and exploring national identity.... Nationalism made Cuban art *sui generis* in style and general appearance, but perhaps more interestingly, in the manner in which it should be read and interpreted" (Menocal 1996, 187).

"Landscape" would eventually find its way into the English language as a derivative of the Dutch term *landschap* and the German word *landschaft*. Over the past 500 years or so, the term has moved from one largely

FIGURE 1.4. Detail of *General View of Havana*, 1856, drawn by Eduardo Bara-
ñano and lithographed by Eduardo Laplante. This bird's-eye view of the port from
the north shows Castillo de Los Tres Reyes del Morro and its lighthouse (left
foreground), La Cabaña fort (left midrange), La Punta castle (right foreground),
and the walled city of La Habana (right midrange).

confined to the fine arts to a concept that is imbued with meanings of
power, politics, and ownership (Creswell 2004).

   In cultural geography, Carl Ortwin Sauer introduced the term to
North American scholars in his seminal 1925 essay, "The Morphology of
Landscape." Sauer proposed the study of landscape as an alternative to the
prevalent philosophy of environmental determinism, which emphasized
the role of their surroundings (environment) in shaping the material development of a people or region. Sauer's notion was that the landscape could
be studied scientifically and that one could elucidate the role humans played
in modifying it—the antithesis of environmental determinism (Sauer
1963). In using cultural history and artifactual analysis, one challenge in
studying the transformation of a natural landscape into its contemporary
condition (cultural landscape) is that it remains daunting to reconstruct
the original natural landscape and to designate seamlessly where the mark
of one group of occupants on the landscape ended and where another

FIGURE 1.5. *View of Trinidad from Mount Vigia*, 1852, by Eduardo Laplante. Laplante captures the rise of the sugar industry in this south-central town set back 11 kilometers from the Caribbean Sea, and a gentrifying "sugarocracy," in the words of Moreno Fraginals. More than a score of small mills (*ingenios*) lined the Sugar Mill Valley (*El Valle de los Ingenios*) just to the west (left) of the image. The detail at right enlarges the main plaza and reveals a turrett used by a wealthy slave trader. Courtesy Museo Nacional de Cuba.

13

began. Subsequent cultural geographers such as D. W. Meinig (1979) and Wilbur Zelinksy (1973) worked with these Sauerian themes in studying the human imprint on the surface of the earth. Their works were highly informative because they synthesized a great deal of information about places and regions and their books reached both academic and general readership. However, such approaches to landscape were often criticized because good description alone—devoid of theory—could not make substantive contributions to basic research (see Soja 1996).

Novel tenets of cultural geography that were grounded in landscape analysis appeared in the 1980s and 1990s. This "new cultural geography" added social and cultural theory to interpret changes in landscape (Back, Kunze, and Pickles, 1989). By emphasizing political and sociocultural processes, this new cultural geography also considered how landscape shapes political and sociocultural processes in a particular region (Schein 1997). No theoretical lens consistently informs these new studies of landscape. Cosgrove (1998), for instance, enlists Marxian analysis to characterize his study of place and landscape, giving particular emphasis to ideology and how it shapes the way social classes view property and land. Others (Duncan and Duncan 1988; Price and Lewis 1993) have furthered this work by focusing on how landscape forms a key ingredient in cultural, political, and social systems. Graham, Ashworth, and Tumbridge (2000, 31) "regard landscape less as places shaped by lived experience than as largely symbolic entities."

We believe this new cultural geographic analysis lends itself nicely to the study of Cuba because of the island's striking historical periods that spawned distinctive political economies: the colonial period based on raw material extraction and slavery (1514–1898); the republican era witnessing the domination of United States investment in sugar, communications, and overall infrastructure, as well as political support and sugar price-fixing for exports (1898–1958); and the socialist era (1959 to the present). Throughout this book, we refer to several examples of *vernacular* or *ordinary landscapes*. These make up the everyday environment of the island, its elements ranging from schools, streetscapes, sugar cane fields, and rural settlements to the shaded suburbs of its large cities and the increasing blend of tourists with locals. Vernacular landscapes are "lived in" and shape the perceptions, values, and behaviors of the Cubans who occupy them. In Cuban towns and cities, for example, vernacular landscapes include the distinguishing automobiles, largely older Soviet-made Ladas and Moskvich models, as well as American cars of the 1950s and earlier (Figure 1.6).

Today these automobiles give the country a museum-like quality (Baker 2004; Schweid 2004). The neighborhood landscape is peppered with the state-run food stores (*bodegas*), primary care clinics (*policlínicas*),

FIGURE 1.6. One of the predominant features of Cuba's contemporary and vernacular landscape is the presence of American cars from the 1950s. Paint for maintaining the bodies of these relics is often stolen from shipyards or is surplus household latex paint, resulting in strong hues. Havana, 2006.

and schools, and many settlements are marked by high-rise public housing complexes (*vivienda social*) built after the triumph of the Revolution in 1959. In the countryside, traditional rural housing based on the pre-Columbian structures of the *bohío* are common visual markers whose virtues are praised in literature, song, and poetry (Figure 1.7). Vernacular or ordinary landscapes are also celebrated in such popular songs as José Fernández Díaz's adaptation of José Martí's lyrics to form the composition "Guatanamera." This famous song, brought to an English-speaking audience by Pete Seeger's adaptation, evoke images of a pristine, bucolic landscape and the virtuous men and women who live there.

Adhering to the tenets of the new cultural geography, we also point out *symbolic landscapes* in this book. Unlike vernacular landscapes, symbolic landscapes portray the values and power of those agents that finance and modify them. Up until independence in 1898–1902, Cuba was seen as a place where many capitalists could "rationalize" imperialism, whether for economic gains, political domination, or a "benevolent civilizing process." Leland K. Jenks, a U.S. business writer contributing to a series titled "American Imperialism: American Fund for Public Service Studies

FIGURE 1.7. Typical rural dwelling made of palm thatching, palm wood (sides), and a zinc roof modification on front porch, Ciego de Avila Province, 2003.

in American Investments Abroad," described three aspects of this notion plainly:

1. Merchants and bankers recognize the opportunities for pecuniary gain in certainly relatively backward political and economic areas.
2. Their penetration is followed by appeals to the foreign offices of their respective states.
3. These requests lead immediately to military intervention and the political administration of such areas. (1928, x)

It was often popular in European circles to refer to colonial Cuba (before the massive introduction of slaves, railroads, and sugar cane) as "a lemon not worth squeezing" because it lacked the gold and silver of Alto Peru and Mexico. However, Jenks's summation about conditions in the early 20th century indicates a sharp change in opinion about the island. Its proximity to the United States created a strong movement toward annexation in the U.S. Congress and a belief, bolstered by the Monroe Doctrine, that perhaps Cuba really should form part of the Union. American politicians saw Cuba as presenting an opportunity to complete the expansion of the U.S. Atlantic seaboard into the "American Mediterranean" and expel Spain forever from the Western hemisphere (Herring 1960).

In the republican era, strong elements of a market economy and concentrations of a consumer society in Havana and selected provincial capitals manifested U.S. affinity through print and radio advertising, billboards, clothing stores, automobile dealerships, and other venues. Promotion of the island as a safe yet exotic tourist destination (Figures 1.8 and 1.9) in the early 20th century drove a growing steamship industry, with steady traffic between U.S. ports and Havana, Matanzas, and Santiago (Schwartz 1997).

Other representations by or for non-Cubans formed a powerful force in the electronic media of the 20th century. Although the contemporary tourist landscape is explored more fully in Chapter 5, this historical pause may provide useful background for the reader. The Hollywood motion picture industry, Broadway musicals, songs, and other forms of U.S. popular culture played a huge role in disseminating an image of Cuba, arguably very distorted, to a global audience (Table 1.1). These representations included a set of practices through which meanings about the island of Cuba were constituted and communicated. And although the socialist government would embark on a long process of contesting these images and reconstructing new social identities of Cuba and Cubans, the "Cuban sensation" worldwide was deep and enduring. Cuba was different: It had swing and pizzazz; it was sexy and tempting.

During Prohibition in the United States, for instance, Cuba was cast as a forbidden but accessible place, as Irving Berlin made popular in his song "I'll See You in C-U-B-A" (© Copyright 1920 by Irving Berlin; © Copyright Renewed. International Copyright Secured; All Rights Reserved; Reprinted by permission):

Not so far from here
There's a very lively atmosphere
Everybody's going there this year
And there's a reason; the season

FIGURE 1.8. This 1953 guidebook cover has all the trappings of promoting Cuba as a safe yet exotic destination. The man is wearing a (dark midlatitude) suit and hat; the Capitolio building (completed in 1930) stands as a (familiar) replica of the U.S. Capitol in Washington, DC. Perhaps the only difference setting the two cities apart is the appearance of the palm trees and bouquet of flowers that proliferate in tropical climes. From Levi and Heller (2002, 39).

> Opened last July
> Ever since the U.S.A. went dry
> Ev'rybody's going there,
> And I'm going too;
> I'm on my way to
> [Refrain:]
> Cuba—That's where I'm going
> Cuba—That's where I'll stay

Cuban musician Ernesto Lecuona (1895–1963) was a versatile artist known as a composer, arranger, and bandleader. Exotica lovers sought his music for the rhythms, excitement, romance, and mystery they conveyed. He was a popular crossover artist between Latin and big band musicians of the pre–World War II era. Some called him a "Latin Gershwin," though his

FIGURE 1.9. This 1940 postcard reinforces the safe-but-exotic theme. It promotes "gay" Havana as "The Paris of the Western Hemisphere" and juxtaposes familiar leisure activities such as casino entertainment and horseracing against castles, cathedrals, and European-like promenades (the Prado). From Levi and Heller (2002, 31).

TABLE 1.1. Sampling of Popular Music and Motion Pictures in the United States about Cuba, 20th Century, before the 1959 Revolution

Medium	Title	Year	Authors/actors
Music	"On the Shores of Havana, Far Away"	1898	Paul Dresser
Music	"The Cubanola Glide"	1909	Vincent Bryan and Harry von Tilzer
Music	"There's a Girl in Havana"	1911	E. Ray Goetz and A. Baldwin Sloane
Music	"I'll See You in Cuba"	1919	Irving Berlin
Music	"Cuban Moon"	1920	Joe McKiernan and Norman Spencer
Music	"Siboney"	1929	Ernesto Lecuona; English lyrics by Dolly Morse
Music	"The Cuban Love Song"	1931	Herbert Sothart, Jimmy McHugh, and Dorothy Fields
Music	"Maria My Own (Maria la O)"	1931	Ernesto Lecuona
Music	"El Frutero"	1932	Ernesto Lecuona
Music	"Cuba Cabaret"	1933	Eduard Herpman, Bert Kaplan, and Reggie Childs
Motion picture	*Havana Widows*	1933	Glendal Farrell, Guy Kibbee, Joan Blondell, Lyle Talbot, Allen Jenkins, and Frank McHugh
Music	"Street in Havana"	1935	Don Marzedo
Music	"Cubanita: The Daughter of Mam-inez, Rhumba"	1939	Lew Abrosio, Lew and Dolph Ambrosio, and Juliet Flores
Music	"Little Havana Girl"	1942	Lewis Brown
Motion picture	*Moonlight in Havana*	1942	Allan Jones, Jane Frazee, Marjorie Lord, Don Terry, William Frawley, and Grace and Nicco (dance team)
Motion picture	*Holiday in Havana*	1949	Desi Arnaz and Mary Hatcher
Music	"Cuban Pete"	1952	Desi Arnaz
Music (album)	*La Sonora Matancera*	1955	La Sonora Matancera with Celio González
Music (album)	*Cha Cha Cha*	1955	Monchito and the Mambo Royals
Motion picture	*Ole Cuba!*	1957	Julito Díaz, Tete Machado, and Alicia Ricú
Music (album)	*El Bárbaro del Ritmo*	1958	Beny Moré
Music (album)	*Lecuona Cuban Boys*	1958	Lecuona Cuban Boys

Note. Data from Levi and Heller (2002).

music was exceptional in its own right. Through some 850 compositions, he cultivated a remarkable number of musical forms such as *pasodoble*, waltz, *habanera, bolero*, and *son* (de León 1995). Reflecting his homeland, his hybrid musical form borrowed widely and integrated a variety of genres.

Perhaps no single Hollywood actor and executive did more to bring Cuban music into American households, including that of Ernesto Lecuona, than did Desi Arnaz, born Desiderio Alberto Arnaz y de Acha III in 1917 in Santiago, Cuba. Desi's father was a rich rancher and politician. He owned several farms and served as the mayor of Santiago. However, the 1933 uprising by Sergeant Fulgencio Batista led to the overthrow of the dictatorship of Machado, and young Desi's family assets were seized and his father was imprisoned. Desi and his mother, Dolores, sought exile in Miami, where he worked various jobs until graduating from high school, then working with Xavier Cugat's band. One of his most famous Broadway and cinematic scenes was his famous Conga line, which he performed in theater in 1939 and 1940 in the musical *Too Many Girls*. In his autobiography, *A Book*, Arnaz writes about his struggles in getting American musicians to conform to his Cuban rhythms:

> After that whachamacallit group and I struggled with a few rumbas, they didn't sound like anything. It was a pitiful sound. The boys weren't bad musicians but we had no arrangements, they had never played Latin music, and the instrumentation was all cockeyed for it.... And my mind did a flashback to the yearly carnivals in Santiago, when thousands of people in the streets form a conga line, and they go all over the town, singing and dancing for three days and nights to the beat of African conga drums. They also use frying pans, nailed to boards, bottom side up, which they beat with hard sticks, making a sharp ding-ding-ding it-ding it-ding-ding sound, keeping tempo with the conga drum going boom-boom-boom-BOOM. It's a simple beat. You can hear this sound approaching from ten blocks away and it keeps getting louder and louder and more exciting. (1976, 59)

What debuted on the U.S. scene as a conga line in the film *Holiday in Havana* in 1949 would years later become an annual tradition during carnival celebrations throughout the Americas. The three-shuffle step progression, derived from African slaves who were chained together, allegedly brought an ensemble of nearly 120,000 dancers to Little Havana, Miami, on March 13, 1998 (Longest List 2006). Arnaz's successful partnership with Lucille Ball allowed snippets of Cuban culture to be portrayed, such as the conga line in the hit syndicated show *I Love Lucy*, which was launched in October 1951 and reached an unprecedented 44 million U.S. households in 1953—an astounding figure in television's infancy. That series, moreover, lives on in reruns, especially through the syndicated cable television network TV Land. Arnaz introduced millions of viewers to Latin pop music and the fictitious Tropicana nightclub on television and perhaps planted a seed for future tourists to visit the real Tropicana in the Marianao district of Havana (which has been operating continuously since 1939; see also Pérez 1999).

In addition to Arnaz's music and memories of Cuba, other images of gaiety in the island can be found in songs such as *The Cubanola Glide*: "Way down in Cuba where skies are clear/Where it is summertime all of the year." All of these sparked the tourist's imagination and representation of Cuba, forged both within and outside the Caribbean.

In contemporary socialist Cuba, only the state has the power within the realm of national culture to invoke symbolic values, and naturally its intentions are largely political and represent the ideology of the Cuban leadership and the Cuban Communist Party. The island's relative lack of commercial advertising and limited private enterprise (Peters and Scarpaci 1998) have provided ample opportunity for political slogans and pronouncements to line the walls of factories, schools, and government buildings, as well as the occasional billboard (Figure 1.10), which we explore further in Chapter 6.

Symbolic landscapes dominate contemporary Cuba because the state has replaced the market as the principal source of ideological dissemination. Instead of visual markers about private businesses, shopping centers, and private retail stores, government institutions mostly dominate the

FIGURE 1.10. Political billboard in the countryside that reads "They showed us the road to follow ahead" and consists of colonial (from left, Antonio Maceo, Máximo Gómez, Ignacio Agramonte, and José Martí), Republican-era (a.k.a. neocolonial), as indicated by José Antonio Echeverría, third from right (an anti-Batista student leader who was killed by security forces in 1957), and socialist political figures (Camilo Cienfuegos and Ernesto "Che" Guevara, second and first from right). In a globalized world of mass marketing, the Cuban landscape is conspicuously void of commodity and service advertising.

public realm. These include political billboards, painted murals with slogans, neighborhood vigilante groups (Committees for the Defense of the Revolution), clinics and schools, busts of José Martí (the 19th-century "apostle" of the Cuban Independence Wars), and uniformed police. Within this realm of symbolic landscapes, we identify two manifestations of power that are at once apparent. At one end, we see landscapes of power that include military and security (police) personnel and facilities. At the opposite extreme, there exist "landscapes of despair" that include the most destitute of Cuban society who reside in urban and rural penury and who stand in contrast to the achievements of social equality that the socialist government portends. Within those extremes there are, on a daily basis, scenes of uniformed Cubans such as white-shirted and red-kerchiefed grade schoolers (*pioneros*) (Figure 1.11), militiamen and women (*milicianos*), and others whose symbolic manifestations of the state are readily identifiable.

FIGURE 1.11. Elementary school children, many of whom become *pioneros* when they join the José Martí Union of Pioneers at the age of 7, enter their school in Habana Vieja, 2006. Busing children to school is rare in Cuba, and parents often escort children to and from school. The red jumpers and white blouses (short pants and shirts for boys), as well as their colored kerchiefs are transient but major components of socialist Cuba's vernacular landscape. They symbolize the state's commitment to free and universal education in a country where private education does not exist. However, this commitment comes with a dose of patriotism—some would say "indoctrination." This is evidenced by the school-age saying *"¡Pioneros por el comunismo!"* (Pioneers [young students] for communism!) and *"¡Seremos como el Che!"* (We'll be like Che!).

A PLACE CALLED CUBA

Geographers' concern with the study of place and territory has a long-standing tradition. Cartographers, kings, military architects, and formal decrees often impose boundaries over the surface of the earth, which are later contested, traversed, negotiated, and renegotiated. Borders between nations are examples of "formal regions," such as the divide between Mexico and the United States or between Ecuador and Peru. However, these are artificial lines on land—continental bodies at large—whose physicality is much more subject to negotiation, conflict, and change than that of islands. These formal regions contrast with "functional regions," which are the lived-in spaces identified by a distinct activity or attribute and ignore political divisions.

Cuba's insularity has been a key feature in the nation's political geography. Early maps emphasized ports and bays so that merchants and navigators could access the hundreds of transshipment points for the exportation of sugar and precious woods to the world beyond (Figure 1.12); this feature has led many writers to reflect tragically on "the cursed circumstance of water everywhere" (Mosquera 1999, 23). Although Spain preferred to interpret Cuba's lingering 19th-century status as a sign of the colony's loyalty to the Spanish Crown, Martínez-Fernández (2004) argues that the Spanish American liberators' lack of a navy impeded the ability of Cuba and Puerto Rico to resist Spanish domination. To be sure, the *criollo* elite knew that being a colony meant Spanish protection against possible black uprisings and the continuation of the slave trade. Moreover, a Spanish Cuba was perhaps preferable to an independent Cuba that might align itself with either England or the United States; Cuba and Spain likely formed a tacit agreement on this point. However, insularity was of singular importance when, in about 1820, the liberation of Spanish American colonies, through the efforts of Simón Bolívar and José San Martín, was fought for in land wars throughout Mexico, Central America, and South America. Although Spanish territories, ranging from the Great Salt Lake of Utah all the way to Tierra del Fuego in Argentina, had thrown off the yoke of colonialism by Spain, Puerto Rico and Cuba would have to wait until 1898 and the Spanish-American-Cuban War to capture their independence. Even then, true independence and sovereignty were subject to debate; Puerto Rico became a possession of the United States and then a Free Associated State in 1952 (*Estado Libre Asociado*), and Cuba was occupied by the United States from 1898 to 1902. The Cuban Revolution of 1959 would interpret the 1902–1958 era as the "neocolonial" period versus the "republican" period, the traditional label used by others. Louis

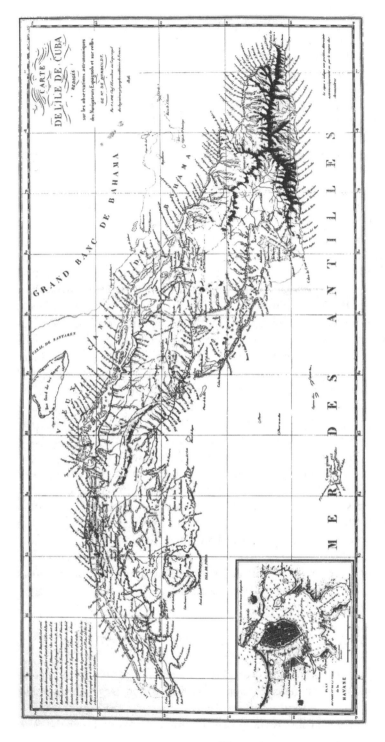

FIGURE 1.12. Map of Cuba, 1814. Almost all of the toponyms identify ports, bays, keys, coves, beaches, capes, peninsulas, estuaries, and other littoral features even though this is not a maritime map. Atlas *Géographique et Physique des Regions Equinoxiales de Noveau Continent,* sheet 23. Librairie Grecque-Latine-Allemande, Paris, 1814. From Humboldt (2001, 2).

25

A. Pérez (1999) argues that the Revolution was a partial response to the Cubans' dissatisfaction about the way America achieved rampant modernity while Cuba did not. With the island geographically discrete and disconnected, insularity, then, has conditioned Cuba's geopolitical fortunes in undeniable ways.

Insularity also defines the ways in which the island has historically responded to its surroundings, or "relative location," as geographers might describe it. Although its attribute as an island has proven to be a strong allure in developing a tourism industry, neither colonial, republican, nor socialist Cuba has always welcomed insularity. Pirates, corsairs, buccaneers,[2] and European navies lurked offshore in the colonial era. In the republican phase, proximity to the United States might have ensured a steady flow of tourists and investment, but it also established a small part of the island as a corner point in a triad of gambling and prostitution that included Miami and Las Vegas (Scarpaci, Segre, and Coyula 2002, 77; Schwartz 1997). Proximity to the United States during Prohibition (enacted by the 18th Amendment to the U.S. Constitution in 1917) triggered investment in molasses production and rum running between the island and the southeastern states, at least until the 21st Amendment ended Prohibition in 1933. And the ill-fated Bay of Pigs invasion of April 1961 by nearly 1,500 Cubans who were trained by the U.S. Central Intelligence Agency (CIA) resulted in good measure from Cuba's closeness to the United States. In October of the following year, 1962, the world was brought to the brink of nuclear war as Nikita Khrushchev and John F. Kennedy had a showdown about the presence and removal of nuclear weapons on the island. The Cuban Missile Crisis stemmed from Washington's objection to Soviet-supplied missile systems in Cuba. That these missiles could strike targets in many areas of the United States once again underscored the importance of Cuba's relative location and geographical character. Even though its insularity had impeded land invasions by foreign armies, it also made the island vulnerable to the vicissitudes of the Cold War when intercontinental ballistic missiles rendered the 90 miles between the United States and Cuba meaningless.

PHYSICAL AND ENVIRONMENTAL FEATURES

Cuba's shape and surface features derive in large measure from diverse rock formations. They generally appear as folded and overthrusted belts of limestone, marble, schist, tuff, serpentine, granite, and amphibolites. The sedimentary coat forms the relatively ample plains of Pinar del Río,

Havana and Matanzas, Ciego de Avila and the Cauto River valley. It is a generally gentle sequence of limestone and marls whose only deformations correspond with some minor vertical horst and graben ruptures (caused by fault lines or cracks in the crust). With 109,886 square kilometers (42,444 square miles) Cuba remains a small, long, and narrow island comparable in size to the state of Tennessee (42,143 square miles) or the European nation of Bulgaria (42,683 square miles) (see Figure 1.13, a general map for this and later chapters).

Cuba's landscape diversity strikes visitors and specialists alike. A trip from the coast to the inland reveals dry (xerophytic) marine terraces carved in limestone and bored by caves, mangrove wetlands, and boney hills. There are a series of low karstic mountains in just a few miles of cross section. Geology and isolation account for such diversity. The island is part of an intricate folded belt created by the collision zone between the North American and Caribbean tectonic plates, which were formed by a series of orogenic (i.e., mountain building) episodes lasting from the mid-Eocene to the Quaternary period (roughly 1.8 to 15 million years ago).

Two main and neatly distinctive groups can be identified in the island's geology. The first is a complexly folded sedimentary and volcanogenic belt encompassing Early-Middle Jurassic to Late Eocene rocks (about 30 to 200 million years ago) with frequent inclusions of ultramafic and granitic rocks. This ancient folded belt stretches from east to west for most of the island and is partially covered by a thin deformed coat of sedimentary rocks, mostly carbonated and ranging in age from the Oligocene (24 to 33 million years ago) to the present (Iturralde-Vinent 1998). This diverse geological foundation is essential for the development of the rest of the physical geographic components of the landscapes and directly or indirectly determines the characteristics of the relief, soils, runoff, and natural vegetation. It also sets a frame for the cultural shaping of the landscapes.

Cuba's ample plains rise from 0 to 200 meters high (650 feet) and in some cases reach 260 meters (845 feet). Terraces at different heights grade these largely marine or deltaic plains. On the surface, they often show the scars of karstic dissolution. For a predominantly flat island, a small group of elevations rising several hundreds or thousands of feet above the surrounding lands gain immediately the sometimes pretentious category of mountains (Figure 1.13). There are in Cuba four mountainous areas: the Sierra Maestra and Nipe-Baracoa mountains in the east, the Guamuahaya mountains (more often called Escambray) in the center, and the Guaniguanico range in the western end. They rise abruptly from the surrounding plains or the seashore to a top altitude of 1,974 meters (6,476 feet) at the Pico Turquino in the Sierra Maestra; 1,231 meters (4,039 feet) at Pico

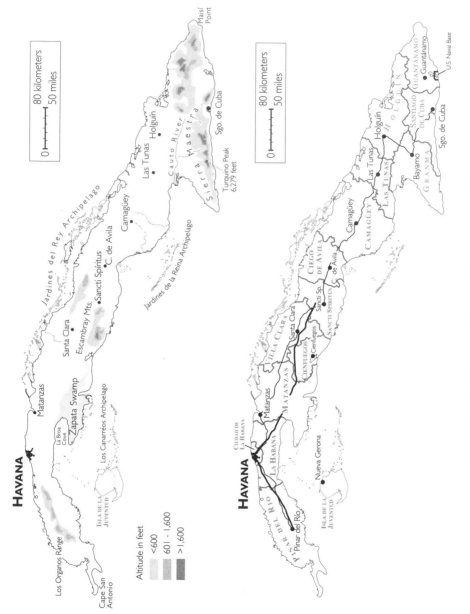

FIGURE 1.13. General political and location map of Cuba.

Havana

80 kilometers
50 miles
0

Maisí Point
Sierra Maestra
Sgo. de Cuba
Turquino Peak
6,279 feet
Holguín
Las Tunas
Cauto River
Camagüey
Jardines de la Reina Archipelago
C. de Avila
Sancti Spíritus
Escambray Mts.
Santa Clara
Jardines del Rey Archipelago
Zapata Swamp
La Broa Cove
Los Canarreos Archipelago
Isla de la Juventud
Matanzas
Los Organos Range
Cape San Antonio

Altitude in feet
<600
601 - 1,600
>1,600

Havana

80 kilometers
50 miles
0

U.S. Naval Base
Guantánamo
GUANTÁNAMO
Santiago de Cuba
SANTIAGO DE CUBA
Sgo. de Cuba
Bayamo
GRANMA
Holguín
HOLGUÍN
Las Tunas
LAS TUNAS
Camagüey
CAMAGÜEY
Ciego de Avil.
CIEGO DE AVIL.
Sci. de Avila
Sancti Sp.
SANCTI SPÍRITUS
Santa Clara
VILLA CLARA
Cienfuegos
CIENFUEGOS
MATANZAS
Matanzas
CIUDAD DE LA HABANA
LA HABANA
PINAR DEL RÍO
Pinar del Río
Nueva Gerona
Isla de la Juventud

28

Cristal in Nipe-Baracoa; 1,140 meters (3,740 feet) in Guamuhaya at Pico San Juan, and 692 meters (2,270 feet) at the Pan de Guajaibón in Guaniguanico.

Cuba lies in a climatic zone characterized by a high hydrothermal balance. The annual average temperature is 25.2°C (77.4°F), and average rains reach 1,375 millimeters (54.1 inches) annually. A wet season, extending from May to October, accounts for roughly 80% of the precipitation, and a dry season, from November to April, includes the rest. Droughts are not uncommon and often inflict serious damage on crops and the economy. However, some years are extraordinarily humid, especially during the hurricane season (June 1 to November 30). Extreme rainfall generally associated with hurricanes can be catastrophic, as evidenced by the deluge that accompanied Hurricane Flora in October 1963; it dropped 1,500 millimeters (59 inches) of precipitation in 3 days and changed the course of some rivers and the shorelines in eastern Cuba.

The rich medley that constitutes Cuba's roughly 7,000 plant species, more than half of them endemic to the island, results from its proximity and one-time connection to North, Central, and South America. It is not surprising, therefore, that certain pines, palms, and hardwoods found in Cuba also exist in Florida, Hispaniola, Mexico, and Central America. It is estimated that about 90% of the island was forested in 1492. However, tree clearing for sugar cane and citrus production, cattle ranching, shipbuilding, and urbanization have today reduced that surface area to just under one-fifth. Nearly 75% of the island is in the form of cleared plains or savannah, just less than one-fifth is confined to mountains, and about 4% is swampland. Other vegetation types include a variety of scrub (upland, rain forest, coastal) and those that are unique to the bedrock found in the limestone outcrops of tobacco-rich Viñales in the western province of Pinar del Río (Figure 1.14).

There are hardy savannah vegetation formations that survive quite well in nutrient-deprived silica soils, as well as drought-resistance (xerophytic) woodlands and scrublands found along the "rain shadow" areas of southern and southeastern Cuba (Figure 1.15). More than 30 species of palm trees have generated more than 20 million palms on the island. One species, the royal palm (*palma real* in Spanish, or *Roystonea regia*— its Latin botanical classification), forms part of the Cuban coat of arms (Barredo 2003, 21–22).

High levels of endemism and biodiversity also characterize Cuba's fauna landscape. The Atlantic coast traffic of migratory birds relies heavily on Cuba for food, water, and rest as the birds island hop from North America to South America. Cuba's abundant wetlands, especially along

FIGURE 1.14. Limestone formations called *mogotes* (haystacks) in the Viñales Valley sprout a unique vegetation cover growing in bare vertical cliffs and on soil where some of the world's finest leaf tobacco is produced.

FIGURE 1.15. Cacti and other drought-resistant plants (xerophytes) thrive in the rain shadow of Cuba's southern coast, along the Caribbean Sea, in Guantánamo Province, and on the lee side of the Nipe-Baracoa mountains.

the north coast, provide ideal habitat for both resident and migratory birds (Figure 1.16). The island is home to more than 13,000 bird, reptile, amphibian, insect, fish, and mollusk species. Barredo (2003) argues that the island's natural landscape is unique because of the number of small animals located there. He cites the froglet (*Eleutheraodactylus limbatus*), dwarf bat (*Nyctiellus lepidus*), and bee hummingbird (*Calypte helenae*, no larger than a grasshopper at just 2 grams) in this diminutive category. Cuban coastal waters contain nearly 900 species of fish, most of which are edible, even though the island remains a net importer of fish (Silva 1997). The vast array of species forming Cuba's natural heritage has, according to Linden (2003, 2), given Cuba "by design or by default" some of the best-kept wildlands in the Caribbean. One explanation for this wildland condition is that Cuba boasts a very low population density, despite a population boom in the 20th century (noted later in this discussion). With just 97 persons per square kilometer, only five other island-nations are less densely settled (Table 1.2).

Soon after the 1959 revolution, the government reconceptualized the relationship between society and nature. The sudden disappearance

FIGURE 1.16. Pink flamingos, a.k.a. Caribbean flamingos (*P. ruber ruber*), Cayo Coco, Ciego de Avila Province, 2004. The island's extensive archipelago with saline lagoons and muddy lakes provides a fine habitat for a variety of fowl.

TABLE 1.2. Range of Caribbean Population Densities in Ascending Order

Country	Rank	Population density (people/km^2)
Anguilla	24	20.9
Bahamas	23	27.8
Turks and Caicos Islands	22	34.9
Dominica	21	88
Virgin Islands, British	20	93.3
Cuba	19	99.6
Montserrat	18	130
Antigua and Barbuda	17	145.5
Cayman Islands	16	146.2
Saint Kitts and Nevis	15	156.1
Dominican Republic	14	165.3
Trinidad and Tobago	13	217.7
Netherlands Antilles	12	221.9
Jamaica	11	243.2
Guadeloupe	10	243.8
Haiti	9	246
Saint Lucia	8	249.2
Grenada	7	282.4
U.S. Virgin Islands	6	338.1
Aruba	5	352.3
St. Vincent and the Grenadines	4	352.9
Martinique	3	384
Puerto Rico	2	430.5
Barbados	1	602.3

Note. Data from International Center for Tropical Agriculture (2003).

of private property, along with the centralization of the economy and the launching of large-scale, compulsive, and often erratic campaigns for the transformation of the countryside, left a lasting imprint on the landscape. This relationship developed after centuries of agriculture had led to intense and widespread erosion. With a diffuse runoff of 5–10 liters/second/square kilometer (Lebedeva 1970), it is not surprising that the upper horizons of soils are gone, especially those lying in slopes of more than 3° inclination. Herrera and Seco (1986) calculated the erosion reaching 21 tons per hectare per year in tobacco fields, and Karasik (1989) estimated the leaching of 20–100 tons per square kilometer per year in the plains, a figure that can be doubled or tripled in the mountains. One quarter of the island is heavily eroded, meaning that the soil horizons A and B (anywhere from 1 to 3 feet) in the profile have disappeared. More than 68% of the soils devoted to sugar cane suffer from some form of erosion; in tobacco the figure reaches 97% (Karasik 1989).

Deforestation, massive river damming, and soil erosion changed forever the landscape in Cuba. Although it was largely forest covered upon the arrival of the conquistadors in the 16th century, today Cuba is probably 18% forest covered (authorities claim 21–23% coverage, but the veracity of the official estimate is arguable). More than a quarter of the total water resources in Cuba are controlled. Nearly 9 billion cubic meters (2.3 trillion gallons) of water are retained in dams, and underground aquifers are exploited to the limit. Salinization hampers the natural productivity of 15% of the agricultural soils in Cuba (Arcia Rodriguez 1989).

Because of its long history of human impact on the environment, no natural ecosystems remain on the island. All of them have been transformed by human activity, sometimes with devastating consequences, especially in the 20th century, following the expansion of the sugar industry. The demographic boom in the past century (the population soared from 1.5 million in 1899 to nearly 11 million in 2000), along with the agricultural and industrial growth, deeply altered all the ecosystems in the plains and hills, leaving some natural remains in the most intricate mountain ranges, the peripheral keys, and the swamps (Iñiguez-Rojas 1989).

CONCLUSIONS

Landscapes, those eclectic elements that define our everyday existence, can be approached several ways. This introductory chapter has offered glimpses of these cultural geographic interpretations through sampling a smattering of travel logs, diaries, landscape paintings, field notes, music, film, cigar labels, posters, responses to disasters, wildlife ecology, geology, and population data to outline some of their defining features in Cuba. Our approach has been deliberately broad, encouraging the reader to take an equally catholic view of vernacular and symbolic landscapes. The former, we noted, include the lived-in and everyday spaces, and the latter are decidedly imbued with doses of ideology. Such ideological underpinnings are not confined to just the socialist government in power since 1959. Rather, Cuba's broad political epochs—colonial, republican, and socialist—lend themselves to displaying the values and power of those agents that finance and modify them. Its history of slavery, capitalists' pursuit of sugar profits (and the subsequent rabid deforestation of the island), and socialism's elimination of consumerism have etched their marks on Cuban landscapes. These forces have given a poetic birth to the island's vernacular and symbolic landscapes embody *cubanidad*, and thread out among the wider interests of Cuba's social geography, the foci of the chapters ahead.

NOTES

1. Landsea (2008) claims even more names: "Hurricane derived from 'Hurican,' the Carib god of evil … alternative spellings: foracan, foracane, furacana, furacane, furicane, furicano, haracana, harauncana, haraucane, haroucana, harrycain, hauracane, haurachana, herican, hericane, hericano, herocane, herricao, herycano, heuricane, hiracano, hirecano, hurac[s]n, huracano, hurican, hurleblast, hurlecan, hurlecano, hurlicano, hurrican, hurricano, hyrracano, hyrricano, jimmycane, oraucan, uracan, uracano, and urycan."

2. Though these three terms are often used interchangeably, there are historic distinctions. "Pirates" refers to plunderers who commit violent acts at sea or on shore. "Corsairs" is often used synonymously with "pirates," though the latter are technically from the Barbary Coast (Morocco, Tunisia, and Algeria, derived from the sociocultural term "berber"). Corsairs were also known as Arab slave traders. The term "buccaneer," derived from the French *boucanier* (literally, one who barbecues), is largely associated with pirate raids in the Atlantic and Caribbean, especially in the late 17th century. Buccaneers were also known as naval mercenaries and learned their meat-cooking skills from the Arawak peoples of the Caribbean who smoked meats on wooden barbecue frames called boucans. For a lucid account of these distinctions, see Rogozinski (1999, 34–44).

CHAPTER 2

★

HUMBOLDT'S LANDSCAPE
Connecting Then and Now

Alexander von Humboldt's uncanny ability to interpret and synthesize landscapes highlights his work as the engaged Enlightenment scholar-intellectual. Nowhere is that plainer than in his observations in *The Island of Cuba*, written during relatively brief visits to the island in 1800 and 1804. In this seminal work, he casts his classic external gaze upon slavery and the sociopolitical structures of Havana. The book, although delayed until 1826 and not widely disseminated until a controversial 1856 English-language translation from his original French text and subsequent publication (Martínez-Fernández 2001, 4), serves at least four purposes examined in this chapter. First, it was a powerful abolitionist work for denouncing the institution of slavery throughout the West Indies. Slavery left a permanent mark on the landscapes of colonial cities and towns. Second, the book provided fodder for American expansionists who coveted the island's wealth and conceptualized it as a buffer between the United States and the slave rebellions in the Caribbean. Third, the work gives insight into the economic geography of early 19th-century sugar production. Finally, it allows the socialist revolution to draw on Humboldt's works to promote nationalism and advocate its own agenda through myriad discourses.

The Island of Cuba documented both the physical and human landscapes of colonial Cuba. So revealing was the book in denouncing the cruelties of slavery and its living conditions that it provoked Spanish authorities to ban the work on the island. An English translation emerged two decades after the French version (1856). The American expansion-

35

ist James Thrasher, a merchant living in Havana, translated the original. Regrettably for scholars and the public at that time, Thrasher eliminated Humboldt's chapter on slavery in which the German scholar had vehemently denounced the institution as inhumane, writ large. Such editorial twists were part of a plan to persuade President Polk and Congress to yank Cuba out of the American Mediterranean and place it squarely within the Union. Nevertheless, *The Island of Cuba* captures the character of early 19th-century Cuba and details the conditions of slavery in the West Indies. Humboldt also draws on a variety of disciplines that allow contemporary scholars a context for tracing U.S.–Cuban relations and contemporary Cuban studies.

Fidel Castro issued a bicentennial anniversary edition of Humboldt's original work in 2002. This book serves as a rallying cry for the continued struggle against U.S. hegemony. A museum celebrating Humboldt's research operates in Old Havana and provides an interesting juxtaposition between the contemporary geopolitical situation of Castro's Cuba and the colonial economy of the early 19th century.

This chapter assesses these matters by reviewing Humboldt's descriptions of Havana, slavery, racism, and the production of sugar. In the last section, we comment on the way in which the Cuban revolution has enshrined this seminal publication and its author, a model of the engaged Enlightenment scholar-intellectual. We argue that the Humboldt discourse gives contemporary leaders in Cuba an opportunity to use a different lens in viewing the island's evolution over the past two centuries.

HUMBOLDT: ELITE GERMAN RENAISSANCE MAN AND ABOLITIONIST

Before postmodernism took hold in Anglo-American human geography in the 1980s, one might have easily posited that Alexander von Humboldt was a role model for young geographers and other students of landscape. He was a broadly trained explorer, geographer, natural scientist, archeologist, and geologist. In addition, he spoke English, French, Russian, Spanish, and Portuguese. He was, perhaps, "the last great *universal* man and a humanitarian liberal" (Aber 2003, 2; emphasis in original). Alexander von Humboldt was born into an aristocratic family in Berlin in 1769. Much of his childhood was spent at Schloss Tegel, a family estate some 12 miles north of Berlin. His father, Alexander George, was a member of the Prussian noble class and his mother, Marie Elisabeth, belonged to a family of French and Scottish Protestant refugees (Ramos 2003). At Göttingen

University in 1789, he joined his brother in university studies. There he met Georg Forster, who had been with Cook on his second circumnavigation of the world (1772). The two men then traveled to England, a trip that proved to be "a revelation to Humboldt, and after one year in revolutionary France he became a lifelong liberal" (Aber 2003, 2).

His formal training in mineralogy in Freiberg led him to a series of government positions until 1796, when he decided to pursue scholarly travel full-time (Aber 2003; Martínez-Fernández 2001, 4). Humboldt's travels through Cuba in particular, and through Spanish America in general, were extraordinary for several reasons. First, the Spanish king granted him a general license to travel unfettered throughout the empire. This unusual honor meant that the German scientist was detached from the services of any commercial enterprise or European government. In Cuba he was the guest of wealthy planters, who facilitated ample access to many sources of the information that he brought back to Europe upon his return. This generous hospitality may have overwhelmed him and lengthened the lag time between the completion of his draft manuscripts and field notes and the publication of his work.

Although Humboldt is known for his contributions to geology, astronomy, naval sciences, botany, and biology, he also had a keen eye for detailing social conditions in the Americas with uncanny accuracy. A good deal of his work addressed the flora, fauna, and geology of the Orinoco watershed. He and Aimé Bonpland doubled the identification of known species in the New World (Raby 1996, 13). Less is discussed about his brief but important stay in Cuba, yet his contributions are many, particularly his discussions of Havana, slavery and racism in Cuba, and the economic geography of sugar production. This broadly trained scientist, the ultimate geographer and Renaissance man, preceded much of the intellectual and scientific community by decades in his categorical denunciation of the institution of slavery. His writings refer often to the slave revolt and new government that occurred in the adjacent Saint-Domingue (Haiti) in 1791, highlighting this unprecedented first black republic of the modern era. The implication for white societies in the Antilles was that some amelioration and acceleration of manumission (a process for slaves to acquire freedom) was now a serious imperative. By 1820 his writings had come to the attention of the Spanish Crown and the governor of Cuba, and though his works did not lead to a ban on slave trafficking between the Caribbean and Africa (300,000 slaves were imported to Cuba between 1790 and 1820), it heightened focus on this issue (Murray 1980). Regrettably, slavery would persist on the island until 1886. Humboldt's was an enlightened agenda for a European scholar who could have settled for a comfortable life of lecturing and nature travel

(Pratt 2003). His most frequently cited assessment was that Cuba was "an island of sugar and slaves," and these words would cast light on this issue of social justice during the 19th-century Independence Wars and in the European press long after they were written.

HAVANA'S COLONIAL LANDSCAPE

Humboldt and Aimé Bonpland, his travel companion and botanist colleague, first arrived in Cuba on December 19, 1800. Ostensibly, Humboldt's purpose for visiting Cuba was to store specimens[1] he had gathered in Venezuela (Aber 2003). His meetings with the Cuban intelligentsia and leadership of the day, Romay, Espada, and O'Reilly, read like a Who's Who of Cuban history. Most of Humboldt and Bonpland's time was confined to Havana (and nearby Regla and Guanabacoa). They traveled only nine days outside the capital to visit the sugar mills in Güines Valley, Managua, San Antonio de las Vegas, Wajay, and Bejucal (as noted in Chapter 4, the contemporary park that carries Humboldt's name is located in eastern Cuba, hundreds of miles from where he traveled and observed). From peripheral points outside Havana, Humboldt traveled on to the Caribbean port of Batabanó, where he groused about not being able to procure specimens of the *caimán* (alligator) and *cocodrilo* (crocodile). From Batabanó he sailed to the Isle of Pines (today, the Isle of Youth) and Cayo Bonito before reaching Trinidad, his last port of call on the island. On March 15, 1801, he sailed off to Cartagena, Colombia, where his South American research would consume most of his professional writing and research in the New World.

Humboldt's demographic estimates separated whites from blacks and distinguished between free and enslaved blacks, a common census-taking protocol for that era. He wrote that the Cuban capital had 96,000 residents, of which 29,000 were slaves and 26,000 were free colored (2001, 82). The size of Havana's population in the first decade of the 19th century was the same as that of New York, the largest U.S. city at the time (2001, 83). However, by 1825, New York City's population had climbed to about 140,000.[2]

Havana was, at first glance, appealing to the German for both its natural beauty and vibrant industries. Although it lacked the lush vegetation of the port of Guayaquil or, as discovered in his reading, the rocky grandeur of Río de Janeiro, he described Havana Bay as "one of the most picturesque and pleasing bays on the equinoctial shores" (Humboldt 2001, 78). Another translation notes Humboldt's words as "one of the gayest and most picturesque on the shores of equinoctial America, north of the Ecuador" (Humboldt and Bonpland 1849, 156). He was impressed with the synchronization of the lumber industry with shipbuilding, building construction, and street paving. The generous supply of data given to him by the island's wealthy allowed him to calculate that between 1724 and 1796 Havana's shipyards had constructed 114 ships that wielded 4,902 canons. Humboldt remarked that Cuba's hardwoods (mahogany and cedar) were much harder than European timber (2001, 85–90). Steamers and machine shops, as well as all manner of innovations that reflected advances brought on by the industrial revolution, were kept in Cadiz (2001, 89). Since the collapse of the Haitian economy after the slave rebellion, "the port of Havana [had] risen to a first-class mart in the commercial world" (2001, 77).

Despite its vibrant port activity, pockets of pristine nature were observed. Witness, for instance, the description of the back bay neighborhood of Atarés: "Atares . . . containing several springs of fresh water" (Humboldt 2001, 79). Today, remnants of a garbage dump are found there and because it is the backwater section, the waters around Atarés retain a high amount of concentrated raw sewage and petrochemical wastes from the nearby refineries (Scarpaci et al. 2002, 181). Because Havana Bay requires nine days to replenish itself, industrial waste is "naturally" cleansed at a slow pace (Díaz-Briquets and Pérez-López 2000).

Havana's public streets were unusual for the Americas, observed Humboldt. Because building stone was shipped in from Mexico via Veracruz, it was a costly road building material.[3] He was struck by the governor's mandate that mahogany tree trunks be set in the ruts of roads (as was done in Germany and Russia). Remnants of these trunks were still visible in the streets of Havana. However, this method was abandoned inasmuch as it proved to be costly as well (Humboldt 2001, 79). (It is noteworthy that no virgin stands of mahogany remain in Cuba today.) Deforestation was fast approaching two centuries ago: "Civilization advances with rapid pace, but [little] remains of [the royal palm and bamboo] former wild abundance" (2001, 81).

Carriages (*volantes*) filled the streets, and their drivers were described by the German as "rude." This made walking through Havana both "vexatious and humiliating" (Humboldt 2001, 79), which was exacerbated by poorly ventilated houses and inhospitable streets (2001, 79–80). He believed there was a need for police in the streets and lamented that people often walked in them with mud up to their knees. Old Havana was especially congested. He described the walled city as roughly 3,000 yards long by 1,000 yards at its greatest width, within which 44,000 people were jammed (2001, 81). Significantly, that is the same population size that planners claim Old Havana should have today (Scarpaci et al. 2002, 328–331). More than half of this population (26,000) was black or mulatto, most of whom worked as slaves.

Humboldt anticipated late 19th-century suburbanization, although its original impetus derived from public health and military concerns. When yellow fever outbreaks occurred, those who could afford to often retired to their country houses in the hills between Regla and Guanabacoa (2001, 81). The Spanish engineers had complained that the suburbs in the *extramuros* (areas outside the walled city) were too close to the fortifications and should be eradicated (for fear that an enemy would hold the residents hostage). This foreign observer lamented that no one showed the firmness to eradicate the houses (Humboldt 2001, 81).

RACE AND SLAVERY
IN THE EXPANSIONIST DEBATE

Humboldt's adamant posture on abolition derived from a complex set of enlightened (for his time) values, his German schooling, and the citations of Bartolomé de las Casas. It is in Chapter 6 of his book, "Slavery," that his treatment of the negro in Cuba deepens. Ever concerned with population estimates, Humboldt posited that 2.8 million slaves toiled in the Caribbean islands, mostly in Cuba, Hispaniola, and Jamaica, at the time of his visit (2001, 76). He was alarmed by the low wages paid to the "free slaves." An African slave in Havana earned only 52–60¢ a day (2001, 189).[4]

Humboldt believed that manumission was much more common in Cuba than in any of the French or British islands (2001, 121). Little did he know that another 86 years would pass before Cuba would abolish slavery, which he characterized like this:

> What a sorrowful spectacle is presented by Christian and civilized nations disputing whether England (Jamaica) or Spain (Cuba), in three centuries, has destroyed the least number of Africans, by reducing them to slavery! (2001, 142)

Alexander von Humboldt was shocked to hear masters speak with the "greatest coolness" about whether it was better to get slaves and work them as hard as possible for a few years to get as much as possible out of him, or to treat them gently so as to extend their lives. Alarming too were the discussions about whether it was worth using women to care for male slaves over a longer period or not to work them so hard (2001, 143).

Humboldt's observations on the economic geography of slavery high-lighted the vast differences in experience between an enslaved carriage driver in Havana and a slave on a coffee plantation (Figure 2.1). He decried "wily writers [who have] tried in vain to mask the barbarism of this situation with deceptive language. They invent terms such as *Negro peasants of the Antilles, black vassalage,* and *patriarchal protection*" (2001, 255; emphasis in original). He captured a historical geographical dimension that few observers have matched:

> A measure of the hierarchy of human deprivation can be seen in the threats leveled against disobedient blacks. The *calesero* [coachman] is threatened with *cafetal* [coffee planting], the slave working in the *cafetal* fears transfer to sugar planting. In this latter situation, the Negro who is married and lives in a separate hut and, with all the characteristic tendencies of Africans, finds comfort in the lap of his family at the end of his workday, has an immeasurably better lot than the isolated slave who gets lost in the crowd. This disparity of situation is altogether unfamiliar to anyone who has not personally seen the Antilles. Progressive improvements in the circumstances of the slave caste on

FIGURE 2.1. *Los negros esclavos.* From *Revista Bimestre de Cuba,* 1916.

the island of Cuba make it comprehensible how the luxury of the masters and the opportunity of earning a living wage could lure more than 80,000 slaves to the cities and how the emancipation that was favored by judicious laws turned out to be so effective that, in the current epoch alone, over 130,000 freed colored people live there.... Philanthropy is not a matter of meting out "a little more dried cod and somewhat fewer thrashings"; genuine improvement of the servant class must extend to all physical and moral facets of the people involved. (2001, 256–257)

Much of Chapter VI, "The Political Essay of Cuba," in *The Island of Cuba* is written with a detached style as Humboldt aims to describe the human condition of slavery: "It would be unjust to deny that the mortality of blacks in Cuba has greatly diminished ... within the past fifteen years" (2001, 143). He also recognizes the variety of living conditions among the slaves. "The slave who has a cabin and a family, is not so unhappy as he who is folded as if he were one of a flock of sheep" (2001, 143). And, finally, "In the hot months, the mortality *during the sale* is sometimes four percent, as was the case in 1802" (2001, 143; emphasis in original).

These denouncements of the inhumane living conditions of Africans in Cuba were what the American, Thrasher, did not want the U.S. public to read. Thrasher used his racism and ethnocentrism to demonize the Chinese, calling them the "lowest of the low." Fears of the Africanization of the island as evidenced by the Haitian slave revolt of 1791 as well as the perils of miscegenation (*mestizaje*) permeated Thrasher's writings. The American confederate (he called the southern states the Pacific States) contended that the intermixing of black slaves and Chinese brought "neither host principles nor good morals" (Humboldt 2001, 145). New Englanders, Thrasher argued, feared that the black states of the south and the Caribbean divided just below the Florida Keys posed a threat to the rest of the Union. "Therefore, [New Englanders] do not wish to cross the Straits of Florida, the boundary of the great American confederacy, except for the purpose of free commerce" (Humboldt 2001, 76).

Fearmongering was inflamed through claims about the "Africanization" of the Caribbean. That prevailing discourse justified the continuation of slavery. However, it stood in opposition to Humboldt's pleas for social justice. At the end of Chapter X, Humboldt argued that the population of Cuba could reach a million within 50 years and that coffee and sugar production would not require a slave population to expand. In addition, abolition would produce "an intelligent and free agricultural people [that] would succeed a slave population that is without foresight or industry" (2001, 187). Humboldt's careful description of social structure led historian Luís Martínez-Fernández (Figure 2.2) to recreate a 19th-century social hierarchy of power and control by class, race, and slave status.

Thrasher, though, appended an editorial note in his translation of Humboldt's writings in French, stating that the naturalist's "social theory" was in error inasmuch as his predicted outcome did not happen, as based on the "sad experience" of Jamaica (Thrasher, noted in Humboldt 2001, 187). Thrasher claimed that the population of former slaves increased in Jamaica after abolition and that a "semi-intelligent" group of black slaves was "retrograding toward barbarism" (Thrasher, noted in Humboldt 2001, 180). Jamaica's moral decay in a postslavery society was also evidenced by the decline in the status of women, the fleeing of pastors from the island, the closing of churches, the physical deterioration of schools, and the poor maintenance of churches on the island (Humboldt 2001, 180). Thrasher's powerful images of racism conditioned the way Humboldt's essay was received in the mid-19th century.

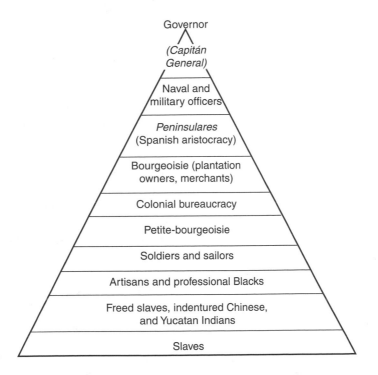

FIGURE 2.2. Cuban social pyramid, 1800–1868. Data from Martínez-Fernández (2004).

Despite the countervailing arguments of Thrasher for a more racially unjust island, Humboldt's contribution to race and social justice has prevailed. Ottmar Ette (2003) goes so far as to claim that Humboldt set the stage for a global consciousness (*Weltbewubsein*) that links ethics in the natural sciences and the humanities, in much the same way that the force of Gaia has been used in geography. To be sure, Humboldt attacked slavery from a variety of fronts: humanitarian, economic, and political. In doing so, he was able to garner support among *peninsular* reformists in the mother country as well as among Spanish American progressives (Naranjo 2003).

THE EARLY SUGAR LANDSCAPE

Humboldt had a great sense of spatial relations and drew on comparisons in the natural and social realms to make his point. In the preface to *Equinoctial Regions of America*, he stated that one of his goals was to examine "the quantity of colonial produce necessary to Europe" (1851, xvi–xvii). Subsequent Victorian travelers found his contributions to place description, science, and trade patterns useful to nonacademics, especially investors, bankers, and traders. Barby (1996, 45) argues that the word "commerce" was never used in the discussions of faraway places in Africa, Asia, or the Americas; such fiduciary matters were considered crass and inappropriate in European circles. Nonetheless, the data proved helpful for targeting investments and spotlighting overseas adventures.

Cuba's networks of sugar mills around Havana connected well to the port. The use of bagasse, molasses, brown sugar, and processed sugar formed part of a well-integrated marketing system. Driving that system, argued Humboldt, was slave labor, and he could never decouple sugar production from the human tragedy that drove it.

The German naturalist also argued that Cuba's geographic and political importance to Spain stemmed from the "geographic position of the city and port of Havana" (Humboldt 2001, 75). He also wrote "that Havana and Veracruz are to the rest of America what New York is to the United States" (2001, 180). Closer economic ties between the United States and Cuba were a possibility if tariff regulations could be balanced. For example, in 1852 U.S. flour had an "impost" (tax) of U.S. $7 per barrel and therefore represented only a small portion of the flour reaching Cuba. Yet Spanish flour from Santander could not compete with the quality of the U.S. flour (2001, 188), a situation that is repeated with the sale of U.S. flour in Cuba in 2009 after more than four decades of a trade embargo.[5]

International restrictions on Cuba imposed by third-party nations prevail throughout the island's history. Whether the result of Spain's will in the colonial era or the U.S. trade embargo over more than four decades, Cuba has been at a disadvantage in the realm of international commerce. Humboldt wrote about the important role of contraband in relations between Mexico and Cuba in the early 19th century.[6] Another historic parallel is that Mexico paid all of colonial Cuba's administrative costs (2001, 76), not unlike the Soviet Union's underwriting from the 1960s to late 1980s.

Humboldt did not decouple slavery from sugar production. He realized that the free labor input sustained the colonial economy, but was willing to denounce that wealth even though his many hosts in Cuba extracted their wealth from slave-produced sugar and molasses. Humboldt countered the fear about African uprisings and the Africanization of the world with the premise of manumission: Free and educated slaves would pose no threat to the Western world. That education and liberation were desirable goals of government is a theme that would echo on the island a century and a half later.

HUMBOLDT IN THE SOCIALIST ERA

Humboldt has been virtually canonized in contemporary Cuba. The German naturalist is honored today in Cuba by a national park named after him, as well as a museum. The park, 700 square kilometers, is located at the eastern end of the island in the provinces of Holguín and Guantánamo (Soroa and Merencio 2003). At the other end of the island, the Havana City Historian's Office opened a museum in the 1990s that is dedicated to the contributions that Humboldt made. Fernando Ortíz (1881–1969); he is considered the island's third discoverer, and the government eulogizes him for both his contributions to the natural sciences as well as his staunch antislavery platform. As is common in the socialist appropriation of property and land uses, the museum is housed in a former elite residence (owned by the Recio family in the 19th century); the symbolism of taking from the rich and sharing with the general public is a key feature of the island's curatorial expositions. One of the museum's exhibits depicts drawings of the harsh conditions of slavery juxtaposed with excerpts of Humboldt's writings, insects and plants that he collected, and the desk of Fernando Ortíz. It is a main attraction for foreign tourists, especially Europeans. The museum is the highest praised of Germany or German citizens anywhere on the island. Like the 19th-century figures of the Spanish priest Felix Varela and a plethora of Independence War figures (Calixto García, Antonio Maceo), Humboldt is cast as a foreigner and friend of Cuba whose ideals, commitment to social justice, and principles transcend time and place. One exhibit compares the life of the negro during slavery with lists of celebrated black Cuban politicians, sports figures, artists, writers, and other accomplished Afro-Cubans.[7] A few blocks away, in the Revolution Museum, numerous exhibits illustrate the deplorable conditions of blacks in Cuba during the Batista dictatorship (1952–1958).

The economic conditions and social pyramid of contemporary Cuba would be nearly unrecognizable to Humboldt. Sovereign Cuba no longer relies on sugar, and the saying "sugar is king" holds little meaning on the island today. Half of the island's 140 sugar mills have closed in the past few years. Blacks and mixed-blooded Cubans (mulattos) form the majority of Cubans, and slavery was abolished more than 120 years ago. However, as in Humboldt's era, monoculture and a complicated international sugar market full of market distortions (Soviet subsidy for 30 years) and political imperatives (the U.S. trade embargo) still condition the island's economic well-being. This historic legacy remains part of Cuba's new political discourse.

CONCLUSIONS

Alexander von Humboldt's intrepidity is most widely recognized in the natural sciences. His field research in the Spanish New World Empire helped erase the ignorance surrounding this vast expanse of *terra incognita*. Although most of his research aimed to discover the unity of the natural landscape, his humanism and social empathy were also powerful. Humboldt was not only a great naturalist and student of the physical landscape, but he was also committed to social justice and abolition in describing the island's myriad landscapes. Whether his "social-science" bent derived from the impact of the French Revolution on him, his diverse schooling and travel in Europe, or some combination of these forces is a matter of speculation. Not long before his death, he wrote of his contributions: "I have never been able to hoodwink myself as I have always been surrounded by people who were superior to me" (Kellner 1963, 233). His humility and keen observation of the human condition connect him with the Cuba of today as well it did with the island 200 years ago.

Cuba's second discoverer serves the socialist government as a historical and cultural symbol that links the 19th and 21st centuries in three key ways. First, Humboldt will live on through a museum in Havana and a national park named for him (see Chapter 4), located far from where he traveled. Second, his ideas of social justice and human dignity echo social-ist and progressive chords. He set the stage for this and related studies about Cuba's political and economic issues that form the cornerstone of Cuban studies as an intellectual field of social-science inquiry. Third, the socialist government promotes a color-blind society and has coupled that value with casting off the yoke of United States imperialism. We revisit this theme in detail in the discussion of information and political land-scapes in Chapter 6.

NOTES

1. According to Thomas (1960, 131–132), the specimens never made it to Cadiz, although they left the port of Havana while Humboldt was there: "Some-where at the bottom of the sea between Africa and America lie the ship and, bur-ied in it, all the butterflies, the plants, the minerals—and the bones of the Atoribe skeletons."

2. Many of the statistics were updated between 1804 and the time of subse-quent publications.

3. Ship ballast was also a source of street paving material.

4. Although the currency and purchasing power are different, it is curious that such a daily wage is not much less than the amount a state worker earns today.

5. The popularity of the plump chickens occasionally finding their way into the current rationed food diet today is an interesting parallel; the Cubans imme-diately notice the differences between the *pollos yuma* (American chickens) and the locally raised ones.

6. Its dealing in contraband in the early 1800s is not unlike Cuba's contin-ued strategic role as a go-between for drug runners between South America and the lucrative U.S. market. As proof, the eastern edge of the island, Punto Maisí, is off-limits to tourists (and other foreigners) inasmuch as cigarette boats pass through the area to pick up bales of drugs dropped from aircraft. In turn, those drugs are conveyed northwesterly along the Bahaman chain of islands and into the United States. Rosalie Schwartz's study of pirates and buccaneers covers this topic well. See Schwartz (1989).

7. On December 9, 2003, one of us (J. L. S.) witnessed a local elementary school class taking a tour of the museum. The instructor gathered the students into the exhibit hall seating area and imparted what seemed to be an impromptu lecture about Humboldt's antislavery stance. It seemed significant, that the teacher and all but two of the nineteen students were Afro-Cuban. The author observed a similar event in the same museum on April 17, 2008, but this time with a Cuban tour guide and group of Brazilian tourists.

CHAPTER 3

★

SUGAR[1]

Cuba's geographical setting in the subtropics, access to the large United States market, and dependence on African slaves gave sugar cane production on the island an unprecedented advantage. No single human-environmental action has modified Cuba's landscape as much as sugar production. The history of sugar production, however, developed unevenly over four centuries. Plantations spread quickly in the 18th century, especially after the Haitian slave revolt. Planters and slave traffickers in Saint-Domingue (Haiti) and French Louisiana found a safe haven in Cuba. It was not hyperbole in Cuba to claim for well over two centuries (1792–1992) that "sugar is king." This agricultural system began as simple sugar mills (*ingenios*) and evolved into modern facilities (*centrales*). In the process, planters felled virgin forests and disturbed complex ecosystems. Today, sugar does not reign supreme. In fact, it eventually cost the Cuban government nearly three times as much to produce a pound of sugar as it earned on the world market (Peters 2003). As a result, more than half the island's 156 sugar mills had closed by 2006.

This chapter explores sugar production as a major agent of landscape change. It does so by employing a historical-geographic assessment. We begin with the rise of sugar plantations and cultivated fields around Havana and in parts of central and eastern Cuba, and then trace their diffusion. We use a series of maps to show how rail lines expanded the cultivation of sugar cane. Next, we examine four stages of sugar production in the post-1959 era: (1) nationalization of mills, production, and distribution; (2) Cuba's membership in the Soviet trading bloc, the Council for Mutual

Economic Assistance (CMEA); (3) the demise of the Soviet Union and its subsidized markets; and (4) the dismantling of the sugar industry.

We conclude with an assessment of how these historical periods have changed the natural and cultural landscapes of the island. Centuries of infrastructural developments in roads, factories, telecommunications, rail lines and port facilities have left an ineffaceable mark on the island's industrial and rural infrastructure. Mill closings in the early 2000s, though, seemed to offer modest respite in reviving the economy. These actions included switching over to molasses production and establishing industrial museums for heritage tourism. The state's challenges in handling massive un- and underemployment, as well as retraining its labor force, are seemingly daunting. A recent spike in the market for ethanol in 2006–2008 may provide a key impetus for reviving the sugar landscape. As one analyst notes: "Cuba is more and more venturing out into the capitalist-dominated, fast-growing alternative energy fields to develop new possibilities for its perennially straitened economy" (Council on Hemispheric Affairs 2006).

ESTABLISHING CUBA'S SUGAR LANDSCAPE

Ever since Columbus carried sugar cane to Cuba on his second voyage, the plant has been commonplace in the gently rolling plains of the island. So widespread is this Old World crop, which is the principal contributing species to cane cultivation (*Saccharum officinarum,* also called "noble cane" or "cultivated sugar cane") that it has been called the "grass of Cuba." Yet Cuba's ascent and recent decline in sugar production have been tied to world demand. Sugar became a luxury product in 17th-century Europe. Only when production levels in the West Indies and Brazil grew did sugar enter into common use by the masses in both the Old and New Worlds. Increases in sugar production lowered prices worldwide. Cuba benefited greatly as industrialization incorporated sugar as the primary sweetener for processed foods and beverages. Even Cubans had high consumption levels as recently as the 1990s (greater than 80 kilograms per capita), though by the new millennium levels had dipped to about 60 kilograms per capita (Kiple and Ornelas 2000).

Sugar in Cuba flourishes in the red clay Matanzas soils, which reach a depth of 8 meters or more. Such permeable and fine-grained bodies possess a clay content between 75 and 90%. High-clay soils can naturally absorb large quantities of water, which is essential for cultivation, even after heavy tropical rains. Matanzas soils cluster along the middle of the

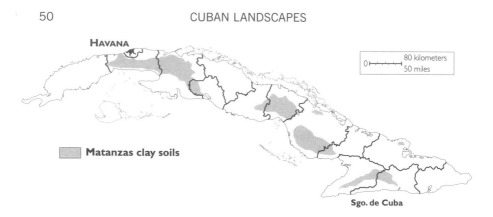

FIGURE 3.1. Distribution of Matanzas soils.

island and stretch from Artemisa in Pinar del Río to Ciego de Avila (Figure 3.1). Rarely is cane produced in places greater than 304 meters or so (about 1,000 feet) above sea level, and the crop has prevailed in areas less than 91 meters (300 feet) in elevation. Even though railroad expansion in the 20th century propelled cultivation eastward (into Camagüey and eastern provinces with poorer soil conditions), Cuba's richest sugar-growing areas have always done well where high-clay soils abound (West and Augelli 1966, 115).

Sugar and Population

Cuba's population growth and racial composition have been closely tied to the island's plantation agriculture. We can trace a high association between the elimination of certain infectious diseases (malaria and yellow fever) and political disturbances on the island and in nearby islands. For example, the barbaric introduction of 65,000 African slaves to work on the small *trapiche*-type (stone-roller cane mill) sugar industry characterized the pre-plantation period. Neighboring Haiti's slave rebellion in 1791 released waves of French sugar growers to Cuba and drove the demand for more slaves (about one million). Political instability and warfare during the Wars of Independence (roughly 1868–1898), along with the abolition of slavery (1886-87), led to a leveling off in population growth. Cuba's quadruple population rise between 1899 and 1959 was spurred by the advent of free black laborers from Haiti (190,000 between 1902 and 1932) and Jamaica (121,000 during the same period), as well as European immigrants (who did work as sugar laborers) (West and Augelli 1966, 122–124). A ruinous collapse of the sugar market in 1921, coupled with a xenophobic movement to "keep Cuba white," severed black West Indian migration to Cuba. Geographers Robert West and John Augelli described the demographic and economic relationship (before the provincial reorganization of 1976) like this:

> The correlation between population growth and sugar production has been all but absolute in the history of Cuba. Not only has the total number of inhabitants risen in almost direct proportion to sugar output, but also the greatest population increases have taken place precisely in the provinces of rising cane production. For example in 1911, the eastern provinces of Oriente, Camagüey, and Las Villas contained 52 per cent of the total population and accounted for 60 per cent of the island's sugar output; in recent years [1950s] the percentage of population and sugar production in these same provinces has risen to roughly 60 and 75, respectively. The correlation is even more striking when one considers the fact that the three western provinces (Pinar del Río, La Habana, and Matanzas) include the huge concentration of metropolitan Havana. (1966, 123)

Precursors to Sugar as a Landscape Modifier

In considering how sugar came to dominate Cuba in the 19th century, it is important to identify the processes of landscape modification that preceded the planting of this cultivar. Felling trees for agriculture and cattle ranching began well before sugar plantations took hold in Cuba. Precious woods, especially termite-resistant and sturdy species, supplied the Spanish palaces of Havana and the royal fleet. The local *guayacán* tree (*Guaiacum sanctum* or Hollywood lignum vitae, and *Guaiacum officinalis* or common lignum vitae), used today for wooden percussion instruments and sculptures, was especially abundant in riparian, coastal, and mountain settings where limestone-derived soils prevail. Its high resin content (up to 26%) makes it scratch-, insect-, and water-resistant. Although it is difficult to nail, its natural attributes made it quite useful for shipbuilding, especially as part of the pillow block used in making wooden ship propellers. Today, though, it is relatively scarce (Fors 1956, 62). A number of colonial buildings—particularly the Convento de Santa Clara in Habana Vieja (Figure 3.2) reveal very similar construction techniques for both roofs and ship hulls (*Urban Design and Planning in Havana, Cuba* 2002). Road building, especially around the capital, consumed vast forest resources. Given that road stone was often shipped in from Mexico, that source proved to be too costly for highway construction. Cuba's endowment of limestone and other softer sedimentary rocks was fine for building construction but less suited for road projects. As noted in Chapter 2,

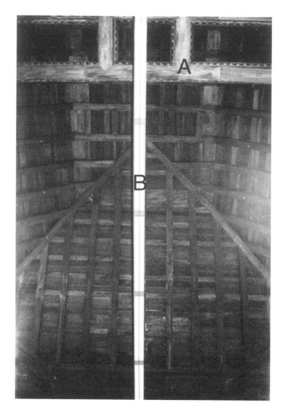

FIGURE 3.2. Ceiling of the Convento de Santa Clara chapel, Habana Vieja, 2007. Looking upward at the ceiling, A indicates the decorative cross-bracing used for support; B is the dual track of fluorescent lights hanging from the ceiling. The concave form of the ceiling reflects the similar design of ship hulls built during the colonial era. Building construction trades and shipbuilders often worked in tandem in the 17th and 18th centuries.

Alexander von Humboldt observed the use of mahogany tree trunk inserts in the ruts of roads so that carriages could pass through Havana's muddy streets during the rainy season (2001, 7). Humboldt remarked that using tree trunks in roads was also a rudimentary yet common practice in late 18th-century Germany and Russia.

Spain's monopoly over trade with the island and its strict control over what ships could dock at Cuban ports contributed to the island's lagging behind other Antillean colonies by at least two centuries. Only in the late 18th and early 19th centuries did sugar production and maritime commerce increase significantly. There were monumental chapters in the Caribbean's environmental history. Richardson (1992, 28–34) calls the spread of sugar production throughout the Caribbean as "the great clearing," and Moreno Fraginals (1976) describes the process in Cuba as "the death of the forest." Although the need to fell trees in Cuba was certainly no exception in the Caribbean, deforestation had already begun before widespread sugar cane planting because of the demand for the island's precious woods. Sturdy and termite-resistant hardwoods served in building the Spanish fleet as well as in road and building construction, especially in the areas surrounding Havana because of the shipbuilding industry in Havana Bay. Moreno Fraginals (1976, 76–77) describes Cuban forest clearings:

> Sugar exterminated the forests. Deaf and blind to history, focusing on the present, the sugarocracy [a term he coined by combining "sugar" with "aristocracy"] destroyed in years what only centuries could replace—and at the same time destroyed much of the island's fertility by soil erosion and the drying-up of thousands of streams.

By 1768 about three dozen sugar mills ringed Havana within a 5- to 15-mile radius (Figure 3.3). Traditional mills (*ingenios*) relied heavily on slave labor to harvest and transport the cane and to turn the grinding stone (*trapiche*) for extracting and then boiling the juice (Knight 1970). Proximity to ports for exporting processed sugar determined the location of these *ingenios*. Accordingly, most sugar production clustered in the shallow valleys and plains that flanked the ports in the western provinces (Havana, Matanzas) and, after the settling of the port of Cienfuegos by the French in 1819, the central portions of the island (Figure 3.4, top panel) entered into sugar cane production. Demand for slave labor mounted in the 1840s and most of these workers were utilized on sugar plantations (Piqueras Arenas 2003).

Sugar and Technology

Two key technological developments in the 19th century catapulted the spread of cane growing. The first was the introduction of the railroad. No longer were the plantation owners reliant on primitive oxcarts and the muddy roads traveled by the carts; railroads allowed them to settle new lands and extend cultivation inland. Allied with foreign capital, sugar planters were no longer confined to areas near ports and could increase efficiency (Zanetti and García 1998). Even during the Independence Wars, sugar production was formidable; it averaged about one million tons annually between 1892 and 1898 (Santamaría García 2003).

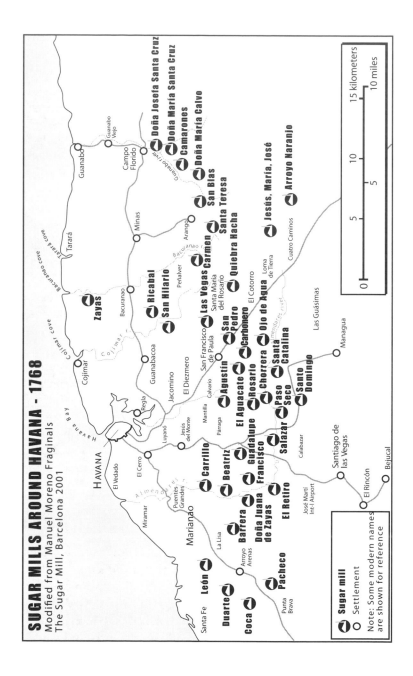

SUGAR MILLS AROUND HAVANA - 1768
Modified from Manuel Moreno Fraginals
The Sugar Mill, Barcelona 2001

Sugar mill
Settlement

Note: Some modern names
are shown for reference

0   5   10   15 kilometers
     5   10 miles

54

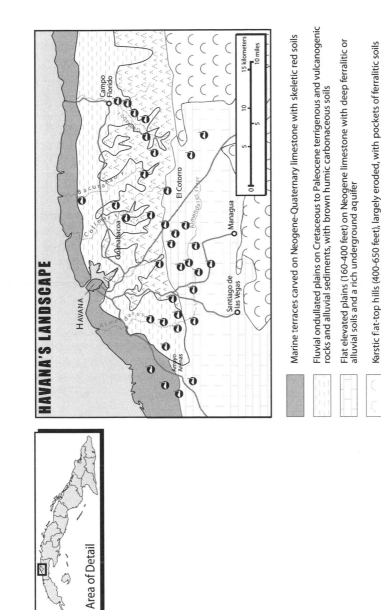

FIGURE 3.3. Sugar mills surrounding Havana, c. 1768.

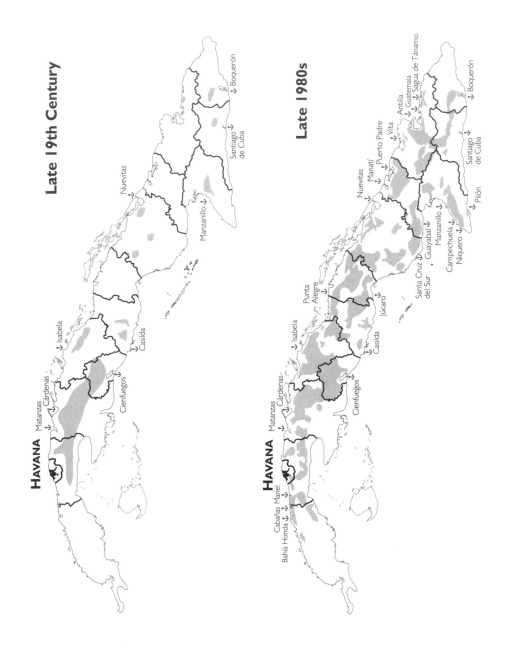

Late 19th Century

Nuevitas

Isabela

Matanzas
Cárdenas
HAVANA

Cienfuegos

Casilda

Manzanillo

Santiago
de Cuba

Boquerón

Late 1980s

Nuevitas
Manatí
Puerto Padre

Antilla
Guatemala
Sagua de Tánamo
Vita

Punta
Alegre

Isabela

Casilda

Júcaro

Santa Cruz
del Sur
Guayabal
Manzanillo
Campechuela
Niquero

Pilón

Santiago
de Cuba

Boquerón

Matanzas
Cárdenas
HAVANA

Cienfuegos

Bahía Honda
Cabañas Mariel

56

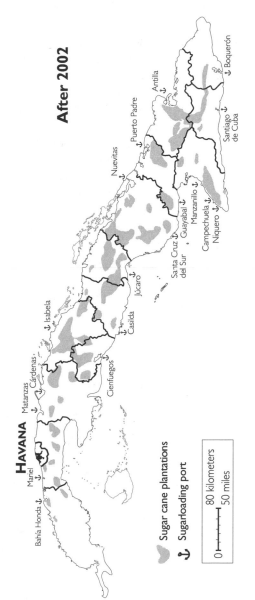

After 2002

HAVANA

Bahía Honda ⚓
Mariel ⚓
Matanzas ⚓
Cárdenas ⚓
Isabela ⚓
Cienfuegos
Casilda ⚓
Júcaro ⚓
Nuevitas ⚓
Puerto Padre ⚓
Antilla ⚓
Santa Cruz del Sur ⚓
Guayabal ⚓
Campechuela ⚓
Manzanillo ⚓
Niquero ⚓
Santiago de Cuba ⚓
Boquerón ⚓

Sugar cane plantations
⚓ Sugarloading port

0   80 kilometers
0   50 miles

FIGURE 3.4. The spatial distribution of sugar cane plantations at three points in time.

A second innovation was the shift to modern central plants (*centrales*) that used large efficient boilers for extracting cane juice. These more sizeable modern sugar mills were largely built by U.S. companies, especially on new lands purchased in Camagüey province in the 20th century. Cuba was one of the first Caribbean territories to use a steam engine (1797, in the Seybabo mill) that was capable of grinding stalks.

Practically every Cuban schoolchild knows that the first railroad in Cuba ran between Havana and the small town of Bejucal in 1837, even before the "mother country" (Spain) had a rail line. Over the next 14 years, 11 railroad lines expanded the rail network an average of 37.2 kilometers per year, or 558 kilometers in all (Zanetti and García 1998, 56). Four-fifths of that network was concentrated in the western half of the island. It spread south from Bejucal (just outside Havana) to the Caribbean port of Batabanó and then east to Macagua (roughly halfway between Matanzas and Santa Clara). It would take another decade for Santa Clara to be connected with Havana; again, rail expansion was linked to sugar cane planting and new cultivation (Zanetti and García 1998, 46) (Figure 3.5). The eastern rail network spread much more slowly and unevenly. Between 1837 and 1854 one line ran from Puerto Príncipe (Camagüey) approximately 50

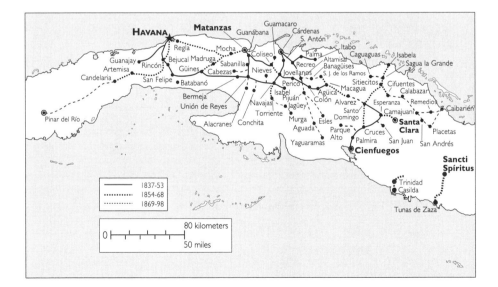

FIGURE 3.5. Expansion of the western rail network, three 19th-century time periods.

miles to the north coast port of Nuevitas. However, not even Trinidad—arguably the most productive sugar-producing region of the world in the 1840s—benefited from railroad investment during that time. The only other connection between 1837 and 1853 was a short spur between Santiago de Cuba and El Cobre.

Cuba's contribution to world sugar production has dropped steadily since the 19th century. In 1860, the island produced about one-fourth of the global total. By 1895, Cuba's global contribution fell to just one-sixth, resulting, no doubt from the complications of the Independence Wars. Output hovered at this level up to the beginning of World War I. After the war, it rose slightly and continued until 1948, when Cuba accounted for 18.4% of the world's sugar output (Marrero 1950, 203, Figure 151).

Cuba's transition from a political colony of Spain to an economic outpost for the United States quickened with the spread of rail lines. Ortiz describes the "tentacles" of rail lines emanating from the large sugar mills as "monstrous iron octopuses" with a seemingly endless demand for cane (Ortiz 1947, 51–52). Even holdings by U.S. banana producers such as the Boston Fruit Company, which had established plantations in Cuba in the 1880s, converted to sugar production. During the 1920s and 1930s the profits of railroad companies were inextricably linked to the value of the sugar harvest (Zanetti and García 1998, 326).

Between 1899 and 1929 the number of sugar mills fell from 1190 to 163, but higher efficiency and more plantings made the sugar crop soar from a half million to five million tons. Mill closings reflected the destruction of the Independence Wars. Less than one-fifth of the mills operating in 1894 survived until the end of the war in 1898. Cane fields had been intentionally burned by the Spanish and equipment was sabotaged or destroyed. Moreover, Cuban planters were unable to come up with sufficient capital to revive their industry. Under the terms of the U.S. occupancy of Cuba spelled under the Platt Amendment (1898–1902), there were few options for these planters to secure capital, and U.S. investors were only too pleased to purchase cane fields and production facilities for pennies on the dollar (McCook 2002, 50).

It was not only through U.S. financial speculation—especially by the Cuban Railroad Company in 1916—that the formerly inaccessible uplands of eastern Cuba came into production (Richardson 1992, 33). The world demand for sugar during and following the First World War resulted in amazingly high prices, high profits, upper-class prosperity, and significant public works projects. Sugar prices hovered around 4.5¢ per pound during World War I, but then soared to 22.5¢ per pound in 1919, only to collapse to 1.6 cents per pound in 1921. Such a frenzy brought unprecedented investment in the nation's industrial and transportation infrastructure during the presidential term of García Menocal (1913–1921). Wartime prices also pushed up the value of sugar and land (Rippy 1958, 406). By 1920, high sugar prices (and profits) were evidenced by the construction of opulent homes in the upscale residential neighborhoods of the Vedado and Miramar sections of Havana. Indeed, the "fat cow" years (literally, *vacas gordas*, or "high on the hog" in idiomatic English) peaked in 1920, only to be followed by a devastating collapse in prices (*vacas flacas*, or "thin cows") (Scarpaci et al. 2002, 59–62). Jenks described this bonanza-like investment setting, as well as the attendant environmental disregard, as follows:

> Vast forests [could] be purchased cheaply, growing on cane-land of unequalled richness.... Corps of wood cutters were set to leveling trees. Where there was hardwood, it was sometimes hauled out by ox and chain. The remainder of the trees lay as they fell for several months, and then were fired—thousands of acres at a time, in a conflagration that drew the entire countryside to prevent its spreading. Cane was planted between the blackened stumps, without the trouble of plowing. (1928, 181)

This sugar frenzy gave rise to the popular saying "Without sugar, there is no country" (*Sin azúcar, no hay país*). Two distinct schools of thought interpret this sugar boom. Marxists claim that avaricious capitalists failed to invest in new sugar technologies, which the outdated mills from the late 19th century desperately needed in the decades of the following century. Industrial capitalists—especially predator-like U.S. investors—spun a web between sugar and railroad production. As a monocultural producer, Cuba was extremely vulnerable to shifts in price and demand (Dye 1998; Zanetti and García 1998). Others contend that U.S.- and Cuban-owned companies were rational actors who responded to fluctuations in land, labor, yields, and sugar beet production in Europe (Dye 1998). What is clear, though, is that the Spanish colonial authorities discriminated against *criollo* producers by allowing Spanish producers access to capital that modernized production. As a result, the *criollos* continued to rely on outdated technology and clung to expensive and inhuman slave labor.

If topography and technology shaped the direction and pace of sugar cane production in Cuba, so too did the myriad trade agreements and tariff restrictions between Washington and Havana. To these influences we must add the vicissitudes to which monocultural production is always susceptible.

Subordinated to the needs of sugar production, the railroads remained dependent on market fluctuations in the price of sugar. During the sugar boom, the railroad lines grew. Their expansion was halted each time the price dropped and was finally ended when the restrictive policy expressed in the agreements, legislation, and sugar tariffs imposed by U.S. interests set permanent bounds to the growth of sugar plantations. The last sugar mill in Cuba was built in 1925. The last important section of track laid in the neocolonial period was completed just two or three years later. (Zannetti and García 1998, 407)

Indeed, North American capital transformed Cuba's sugar industry. Small-scale farmers (*colonos*) were displaced quickly as modernized sugar mills dominated the 20th-century landscape. The plantation system (*latifundia*) deepened its hold on the agrarian labor market that, in turn, brought in thousands of Antillean laborers. Although Cuban capitalists would increase their investment in the island's production system between 1938 and 1948, the U.S. influence in ownership, production, and tariff quotas prevailed in the 1950s (Marrero 1950, 204). These issues would drive Cuban sugar production and development over the next four decades of the socialist government.

SUGAR IN THE SOCIALIST ERA: 1959–2008

Our interpretation of the past nearly half century of sugar production in socialist Cuba reveals four distinct periods: (1) rapid nationalization of sugar mills, production, and distribution; (2) Cuba's membership in the Soviet trading bloc; (3) demise of the Union of Soviet Socialist Republics (USSR) and its price-supported markets; and (4) erratic dismantling of the sugar industry.

Nationalizing the Sugar Industry

Shortly after the 1959 Revolution, the sugar industry underwent radical reforms. The new leadership accused the nation's dependence on sugar and the private ownership of mills, infrastructure, and land as being a key variable of Cuba's underdevelopment. In just a few years the government nationalized sugar mills and plantations and port facilities. The state took ownership of landholdings of more than a certain size; the only way to avoid that was to have private owners reallocate their farms to family members. By 1962 the sugar sector was fully in state control and the decision-making process in regard to sugar—previously made up of thousands of discrete decisions—had become highly centralized. Foreign trade (i.e., who sold what and at what price) also fell under the state's purview.

These radical economic development schema of the early 1960s entailed a heavy reliance on a workforce that could mobilize quickly. Sugar labor included conscripts, students, urban blue- and white-collar workers, and even prison inmates to labor in the *zafra* (sugar harvest). An ambitious goal of this early period was a 10-million-ton harvest of 1970—an Olympic effort to raise output by 40%. Reaching that goal centered on the spread of sugar cane plantations and augmenting the number of laborers in this manually intensive process. Although the 1970 harvest produced a record 8.5 million tons, it inflicted collateral cost by ignoring other economic sectors.

Cuba's Entrance into the Soviet Trading Bloc

In 1972, Cuba gained admission to the Council for Mutual Economic Assistance (CMEA), the Soviet-centered trade bloc that joined the communist nations of Eastern Europe with Mongolia and Vietnam. Cuba had lost a trading preference and guaranteed quota with the United States before 1959, and the island nation now sought comparable price support from Moscow during the peak of the Cold War. CMEA offered Cuba secure markets for sugar and demanded that it specialize and become CMEA's only sugar supplier. CMEA and Cuba reflected a complex relationship in providing Cuba a guaranteed market and fixed prices. The complexity stemmed from the varying exchanges and prices that mirrored both nations' needs at key times (Zimbalist and Brundenius 1989). In a relationship not unlike that of the United Kingdom with its Caribbean colonies and ex-colonies, or between France and its territories as stipulated by the Lomé Convention, Cuba and CMEA worked out a complex web of trade and subsidy arrangements. This face of socialist Cuba's sugar policy contradicted earlier efforts to diversify the nation's economic base; Cuba would deepen its reliance on sugar through CMEA.

State commitment to the agro-industrial sector ensured that annual sugar output hovered around 7.5 million tons throughout the 1980s, versus the 6 million tons of the 1950s. With hindsight, it is arguable that such heavy financial, labor, and chemical inputs were not sustainable. Official discourse downplayed the environmental impacts and (subsidized) production costs (Portela and Aguirre 2000). Nevertheless, inputs in the 1980s rose dramatically. Machinery use increased tenfold, hundreds of miles of canals and culverts were built to accommodate sugar production, the water in reservoirs rose nearly 200-fold, and the consumption of agriculture fertilizer reached more than one million tons. Land area committed to sugar cane production grew by 30% (Figure 3.4, middle panel), and eight new sugar mills were constructed, most of them on low-lying and poorly drained lands. One plan entailed draining a large section of the Zapata Swamp to bring more arable land into sugar production; it was, however, discarded at the last minute because of possible irreversible soil salinization conditions that would have been ruinous, resulting in altering one of the largest ecosystems in the Antilles (Díaz-Briquets and Pérez-López 2000, 17). That sugar dominated the thinking in the first decades of the Revolution is revealed in Figure 3.6, where the proposed projects to reclaim land for the sea—mostly to sustain the sugar agro-industry—would have greatly altered the shape of Cuba. Witness, for instance, the land that would have been filled in between the Isla de Juventud and the main island. "These projects, of course, never got off the ground ... [because they were] unfeasible, uneconomical, or both, and [were] quietly abandoned" (Díaz and-Briquets and Pérez-López 2000, 17). Had they been implemented, they would have been the most drastic environmental modification of the island's landscape ever.

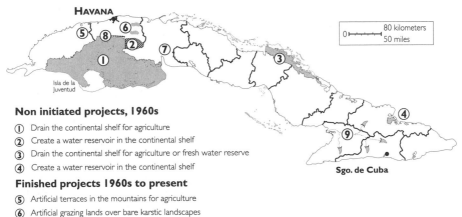

Non initiated projects, 1960s

① Drain the continental shelf for agriculture
② Create a water reservoir in the continental shelf
③ Drain the continental shelf for agriculture or fresh water reserve
④ Create a water reservoir in the continental shelf

Finished projects 1960s to present

⑤ Artificial terraces in the mountains for agriculture
⑥ Artificial grazing lands over bare karstic landscapes
⑦ Desecated the swamp for agriculture
⑧ Levee to stop the freshwater runnoff
⑨ Damming for irrigation and flood control

FIGURE 3.6. Proposed projects to reclaim land from the sea and to drain swamplands. Based on data from Díaz-Briquets and Pérez-López (2000, 16).

The Collapse of the USSR and Its Subsidized Markets

The demise of CMEA in the early 1990s severed the island from its principal trading partners. With the flow of cheap inputs to support the behemoth sugar industry suddenly eliminated, the industry nearly collapsed. Yields fell by half in 6 years. Sugar plantations and mills lapsed into disrepair. Cuba's sugar economy, long accustomed to Soviet subsidies, faced difficulty in competing on the world sugar market. Within a short period, Brazil surpassed Cuba as the world's largest sugar exporter and as Russia's main supplier.

Downsizing the Sugar Industry, Revamping Its Landscape

The same forces that made sugar king would also lead to its rapid demise in the 21st century. Cuba's restructured sugar industry in the 21st century brought to a grinding halt the prevailing role that the crop had played in the island's population, agricultural, and economic geographies (Castellanos Romeu 2001). If the popular saying "Without sugar, there is no country" rang true historically, nothing like that slogan remotely captures the role of sugar today.

In the new millennium, the number of working sugar mills plummeted from more than 140 in 2000 to 70 in 2003 (Figure 3.7). The downsizing of Cuba's sugar sector became evident in the 1990s when the island's production fell in absolute terms and relative to other producers. At the same time, world prices fell and new and strong competition entered the world market from Brazil, China, India, and Thailand. Rising world production confronted a saturated sugar market that also faced alternative sweeteners in the form of high-fructose corn syrup and artificial sweeteners (Peters 2003, 6–7).

Although Cuba's current position in the world sugar market is relatively easy to quantify on the basis of world production and market trends, much less is known about the impacts of restructuring at the local level. Government publications on industry downsizing are vague and erratic. We know little about how sugar's demise affects household consumption (because of decreased government revenues) or about alternative employment opportunities. In 2004 we spoke with workers at a sugar mill in Cienfuegos, who reported that they were learning the basic suite of Microsoft Office software as part of a retraining program. However, attendance at the free training had waned as many become disappointed upon discovering that a transfer into a new line of work was not a sure thing. In 2006 we meet several former sugar cane workers from Matanzas who were liv-

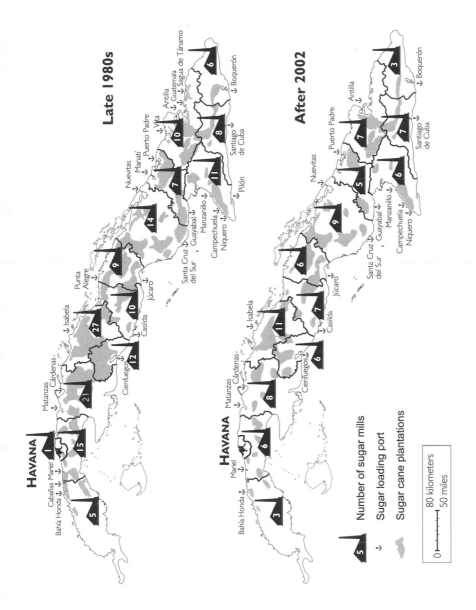

Late 1980s

HAVANA

Bahía Honda
Cabañas Mariel
Matanzas
Cárdenas
Isabela
Punta Alegre
Cienfuegos
Casilda
Júcaro
Nuevitas
Manatí
Puerto Padre
Vita
Antilla
Guatemala
Sagua de Tánamo
Santa Cruz del Sur
Guayabal
Manzanillo
Campechuela
Níquero
Pilón
Santiago de Cuba
Boquerón

15
5
21
27
12
10
9
14
7
11
10
6
8

After 2002

HAVANA

Bahía Honda
Manel
Matanzas
Cárdenas
Isabela
Cienfuegos
Casilda
Júcaro
Nuevitas
Puerto Padre
Antilla
Santa Cruz del Sur
Guayabal
Manzanillo
Campechuela
Níquero
Santiago de Cuba
Boquerón

3
6
8
6
11
7
6
9
5
7
7
6
3

Number of sugar mills

Sugar loading port

Sugar cane plantations

5

0   80 kilometers
0   50 miles

FIGURE 3.7. Downsizing the sugar industry.

65

ing with relatives in Havana, doing "whatever [they] can" (*lo que podamos*) to sustain their families back home. Significantly, those activities were not legally sanctioned and had forced them into an underground status.

CONCLUSIONS

This chapter offers a historical-geographical assessment of Cuba's sugar landscape. It shows how Cuban sugar plantations influenced the racial composition and growth of the island's population. The availability of African slave labor and Europe's demand for sugar were major determinants of sugar's rise in the 18th and 19th centuries. Initially, planters cleared forests south and then east of Havana. Expansion, using African slave labor, allowed the colony to satisfy Spain's demand for sugar, but it also opened markets in Europe and the United States. Nineteenth-century sugar cane production, however, derived from two main factors. One was the expansion of railroad lines after 1837, and the second was the political and economic vicissitudes created by the Cuban colonial struggle and the independence movements in nearby Haiti. Rapid deforestation resulted from these forces.

The diffusion of sugar production left two indelible marks on Cuba's landscape. Cane production spread to parts of Pinar del Río, Matanzas, and Las Villas provinces; rail transportation quickened that expansion. The end of the 19th-century civil wars gave U.S. and, to a lesser extent, British investors a chance to modernize infrastructure and open up new lands in Camagüey. This expansion, in turn, tapped into more ports for international trade.

Sugar cultivation during the 1960s and 1970s increased greatly, in part to meet the 10-million-ton harvest goal of 1970, and to take advantage of the Soviet Union's patronage and the CMEA trade agreements. Although the 1970 harvest reached 8.5 million tons, Cuba would never again reach such a high yield. High chemical inputs proved to be unsustainable once price subsides ended. Fortunately, many of the ambitious land reclamation projects that were proposed in the early decades of the Revolution were not carried out. Since the collapse of the Union of Soviet Socialist Republics (USSR), a changing global economy has altered the pattern of sugar mills and cultivation even further. By 2007 more than half of the mills that were in production at the Triumph of the Revolution had closed. A good number of those mills have been dismantled (Figure 3.8), and others have shifted to molasses production for the rum industry.

FIGURE 3.8. Sugar mill "Central Bolivia" in Ciego de Avila, photographed in 2003 after it had been closed. The main exhaust chimney and elevated cane-loading belt are seen here.

A smaller number have become museums, reflecting the island's substantiated industrial heritage (see Chapter 4).

By July 2006, the price of sugar on the world market rose from about 5¢/pound in 2000 to nearly 17¢/pound, but 2 years later, the commodity plummeted to 9.9¢/pound (illustrating the vicissitudes of the industry). The demand for sugar in the soft drink industry—particularly in China and India—seemed to be driving prices upward (Patton 2006), but the spike appeared to be short-lived. The Cuban government announced that it would consider putting more mills back into production in order to take advantage of this price trend, but doing so meant anticipating the following planting season. U.S. foreign policy toward Cuba has a direct impact on future production levels in Cuba. One of the major forces supporting the U.S. trade embargo on Cuba is the alliance of sugar cane and beet sugar producers in the United States. Reopening trade with Cuba would cut their competitiveness in sugar pricing for the domestic market. Even though these producers are unabashedly free-trade focused, a major sugar lobby in the United States—the American Sugar Alliance—had this to say about sugar pricing and trade:

> Governments of all foreign sugar-producing countries intervene in their production, consumption, and trade of sugar. This makes sugar one of the most heavily subsidized and distorted markets in the world. The result: There is no true "world market" for sugar that bears any relationship to actual global supply and demand conditions. Today, 80 percent of the world's sugar is not traded on an open market. It is sold in the country where it is produced for prices that, on average, are similar to American prices. Only 20 percent of foreign sugar is dumped on the global marketplace for any price it will bring. This surplus sugar is heavily subsidized and historically has received a price that is about half the world average cost of production. (2008)

What is clear, though, is that no single economic, political, or cultural practice has altered Cuba's landscape as greatly as sugar production. The felling of trees, clearing of forests, and planting of "seas of grass" left an indelible mark on the island; so did the reliance on a principal source of foreign exchange. Beet sugar and corn syrup will continue to curtail the global demand for sugar cane, as will artificial sweeteners. Still, reopening the United States to Cuban sugar—either as a sweetener or as a "new" source of fuel in the form of ethanol—might transform the rural landscape of the island, as sugar would once again become king.

NOTE

1. A preliminary version of this chapter appeared in Scarpaci and Portela (2005). Adapted by permission.

CHAPTER 4

▼ ★

HERITAGE

Heritage landscapes are appropriately suited for geographic inquiry because of the concern about location and the array of ecological, social, economic, and political variables that make up these places. Interest in heritage landscapes has risen enormously in recent years (Muir 1999). As noted in Chapter 1, architects, urban designers, historians, archeologists, landscape architects, and especially geographers, pursue this line of study because local objects (monuments, historic sites, national parks) can be situated in different geographic and social scales of analysis. Approaches to the study of landscape are as varied as the number of research topics in the field. Geographers Daniels and Cosgrove (1988, 8) examine landscapes from a postmodernist perspective, claiming that

> landscape seems less like a palimpsest whose "real" or "authentic" meanings can somehow be recovered with the correct techniques ... [like] flickering text displayed on the word-processor screen whose meaning can be created, extended, altered, elaborated and finally obliterated by the nearest touch of a button.

Rose (1992, 10) argues that in human geography, "pleasure in the landscape was often seen as a threat to the scientific gaze." Mitchell (1994, 14) notes that "landscape is itself a physical and multi-sensory medium (earth, stone, vegetation, water, sky, sound and silence, light and darkness, etc.) in which cultural meanings and values are encoded."

Heritage means using the past as an economic resource for the present. Historic districts and monuments allow countries to create national identity, forge ideologies, and "ground" abstract notions of history and heritage in tangible forms (Hall 1995; Hobsbawm 1990; Woolf 1996). The wish to preserve relics of past environments is often tied to an influential elite. However, the tension created over what is to be preserved and whose collective memory should be celebrated is often ignored in official public circles. A bewildering array of places and objects determines what is included in the web of historic preservation projects. As Graham and colleagues (2000, 17) argue:

> Clearly, [heritage] is an economic resource, one exploited everywhere as a primary component of strategies to promote tourism, economic development and rural and urban regeneration. But heritage also helps define the meanings of culture and power and is a political resource; and it thus possesses a crucial sociopolitical function. Consequently, it is accompanied by an often bewildering array of identifications and potential conflicts, not least when heritage places and objects are involved in issues of legitimization of power structures.

Government approaches to the identification, safeguarding, and maintenance of national heritage sites and monuments defy a simple division into whether a nation is a market or a centrally planned economy. For instance, images of historical small town America drive the present construction boom by the Walt Disney Corporation in Celebration, Florida. The town is a planned community that embraces the pre-automobile period that typifies Disney's Main Street pedestrian boulevard at the entrance to Disney World in Orlando, Florida. The United States housing market has displayed a strong demand for neotraditional design structures such as those at Seaside, Florida, and related projects of Andres Duany and Elizabeth Plater-Zyberk of DBZ Associates (Duany, Plater-Zyberk, and Speck 2000). In the community where one of us (J. L. S.) lives—Blacksburg, Virginia—a developer touts a neotraditional community (a.k.a. New Urbanism), the Village at Tom's Creek, this way:

> The Village is a planned "traditional neighborhood development," built according to the principles that shaped traditional Virginia villages. Its character is revealed in its respect for the beautiful rolling landscape of the Tom's Creek Basin. It is designed to create an intimate neighborhood surrounded by and connected to its open meadows and woodlands. Traditional close-knit Virginia communities evolved around distinctive civic spaces. The Village's informal parks, tree-lined boulevards, and small central shops are designed with respect to this tradition. The streets and alleys will provide both intimate lanes of small yards and friendly porches and formal boulevards with flowered medians and small shops. The variety of house styles and sizes will

echo the finest traditional Virginia architecture. (The Village at Tom's Creek 2006)

This example of heritage draws on both cultural (traditional neighborhood development, close-knit Virginia communities, civic spaces) and natural elements (beautiful rolling landscapes, meadows and woodlands, flowered medians). Heritage, therefore, is carefully packaged on the developer's website to conjure up history, lifestyle, and landscape in the roaring U.S. housing market of the early 2000s. Its marketing conveys history, prestige, respectability, and a sensibility toward the fine (middle-class) aesthetics of life.

Yet the question arises: Are such descriptions of heritage so different from promotions of heritage landscapes in Cuba? In the first place, recall from Chapter 1 that islands exude a certain allure as novelty sites. They lend themselves as convenient platforms for all seasons and tastes, for practically any whim or fancy (Baldacchino 2007, 166). Witness, for instance, how historic Trinidad is promoted on the government's national press (Prensa Latina) website:

> The cultural treasure that distinguishes Trinidad gives it a unique distinc-
> tion in the Greater Antilles. Between mountains and sea, the city called the
> "Museum of the Caribbean" expresses a proud and unique natural beauty to
> whoever visits it.... Passing through its narrow cobble-stoned streets allows
> the walker to discover artistic balconies, curved balustrades of precious
> wood, complex iron grillwork, surprisingly decorated walls, and romantic
> patios. (Primeras Villas 2006, our translation)

As in the earlier description of the Virginia village, noting its small-town image, natural and cultural attributes pepper the discourse about the charms of this colonial Caribbean town. Yet assessments of heritage are not always black and white. In the case of Trinidad, there are Cubans who would argue that Trinidad was neglected intentionally in the first decades of the Revolution because the government wanted to punish Trinidadians for the support that some locals lent to the anticommunist guerillas in the Escambray Mountains during the insurgency of the 1960s. When old towns became "fashionable" and when the government discovered that European backpackers were enthralled with Trinidad, the government decided to capitalize on its assets.[1]

In an era of global travel in a deregulated market for the middle classes, heritage is becoming an important niche market in international tourism. Hewison argues that heritage is produced just like any other commodity, "which nobody seems able to define, but which everyone is eager to sell" (1987, 9). If heritage tourism is indeed commodified, then the pressure on developing nations like Cuba is great because the need for hard currency may conflict with what locals want. Cheryl Shanks (2002, 17) describes this paradox as one of the many dilemmas of "artificial authenticity": "Commodifying culture simultaneously preserves, transforms, and destroys it."

This is a sensitive issue for politicians and local officials in developing countries like Cuba because economic development creates pressure to attract dollars or Euros, which, in turn, may corrupt the authenticity of the local culture (Barberia 2002). As examples, we note Ernest Hemingway's favorite bars in Habana Vieja, or dancing the tango in Buenos Aires's San Telmo or La Boca neighborhoods. Both images (Hemingway and tango dancing) garner a disproportionate amount of publicity in promoting heritage even though they may be only marginally related to the history of the neighborhoods in which they are promoted. And the unwitting tourist may know little about the historic veracity of these representations; in fact, he or she may not even care to know (Urry 2002). Nevertheless, as David Lowenthal (1985) has shown, rebuilding historic landscapes offers a familiarity and guidance to present-day residents and tourists even though their historical veracity may be suspect. To be sure, heritage tourism legitimizes the social history of local peoples and portrays positive images of the past. Latin America has no shortage of heritage tourism venues: *favela* (slums) tourism in Brazil (Mahieux 2002), immigrants' heritage tourism in South America (Schlüter 2000), human rights tourism (Burtner 2002; Haddock 2002), and historic district venues (Scarpaci 2005), to name just a few.

Debates internal to Cuba about heritage have thus far been exempt from the neoliberal economic waves rocking other Latin American nations. Breglia (2006) examines heritage in Mexico as an arena in which multiple public and private actors compete for the right to control cultural patrimony. Starting in the early 1990s, she demonstrates how farmers, ethnic minorities, politicians, heritage site managers, and local developers aim to control cultural patrimony as a form of legitimizing how archeological sites should be managed. Her discussion is set against the privatization policies that prevail in Latin America. Although Cuba has thus far been spared these debates, it is unclear how financing heritage projects in a post-Fidel Cuba will unfold and what the role of for-profit management arrangements portends for the island.

Against this backdrop of the debates and issues surrounding heritage, this chapter turns to a brief review of Cuba's heritage sites. These sites have been selected for membership on the United Nations Educational, Scientific, and Cultural Organization's (UNESCO) World Heritage List. In the following section we describe Cuba's participation in UNESCO's program and situate the island's heritage record in an international context. The rest of the chapter summarizes the key features of Cuba's nine World Heritage Sites and the many national landmarks and protected zones. We conclude by revisiting the literature discussed above regarding the meaning of heritage landscapes and their significance in Cuba.

NATIONAL AND INTERNATIONAL HERITAGE SITES IN CUBA

Cuba became a signatory of the World Heritage Convention in 1981, the year before Old Havana was placed on UNESCO's list as a World Heritage Site. The World Heritage Convention promotes preservation of cultural properties and the conservation of rich natural elements. The UNESCO list emphasizes how particular peoples interact with their cultural and natural environments and attempts to preserve the delicate balance between the two. Inscription on the World Heritage List requires that a particular place exhibit "outstanding universal value." Specifically, 10 criteria guide the assessment of heritage sites (Table 4.1), and we refer to these criteria (using lowercase Roman numerals) in our discussion of each site. Cuba has nine entries on this list: seven cultural and two natural (Table 4.2). Given the size of its territory and the absence of a large indigenous population, Cuba places respectably well on the list when compared with its Caribbean and Latin American neighbors, as well as selected European, African, and Asian nations.

By mid-2009, the UNESCO World Heritage List included 878 sites, of which 679 (77.3%) were cultural, 174 (19.8%) were natural, and 25 (2.8%) were mixed properties. And the list keeps growing (United Nations Educational, Scientific, and Cultural Organization 2007). The 2006 annual convention held in Lithuania reviewed 37 nominations: 27 cultural sites, 8 natural sites, 2 mixed sites, and 3 transboundary sites, presented by 30 countries (Doubleday 2006). By 2009, 186 countries had ratified the World Heritage Convention.

CUBA'S WORLD HERITAGE SITES

Cuba boasts nine World Heritage Sites: Six are cultural environments (the Archeological Landscapes of First Coffee Plantations in Southeast-

TABLE 4.1. Selection Criteria for World Heritage Status and Cuban Site Qualification

---

   i   To represent a masterpiece of human creative genius; *Desembarco del Granma National Park.*

   ii   To exhibit an important interchange of human values, over a span of time or within a cultural area of the world, on developments in architecture or technology, monumental arts, town planning, or landscape design; *Urban Historic Center of Cienfuegos, Alejandro de Humboldt Park.*

   iii   To bear a unique or at least exceptional testimony to a cultural tradition or to a civilization that is living or that has disappeared; *Archaeological Landscapes of First Coffee Plantations in Southeastern Cuba; Desembarco del Granma National Park.*

   iv   To be an outstanding example of a type of building, architectural or technological ensemble, or landscape that illustrates significant stage(s) in human history; *Old Havana and Its Fortifications, San Pedro de Roca Castle, Santiago de Cuba; Trinidad and Valley of the Ingenios; Viñales Valley, Alejandro de Humboldt Park; Viñales Valley; historic center of Camagüey.*

   v   To be an outstanding example of a traditional human settlement, land use, or sea use that is representative of a culture (or cultures), or human interaction with the environment especially when it has become vulnerable under the impact of irreversible change; *Old Havana and Its Fortifications, San Pedro de Roca Castle, Santiago de Cuba; Trinidad and Valley of the Ingenios; Urban Historic Center of Cienfuegos; historic center of Camagüey.*

   vi   To be directly or tangibly associated with events or living traditions, with ideas, or with beliefs, with artistic and literary works of outstanding universal significance. (The Committee considers that this criterion should preferably be used in conjunction with other criteria.)

   vii   To contain superlative natural phenomena or areas of exceptional natural beauty and aesthetic importance.

   viii   To be outstanding examples representing major stages of the earth's history, including the record of life, significant ongoing geological processes in the development of landforms, or significant geomorphic or physiographic features.

   ix   To be outstanding examples representing significant ongoing ecological and biological processes in the evolution and development of terrestrial, freshwater, coastal, and marine ecosystems, and communities of plants and animals.

   x   To contain the most important and significant natural habitats for *in situ* conservation of biological diversity, including those containing threatened species of outstanding universal value from the point of view of science or conservation.

Note. Data from United Nations Educational, Scientific, and Cultural Organization (2006a).

TABLE 4.2. World Heritage Sites, 2009,
by Selected Nations

Argentina	8	Guatemala	3
Bangladesh	3	Haiti	1
Belgium	9	Honduras	2
Belize	1	Indonesia	7
Bolivia	6	Japan	14
Brazil	17	Kenya	4
Canada	13	Lebanon	5
Chile	4	Mexico	29
China	31	New Zealand	3
Colombia	5	Nicaragua	1
Cuba	9	North Korea	1
Costa Rica	3	Norway	7
Czech Republic	12	Panama	5
Congo	5	Peru	10
Dominican Republic	1	South Africa	8
El Salvador	1	Syria	5
France	33	United States	20
Greece	16	Venezuela	3

Note. Data from United Nations Educational, Scientific, and
Cultural Organization (2009).

ern Cuba, Urban Historic Center of Cienfuegos, Habana Vieja and its
fortifications, San Pedro de Roca Castle in Santiago de Cuba, Trinidad,
and Viñales Valley) and two are natural settings (Alejandro de Humboldt
National Park, Desembarco del Granma National Park) (Table 4.3). These
landscapes are evenly distributed throughout the island (Figure 4.1).
Since 1992, UNESCO has used the term "cultural landscape" to refer
to the interaction that exists between the cultural and natural environments (United Nations Educational, Scientific, and Cultural Organization
2006a). UNESCO inscribed Tongariro National Park (New Zealand) as
its first cultural landscape on the World Heritage List because it displayed
spiritual links of the indigenous Maori people with their land (Rössler
2004b). Cuba's Viñales Valley and the Archaeological Landscapes of the
First Coffee Plantations in Southeastern Cuba are two "cultural landscapes" out of 37 recognized by UNESCO (United Nations Educational,
Scientific, and Cultural Organization 2006a). In the sections that follow
we first discuss the natural heritage sites and then the cultural ones.[2]

Natural Heritage Sites

Well before the demise of the former Soviet Union and the disbanding of
the Eastern bloc nations, there was legitimate concern about the impact

TABLE 4.3. Cuba's UNESCO World Heritage Sites

Site	Location	Cultural or natural site (year established)	Attributes
Alejandro de Humboldt National Park	Holguín and Guantánamo Provinces N20° 27′ W75° 0′	Natural (2001)	Large concentration and high diversity of endemic fauna and flora. Landform variety, altitudinal diversity, and rich lithologies. Freshwater biological diversity stems from one of the largest watersheds in the Caribbean. Named after Alexander von Humboldt for his research in Cuba in the early 1800s.
Archeological Landscapes of First Coffee Plantations in Southeastern Cuba	Santiago and Guantánamo Provinces N20° 01′ 48″ W75° 23′ 29″	Cultural (2000); also a designated "cultural landscape"	Remnants of 19th-century coffee plantations in Sierra Maestra foothills stand as testimony to an enterprising agricultural system carved out of steep topography. Construction highlights the technological, social, and economic conditions, of the Caribbean at that time.
Cienfuegos: Urban Historic Center	South central port city of 150,000 residents N 22° 08′ 50″ W80° 27′ 10″	Cultural (2005)	Settled by French settlers rather late in Cuba's history (1819), Cienfuegos became an important agricultural trading center and port. Its historic core displays an eclectic architectural ensemble that embraces the ideas of modernity and hygiene in 19th-century Latin America.
Desembarco del Granma National Park	National Park, southeast corner of Cuba N19° 53′ W77° 38′	Natural (1999)	Established in 1986 as a national park, its 26,180 hectare area includes some of the best examples of elevated marine terraces and karst topography. Considered one of the finest natural landscapes along the Atlantic Ocean.
Old Havana (Habana Vieja)	City of Havana Province N 23° 8′ W82° 21′	Cultural (1982)	Settled in 1519 by Diego Velázquez de Cuéllar as one of the island's seven initial settlements (*villas*). Includes the core of the historic settlement of San Cristóbal de La Habana and its fortifications from the 16th through 18th centuries. Encompasses most of the municipality of Habana Vieja, which is one of 15 such jurisdictions in Havana City Province.

(cont.)

TABLE 4.3. *(cont.)*

Site	Location	Cultural or natural site (year established)	Attributes
San Pedro de Roca Castle, Santiago de Cuba	Santiago de Cuba City N19° 58′ 0″ W75° 52′ 15″	Cultural (1997)	Citadel located at the entrance to the harbor of Santiago de Cuba. Considered a prime example of Spanish colonial military architecture derived from Renaissance and Italian designs.
Trinidad and Valle de los Ingenios	South central Cuba, Sancti Spiritus Province N21° 48′ 11″ W79 59′ 4″	Cultural (1988)	The town of Trinidad and valley adjacent to it where sugar production in the 18th and 19th centuries reigned supreme and sugar mills (*ingenios*) dominated the landscape, especially in the first half of the 19th century.
Viñales Valley	Pinar del Río Province N22° 37′ W83° 43′	Cultural (1999); also a designated "cultural landscape"	A visually striking valley because of large limestone erosive remnants called haystacks or *mogotes* (in Spanish). Includes the island's prime tobacco production system, largely unchanged over the centuries. It possesses unique vernacular architecture and a multiethnic population that mirrors that of the broader Antilles region.

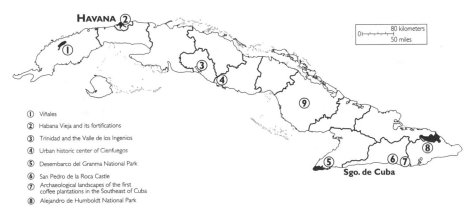

① Viñales
② Habana Vieja and its fortifications
③ Trinidad and the Valle de los Ingenios
④ Urban historic center of Cienfuegos
⑤ Desembarco del Granma National Park
⑥ San Pedro de la Roca Castle
⑦ Archaeological landscapes of the first coffee plantations in the Southeast of Cuba
⑧ Alejandro de Humboldt National Park
⑨ Historic center of Camagüey

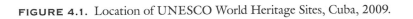

FIGURE 4.1. Location of UNESCO World Heritage Sites, Cuba, 2009.

that centrally managed economies were having on the natural environ-ment. Crucial to this preoccupation was the idea that "scientifically" guided centrally planned nations were paying little attention to industrial and urban externalities. Verifying health statistics and validating environ-mental impacts were virtually impossible for outside agencies such as the United Nations Development Programme (UNDP). Stalinist and post-Stalinist industrialization policies proved to be the culprits, as the Soviet bloc nations forged their own industrial-military complexes in the zero-sum game that cast the Cold War into two distinct camps. Although the communist camp argued that environmental destruction could stem only from industrial capitalism's relentless pursuit of profits, there was legiti-mate concern—corroborated later by a postcommunist "autopsy" of envi-ronmental impact—that the Soviet bloc was destined for a sort of "eco-cide." As Feschback and Friendly (1992, 1) noted in regard to the Soviet Union soon after the fall of the Berlin Wall, "No other great industrial civilization so systematically and so long poisoned its land, air, water, and people. None so loudly proclaiming its efforts to improve public health and protect nature so degraded both." Given Cuba's three-decade attach-ment to the Soviet bloc's trading group (CMEA, Council for Mutual Eco-nomic Assistance), it is appropriate to ask the question: What about the environmental record of the "Pearl of the Caribbean"?

Law 33, passed in 1981, was a thin document (just 25 pages) that addressed environmental protection based on the "principles of the Cuban Communist Party concerning the environment" (Segre, Coyula, and Scar-paci 1997, 169). As in the former Soviet Union, environmental degra-dation was seen as a by-product of industrial capitalism. Other analysts summarized socialist Cuba's environmental policy this way: "[The] wise use of natural resources by communist countries versus the indiscriminate use of natural resources by the Capitalistic World" (Barba and Avella 1996, 34–35). Cuba's environmental record has been rightly criticized by others, particularly because of its disregard for industrial waste, expansive land-clearing projects in the early years of the Revolution, and lack of urban water and waste treatment facilities (Díaz-Briquets and Pérez-López 2000; Scarpaci et al. 2002, ch. 10). Nevertheless, the past half-century has seen a gradual reforestation of the island.

In 1812, for instance, it was estimated that 90% of the island was forested. By 1900, that figure dropped to 54% as a result of the spread of sugar cane cultivation (Scarpaci and Portela 2005) and continued to fall to 14% in 1959. By 1975, however, reforestation programs produced a comeback in forest cover (to 18%), and today that figure hovers around 20% (*Atlas de Cuba* 1978, 40; Linden 2003). A relatively low population density, areas that are topographically difficult to access, and early land conservation in the eastern part of the island may account for this recovery. Linden (2003, 102–103) argues that when an illiterate farmer provided protection for Castro's guerrillas after they landed the boat *Granma* on the shores of then Santiago de Cuba Province in 1957, this farmer—Guillermo García Frías—assumed political positions in the Castro government once Batista was overthrown. "A nature lover," writes Linden, "García turned to preserving the Sierra Maestra" (Linden 2003, 102). Regardless of the reasons, Cuba does boast some spectacular natural heritage sites, to which we now turn.

Alejandro de Humboldt National Park

Located in the southeastern corner of the island in the province of Granma is Alejandro de Humboldt National Park; this protected area is perhaps the most important biodiversity spot in the nation. As discussed previously, it is named after the German naturalist who briefly visited the island in 1800–1801 and then in 1804 (Humboldt 2001).

The flora and fauna inventory of the park encompasses an extensive array of landscape elements: mountains, valleys, plains, marine terraces, keys, bays, and coral reefs. The park holds key natural habitats for conservation and terrestrial biological diversity for the insular Caribbean region. It is home to 16 of 28 plant formations that are specific to Cuba, making it a distinct biogeographic realm. According to León Moya (2001), along with New Caledonia in Australia, the park is a place with one of the greatest density of endemic species on the planet. Of 905 endemic species— one-third of the island's total—are within the park's limits. Almost 70% of the 1,302 spermatophytes (seed plants) found are endemic to the park. Accordingly, it "is one of the most biologically diverse terrestrial tropical ecosystems in an island setting anywhere on earth" (United Nations Educational, Scientific, and Cultural Organization 2008).

The steep Cuchillas del Toa (Toa Peaks) biosphere occupies half of the park's area, which is one of six biospheres on the island (the others are Baconao, Buenavista, Ciénaga de Zapata, Península de Guanahacabibes, and Sierra del Rosario). The Sagua Baracoa mountain ranges forming the northern edge of the park are geologically some of the oldest on the island, dating to the Mesozoic era, Jurassic period (169 million years old) (León Moya 2001; Marrero 1957, 33), and form the core of the park's mountains. Particularly noteworthy in the mountains is the Cuban dragon tree (*Dracaena cubensis*), whose botanical relatives stem from the Canary Islands, North Africa, and Madagascar. The elusive royal woodpecker (*carpinerto real* in Spanish, or *Campephilus principalies bardili*) is also sought by the most avid bird-watchers (*Atlas de Cuba* 1978, 41).

There is further speculation about the existence of another woodpecker on the island: "If the ivory-billed woodpecker still exists anywhere on the earth, it is likely to be atop a plateau deep inside Humboldt Park" (Linden 2003, 98).

Desembarco del Granma National Park

In 1999, UNESCO added the Desembarco del Granma National Park to its World Heritage List. It is named after the landing (*desembarco*) of Fidel Castro and 82 rebels who had traveled from Mexico to Cuba in 1956 to overthrow the government of Fulgencio Batista. The ship they had purchased in Mexico was called *Granma*, a name that was later given to one new province (of three) created out of the former province of Santiago de Cuba in 1975. The daily official newspaper published by the Cuban Communist Party is also called Granma.

The park is noteworthy for the layers of marine terraces and its well-defined karst topography. The area is a good example of the tectonic forces that create uplifting as the Caribbean plate collides with the North American plate. Dramatic stair-step terraces and cliffs create unique ecosystems. UNESCO considered the coastal cliffs in the region to be some of the most pristine along the Western Atlantic region between South America and the Canadian Maritime provinces (United Nations Educational, Scientific, and Cultural Organization 1999).

In a 1999 pronouncement, UNESCO commended the Cuban government for its conservation efforts in the park, despite the difficult economic conditions gripping the nation (United Nations Educational, Scientific, and Cultural Organization 1999). The national commission of ICOMOS (International Commission on Monuments and Sites) petitioned the World Heritage Fund for technical assistance so that a tourism management plan might be included for the park's administration.

Cultural Heritage Sites

Archeological Landscapes of First Coffee Plantations in Southeastern Cuba

Chocolate drunk by the elite at leisure, was the principal nonalcoholic beverage consumed during the first two centuries of the colony's history. It was not until the introduction of coffee about 1750 that the beverage became popular. Coffee production in nearby Haiti and the Dominican Republic was firmly established at this time, and it is alleged that traders brought coffee to Cuba from Santo Domingo. As discussed in Chapter 3, it was the Haitian slave rebellion of 1791 that pushed producers and traders out of Hispaniola, and many settled in Cuba and New Orleans (at that time, French territory). Santiago de Cuba became the first coffee producer on the island. Production takes advantage of the humid, cool, and forested slopes of the Sierra Maestra (Portela 2003). UNESCO considers these old coffee plantations a designated "cultural landscape" because of the unique way it represents how humans interacted (i.e., terraced, planted, harvested, and processed) with the natural landscape.

Reflecting the French colonial origins of coffee in Cuba, other French cultural practices established a foothold in the Spanish colony. In the early 1800s cafes sprang up in Havana and Santiago, accompanied by an interest in French music and culture (Segre et al. 1997). Climatic conditions in the Sierra Maestra mountains and their foothills were conducive to coffee plantations and cultivation. French émigrés etched their estates into the lush vegetation of southeastern Cuba, and coffee soon rivaled sugar as a profitable investment for both local consumption and export. However, competition and greater yields from investments in Costa Rica, Brazil, and Venezuela hurt the Cuban coffee market. By the late 19th century the island was cast in intermittent war with Spain, most notably the Ten Years' War (1868–1878).

In 2000, UNESCO acted favorably on the Cuban petition to include the remnants of these 19th-century coffee estates on its World Heritage List. Several coffee plantations in the vicinity still operate. Cuba produces mainly Arabica beans, known for their full flavor and relatively low levels of caffeine. Among the most popular brands of coffee for domestic and international consumption are Caracolillo, Cristal Mountain, Cubita, Serrano, and Turquino.

Cienfuegos

The historic quarter of Cienfuegos is the most recent addition to the island's list of cultural heritage sites. Unlike Havana and Santiago, Cienfuegos was not settled by the Spanish in the 16th century. Rather, a group of French immigrants from Bordeaux and Louisiana petitioned then-governor José Cienfuegos for permission to establish this port town on a deepwater bay on the Caribbean Sea. Table 4.1 shows that the World Heritage List attributes of Cienfuegos are cultural criteria (ii) and (iv). Specifically, the historic town center of Cienfuegos displays key influences of architectural design and planning that hark back to the Spanish Enlightenment. It also includes a choice selection of urban planning in Latin America in the 19th century (Figure 4.2), with its emphasis on segregating different land uses (industry from residences) and its strict adherence to an orthogonal grid plan (Hardoy 1992).

FIGURE 4.2. *Bottom:* Cienfuego's town hall (*ayuntamiento*) located on the south side of the main plaza in the heart of the UNESCO World Heritage Site is presently the seat of the provincial government. Its dome is allegedly modeled after Havana's Capitolio (completed in 1930), which, in turn, is modeled after the U.S. Capitol building in Washington, DC. *Top:* Gazebo and church on same plaza.

Cienfuego's main town square is, according to the "decision text" of ICOMOS' commission, "an outstanding example of an architectural ensemble representing the new ideas of modernity, hygiene and order" (United Nations Educational, Scientific, and Cultural Organization 2006b). An interesting complex of buildings cluster around the main plaza (Parque Martí), including the Cathedral of the Purísima Concepción (1833–1869), Provincial Museum (1896), Palacio Ferrer (Figure 4.3), and Tomás Terry Theater (1886–1889). These attributes are partly why Cubans call Cienfuegos the "Pearl of the South."

FIGURE 4.3. Palacio Ferrer sits at the western edge of Parque Martí in the heritage site of Cienfuegos. Built in the early 1900s by a wealthy sugar baron, José Ferrer Sirés, it is unique because of the blue mosaic cupola and spiral staircase. Famous opera stars, such as Enriquo Caruso, who sang at the nearby Terry Theater, purportedly stayed at the Palacio Ferrer during visits to Cienfuegos.

Old Havana and Its Fortifications

The 142 hectares that constitute Old Havana (Habana Vieja) are part of a legally protected area that contains a spectacular layering of historic buildings and public spaces spanning nearly half a millennium. If Lewis Mumford's (1986) legendary statement that "in the city, time becomes visible" has any veracity, then surely it is so in Havana. Founded in 1519 as one of the original *villas*, the city changed its location twice before settling on a cape at the western edge of the bay, originally called Puerto Carena (today called Havana Bay or *Bahía de la Habana*). The first site in 1516 was on the southern (Caribbean) shore of the island, near the present port of Batabanó. Adjacent swamplands and an unprotected bay led the military expedition that followed Diego de Velázquez's party to relocate to the northern (Florida Straits–Atlantic Ocean) site, near the Almendares River (the present-day divide between Vedado and Miramar municipalities). Soon thereafter the current site of Habana Vieja was selected because of its bag-shaped harbor and more defensible port.

Perhaps no other heritage site in Latin America and the Caribbean has received as much attention as Habana Vieja, the historic municipality in Havana City province. Because much has been written about the district, our remarks here are brief. It is a relatively large UNESCO designation and is home to about 85,000 residents. Long neglected by many governments before and after the Revolution, the property was admitted to UNESCO's heritage list in 1982, but it was not until the creation of Habaguanex and a number of related construction and real estate firms tied to the City Historian's Office (directed by Dr. Eusebio Leal) that the systematic restoration of Habana Vieja began in the mid-1990s. It includes some the largest collections of Spanish colonial architecture in the Americas (Figure 4.4). Three key plazas (Catedral, Armas, and Vieja), as well as several pedestrian boulevards (Prado and Obispo), anchor the historic preservation projects (see also Colantonio and Potter 2006a, 2006b; Edge, Woofard, and Scarpaci 2006; Scarpaci 2000; Scarpaci et al. 2002).

The City Historian's Office has been an engine of economic development, not just for Habana Vieja, but also for all of Cuba. Its annual budgets rocketed from just U.S. $3 million in 1993 to more than U.S. $60 million in the new millennium. It employs perhaps as many as 6,000 workers spread among construction (Puerto de Carena), real estate (Fénix and Aurea), historic preservation and tourism (Habaguanex), travel (San Cristóbal), monument restoration, and other agencies (Scarpaci et al. 2002, 340–343). The City Historian's Office (the office, henceforth) rightly boasts a huge list of redevelopment projects. What is unclear, however, are the actual revenues generated by heritage tourism in the old city, the

FIGURE 4.4. San Francisco Plaza with the former San Francisco Church in the background, and the Sierra Maestra warehouse and ocean terminal to the left (on Havana Bay). The former church is used mainly for conferences, meetings, and concert recitals as administered by the Office of the City Historian, not the Roman Catholic Church.

portion that is directed to the national treasury, and the percentage that actually reaches local residents (Colantonio 2004). It may be significant that the southern tip of Habana Vieja contains the poor neighborhood of San Isidro, which has been targeted by the office for residential rehabilitation. Unlike the approach in Trinidad, though, the office labors in multiple areas and its efforts are a powerhouse in a city and national economy that has faced setbacks in tourism and sugar production.

Another contentious issue is the extent to which residents of Habana Vieja are displaced, especially across the bay to the sprawling public housing complexes in Habana del Este. Foreign tourist investment and public–private partnerships with foreign capital are a top priority policy objective in Cuba, where the office contracts with mostly European investors in revitalizing Habana Vieja. Historic preservation enhances social stability while supporting the country's environmental and socioeconomic resources. Colantonio (2005) argues that the revitalization of Habana Vieja is drawing key personnel from other "badges of honor" touted by the Revolution: health care and sports. This labor transfer has resulted from the higher-paying jobs in national currency and access to hard currency (gratuities) in tourism. Focus groups conducted by Scarpaci (2005, 141–145) showed that residents of Habana Vieja are generally pessimistic about the benefits of heritage tourism that will accrue to them, but their cynicism is not much different from that of residents in the UNESCO historic sites of Cartagena, Colombia, or Cuenca, Ecuador. Nevertheless, restoration efforts cannot proceed fast enough to rescue the historic shell of the old quarters, which have been debilitated by humidity, storms, high temperatures, and a lack of maintenance.

UNESCO also included military fortifications in its designation. The fortresses of El Morro (Figure 4.5), Real Fuerza, La Punta, and La Cabaña constitute the largest collection of colonial architecture concentrated in one district in the Western hemisphere. Inspired by Renaissance and Italian military designs from the 16th to the 18th centuries, these garrisons complement the ramparts that surrounded Habana Vieja until 1861, at which time they were torn down because of their military obsolescence. During the colonial era this network of forts guarded the riches pouring out of Mexico and South America, which found their way as part of the famous flotilla sailing from Havana to Cádiz, Spain, at the end of the hurricane season in late October.

FIGURE 4.5. El Morro Castle.

These former castle-fortresses now serve largely as museums and mixed heritage venues. La Punta (built between 1589 and 1600 to guard the "point" or western entrance to the bay) houses a naval museum. Castillo de los Tres Santos Reyes del Morro (or simply El Morro), built between 1589 and 1630, is an impressive polygon-shaped fort sitting on a rocky bluff at the eastern mouth of the bag-shaped bay. Its museum holdings focus on military and naval themes, and many visitors are drawn to its lighthouse dating from the 1840s.

La Cabaña (Forteleza de San Carlos de la Cabaña) was completed in 1774 in response to the British taking of the city in 1762. It sits on a high ridge overlooking Habana Vieja and was designed to thwart repeat land attacks from the east. Each evening there is a colonial reenactment of the canon firing ceremony that announced the closing of the city gates (Figure 4.6).

La Cabaña also has a complex history and allows myriad interpretations of the meaning of heritage landscapes in contemporary Cuba. It houses a museum dedicated to Che Guevara. However, there is little curatorial attention given to Guevara's role as head of the military tribunals (*Comisión Depuradura*) held immediately after the Triumph of the Revolution in 1959, in which suspects were tried and executed; some allege that these "puppet" courts ignored well-established judicial review and instead opted for military court procedures that are enacted during states of siege and national emergencies (Brown and Lagos 1991; Valladares 1986; Vargas Llosa 2005). La Cabaña is also where political prisoners were kept, including the Cuban author Reinaldo Arenas (1943–1990). His life in Cuba as a persecuted political dissident, author, and homosexual led to his imprisonment (see Arenas 1991). In 1973 the authorities arrested him for "ideological deviation." He was tortured in La Cabaña, where the harsh living conditions included backed-up sewage and whose visual portrayal reached mass audiences in Julian Schnabel's film *Before Night Falls*. Spanish actor Javier Bardem played Arenas, and the movie was based on Arenas's original Spanish-language book *Antes de que Anochezca* (1993). While imprisoned, Arenas was threatened with death if he failed to renounce his writings. Arenas's amusing yet tragic statement about the differences between capitalism and communism reads:

> The difference between the communist and capitalist systems is that, although both give you a kick in the ass, in the communist system you have to applaud, while in the capitalist system you can scream. *And I came here to scream.* (Reinaldo Arenas, shortly after arriving in Miami, 1980, cited in *The Sunday Times*, May 14, 2006; emphasis added)

FIGURE 4.6. La Cabaña's evening ceremony reenacts the closing of the city gates in Habana Vieja, across the bay from the fortress. This historic reenactment is one of the few ceremonies where international tourists (paying the equivalent of U.S. $5) and Cubans (paying about U.S. 25¢) mingle in the same public space. Soldiers from Cuba's Revolutionary Armed Forces don Spanish colonial military garb as they march from the barracks to the canon, load it, and fire it at 9:00 P.M.

Information presented at La Cabaña fortress and museum reveal no history of either political prisoner holdings or summary executions. Estimates of the number of executions carried out there and over which Che Guevara presided range from 179 to several thousand (Brown and Lagos 1991). Mario Vargas Llosa (2005) describes Che's actions as comparable to those of Lavrentiy Pavlovich Beria (1899–1953), who was Joseph Stalin's head of Soviet security and police apparatus during the Great Purge of the 1930s. Not surprisingly, La Cabaña's themes of English naval attacks, corsairs, and pirates exclude Arenas and other political prisoners (e.g., prisoners of conscientiousness) who served time in this 18th-century fortress. However, in other nations political imprisonment, torture, and extermination serve as a niche-type heritage industry, as evidenced by Nelson Mandela's South African imprisonment on Robben Island (12 kilometers offshore of Cape Town; *see* Mandela 1994), detention centers that have come to light in post-Pinochet Chile (Scarpaci and Frazier 1993), and the rise of holocaust or atrocity tourism (Ashworth 2002; Ashworth and Tunbridge 1990), respectively. As this chapter has shown, heritage interpretation and the development of curatorial displays are an evolving process in Cuba, and such recognition of the darker side of La Cabaña's Spanish colonial façade may some day be revealed.

San Pedro de Roca Castle, Santiago de Cuba

Santiago de Cuba, one of the original seven *villas* on the island founded by Diego de Velázquez, was the colonial capital until 1592, at which time the Spanish Crown transferred the main government powers to Havana. Santiago was the target of pirate and corsair attacks, and its isolation from the capital led to a productive contraband trade during the colonial period (Martínez-Fernández 2003). Like many Cuban cities, Santiago de Cuba possesses a bag-shaped (or pocket) bay, consisting of a narrow entrance that widens in the back bay area. San Pedro de Roca is perched on a cliff at the top of the eastern side of Santiago de Cuba's harbor (Figure 4.7).

Colonial Governor Pedro de la Roca commissioned Italian military engineer Giovanni Battista Antonelli to design this fortress in 1637, about 10 kilometers southwest of the city of Santiago de Cuba. The citadel, built between 1638 and 1700, was capable of housing 400 soldiers. As is true of much colonial and institutional architecture (convents, hospitals, forts, castles), its uses have changed from a fort protecting the city against pirate trades, to a prison in 1775, and then again to a fort in 1898 during the Cuban-Spanish-American Wars.

FIGURE 4.7. El Morro Castle, UNESCO World Heritage Site, evening canon ceremony in Santiago de Cuba.

The fort was included in the list because of its outstanding features noted in criteria (iv) and (v). Specifically, UNESCO recognized that the military construction "constitute[s] the largest and most comprehensive example of the principles of Renaissance military engineering adapted to the requirements of European colonial powers in the Caribbean" (United Nations Educational, Scientific, and Cultural Organization 2006c). The casemates on one of the upper levels house a permanent display of prints that highlight the history of forts in the Santiago de Cuba region. An original winch at the drawbridge that covers a moat, and an intricate set of stone stairways lacing through six distinct levels, give San Pedro de la Roca considerable tourist appeal.

Trinidad and Valle de los Ingenios

Trinidad was also one of the island's original villas founded by Diego Velázquez de Cuéllar. It was settled in 1514 and named after the Holy Trinity (called *Santísima Trinidad* in Spanish). The town was a key transshipment and refurbishment point for maritime traffic between eastern (Santiago de Cuba) and western (Havana) ports. One point reflecting Trinidad's fame, or infamy, is that it was the last refurbishing point for Hernán Cortez in 1519 before he set out to conquer the Valley of Mexico and embark on what turned out to be one of the largest genocides in the European domination of the Americas (Figure 4.8).

Trinidad's relative isolation fostered a regional economy based on illegal trade with Dutch, English, and French merchants, while also leaving it vulnerable to attacks by corsairs, buccaneers, and pirates. As in other parts of Cuba, the Caribbean, and North America, the Haitian slave revolt sent French colonial sugar cane growers in search of new lands and their settlement in eastern Cuba introduced distinctive vernacular architectural details (Figure 4.9).

Trinidad's elite benefited greatly from this sugar investment and took advantage of the fertile soils located in the adjacent valley, where the periodic floods from local rivers draining the Escambray Mountains provided rich alluvium for sugar cane production. In the first half of the 19th century, Trinidad and its adjacent valley (called the *Ingenio,* or grinding-stone sugar mill) attracted significant investment and, in turn, produced considerable exports of sugar (Figure 4.10). The elite built opulent palaces in town, such as the Palacio Cantero, mansions in the adjacent valley, and religious architecture (Figure 4.11). This slave-based production (Figure 4.12) peaked in the 1850s or so as the local cane growers failed to update their *ingenios* with more modern mills (*centrales*) that used steam-powered processing and grinding mechanisms.

FIGURE 4.8. A statue in Trinidad dedicated to the memory of Friar Bartolomé de las Casas, one of the few clergymen who objected to the enslavement and mistreatment of Native Americans during the 16th century. Located at the entrance to the Hotel Las Cuevas in Trinidad. Neither Trinidad nor the rest of the island had a particularly large indigenous population, but the native Tainos and Arawaks were quickly decimated as a result of infectious diseases, warfare, and their mistreatment as slaves who labored in the mines.

Railroad expansion in western Cuba (Havana and Matanzas provinces) gave sugar cane growers greater proximity and lower transportation costs to the United States market. Eventually, other sugar cane regions in Cuba and Latin America exceeded Ingenio Valley production levels. The shift in sugar production and investment left a museum-like cluster of colonial homes, palaces, churches (Figure 4.13), and streets in Trinidad, many of the latter adorned with ship ballast from Hamburg, Germany, as well as a blending of cut stone with stream rock, called *chinas pelonas* (Figure 4.11). Relative isolation from the larger port of Cienfuegos (a paved road did not connect the two places until the 1950s) indirectly resulted in a rich collection of 19th-century artifacts, less by design and more by default; Cubans call the town the "museum city" (Scarpaci 2005, ch. 7).

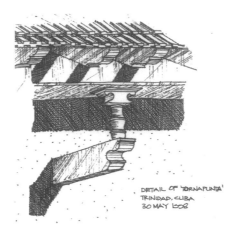

DETAIL OF 'TORNAPUNTA'
TRINIDAD, CUBA
30 MAY 2008

FIGURE 4.9. French migration to Cuba introduced minor but interesting changes into the vernacular design. French roof tiles, for instance, consisted of a series of rectangular "locking" pieces that contrasted with the traditional Spanish tile. The latter were "curved" by traditional artisans, who molded the clay tiles on their thighs before firing them in kilns. Trinidad's homes also contain a cantilever bracing system called *tornapunta*, seen above. It is a mounted spindle fastened to a beam protruding from the exterior wall of Trinidad homes. Courtesy of Marisa Masangkay.

FIGURE 4.10. Valley of the Ingenios, UNESCO World Heritage Site, adjacent to Trinidad.

FIGURE 4.11. Many of the streets in Trinidad are built with a blend of local river rock and ship ballast from European ports.

FIGURE 4.12. The former San Francisco Convent and Monastery in Trinidad, now a school and a museum dedicated to the revolutionary fighters who fought against the anti-Castro uprising in the Escambray Mountains (called the "Cleansing of the Escambray") between 1961 and 1965. It is now called the Museo de la Lucha contra los Bandidos (Struggle against the Bandits Museum). The bell in the tower dates from 1853.

FIGURE 4.13. This tower built in the 1840s, called the Iznaga Tower (after the plantation owner), allowed the overseer (*mayordomo*) to keep an eye on slaves working the sugar fields. When the Restoration Office in Trinidad was established in 1988, rebuilding the steps in the tower was the first project completed.

An expanding team of talented professionals, headed originally by the late Trinidad native and architect Roberto "Macholo" González and later by architect Nancy Benítez, maintains the properties in much of the historic district. A 2% tax imposed on hard currency operations (hotels, restaurants, taxis, bars, art galleries, etc.) and a 1% tax on peso-run establishments produced an annual budget of more than $400,000 in the early years of the millennium. Significantly, the Trinidad restoration team does not prioritize restaurants, art galleries, museums, or other entities devoted strictly to tourism. After an early phase (1988–1992) of restoring key "elite" structures from the 18th and 19th centuries, the group has focused largely on improving run-down residential structures in the Three Crosses Neighborhoods (*Barrio Tres Cruces*), with the assistance of the Barcelona-based nongovernmental organization (NGO), Architects without Borders (*Arquitectos sin Frontera*). Efforts are under way to develop a network of bed-and-breakfast facilities and an agricultural museum (Figure 4.14) in the Valley of the Ingenios, as well as to curtail impending beachfront hotel

FIGURE 4.14. The former living room of Guaímaro Plantation, in the Valley of the Ingenios, about 8 kilometers outside Trinidad. The house dates from the 1830s and contains frescoes by Italian muralists. The Restoration Office of Trinidad has plans to convert the former plantation into an agricultural heritage and machinery museum in an effort to decentralize heritage tourism away from urban Trinidad and into the valley.

development along Ancón Peninsula, some 11 kilometers from Trinidad proper (Scarpaci 2005, ch. 7).

Viñales

UNESCO's "cultural landscape" classification stems from the long-standing tradition of tobacco cultivation as well as the area's tobacco sheds and other distinctive vernacular architecture (Figure 4.15). This valley's proximity to the capital makes it a common day trip for visitors to Havana. It is located about 112 miles (180 kilometers) west of Havana in Pinar del Río Province. Its green tobacco fields, coffee, and mixed cropping convey a postcard-perfect beauty (Figure 4.16). Moreover, a unique combination of even temperature, hills and valleys (Figure 4.17), humidity, solar exposition, and soil conditions create a unique biogeographic realm and microclimate that produces some of the world's finest tobacco leaf.

FIGURE 4.15. UNESCO was impressed with the Viñales tobacco-based agricultural system, which has remained fairly unchanged throughout the years, thus leading the Geneva-based institution to designate it as a "cultural landscape." Tobacco drying sheds such as these have changed little over time in terms of design and building materials. Thatched walls consist of local palm leaves and the roof is made of the traditional ceramic tile, not zinc. Local farmers claim that the tile roofs "breathe" better than metal ones and, in turn, produce ideal drying conditions for the tobacco leaf.

FIGURE 4.16. Viñales Valley, Pinar del Río Province, in western Cuba.

FIGURE 4.17. This detail of a pen-and-ink relief map popularized by Cuban cartographer Gerardo Canet and Harvard professor Edwin Raisz reveals the knoblike hills (*mogotes*) and mountains (Sierra de los Organos and Rosario chains) that run northeast–southwest in the Viñales Valley (right middle of map) in Pinar del Río Province. From Marrero (1957, 406, map insert). Courtesy Harvard University Press.

Unlike sugar production elsewhere in the island, tobacco production was mostly a nonslave agricultural system, and therefore the majority of the population is largely made up of white descendents from the Canary Islands who settled there in the late 17th century. Cultivation has remained relatively unchanged since the 18th century except for the use of chemical fertilizers and some diesel-powered tractors (though ox-driven plows prevail). Fine shade and filler tobacco is well suited to the local climate and soils (Marrero 1957).

A series of underground streams has carved out the striking limestone haystack (*mogotes*) hills, offering photographers and sightseers a spellbinding view of the valley (Figure 4.18). Geomorphologically, the *mogotes* are "transported mountains" or "mountains without roots" (*klippes* in German) because, through heavy erosion, uplifting, and deposition, the mogotes are huge fragments of rock that have been superimposed over strata to which they have no affinity—in this case, limestone overlying shale (Marrero 1957, 410). Viñales offers an ideal venue for speleology and leisure boat rides throughout its many caverns and caves. The *mogotes* date back to the Jurassic period (roughly 146–198 million years ago) and contain a mixed and endemic plant cover.

FIGURE 4.18. Haystack (*mogote*) karstic formation in a Viñales landscape.

HERITAGE AT RISK

Cuba's economic downturn in the 1990s increased competition for scarce public resources. Not surprisingly, matters of food provision, health care, and energy tended to receive priority over matters of cultural patrimony. In 2001, ICOMOS identified scores of heritage sites in Cuba that were considered "at risk." This entailed a list of establishments and types of structures designated as Agro-Industrial Heritage (mostly sugar mills), Wooden Architecture (largely late 19th-century buildings and verandas), Urban Industrial Heritage (mostly cigar, beer, timber, electricity, and paper production facilities), and 20th-century Legacy (mostly Art Nouveau, Art Deco, and Eclectic structures) (International Commission on Monuments and Sites 2001–2002).

   Of special significance are the famous art schools (*Escuelas de Arte*) located on the former golf course of Havana's western suburbs. The World Monuments Fund placed them on its "100 Most Endangered Sites" list in the early 2000s. The schools, designed and built (1961–1965) by Italian architects Roberto Gottardi and Vittorio Garatti and Cuban architect Ricardo Porro, were never fully completed and fell into disrepair. Some *machista* (macho) interpretations of the sinuous shape of the walkways, the bulbous forms of the pavilions, and the earth tone colors of the brick and tiles conjure up images—in the minds of some viewers—of a beautiful dark-skinned woman. The schools were to house higher education classes in dance, music, and the plastic arts. All of the schools have been functioning for four decades, but not all have been completely built (Loomis 1999) (Figure 4.19).

In general, their maintenance has been lacking (Figure 4.20). Built from local clay tiles and drawing on colors, forms, and textures of the island, they are perhaps among the best examples of modern architecture done since the 1959 Revolution (Loomis 1999). However, in the early millennium, the Cuban government prioritized the repair of these structures and a multimillion-dollar project is under way. The Havana City Historian's Office heads up a major part of the renovation. The schools were removed from the World Monuments Fund endangered list in 2004.

One of the iconic images of Havana that would not seem to form part of heritage or tourism landscapes is that of American writer and Nobel laureate Ernest Hemingway. A longtime resident of Cuba, the writer frequented many of the bars, restaurants, and hotels in Habana Vieja. Between 1959 and the early 1990s, there was hardly an image of him to be found in

FIGURE 4.19. A portion of the incomplete Escuelas de Arte, in Cubanacán, western Havana City Province. Construction started in the early 1960s.

FIGURE 4.20. Cuba's Escuelas de Arte. One of the finest complexes built in Cuba since 1959. The schools are known for the use of local building materials that draw on red clays that characterize most of the island's soils. Terra-cotta materials and Catalan vaulted ceilings symbolize both the authenticity and optimism of the design. The domes seen in the top and bottom images grace the complexes, and are framed by concrete lattice sunscreens that serve as glassless "windows." High-vaulted domes (light colored, top image) allow for rising warm air to escape through the ceiling tops. These pod-like domes serve as art and dance studios. Cracked and flaking brick and tiles can be seen in the ceilings of both images, taken in 2004.

the old quarters. Today, though, hotels, restaurants, T-shirt vendors, and bartenders pay tribute to him (Figure 4.21). His permanent residence was Finca Vigía (Lookout Farm), located in the Havana southeastern suburb of San Francisco de Paula. This is where the Nobel laureate penned *For Whom the Bell Tolls* and *The Old Man and the Sea*. The original structure was built in 1886 and Hemingway acquired the house in 1939, where he resided until 1960 (a year before his suicide in Idaho).

The house serves as the official Ernest Hemingway Museum, and foreigners pay a hefty $25 to visit the site. However, the house has not been well maintained during the period of the socialist government. In the early millennium the house was identified as being at risk, and by 2006 it had remained on the World Monuments Fund and ICOMOS lists of endangered structures. Tourists have never been allowed inside the home. Instead, they peer through windows to see Hemingway's books, clothes, photographs, office, and paintings. The house-museum suffers from foundation instability and problems induced by the high humidity of the region. Normal aging, high winds, tropical rains, and storms have debilitated the structure. According to the Cuban government, it has no funds to restore the facility, despite the hefty entrance fees.

A binational effort between the United States and Cuba has led to the gradual renovation of the house. Relatives of Hemingway, his former edi-

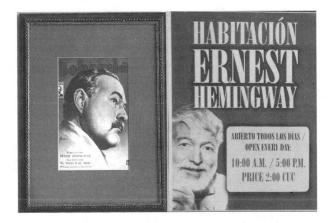

FIGURE 4.21. Two images from the Ambos Mundos Hotel, in Habana Vieja, where Ernest Hemingway was a frequent guest. Hemingway was a popular figure, as illustrated by his picture on the cover of the Cuban weekly news and arts magazine, *Bohemia* (left). The hotel has recreated the room where Hemingway was a guest and where he often wrote (right). Tourists can visit the room for the price of approximately U.S. $2.

tor Maxwell Perkins, and several film stars founded the Hemingway Preservation Foundation, Inc. In an unprecedented arrangement under the U.S. trade embargo on Cuba, the foundation made a case for "binational heritage" before the U.S. government. Roadblocks imposed by the U.S. Department of the Treasury have kept funds from reaching the project directly. However, the restoration efforts have involved the microfiching of some draft manuscripts found in the basement of Finca Vigía, part of a joint project between Boston University and the National Library of Cuba. Finca Vigía found its way on the U.S. National Trust for Historic Preservation's 2005 list of America's 11 Most Endangered Places.

OTHER FORMS OF HERITAGE

The Cuban government administered 289 museums in 2006. According to UNESCO's classification system of museums, 164 are general museums, 14 are art museums, 68 are historical museums, 9 are specialized museums, 9 are history and science museums, 4 are archeological museums, and the remainder are unclassified (Consejo Nacional de Patrimonio Cultural 2008). Most are dependent on central funding from the Ministry of Culture. Cubans enjoy free admission to most museums or are nominally charged in local currency; foreigners always pay in hard currency when admission is required.

Since the demise of the Soviet Union and CMEA, Cuba has embarked on a strong movement to rescue historical places, promote museums, and celebrate nationally and internationally acclaimed sites and monuments (Scarpaci 2000, 2005). One of the catalysts of this movement has been the city historian of Havana, Dr. Eusebio Leal Spengler. He was perhaps first known to millions of Cubans for a television show he hosted, *Andar La Habana* (Walking through Havana), in which he highlighted the city's historical and cultural assets. An elegant speaker and an elected member to the National Assembly, he describes the nation's pursuit of heritage this way:

> We have brought life back to every neighborhood in all aspects, as a worthy place to live where schools, cultural institutions, and health facilities proliferate. Resurrecting what once seemed to be lifeless provokes confused looks at such a romantic crusade. And even if it were that way, we would not feign ignorance nor feel ashamed of being romantics in an age defined by apocalyptic events. Our work projects other forms of hope: that which is born from recovering memory, from dreams shared by many to create a new order. (Oficina del Historiador de la Ciudad de la Habana 2006; our translation)

Perhaps no single Cuban has been more affiliated with heritage preservation than Dr. Leal.

LOST HERITAGE:
DISPLACED OR TEMPORARILY ON LOAN?

Revolutions are messy. They divide nations, neighborhoods, and families. The Cuban Revolution is no exception. The population of the Cuban diaspora since 1959 easily approaches 2 million individuals who consider themselves Cuban even though they live outside the island. Without delving into the polemics surrounding the Revolution, one current of discussion about heritage concerns the definition of what is "Cuban" (*lo cubano*) and whether or not one must reside on the island to contribute to this debate. A related aspect of the Revolution and heritage concerns the socialist government's use of personal and corporate property before the Revolution. Émigrés leaving the island were usually allowed to take only a small amount of personal property; often they could leave with only the clothes they were wearing. Personal artifacts (jewelry, photographs), family heirlooms, and artwork stayed behind. Although these items do not individually constitute significant parts of a heritage landscape, they may form parts of curatorial exhibits in museums, which, in turn, make up Cuban heritage.

Alberto Bustamante, a fervent anti-Castro exile and chairman of the board of Cuban National Heritage in 2001, is one of many advocates who claim that Cuba is losing its heritage. Writing in a special issue devoted to Cuban culture and heritage in *Herencia* magazine, he argued that

> with tremendous sacrifices we have presented the truth [about Cuban heritage] because the search for it is a condition of liberty.... The loss of our patrimony is doing irreparable damage to young Cubans in the island as well as to those in exile.... Many bright and honest people inside Cuba are dedicated to saving our patrimony and we have recognized their effort in the restoration and preservation of historical buildings in Havana, Cienfuegos, Trinidad and other cities. (Bustamante 2001, 3)

He also contends that some of the island's personal property and artwork has been either sold abroad or "taken" without proper compensation. Table 4.4 lists a few of his concerns surrounding this matter. If the eastern European countries and former Soviet Union serve as examples in regard to indemnifying the previous owners of heritage items, it appears that the matter of compensating and repatriating Cuban heritage will not be easy.

TABLE 4.4. The Appropriation of Cuban Heritage since 1959

1. Since 1959 thousands of artistic artifacts of Cuban patrimony, most from private residences of families that had fled the country, were disposed of by prominent members of the regime. Most were taken to large warehouses on the Avenida del Puerto and sold.

2. Between 1960 and 1970, approximately 30 million dollars' worth of books, most from private libraries, and small valuables were sold to Western Europeans through East Berlin. There were also sales to dealers in Buenos Aires, Mexico City, Madrid, and Barcelona. Many auctions were held in Toronto and Montreal. Advertisements were placed, describing lots as being furniture, paintings, and jewelry from the palaces of Havana and other Cuban cities. There is a documented example of this type of sale in Canada, held at Montreal's Frazer Brothers Auctioneers in 1969.

3. For the past 39 years [*Note*: written in 1998] the Communist Cuban government has aggressively pursued smaller family heirlooms. To gain access to precious metals and gemstones, the government manipulated the chronic scarcity of consumer goods by establishing "trading centers" where ordinary citizens were encouraged to exchange jewels and artifacts for necessities such as electronic appliances, household goods, and cash. The exchange rates were so abusive that the centers were soon nicknamed "centros Hernán Cortez," referring to the beads-for-gold deception practiced by the early conquistadors.

4. In May 1994 in Milan, Italy, the Casa Delle Aste, Instituto Italiano Realizze, sold, at auction, 700 lots that were described as decorations and objects from the diplomatic residences of Cuba. The "diplomatic residences" were, in reality, the private homes of Cuban families. The total sale of 138 paintings alone was estimated at more than U.S. $8 million. Notice of the auction by the Italian press indicated that the items had received approval for export from the Cuban Ministry of Culture on March 12, 1994.

5. Periodically, shipments of Cuba's cultural heritage were moved through the Port of Barcelona to supply multiple dealers active in the Costa Brava.

6. The Cuban government, capitalizing on the Cuban people's need of dollars for basic survival, has encouraged and allowed the Galeria Las Acacias in Havana to accept art and antiques on consignment for sales overseas. Upon completion of a sale, the owner receives 70% and the state retains 30% of the proceeds. Officers of the Museum of Fine Arts have often sold museum works at this gallery.

7. From the archival heritage, the loss has not been any less. Thousands of documents from the National Archives and the National Library have been systematically sold to dealers worldwide. The stamps and seals of these institutions are easily identifiable on books and documents, clearly indicating their place of origin.

Note. Based on Bustamante (n.d.; c. 1998).

NATIONAL SITES AND MONUMENTS
AND PROTECTED ZONES

Aside from Cuba's nine World Heritage Sites, the Ministry of Culture has developed an extensive list of national monuments, local sites, and protected zones (Table 4.5). In this section we briefly discuss these national monuments and protected zones.

Cuba's "national sites" encompass all urban historic centers and all construction sites or objects that possess exceptional character and deserve to be conserved for their cultural, historical, or social significance to the country. A National Commission of Monuments makes such a determination. It should be noted that "social" significance also entails political importance. Our analysis shows that about 10% of the sites discussed below have "sociopolitical" significance based on the Triumph of the Revolution from 1959 onward. This may mean that the naming of national heritage sites and monuments in socialist Cuba is not as politically charged as some have suggested (Préstamo 1995).

TABLE 4.5. Cuban National, Local, and Protected Zones and Sites, 2008

Province or municipality	National sites	Local sites	Protection zones	Province/ municipal totals
Pinar del Río	10	14	3	27
La Habana	7	19	2	28
Ciudad de la Habana	35	6	11	52
Matanzas	14	14	4	32
Villa Clara	9	3	7	19
Cienfuegos	11	12	0	23
Sancti Spiritus	10	22	1	33
Ciego de Avila	2	7	25	34
Camagüey	7	7	0	14
Las Tunas	3	2	1	6
Holguín	10	7	2	19
Granma	15	5	1	27
Santiago de Cuba	47	41	8	96
Guantánamo	10	18	3	45
Isla de la Juventud	4	9	1	14
Dispersed	1	0	1	2
Totals	215	186	70	471

Note. Data from Consejo Nacional de Patrimonio Cultural (2008).

"Local monuments" include all elements of the built environment, sites, and objects that do yet entail the necessary conditions to be declared national monuments. Still, the National Heritage Commission deems them to be worthy of conservation because of their historical, cultural, or social interest to local communities.

"Protected zones" are sites with the potential to be declared national monuments. A protected zone is reviewed for a final evaluation and is subject to special regulation to guarantee its protection as a monument or as an urban zone of historical-cultural value that deserves to be protected. In 2006, 70 such zones existed (Consejo Nacional de Patrimonio Cultural 2008).

CONCLUSIONS

For a relatively small nation—not much larger than the U.S. state of Tennessee—Cuba has a remarkable array of insular heritage. Its cultural and natural sites, national landmarks, and cultural landscapes are varied and special. Not all of the heritage sites have developed under carefully designed management plans; Trinidad and other sites evolved as museum-like places as much by default as by design. A relatively low population density on the largest island in the Caribbean may be an important criterion in accounting for the preservation of these sites. Idiosyncratic and technological factors have led to the destruction of historical landscapes; politicians and private owners have dispensed with properties for various reasons. For instance, Havana's walls were torn down because they were militarily obsolete and exacerbated crowding. Although heritage preservation was not particularly well supported or encouraged in the decades following the Triumph of the Revolution, it has recently received considerable attention. To be sure, heritage sells, and the Cuban government unabashedly seeks—in the parlance of free-market economics and neoliberalism—new comparative advantages to sustain the economy. It will be a test of time to determine whether the Revolution is successful in defining its own version of socialist heritage that will add to the national stock. As Graham and colleagues (2000, 25) note, "It follows that once a subversive heritage succeeds to power, it quickly loses its revolutionary intent and becomes a conservative force in itself."

There is a trend in heritage preservation to acknowledge the spiritual values tied to historical monuments, natural features, and cultural landscapes. In a similar vein, Anthony Tung poses an almost anachronistic question, in this age when technological gains capture the public's imagination about what is new, not what is old:

If the historic cores of major cities are vigorously protected and their architectural forms are fixed in time, as if they were living museums, can such metropolises prosper in the unforgiving world of global economic competition? Have we arrived at a moment when … conservation assumes an unprecedented urgency because of the historically unparalleled power of modern humans to alter whole cityscapes overnight? (2001, 1)

This urgency to conserve without being reactionary also entails documenting rituals, belief systems, and oral traditions. Given Cuba's low level of formal religious participation, we might expect to see some movement whereby the "spiritual" and "belief systems" could, over time, incorporate many more political values embraced by the Revolution, or by Cuba's African heritage, which has only since the 20th century been celebrated and recognized (de la Fuente, Garcia del Pino, and Iglesias Delgado 1996; Ortiz 1975; Tannenbaum 1992). Behind most of the UNESCO cultural sites described in this chapter are the blood and sweat of anonymous slave labor. Indeed, there is a huge resurgence of Afro-Cuban heritage tourism throughout the island (Figure 4.22) that also consists of microenterprises.

FIGURE 4.22. An Afro-Cuban priest who practices *palo monte* (derived from African religions grounded in nature) spits rum into an altar devoted to several syncretic deities in his home in Atarés, Havana, in 2001. He lists his home as a "cultural center," though government authorities turn a blind eye to centers like this, which may, on occasion, receive compensation from heritage tourists in remote corners of the island.

Because the transmission of national values to young people is a celebrated form of promoting national cultural identity that UNESCO supports (Rössler 2004b), such a trend is quite likely, particularly as the Revolution approaches its 50-year anniversary. To date, however, the number of national sites (non-UNESCO) in Cuba is just 10% of the 215 sites. We might even envision a new kind of heritage landscape emerging at the U.S. Naval Base in Guantánamo, Cuba, once it returns to Cuban control. Fidel Castro claims that he will turn the facility into a free education center for the people of Latin America. At present, tourists can observe the base from only a single observation town several kilometers north of the base (Figure 4.23). The international uproar over the use of the U.S. Camp X-ray for detaining alleged terrorists has resulted in unprecedented scrutiny of what was once a sleepy coaling station negotiated dubiously from the Cuban nation in the Platt Amendment of 1902. In fact, Cuban maps since 1959 make no reference to the U.S. naval base. Nevertheless, new venues of atrocity heritage tourism lurk on the horizon, whether it denounces political oppression (e.g., La Cabaña) or international violations of human rights (Camp X-ray). The possibilities for new heritage landscapes are unlimited:

FIGURE 4.23. European and U.S. tourists observe Guantánamo Naval Base (a.k.a. "Gitmo") and search for a glimpse of Camp X-ray from a hilltop north of the base in Cuban territory. The restaurant-bar is draped in guerrilla-chic camouflage netting and is run by the government's military tourism branch, *Gaviota* (meaning "seagull").

Camp X-ray could some day be a sort of international Islamic heritage or antiwar site in a post-Iraq war, postembargo, and post-Fidel era. Regardless of its future use, it is in many ways the Cuban version of Abu Ghraib prison, even though Camp X-ray is in U.S. and not Cuban territory. One of President Barack Obama's first acts in office was to order the closing of this detention center at "Gitmo."

Given that Cuba is a socialist island, there are relatively few political monuments from the revolutionary era. For instance, although there are communist monuments to Mao in China, Kim in North Korea, and Soviet leaders in the former USSR, there are no monuments to Fidel (until now, during his lifetime); there is a small plaque in Vedado on the corner of intersection where he declared his revolution to be a communist one (Figure 4.24). Havana's Plaza de la Revolución, formerly Plaza Cívica, was completed for the most part during the Batista government of the 1950s. Havana does contain a few smaller civic art projects commissioned during the Revolution that may someday approach national landmark status. This includes the Student Martyr Park in Centro Habana and the monument in Colón Cemetery (Figure 4.25) to students who attacked the Presidential Palace on March 13, 1957, nearly killing Batista.

The structure enduring the most significant architectural neglect is Havana's School of Arts, which in 2000 was placed on the World Monuments Watch List of 100 Most Endangered Sites. However, it is now undergoing a multimillion-dollar repair. The island's checkered attempts at environmental stewardship may some day endanger its cultural land-

FIGURE 4.24. Bronze plaque designating the location where Fidel Castro declared his socialist revolution, in Vedado, Havana, Avenida 23 and Calle 12.

FIGURE 4.25. Student martyr monument and burial ground at Colón Cemetery, Havana (cemetery basilica on right center horizon). Built and designed in 1983 by Mario Coyula, Emilio Escobar, Orestes del Castillo Sr., and José Villa. The site consists of small rises that represent the "sierras" where the Revolution was launched and uses rough cobblestones that force pedestrians to look down as they walk, which, at the same time, is a sign of respect to the 13 fallen students the monument commemorates. At the exact time of the attack on President Batista's presidential palace, 3:20 P.M. on March 13, the sun casts a shadow along the axis of the stainless steel Cuban flags (one for each fallen student) and culminates at a torch in the ground, which is lighted. The ceremony takes place annually. A large yagruma tree (*Cecropia* spp.) sheds leaves that are gray and somber on one side, and bright and green on the other, in reference to the lives and deaths of the deceased.

scapes and natural sites. To be sure, heritage evolves and is ongoing. The revolutionary government has done much recently to promote its hundreds of UNESCO and national sites and protection zones, endowing the island with a plethora of heritage sites. Cuba's relative standing vis-à-vis Caribbean and other nations is considerable. Perhaps the greatest challenge may lie in marshaling the necessary resources to manage these landmarks as the economy struggles to regain the level of the 1989 Soviet era. *New York Times* architecture critic Paul Goldberger (2001) identifies the risk in leaning toward too much free-market activity and too much state control:

> It is a striking paradox that right now in Cuba, the Communist regime seems quite eager to sell anything it can to bring in short-term income—whereas it

is here, in the United States, this citadel of capitalism, that so many people are looking at Cuba with more of a long view, and urging it to move slowly, to make rules, to enforce a certain amount of governmental authority to limit and guide development. . . . The answer for [Cuba]—this "third way"—is not merely a matter of preserving what is there and preventing new construction which is absurd and impractical. And it is emphatically not the theme park. . . .

Future heritage projects in Cuba will be ambitious but necessary. And they will not be confined to just land projects either. They might include underwater cultural heritage as it is fast becoming a focus of extrainsular relevance as international agencies explore shipwrecks and preserve fragile coral reefs surrounding Cuba (Grenier, Nutley, and Cochran 2006). Heritage landscapes will continue to offer constructive lenses through which we can interpret Cuban history, culture, natural resources, and politics.

NOTE

1. We are grateful to architect Orestes del Castillo Jr. for making this point.

2. The inclusion of a more detailed discussion of the historic center of Comagüey in 2008 came about while this book was in production and, therefore, we could not give it more attention.

CHAPTER 5

TOURISM

The rise of international travel in the 20th century is inextricably linked to an increase in leisure time and expendable income in the advanced capitalist nations. A mass market makes travel and lodging relatively affordable to a rising middle class across the globe. No less important is today's tourists' perception of possible destinations; whatever forces shape the tourists' gaze, advertising, media portrayals, and information technologies—rightly or wrongly—spark an interest in travel, exploration, and relaxation (Urry 2002). The confluence of these forces is powerful, and there are crosscurrents touting both merits and detriments in exploring the island of Cuba. Indeed, as discussed in Chapter 2, Alexander von Humboldt noted this contradiction: Its institution of slavery was abhorrent, yet the island's natural beauty and variety were astounding (Humboldt 2001).

Fast-forward two centuries from Humboldt's 1802 observations, and similar ironies arise. For instance, international organizations lambaste the island for its human and civil rights records. The European Union—often a supporter of Cuba, especially when the latter is confronted by U.S. exigencies—concluded that it would continue to "condemn acts of repudiation ... [and] call for the unconditional release of all political prisoners ... [and] facilitate the free flow of information" (2006, 1). In a similar denunciation, the Heritage Foundation's 2008 Index of Economic Freedom situated Cuba 156th in regard to the 157 countries among political, economic, and social liberties (Heritage Foundation 2008). The Heritage Foundation ranks Cuba 29th out of 29 countries in the Americas, and the island's overall score is less than half the regional average. Cuba performs least egregiously in corruption, trade freedom, and monetary freedom. Its business freedom, investment freedom, financial freedom, property rights, freedom from corruption, and labor freedom are all weak. It is significant that Cuba ranked just ahead of North Korea, which scored at the bottom of all "economically repressed regimes." At the heart of these assessments lies the argument that the government of Cuba violates basic human rights. Moreover, the Cuban government dominates matters of labor organization, higher education, media outlets, and the national economy. Carlos Alberto Montaner argues:

> Cuba must eventually face up to history. The country cannot continue as an anachronistic, collectivist, communist dictatorship in a world where Marxism has been completely discredited. Cuba belongs to Western civilization. It is part of Latin America, and it makes no sense for its government to keep the country isolated from its surroundings.... After all, the dictatorships of Latin America, both on the left (like Velasco Alvarado in Peru) and on the right (Augusto Pincohet and the military regimes in Argentina, Brazil and Uruguay), were all replaced by governments legitimized at the ballot box. (2007, 58)

If Cuba is so horrible, what drives its tourism industry? Why are countless Americans clamoring to get to their island neighbor? The charges previously noted are not new in this long-standing global polemic. To be sure, the Cuban government counters that it conceptualizes human rights differently. It does not profit from medical care to the masses and the government prioritizes housing and food subsidies, despite the poor quality in both realms. The nation is proud that there are no homeless people and contends that it could do more if it were not for the 1961 trade embargo that frustrates the government and impedes access to U.S. markets, credit and finance capital, consumers, and distribution networks. Cuba points to other "badges of honor" to counter charges of economic and political repression. For instance, its life expectancy ranks 53rd (77.4 years) as compared with the United States' 46th place (77.9 years), and the Central Intelligence Agency (2007) estimated the 2006 Cuban infant mortality rate (6.22 deaths within the first year of life per 1,000 babies born) to be lower than that of the United States (6.433). Ignacio Ramonet, countering the claims made by Carlos Alberto Montaner in *Foreign Policy*, argues:

> No serious organization has ever accused Cuba ... of carrying out "disappearances," engaging in extrajudicial executions, or even performing physical torture on detainees. The same cannot be said of the United States in its five-year-old "war on terror." ... [Cuba] has succeeded in increasing life expectancy and lowering infant mortality.... These successes constitute a great

legacy of Fidel Castro's, one that few Cubans, even those in the opposition, would want to lose.... Cubans enjoy full employment, and each citizen is entitled to three meals a day, an achievement that continues to elude Brazil's [President] Lula [da Sliva]. But Castro will not only be remembered as a defender of the weakest and poorest citizens. Historians 100 years from now will credit Castro with building a cohesive nation with a strong identity, even after a century of the white, elitist temptation to side with the United States out of fear of the numerous and oppressed black population. They will remember him correctly, as a preeminent pioneer in the history of his country. (Ramonet 2007, 61)

We will not enter this perennial debate between Washington, DC, and Havana, as there is already a broad literature on the subject. Both sides question the conceptual assumptions that buttress the data hurled back and forth in this dispute. And each party contends that the data and conceptual underpinnings of the other camp are suspect. Suffice it to say, the positions staked out in this exchange are firm and no review of the literature will resolve the impasse. As Ramón Vázquez astutely noted about the bipolar and entrenched positions between the exile community in Miami and the government in Havana: "Nothing is more similar to a Cuban Communist than a Cuban anticommunist" (Vázquez 1994, 7–8; our translation).

Our concern in this chapter is to trace the magnetism of Cuba for the international tourist, regardless of the merits and detriments of the communist government. As the sixth decade of the Revolution begins, few would have expected Cuba to resort to a conventional neoclassical economic tenet—comparative advantage—as an economic development tool. Allegedly, Fidel Castro stated in the early years of the Revolution that he did not want an island of bartenders and chambermaids; his vision of Cuba was that it would become a "different America" that supports social justice and equality (Chafee and Prevost 1992). What advantages does Cuba hold in the tourist market? Geography and political perception explain some of Cuba's advantage in this enterprise.

First, Cuba is 90 miles from one of the largest pools of tourists in the world. Although the halcyon days of the 1950s are over—when hourly flights carried gamblers and adventure seekers from Miami to Havana—airlines and hotels today are primed to tap into this new and exotic market once again. The international tourist industry suffered significant setbacks in the early years of the new millennium. Y2K spooked potential travelers and then the attacks of September 11, 2001, deepened the shock. A strong global economy in the late 1990s dissipated when the information technology bubble driving the stock market broke in March 2000. Cultural and economic exchanges between United States citizens and Cubans increased from the mid-1990s until June 2004, and the executive order imposed by President George W. Bush (to curtail undergraduate student and cultural trips) could easily be rescinded by the stroke of a different presidential pen. Cuba is closer to most Americans who live east of the Mississippi River than to those in the desert southwestern states.

Second, the Cuban landscape remains largely unexplored by international tourists, who have visions of tall palm trees and clear blue seas. Washed by the warm waters of the Gulf of Mexico, the Atlantic Ocean, and the Caribbean, it remains indelibly enticing. It bears repeating that Cuba has a relatively low population density, thanks in part to its being the largest island in the Caribbean and its moderate population growth. Only the Bahamas (27.8 people per square kilometer), Dominica (88), and the British Virgin Islands (99.3) display lower population densities than Cuba (99.6) (Overpopulation.com 2007). It is also noteworthy that its 11.2 million residents are sprinkled along a 1,250-kilometer (775-mile) length, which is comparable to the distance between Long Island (New York) and Chicago. An average width of just 60 miles allows tourists to visit the northern Gulf/Atlantic side and the southern/Caribbean shores within a short drive. Unlike those on other West Indies islands, Cuban settlements are not largely confined to narrow coastal plains, narrow valleys, or restricted back bay locations. Instead, the island's broad expanse of inland plains affords a different kind of settlement geography. The Dominican Republic is the only Caribbean nation with a larger percentage (72%) of its population living beyond 10 kilometers of the coast; in Cuba, 59% live beyond that 10-kilometer band (World Resources Institute 2007). To the delight of some tourists, this means there are large tracts of open spaces (much of it waterfront), dotted with small and medium-size settlements, all potentially waiting for a burgeoning U.S. market to explore them. And if there is any hope that proper wastewater and industrial management might someday safeguard Cuba's coral reefs, it will be helped by the relatively large "inland" population, as compared with those of other Caribbean nations (Burke and Maidens 2005). All of this, of course, assumes the necessary environmental and civil engineering investments as well as the political and economic will to thwart coastal degradation.

Third, international visitors to Cuba seem to relish finding themselves in a place where most Americans cannot travel, whether they are British citizens commenting on the relative absence of "Yanks" on the island, Mexicans remarking about the few *gringos*, or Spaniards noting the lack of *norteamericanos*. Cuba is generally off-limits to U.S. citizens except for journalists, academicians, and religious groups. As America's popularity wanes in the new millennium—not least because it has waged a highly unpopular war in Iraq—America bashing has found a new source of comfort: Cuba. British writer James Leavey sums it up this way:

> "So what was it like?" asked the man serving drinks at Bar Cuba, in Kensington High Street.
> "Cuba was the place I dreamt about for 30 years," I told him, "after reading Hemingway's novels and Graham Greene's *Our Man in Havana*. It's funny how over the years little things fix an impression of a distant country in your mind. Cuba was the place I thought you only got hijacked to.... Cubans were some of the friendliest people I had met anywhere, bearing in mind that only a few years ago they would have been arrested for talking to a foreigner.... What's suprised [sic] me is how well-educated [Cubans] are, which explains why Cuba probably has the world's most literate beggars. Where else could you discuss Bertolt Brecht and Karl Marx with a doctor or dentist who is working ... [not to mention a] *total lack of American tourists.*" (2007; emphasis added)

There is more evidence that anti-Americanism and Cuba are a perfect match. A BBC public opinion poll in 2007 queried 11,000 adults in the United Kingdom, France, Russia, Indonesia, South Korea, Jordan, Australia, Canada, Israel, Brazil and the United States about their views and opinions of America (British Broadcasting Corporation 2007). When asked, "In general, how would you say you feel toward America?" just 18% of the sample gave a "favorable" response (among favorable, less favorable, or average), and that figure included the American respondents in the fold (British Broadcasting Corporation 2007).

Contemporary journalistic accounts echo similar themes, albeit with the usual dose of misinformation. The following quote posted on the popular MSN home page corroborates this:

> Cuba. American traveler's forbidden fruit. Palm trees tower over cobblestone streets. Taxi drivers careen through the Old City. Lovely verandahs create the perfect atmosphere to enjoy a rum-and-coke. The smell of sweet cigar smoke and the sound of *merengue* are everywhere. And Americans, for the most part, aren't allowed to visit. (Isenberg 2007)

The "forbidden fruit" image permeates the popular press (even though merengue music is more likely to be heard in the Dominican Republic than in Cuba). This description captures key visual elements of the tourist landscape (cobblestones, palms, verandahs) as well as leisure pastimes (cigar smoking and drinking) carried out in an exotic place.

Fourth, Cuba is unabashedly appealing on the global political stage. In a classic David-and-Goliath saga, a small island has stood up to the most powerful nation in the world. One of the more poignant scenes to reach a world audience might be found in Mario Puzo and Francis Ford Coppola's famous 1974 Hollywood blockbuster *Godfather II*—part of a film trilogy that earned more than $1 billion in worldwide revenues—which captures well the discontent of Cuba in the 1950s (Maiello 2002). The following exchange between the fictitious organized father–son crime figures Hyman and Sam Roth and the junior mafia don Michael Corleone (played by Al Pacino) takes place at the senior Roth's birthday party.

> MICHAEL: I saw an interesting thing today. A man was being arrested by the military police; probably an urban guerrilla. Rather than be taken alive, he exploded a grenade hidden in his jacket, taking the command vehicle with him.

> *The various men look up as Michael eats his cake, wondering what the point of it is.*

> MICHAEL: It occurred to me. The police are paid to fight, and the rebels are not.
> HYMAN ROTH: So?
> MICHAEL: So, that occurred to me.

> *View on Roth: He understands Michael's point, if the others do not.*

> HYMAN ROTH: This country has had rebels for the last fifty years; it's part of their blood. Believe me. I know.... I've been coming here since the twenties; we were running molasses out of Havana when you were a baby. To trucks owned by your father (*he chuckles warmly over the memory*). We'll talk when we're alone.

> *And he returns his attention to the men who are gathered with him on his birthday.*

> HYMAN ROTH: You have to be careful what you say in front of the others ... they frighten easy. It's always been that way, most men frighten easy. (Puzo and Coppola 1996, 110–112)

The presence of organized crime in Havana was well known. The 1950s cabarets and gaming tables at the Caribe, the Sans Souci, the Riviera, the Capri, and the Nacional were of international renown (Palero and

Geldof 2004, 254). The 1959 Revolution, however, tarred and feathered them as symptoms of runaway capitalism, neglect by Fulgencio Batista's corrupt government, and the result of vice and prostitution. Alas, Cuba's tourist landscape had turned Havana into the "brothel of the Caribbean" (Robaina 2004).

As of this writing, Fidel Castro has survived ten American presidents, avoided several assassinations, weathered international economic sanctions, and defeated the American-funded Bay of Pigs invasion that was hatched under the Eisenhower administration (but launched during John F. Kennedy's first hundred days in office in April 1961) (Szulc 1986). The Cuban Revolution champions the causes of antiglobalizationists, denounces neoliberal economic policies, and supports antihegemonic forces. And even though Fidel Castro is the man who has personified the Revolution for nearly five decades, it has been embodied in no small measure by the Argentine physician-turned-revolutionary, Ernesto "Che" Guevara. Perhaps no counterculture icon of the 20th century has been more widely disseminated than that of Che's. In both public and private spaces within Cuba (Figure 5.1), as well as in a mass consumer culture outside the island, Che's image embodies a defiant idealism of revolution, charm, and anti-imperialism. This has endeared him to countless millions worldwide.

Finally, Cubans have a strong cultural allure; they are internationally appealing at many levels, and, perhaps, always have been. Cuban fashion, the Cuban sense of street humor (*choteo*), and a grand display of style are endearing attributes (Kapcia 2000, 2005; Levi and Heller 2002). Whether through racial blending (miscegenation, or *mestizaje*) or the cross-fertilization of cultures that constitute the island, Cuba and its landscape—with all its sensory components—is powerfully attractive. Witness Hermer and May's visual description of Cuban fashion and style back in 1941:

> Color is exciting to Cubans of every class. If they err in taste, it will be by wearing florid shades or combining too many. The Parisian love of detail and intricate fabrics is also quite Cuban, and the most common fashion blind-spot is in the failure to ensemble properly. (Hermer and May 1996, 61)

Perhaps the most endearing element of the Cuban tourist landscape, therefore, is the Cuban people.

In sum, Cuba embodies geographic, cultural, and political attributes that make it highly appealing to international visitors. It is the consummate underdog in a classic David-and-Goliath showdown. That it is so close to the United States, yet surprisingly inaccessible to Americans, adds

FIGURE 5.1. The ubiquitous Che (Ernesto Guevara de la Serna). Ever since Alberto Korda snapped a somber photograph of Che Guevara, who was attending a funeral in March 1960, the face of this revolutionary has become a universal icon. *Clockwise from upper left:* A street mural painted in Baracoa, Cuba; a T-shirt on sale in a hotel gift shop in Santiago de Cuba; a teenager in Sikkim, India, who was unaware of whom the face represented but liked the shirt's design; and a monument to Che Guevara built in Santa Clara (designed by sculptor José Delarra)— as Che gazes toward Bolivia, where he was killed in 1967 by Bolivian soldiers as he tried to spread the revolution in the Andean nation.

a particular charm. And if the political and anti-American sentiments are not enough for the potential market of 5.7 billion non-U.S. travelers, there is a unique blend of African culture and music giving further impetus to visit the island—at least once. Wim Wender and Ry Cooder's 1997 musical documentary, *Buena Vista Social Club*, pulled in $23 million in box office receipts by promoting the island's unique blend of *son, guajiro, boleros, danzón, mambo, cha cha chá*, and other rhythms (The Numbers 2007). Even the island's largest exporter of rum, Havana Club, has tapped into promoting the sultry look of brown-skinned beauties dancing in the Caribbean moonlight and in the shadow of Spanish colonial architecture (Figure 5.2). Cuba beckons.

FIGURE 5.2. Havana Club magazine advertisement.

HISTORY

Tourism is not new in Cuba (Table 5.1). The drawn-out Cuban independence wars (1868–1878, 1895–1898) in the late 19th century prevented the Spanish Crown from investing in the island's infrastructure. Developments in modern technologies such as public lighting, telegraph, telephones, paved roads, and port infrastructure received short shrift as Madrid tried to snuff out the island's revolutionary fervor. When the Americans arrived in 1898, they found a lackluster and undercapitalized island, ripe for speculation, construction, and investment (Scarpaci et al. 2002, ch. 2). A number of U.S. veterans from the Spanish-Cuban-American War of 1898 became enthralled with the "Pearl of the Antilles" and stayed behind after the war to tap into this new market. A supply officer, Frank Steinhart, became a prominent businessman in the early 20th century, investing in and later owning Havana's electric tram cars (Aruca 1996). He also served as a consular officer for the U.S. embassy in Havana in 1906. His Italianesque mansion still graces Prado Boulevard at the edge of Old Havana and stands as a testimony to the untroubled days of U.S. investment in Cuba.

A rising middle class in the United States and Canada meant more leisure time and new opportunities for travel and exploration. Cuba emerged as a perfect market for an increasingly curious and prosperous pool of

TABLE 5.1. Cuban Tourism Policy, History, and Goals: In the Ministry of Tourism's Own Words

Tourism is not a new activity in Cuba. Just as in the rest of the world, it had its peak in the 1950s. At that time, when tourism affiliated with the largest [nation of the] Antilles, it was very connected with the North American presence of the Mafia. The United States was the main market and gambling and prostitution were the principal offerings of the island. This city tourism allowed little development of our gross domestic product in that stage. The U.S. trade embargo that began with the Triumph of the Revolution ended tourism with United States. Starting in 1959, economic development was directed to other important programs in the country, and for that reason, tourism became basically focused on national tourists, which made lodging not very competitive with international tourism facilities. In the 1980s, tourism reopened to foreigners and in 1990 there was a new focus on this sector. The first [tourist] joint-ventures were created and there was an accelerated rise in visitor arrivals and revenues. Since 1996, when the number of visitors surpassed one million, Cuba has aimed to become a world destination, in addition to a Caribbean destination. To market its tourist product, the largest Antillean island relies mainly on quality local hospitality, exceptional natural attractions, authentic historical heritage, a prolific cultural and artistic life, a healthcare system in a class of its own, political stability, and security for all tourists (our translation).

Note. Our translation. The Cuban Ministry of Tourism describes it this way: "El turismo no es una actividad nueva en Cuba. Al igual que en el mundo, tuvo su auge a partir de los años 50. En esa época, cuando el desarrollo turístico en la mayor de las Antillas estuvo muy ligado a la presencia de la mafia norteamericana en la Isla, Estados Unidos era el mercado principal, y el juego y la prostitución eran las principales ofertas de la Isla. Este turismo de ciudad condicionó el poco desarrollo de nuestro producto natural en esa etapa. Con el triunfo de la Revolución comenzó la política norteamericana de bloqueo y se eliminó el turismo proveniente de Estados Unidos. A partir de 1959, el desarrollo de la economía estuvo dirigido a otros programas importantes del país, por lo cual el turismo era entonces fundamentalmente nacional, hecho que condicionó una estructura habitacional poco competitiva como producto internacional. En los años 80 comienza la reapertura al turismo internacional, pero es en 1990 que se produce un nuevo enfoque del desarrollo de este sector, se crean las primeras empresas mixtas y hay un crecimiento acelerado en los arribos de visitantes y en los ingresos. Desde 1996, cuando se logró por primera vez sobrepasar el millón de visitantes, Cuba se ha propuesto consolidarse como destino mundial y del Caribe. Para comercializar su producto turístico, la mayor de las Antillas cuenta, principalmente, con la hospitalidad popular y calidad de su pueblo, excepcionales atractivos naturales, un patrimonio histórico autóctono, prolífica vida artística y cultural, un desarrollo sanitario único, la estabilidad política y la seguridad para los turistas." From Ministerio de Turismo (2007).

travelers. By the 1920s a growing line of steamships began offering service from U.S. ports. For instance, the Standard Fruit Company accommodated small but regularized passenger traffic on its ships as they plied Caribbean waters in the Antilles and off the coast of Central America to pick up bananas, coffee, and spices (Karnes 1978). Although transatlantic travel between eastern seaports in the United States and Europe flourished, it was not inexpensive, but afforded North Atlantic travelers a kind of "planned serenity" (Coons and Verias 2003). A proximate and more economical market emerged in the interwar years. Galveston, New

Orleans, Biloxi, Tampa–St. Petersburg, Miami, Key West, Jacksonville, Baltimore, Philadelphia, New York, and Boston offered passenger travel to Havana at more affordable rates (Schwartz 1997). Enactment of the Eighteenth Amendment to the U.S. Constitution between 1920 and 1933 (prohibition of alcohol) heightened the attraction of Cuba; so close, yet so far away; familiar yet exotic. Bars such as Sloppy Joe's became icons of Cuba's carefree ways (Figure 5.3). In fact, so entrenched is that icon, that a Sloppy Joe's establishment surfaced in Key West, Florida, on December 5, 1933, the day Prohibition in the United States was repealed (Sloppyjoes 2007). The economic development branch of the City Historian's Office in Havana planned a reopening of the original Sloppy Joe's for 2009.

Tourism boomed in the 1920s as hotels, racetracks, casinos, and dog tracks enticed international visitors. Colonel Charles A. Lindberg's arrival in early 1928 underscored Cuba's position as a prominent tourist destination. However, unlike the 1990s fall of sugar prices, when tourism was there to rescue the national economy, the 1920s decline in sugar prices hurt the tourist industry. President Machado tried to keep beggars off the streets (not unlike the contemporary scene), but tourists became ill tempered with work stoppages and street protests. To offset these troubles and to bolster the new tourism economy, a major $7 million development project was launched atop an old quarry near Havana's Malecón (seaside promenade). This project, the Hotel Nacional, would serve as a powerful anchor in expanding tourism away from the "old" city and into the "new" city (Figure 5.4). However, the stock market crash of 1929, coupled with the mutiny of 1933 led by then-sergeant Fulgencio Batista and other sergeants and corporals against the provisional government of Carlos Manuel

FIGURE 5.3. Advertisement for Sloppy Joe's Bar, Havana, c. 1938. From *Havana Journal* (2007).

FIGURE 5.4. Hotel Nacional (center left with two towers), located on the Malecón, was built in 1930 and anchored the rise of Vedado in Havana's "new" section, in contrast to Havana's old quarters (top center).

de Céspedes y Quesada, was not enough to revive the economy. Even Irene Dupont's plan to make Varadero Beach (2 hours from Havana by car) an exclusive playground for U.S. business executives could not jump-start the island's recovery (Figure 5.5).

The end of Prohibition proved to be the final straw. As Rosalie Schwartz describes it:

> Aside from alterations to the Havana landscape, Cuba had changed little. The impact on traditional Cuban culture was minimal. Few Cubans relinquished cockfights for tennis or replaced the *danzón* [a traditional dance] with the fox-trot. Cubans continued to think the sea too cold for swimming in winter, tourist brochures notwithstanding. (2004, 251)

Cuba's tourist landscape would have to wait until the 1950s for its rebirth.

Capital cities or large prominent ones often exaggerate tourists' perceptions of the larger nation. For instance, it can be argued that New York is a different kind of place within the United States, London is but one facet of England, and Beijing portrays just a sliver of China. So too is the image of Havana, which, rightly or wrongly, becomes the window through which the rest of the island is often portrayed. Graham Greene's novel and subsequent movie *Our Man in Havana* did much to place Havana in the 1950s in the minds of many readers when he wrote:

FIGURE 5.5. Varadero Beach, 2000, with the Dupont mansion on the right and a new joint venture Spanish hotel on the left.

The long city lay spread along the open Atlantic; waves broke over the Avenida de Maceo [Malecón; see Figure 5.6] and misted the windscreens of cars. The pink, grey, yellow pillars of what had once been the aristocratic quarter were eroded like rocks; an ancient coat of arms smudged and feature-less, was set over the doorway of a shabby hotel, and the shutters of a night-club were varnished in bright crude colours to protect them from the wet and salt of the sea. In the west, the steel skyscrapers of the new town rose higher than lighthouses into the clear February sky. It was a city to visit, not a city to live in.... (1996, 122)

Greene's 1958 description of the Malecón captures one of the most spec-tacular waterfront landscapes in the Americas.

ENVIRONMENTAL BACKDROP
TO CONTEMPORARY VENUES

Havana is challenged by issues of proper waste and water treatment plan-ning. Raw sewage drains into Havana Bay and is also pumped into the Florida Straits. Just over two million *habaneros* (Havanans) already tax

FIGURE 5.6. The Malecón: Havana's seaside promenade in Centro Habana looking west toward Vedado, with the 1958 former Habana Hilton, now Habana Libre, at the righthand horizon.

a water system that may leak as much as half of its fresh water (owing to broken water mains). In addition, on any given night thousands of tourists debilitate the system further. The original 1893 Albear aqueduct was designed for a city of 600,000, and although it has been updated, it is inadequate for the burgeoning population (Scarpaci 2006).

Geographers Andrea Colantonio and Robert Potter studied the impact of tourism on Havana's environmental condition and concluded:

> The environmental impact of tourism on Havana ... has been mixed. While in some instances tourism has indirectly prompted environmental improvement, such as the upgrade of the local water and sewerage systems, in others it has been responsible for increasing flooding problems, for example, in Havana's western district. (2006b, 211)

The future of Cuban tourism will also be able to draw upon niche nautical tourism, which includes a growing network of marinas (Figure 5.7). Except for rounding the eastern point of the Windward Passage between Haiti and Cuba, the island is well endowed with marinas to accommodate yachters. More than a dozen marinas on the Atlantic and Caribbean shores are within a day's sail from each other. They are poised to tap into the market made up of yachters who travel from the United States: There are

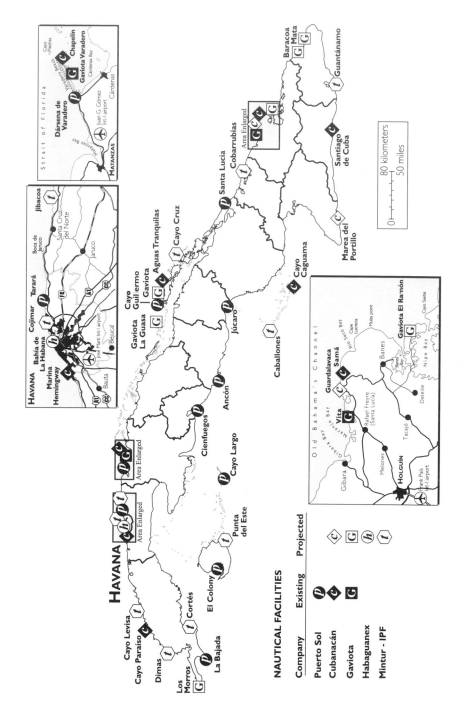

FIGURE 5.7. Cuban nautical facilities.

NAUTICAL FACILITIES

Company	Existing	Projected
Puerto Sol	P	
Cubanacán	c	c
Gaviota	G	G
Habaguanex		h
Mintur - IPF		t

126

thousands of privately owned ships between Tampa–St. Petersburg, and Ft. Myers and Key West, and from Miami to Boca Raton that will be able to circumnavigate Cuba when travel restrictions are rescinded. As unemployment in the rural sugar-growing areas rises, port-, marina- and resort-based employment will become an important alternative. Polly Pattullo refers to this shift from agriculture to tourism across the Caribbean as the "from banana farmer to banana daiquiri" phenomenon (1996, 52). In terms of marina employment elsewhere in the Caribbean, Conway (2006) has shown how important and lucrative skilled marinas are in this segment of the Caribbean's tourist industry. The development of a network of marinas located about a day's travel from each other, coupled with a regular cruise ship industry coming out of Miami and Ft. Lauderdale, would quickly increase the percentage of Western hemisphere visitors (e.g., from the Americas) beyond its current 50% level (Figure 5.8).

Cuba's principal tourist regions span the island and offer an array of distinctive landscapes, several of which we discussed in Chapter 4. Figure 5.9 shows the geographic distribution of these regions. Most include a

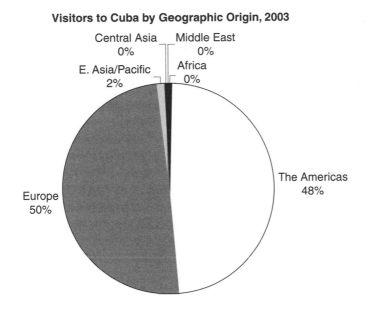

FIGURE 5.8. Visitors to Cuba by region. Data from *Cuba Facts: Tourism in Cuba: Selected Statistics*. Cuba Transition Project, Institute for Cuban and Cuban American Studies, University of Miami and USAID (Funded by USAID under the terms of Award No. EDG-A-00-02-00007-00, Publications, CD-ROM).

FIGURE 5.9. Cuban tourist regions. After Espino (2006).

combination of city-beach locations, for instance, Havana has the Playas del Este (Eastern Beaches) and the Marina Hemingway (in the far western suburbs). Trinidad sits back just 11 kilometers from the Caribbean Sea (Ancón Peninsula) and relies on the unspoiled landscape of nearby Topes de Collante within the Escambray Mountains for ecotourism; this complements Trinidad's cultural heritage, beach, and ecological offerings. North Camaguey includes the UNESCO World Heritage Site of Camaguey, and within a short drive offers access to Santa Lucia beach. Only Santiago de Cuba remains a largely urban setting, with limited sandy beach coves along its Caribbean shores. However, the draw for visitors to the nearby town of El Cobre is the famous basilica. It is just a half-hour drive from Santiago and is the island's most widely recognized place of worship. Cubans pay homage to the island's patron saint—the Virgin of the Charity of Copper (*La Virgen de la Caridad del Cobre*)—at a shrine where thousands make requests in prayer and in small notes and offerings before the black Madonna, draped in a diamond-, ruby-, and emerald-encrusted gown.

Varadero, the Canarreos, North Holguín, and the Jardines del Rey offer mostly beach and aquatic activities. Varadero is located at the end of the Hicacos peninsula and is no more than a 2-hour drive from Havana. Once a playground for the very wealthy, including the heirs of the Dupont chemical empire, it has undergone tremendous hotel development since the early 1990s. A toll both built in the 1990s earns revenues from international visitors and also serves to keep out hustlers who want to work the tourist crowds (Figure 5.10); only those Cubans who work in legitimate establishments or have official business in Varadero are allowed to pass, underscoring what is probably the most tourist-apartheid (i.e., segregated) setting on the island. The Canarreos region in the Caribbean Sea includes

FIGURE 5.10. Varadero/Matanzas toll both at the access point to the Hicacos Peninsula leading from the mainland to Varadero Beach.

the special municipality of Isla de Juventud and bead of small islands that offer prime fishing, snorkeling, and scuba diving. The north shore of the island includes Holguín, which mostly represents the resort of Guardalavaca, hugely popular and affordable for Canadian and European charter groups.

Perhaps the most environmentally criticized new tourist region is the Jardines del Rey, the center of a large archipelago off the north-central shore. A significant feature of the Jardines del Rey is that it contains 1,249 species of flora and fauna, of which 20% are endemic. As early as the 1980s, these islands were eyed as a potential development resource. In 1983, Fidel Castro allegedly stated, "What we have to do here is to throw rocks and not look ahead" (Cepero and Lawrence 2006). The comment preceded the construction of the Cayo Coco Causeway (*pedraplenes*), running through shallow marshes and mangroves, which separated the main island and the archipelago (Figure 5.11).

Cepero and Lawrence (2006) conducted an environmental impact study on the causeway's cutting Dog's Bay (Bahía de los Perros) in half. Using spectral analyses derived from remote satellite images, they examined plant reflectivity before (1990) and after (2000) the causeway was built to assess whether the reduction in water circulation hurt the marsh. The amounts of nutrients and phytoplankton, as well as the interchange of organic matter and temperatures, might be altered because of the road project. Because healthy vegetation absorbs visible light and unhealthy or sparse vegetation tends to reflect it, these researchers were able to measure changes between the two data sets. Focusing on the mangroves—generally a good indicator of tropical marshland ecology—they found an increase in silicates (2.35 micromoles/liter and ammonia (21.07 micromoles/liter),

FIGURE 5.11. Cayo Coco Causeway (*pedraplenes*), 2004. Clockwise from upper left: Looking south from the Jardines del Rey "crown" entrance toward the mainland; a truck along the causeway; one of several intermittent underpasses allowing water to pass from west to east (note water main pumping fresh water from mainland to Coco Key); and marshland to the east of the causeway.

a rise in salinity to between 50 and 80%, and a reduction in fish stock. The most deleterious situation found was that 6.5 million square meters of black mangrove had been destroyed or was in the process of dying (Figure 5.12), all at the expense of building hotels on several islands on the Atlantic beaches.

These findings are sobering, inasmuch as mangroves are nursery grounds and breeding sites for territorial organisms. Sediments, nutrients and carbon, and contaminants collect there. Moreover, mangroves afford protection against coastal erosion (Alongi 2007). Although research like that of Cepero and Lawrence is highly controversial and difficult to corroborate because of restrictions on peer-reviewed field research conducted in Cuba, it does underscore how environmental matters in Cuba—not unlike the situation in the former Soviet Union or even in countries with unfettered market capitalism—can receive low priority when political deci-

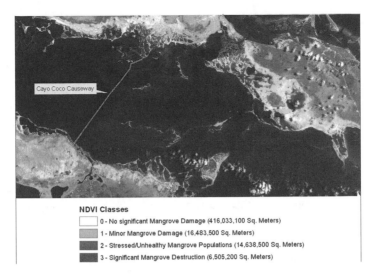

NDVI Classes

☐ 0 - No significant Mangrove Damage (416,033,100 Sq. Meters)

▨ 1 - Minor Mangrove Damage (16,483,500 Sq. Meters)

▨ 2 - Stressed/Unhealthy Mangrove Populations (14,638,500 Sq. Meters)

■ 3 - Significant Mangrove Destruction (6,505,200 Sq. Meters)

FIGURE 5.12. Geographic information system layered image of impacted mangrove in Bahía de los Perros. Note the shading for "significant mangrove destruction" on the island at the bottom center of the image as well as the Cayo Coco Causeway connecting the main island (lower left) with Cayo Coco (top of image). From Cepero and Lawrence (2006).

sions are used in the name of centralized planning or profit making (Diá-Briquets and Pérez-López 2000).

Cuba's international tourism industry was relatively insignificant before the rise of the Special Period in a Time of Peace, ushered in after the collapse of the Soviet Union and its trading bloc. The decade between 1990 and 2000 triggered a significant increase in international visitors to Cuba (Figure 5.13). In the early 1990s tourism increased only slightly; infrastructure was poor, power outages were frequent, and the level of necessary ancillary services was limited (Figure 5.14). By 1996, however, the number of tourists surpassed the one-million mark, and the figure might have surpassed the two-million level 4 years later had Y2K concerns not developed. After September 11, 2001, the upward trend continued. By 2005, just fewer than 2.4 million visitors reached Cuba, a trend that continued until 2008 (Juventud Rebelde 2009).

Anticipated but unfulfilled growth in the tourist industry is shown in Figure 5.14. About 10,000 hotel rooms were added between 2000 and 2004, but occupancy rates actually fell from the upper 40% realm to below 40% during the same period. It is unclear whether the broader global economy, lower return visitation rates, or a combination of factors account for the gap between the number of hotel rooms and occupancy rates.

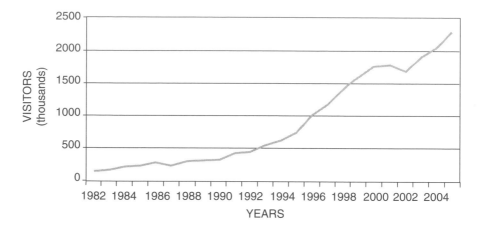

FIGURE 5.13. Tourist arrivals to Cuba and the Caribbean, selected years, 1982–2005. Data from Espino (2006).

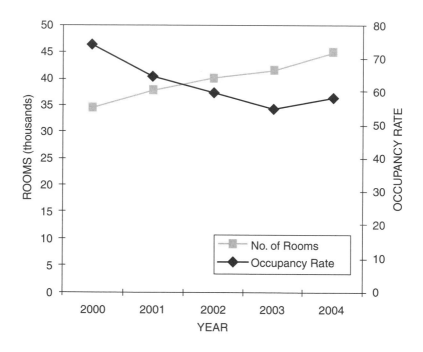

FIGURE 5.14. Cuban hotel rooms and occupancy rates, 2000–2004. Data from *Anuario Estadístico de Cuba*.

Not surprisingly, the vicissitudes of the late 20th- and early 21st-century market trends indicate a significant proportional increase in Cuba's share of the Caribbean market over that of the 1990s. Rising from 3% in 1990 to 10% in 2000, the relative take of the West Indies travel industry appears to have flattened out for Cuba (Table 5.2). It is unclear whether there is dissatisfaction among those who have visited the island for the first time, or whether other travel bargains can be had elsewhere in the Caribbean.

The ranking of leading foreign visitors to Cuba between 2000 and 2004 parallels political and economic trends. Canadians, equipped with purchasing power and good relative location, remain the single largest national group of tourists. In addition, the island's tourism offers prospective Canadian visitors with a survey of investment opportunities. As Seguin (2007, 63) argues in *Canadian Business*, "Canadians can prosper in post-Castro Cuba." Travelers from the European Union make up the second largest block of tourists. Overall, four trends emerge. First, Italians have held steady at a consistent level (about 180,000 per annum; Figure 5.15). Second, the proportion of Germans has dipped while the contribution of British tourists has risen. This may indicate a rise in more affordable tourist packages for the British and a slight shift in more discerning German preferences. Third, Venezuelans were relatively small contributors to the tourist stock until 2002, when their numbers rose sharply. This trend paralleled a growing political alliance between Hugo Chávez and Fidel Castro. Finally, despite the U.S. trade embargo and travel restrictions, the United States was contributing about 100,000 visitors per year

TABLE 5.2. Cuban Tourist Arrivals in the Caribbean Context, 1985–2005, Selected Years

Year	Tourist arrivals to Cuba (thousands)	Tourist arrivals to Caribbean (thousands)	Cuban market share
1985	238	8,000	3%
1990	327	11,400	3%
1995	742	14,025	5%
2000	1,741	17,180	10%
2001	1,736	16,902	10%
2002	1,656	26,058	10%
2003	1,895	17,198	11%
2004	2,017	18,385	11%
2005	2,297	19,028	12%

Note. From Espino (2006). Courtesy María Delores Espino.

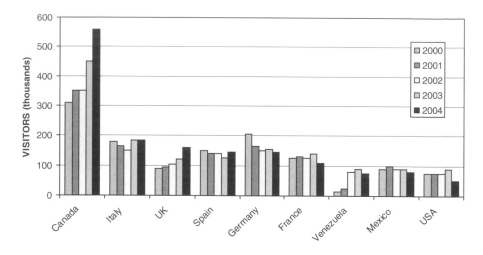

FIGURE 5.15. Leading foreign visitors to Cuba, 2000–2004.

until 2004, when President George W. Bush issued an Executive Order in June of that year, scaling back most undergraduate student travel and all cultural travel (alumni groups, art groups). Workers in the Cuban tourism industry feel the decline in American travelers, who have a reputation as being better tippers than Europeans.

Following the Dominican Republic and the combined ports of Cozumel and Cancún in Mexico, Cuba ranks highly in Caribbean basin tourism. Table 5.3 shows the ranking of tourist arrivals in the region for 2005. As noted earlier, it remains to be seen to what extent repeat tourism can be sustained. This impressive rise has not been without its problems. Cuban art critic Gerardo Mosquera has observed foreign investors realign themselves with the Cuban government since the collapse of the Soviet trading bloc. Also germane is the extent to which the Cubans themselves can enjoy the benefits of Cuban tourism. Mosquera writes:

> The Cuban people have had to confront neoliberal policies without even having the option of legally participating in the informal economy. This curious mixture of "socialist" fundamentalism and "neoliberalism" has created corruption, widespread theft, marginality, the black market, mass exodus, and jinetero [prostitution and illegal hustling] as survival strategies. (1994, 4)

The paradox is not lost on others who observe Caribbean tourism. Although tourists relish walking barefoot on the sandy beaches, going barefoot in the region has always been a sign of poverty. In Cuba, however,

TABLE 5.3. Visitors to the Caribbean Basin, 2005

Country	Visitors (millions)	Percentage
Dominican Republic	3.69	20.3
Cuba	**2.32**	**12.7**
Cancún	2.13	11.7
Bahamas	1.51	8.3
Jamaica	1.48	8.1
Puerto Rico	1.45	8.0
Aruba	0.73	4.0
U.S. Virgin Islands	0.7	3.8
Barbados	0.55	3.0
Martinique	0.47	2.6
St. Maarten	0.47	2.6
Trinidad and Tobago	0.46	2.5
British Virgin Islands	0.34	1.9
St. Lucia	0.32	1.8
Cozumel	0.28	1.5
Bermuda	0.27	1.5
Antigua and Barbuda	0.25	1.4
Belize	0.24	1.3
Curacao	0.22	1.2
Cayman Islands	0.17	0.9
Suriname	0.16	0.9
Guyana	0.12	0.7
Granada	0.1	0.5
Saba	0.1	0.5
St. Eustatius	0.1	0.5
St. Vincent and Grenadines	0.1	0.5
Anguilla	0.06	0.3
Bonaire	0.06	0.3
Monteserrat	0.01	0.1
Total	18.86	100.7[a]

Note. Data from Caribbean Tourism Organization (2006). Figures for Cuba deemed "preliminary."
[a]Figures do not add up to 100% because of rounding.

it is safe to say that the general population understands the reasons for its popularity with international visitors to their island: It is beautiful, rich in history, and full of culture. Less acceptable has been the rise in illicit activities such as Mosquera (1994) notes.

CONCLUSIONS

The somewhat schizophrenic portrayal of Cuba in the international media, on one hand, shows the island as an authoritarian outpost that mistreats civil society. On the other hand, its nearly 2.5 million tourists per annum suggest that despite these concerns, the island has much to offer. In early 2008, Raúl Castro announced that the purchase of cell phones for the masses would be permitted and that the island's hotels would now allow Cubans to lodge there if they paid in hard currency. It is too early to determine whether this suggests a reorientation of the leadership's policies on civil and individual liberties. Moreover, the number of Cubans who have the necessary cash to purchase a cell phone contract or stay in a tourist hotel is likely quite small. Nevertheless, the gesture of liberalizing these two regulations continues to confound Cuba watchers.

This chapter examines selected layers of Cuba's tourist landscapes. It may be useful to recall what the famous landscape architect Kevin Lynch (1972) had to say about Havana's historic cityscape in the 1970s. In his book *What Time Is This Place?*, he argued that the city's unique built environment, rich architectural variety, and impressive vistas and promenades make it a singular place. Hardly the first to remark on this feature, he also focused on the blending of cultures from Europe and Africa and how each had left its imprint. He shows that a city's attractiveness depends largely on how it manages different layers of history and culture. Writing in the era of the "urban crisis" of the 1960s and the "eco crisis" of the 1970s, Lynch makes a clarion call—using Havana's landscape as an example—for planners to become more cognizant of rich historical cities so that they can use the past to inform present and future planning (Ford 1976). In a similar vein, Cuban anthropologist Fernando Ortiz described, decades earlier, the island's cultural mélange—which he calls "transculturation"—this way:

> A steady stream of African Negroes coming from all the coastal regions of Africa along the Atlantic, from Senegal, Guinea, the Congo, and Angola.... And still other immigrant cultures ... Jews, Portuguese, Anglo-Saxons, French ... even yellow Mongoloids from Macao, Canton, and other regions of the sometime Celestial Kingdom. And each of them torn from his native moorings.... The concept of transculturation is fundamental and indispensable for an understanding of the history of Cuba, and, for analogous reasons, of that of America in general. (2004, 27)

Cuba's tourist landscape and imagination make that clear. That tourism has become an engine of economic growth has not been lost on the Cuban leadership. When the World Tourism Organization (2007) claimed that "tourism is firmly established as the number one industry in many countries and the fastest-growing economic sector in terms of foreign exchange earnings and job creation," Cuba could hardly dispute that claim.

The Antillean nation aims to cash in on this market, politics and ideology aside. Cuban tourism officials contend that an immediate suspension of the U.S. ban on travel to the island would produce 1 million visitors (roughly half of the 2006 market) in its first years.

> Americans are expected to flood to Cuba to enjoy its pristine beaches, sip daiquiris at Ernest Hemingway's favorite bars and take a step back in time riding in vintage cars in a city that was once a Mafia playground. (Boadle 2007)

Although the island's capture of the international tourist market is still small, it is sandwiched between the third (United States) and seventh (Mexico) largest tourist destinations in the world. If Cuba could tap into just 10% of Florida's 40 million annual visitors, Price Waterhouse tourism analysts argue, that would bring an unprecedented 6 million visitors to the island and would provide a huge infusion of hard currency into Cuba (Seguin 2007, 66). Enticing tourist circuits of tomorrow might include, for instance, a Disney World–Key West–Havana–Key West itinerary, connected by air, rail, and ship transport. The proposed itinerary would include fantasy, cultural heritage, and conventional mass tourism beach settings, with the option of adding or dropping any of the "s" ingredients in the "sun–surf–sex–sangria" formula. If Cuba's tourist landscape is ambiguous now, then multiple scenarios will surely find a market niche in the world tourism map of tomorrow.

The Cuban diaspora—largely in south Florida but also in Spain and Mexico—will be eyeing their homeland as a possible second home or retirement destination, as well as aging non-Cuban baby boomers in the United States who seek low-cost, high-amenity living in a fiscal era when Social Security payments may dwindle, and even 401(k) retirement funds pose some risk. If health care and long-term care inch up from 14% of the U.S. gross national product to, say, 20% by 2030, then Cuba could become a major economic service provider in the health care, long-term care, and geriatric markets. The island's socialist revolution may have thwarted the fast-food chains and endless miles of commercial strip development that have plagued the United States, but the aging young urban professional (yuppies) segment of the United States—part of the 76 million of the baby boom generation of 1945–1964—will become a cohort of "gray urban maturing professional" (grumpies) that could profoundly transform Cuba's tourist landscape in unexpected ways. An onslaught of American visitors in any capacity (e.g., college students on spring break, retirees, curious travelers, party revelers) has not gone unnoticed by Cuban authorities.

CHAPTER 6

★

INFORMATION[1]

Cuba, like much of Latin America, is often romanticized in the humanities and social sciences because of its striking beauty, diverse peoples, and other distinctive attributes of place (Robinson 1989, 157). As noted in Chapter 1, the imagination of travelers to Cuba—The Pearl of the Antilles—has always been full of hyperbole. William Joseph Showalter, for instance, wrote in the July 1920 *National Geographic* that Cuba had "rivers of sugar flowing out and the streams of gold flowing in" that made the island unique, as did the palm avenues outside sugar plantations, which were "to be seen in almost every landscape" (Showalter 1920, 1, 3). Early republican-era hyperbole about the island's natural beauty lent itself to profit making (e.g., "rivers of sugar ... streams of gold"), a premise derived by annexationist elements that likely persisted at the time. One of the grandest accolades was that given by Christopher Columbus: The island was "the most beautiful land [his] eyes had ever seen." Chapter 1 also stated that Columbus made this comment at other landings, and the veracity of his remark is speculative. However, there is no doubt that the distinctive landscape of the largest island in the Antilles has been widely portrayed in literature, travel accounts, and, recently, in the political discourse of the socialist government.

This chapter examines how various ideologies and political messages surface through the communication media to further the socialist imprint on what we call the "information landscape." Information technology, especially in the form of simple roadside billboards, creates a unique sense of place and landscape in a country where messages encouraging people to consume goods and services are largely absent. We use these selected ideological narratives to explore the rhetoric of place making and the creation of *cubanidad* in socialist Cuba.

We begin with a brief review of some key geographical writings by humanistic geographers that situate the discussion of political landscapes. We posit that an understanding of how places are constructed forms part of the human imagination and creates multiple meanings of place. Here we avoid descriptions of socialism, which often include "perversion," "evil empire," "criminal system," and so on (Juraga and Booker 2002, 2). Instead, we select key iconographic and political symbols of Cuba's 19th- and 20th-century history that are used in the design and dissemination of political billboards. A brief discussion of class, legitimation, and propaganda situates our discussion. The main body of the chapter discusses access to information technology and interpretations of political billboards and representation: patriotism and socialism, U.S. hegemony, conservation, social justice, and civic participation. On the basis of our own experience in living in Cuba and our field research, we believe that such discourses cover the preponderance of the messages disseminated by the communist leadership. Except for conservation and ecological billboards, these icons and political symbols embody the pillars of the revolution and at the same time leave a distinct imprint on the island's landscape. So common are these signs that they are virtually inescapable in the course of quotidian life. We show how ideology, landscape, and the social construction of space manifest themselves uniquely in socialist Cuba, giving the island a distinctive stamp in a world of globalized consumer culture.

ON THE CONSTRUCTION OF "PLACE" IN THE HUMAN IMAGINATION

Images are a part of everyday life, and in every corner of the globe. Some are fabricated by ordinary people, some by companies, and some by governments. Those who witness such images, whether commercially, publicly, or individually fabricated, from various perceptions of each type of image. These perceptions, in turn, carry meanings and symbols that form part of the process of representation. Ideology is a key component of this communication process between individuals and these images (Seamon and Mugerauer 1985). Simply put, an ideology is

> a powerful system of ideas ... [whose impacts] manifest everywhere in geographic landscapes at all scales.... All ideologies, whatever their provenances or manifestations, are involved to varying degrees in the political organiza-

tion of social and spatial relationships involving authority. (Nemeth 2006, 241)

As is by now obvious, Cuba's landscape is largely void of any consumer advertising. Perhaps only North Korea shares this attribute with Cuba. Therefore, the use of political slogans on billboards constitutes the advertising and marketing that most countries permit. In this regard, the historicism that the socialist leadership uses sets it apart from its Caribbean, Latin-, and Anglo-American neighbors. The historical struggles for independence in the 19th century and the socialist rhetoric of the 20th and 21st centuries forge a powerful sense of place identity in contemporary discourse. The Castro government relies heavily on historic events, battlefields, rallying cries from the 19th century and the guerrilla struggle of the 1950s, and images of heroes to advance its political and ideological agenda (Table 6.1). The use of these historical events and images goes beyond, for instance, what in the United States might correspond to respect for a Civil War culture, or reverence for the holocaust in Europe. In those countries there are parks, museums, statues, and commemorative monuments to these historic events. In Cuba, however, historic events, slogans and rallying cries, and historical political figures can be seen daily on television, billboards, and murals or heard on the radio. The contemporary Cuban landscape reveals these messages through myriad political advertisements and special public squares used for protesting, mass organizations, and assorted political art. It is noteworthy that the protesting allowed in this public space is only against the United States, and massive public assembly is usually permitted only when the state has an anti–United States event planned.

A recent diplomatic exchange of cat and mouse between the United States government and the Cuban government illustrates the important role of billboards. In 2006, the U.S. Interests Section* in Havana installed an electronic bulletin board on the upper floors of its building, a modern structure designed by the firm Harrison & Abramowitz, part of the same team that designed the United Nations headquarters in New York. This bulletin board, actually a series of panels, carries news items that are meant to provide alternative interpretations of both Cuban and international news, as well as U.S. sports scores. The United States claims that these news stories are important because Cubans do not have access to them

*The United States does not have full diplomatic relations with Cuba. Instead, it has a consulate there and leases the former U.S. Embassy from the Swiss government. Nevertheless, with more than 50 employees, it is the largest diplomatic staff in Cuba.

TABLE 6.1. Nineteenth-Century Cuban Independence Heroes

Hero	Profile
José Martí	(1853–1895). Author, poet, journalist, and overall "apostle of Cuban Independence," he lived in exile in New York City, Tampa, and Spain. Martí wrote eloquently about the virtues of a free Cuba and the evils of both Spain and the United States as menaces to his homeland. He was killed in battle against the Spanish. Although it was not he who put his poem "Guantanamera" to an already popular tune in the 20th century, his volumes of writings are both scholarly and highly popular among the public.
Carlos Manuel de Céspedes	(1819–1874). A wealthy landowner from eastern Cuba who pronounced the *Grito de Yara* (Cry of Yara) that marked the beginning of the Cuban independence struggle and led to the Ten Years' War (1868–1878). He was briefly the president of Cuba in Arms before being overthrown and executed by the Spanish army.
Antonio Maceo	(1845–1896). Called the Bronze Titan, he was a mulatto Cuban independence fighter and political strategist who was recognized for his fighting in the Ten Years' War, as well as his writings on Cuban independence and sovereignty. José Martí remarked that he was as strong in his mind as in his body (he stood 6 feet tall and weighed 200 pounds). He was killed by the Spanish.
Calixto García	(1839–1898). Born in the eastern province of Holguín, García fought against the Spanish as a teenager until his capture 5 years later. Although he fought with the American troops in 1898 in their brief confrontations with the Spanish, he was not allowed into the surrender ceremony in Santiago de Cuba at the end of the war. He died of pneumonia on a diplomatic mission to New York in 1898 and was buried with honors at Arlington National Cemetery in Virginia.
Father Félix Varela	(1788–1853). A Spaniard born in Havana but raised in St. Augustine, Florida. He returned to Havana to study at the San Carlos Seminary, where he later became a young and distinguished professor of philosophy, religion, physics, and chemistry. In 1821 he was elected to the Spanish legislature, where he argued for Cuban and Spanish American independence. This bold stance earned him a death sentence, and he escaped to New York where he entered the priesthood. While pastor in an Irish neighborhood in New York City, he published *El Habanero* (*The Havanan*), which although published only seven times, became a highly prized and smuggled document in Cuba. He became vicar general of the New York Archdiocese. He died in St. Augustine the same year José Martí was born (1853). His remains were taken to the University of Havana in 1912.

otherwise. In response, the Cuban government retaliated by placing a series of black flags (called the "mourning flags") to block the bulletin board from public view (Figure 6.1). Media sources have referred to this tit-for-tat diplomatic action as the "battle of the electronic bulletin boards." In June 2006, the Cuban government cut off power to the building in a protest against the bulletin board, but it was later restored. Cuban authorities claimed that there was a problem with the local power grid in the Vedado neighborhood where the building is located (Robles and Bachelet 2006). Consular officer Michael Parmley, however, claimed that power was restored only after the *Miami Herald* carried a newspaper headline denouncing the sanctions imposed on the diplomatic building. When Parmley, then chief of the U.S. Interests Section, was asked whether the United States would tolerate a similar bulletin board running Al Jazira news stories on one of Washington, DC's embassies, he responded that the U.S. government probably would not like it, but would tolerate it. Parmly went on to claim that the Havana board was appropriate because of the "total propaganda found [in Cuba]; it helps that it is an island" (National Public Radio 2006). Once again, geography played a key role.

This so-called battle of the billboards between the governments is one indicator of the deteriorating diplomatic condition between Havana and Washington. However, the situation has not been confined to just the electronic bulletin board incident. In 2004, Cuba erected several billboards near the U.S. mission in Havana that included pictures of American soldiers pointing rifles at Iraqi children and bloodied and hooded inmates at the Abu Ghraib prison. These billboards, along with a swastika and the word "fascist" next to it, juxtaposed the U.S. Interests Section display of 75 Christmas lights; each light corresponded to one of the 75 prodemocracy activists (called "dissidents" in Cuba) who were given lengthy prison terms in 2003. On one hand, senior Cuban diplomat Ricardo Alarcón referred to the U.S. Christmas display as a "provocation" and "rubbish." On the other hand, the U.S. State Department remarked, "Any government that puts up swastikas ought to answer its own questions about why it does that.... We think that the remembrance of the 75 people in jail is entirely appropriate to the season. And we intend to leave the lights up" (Franc 2004). Thus, in a geopolitical setting where two nations do not maintain full diplomatic relations with each other, the use of "outdoor advertising" ratchets the tenor of discourse up a notch about the meaning of civil society and government legitimacy. A tropical "cold war" still lingers between Havana and Washington, and Cuba's information landscape is one arena in which this battle is fought.

FIGURE 6.1. The *protestatario* (protest plaza) located on the Malecón seaside boulevard, facing the U.S. Interest Section. Originally built in a very short period of time while the Cuban boy Elián González was awaiting his custody case to be adjudicated in U.S. courts in 1999–2000, it is a place of public protest. Speakers and stage face the U.S. Interests Section (leased to the United States by the Swiss government). In 2006, the U.S. Interests Section began running an electronic bulletin board around the top floors of its building. *Top*: Looking west toward the U.S. Interest Section with the "mourning flags" (banderas de deluto) in the background and the José Martí statue (cradling a young boy in his arms, symbolizing Elián González). *Bottom*: Looking east shows scaffolding for lighting and sound systems.

CLASS, LEGITIMATION, AND PROPAGANDA

In Marxist terms, ideology entails the reproduction of the social relations of production; that is, how society guarantees its social and economic structures from one generation to the next.

> Ideology is how the existing ensemble of social relations represents itself to individuals; it is the image a society gives of itself in order to perpetuate itself. These representations serve to constrain [those who live in a particular society] ... they establish fixed places for us to occupy that work to guarantee coherent social actions over time. Ideology uses the fabrication of images and the processes of representation to persuade us that how things are is how they ought to be and that the place provided for us is the place we ought to have. (Nichols 1981, 1)

In this regard, the work of Jürgen Habermas (1975), in *Legitimation Crisis*, is particularly useful in understanding Cuba's information landscapes. Habermas identified three broad subsystems operating in society: work as formulated in an economic system, language as a sociocultural system, and domination as a political system. These are useful lenses through which we can understand how the Cuban government employs political billboards in Cuba because, as Weinar (1981, 119) shows, these discourses can stop the masses from raising "truth claims" that may challenge the political status quo. The political mark made by any socialist nation can manifest itself several ways. Without competing political parties advertising in the print or electronic media, the single-party system is guaranteed a monopoly on discourses to deliver its messages to the masses. We agree with Kubik (1994, 7), who argues that the use of legitimacy is key in studying the political systems of communist nations. Legitimacy is essentially the regime's successful continuation because it can "allow"—to a certain extent—the claims of a government to maintain control over a people. Seymour Lipset (1960, 19) stated it succinctly a half century ago: "Legitimacy involves the capacity of the system to engender and maintain the belief that the existing political institutions are the most appropriate ones for society."

Political propaganda in the form of billboards is one part of many "spatial vocabularies of power" that individuals, organizations, and governments employ (Allen 2003; Von Blum 2002). Other venues that the Cuban government uses include—but are not limited to—comics, declarations, harangues, public shaming (in Cuba, called *actos de repudio*[2]), mass rallies, focused news programs (recently called *mesas redondas*), newspapers, political manifestos, pictorial magazines, propaganda leaflets, public announcements, revolutionary songs, and speeches, among others (Holm 1991, 18). Together, these venues constitute the rhetorics of place.

The concept of place holds a prominent position in 20th-century Anglo-American geography. It is foremost a portion of geographical space that people or objects occupy. John Agnew (1987) argues that place consists of three distinct attributes. One is the "sense of place" that invokes a local "structure of feeling." A second dimension is the location of things or people in a designated geographical area. This notion shares the concepts of relative location, that is, the relationship of a fixed point (absolute location) with the surrounding area. A third component entails "locale," or those settings where social relations take place. Taken together, these constructs of place provide an alternative to the more positivist positions in human geography and embrace phenomenological approaches to geographic research on place. By "phenomenological," we mean how individuals experience their world without preconceived constructs to categorize their experiences. Rather, a sense of place can be described inductively and uniquely according to each individual (Relph 1976; Seamon 1979).

By the close of the 20th century, however, interest in the concept of place had expanded beyond its original humanistic confines and came to inform studies in economic, social, and political geography (Agnew 1987; Johnston 1991; Kirby 1982, 1993) and communication studies. Place serves as the empirical or observable part of power and political processes, where outcomes can be observed and landscapes reveal these imprints. Studies at a variety of geographic scales show how the study of place sheds light on complex phenomena: urban sprawl; where to build and maintain locally unwanted land uses (or LULUs, such as garbage dumps, incinerators, noxious industries, prisons, mental health and substance abuse facilities, and water treatment plants), and the use of advertising and political propaganda.

Canadian scholar Marshall McLuhan (1967) was among the first to argue that new electronic media (particularly television) were homogenizing our world and invoking plainness. It is important to note that his observation came before "globalization"—the shrinking of time and space through advanced communication technologies—became a household word (Waters 1985). McLuhan, whom *Time* magazine called "The Prince of the Global Village," observed that "ours is a brand new world of all-at-onceness … we live in a global village … created by instant electronic movement. It is at once as wide as the planet and as small as the village" (*Time* 1992). In his conceptualization of space in the precomputer era, the lines between the local and universal become blurred.

The works of Appadurai (1986, 1996), however, bridge the gap between the local and the universal. He joins the roles of media and ideology in his discussion of "ideascapes" in which prominent ideologies are used to leave their marks on landscapes, reshape the relationships between state power and citizens, and summon an allegiance among citizens who are exposed to both overt and covert messages of political propaganda.

CIVIL SOCIETY AND INFORMATION TECHNOLOGY IN CUBA

Cuba's "ideascapes," to borrow Appadurai's (1996) term, embrace the virtues of the Revolution, celebrate the accomplishments of national martyrs, victimize the island as a casualty of U.S. hegemony, and are widely distributed throughout Cuba.[3] Carty argues that the societal role of mass media in Cuba is rather mixed. "On the positive side," he writes, "[the media] do interpret domestic and international events and trends from the Marxist–Leninist perspective in a systematic and rigorous manner. On the negative side, mass communicators do not provide a needed critique of the goals, accomplishments and failures of leaders and organizations" (1990, 134). In other words, there are no open op-ed columns in the state-run newspapers and no opposition press exists. Critiques against state policy must be veiled and indirect, and only the highest public officials can even allude to such criticism. In the electronic media, there is no affordable Internet access in Cuba for private citizens; only select employees at public institutions or joint venture firms can access the Web and maintain e-mail accounts. In addition, there is no cable TV beyond the hotels and restaurants, although there is a thriving trade in illegal satellite dishes and pirated cable TV services (Peters and Scarpaci 1998). Unauthorized access to the Internet and satellite TV carries a punishment under the Cuban legal system. Nonetheless, illegal Internet and cable access is growing through an underground network of dealers, installers, and embezzlers.

A defining feature of the modern nation-state, especially an authoritarian one, is its relationship to the media. Besides control of the armed forces, media control is of paramount importance in how a government projects its legitimacy to civil society. During the Cold War, news agency information pooled by the nonaligned nations (Nonaligned Movement) served as a counter to Western-based news services such as Associated Press, United Press International, Reuters, Cable News Network (CNN), British Broadcasting Corporation, and other sources.

The Cuban government has long seen itself as being "influenced by a barrage of news and commentary from international media but seldom having any input of their own [or other] Third World leaders" (Milner 1979, 17). In Cuba's final declaration of the 1971 Cuban Congress on Education and Culture, the government declared:

> Culture, like education, is not and cannot be apolitical or impartial. . . . Radio, television, cinema and the press are powerful instruments of ideological education and for creation of a collective conscience. . . . The mass media cannot be left to change or used without direction. (*Granma Weekly Review* 1971; cited in Milner 1979, 18)

Despite these restrictions, there are many newspapers, radio stations, and television channels on the island. Although there are about one dozen national Cuban portal servers (Table 6.2), Internet use and access are tightly controlled. Only researchers and bureaucrats at public institutions gain free access to the World Wide Web. Cubans willing to pay in hard currency can rent Internet machines; rates range from about U.S. $3 to U.S. $6 per hour, comparable to about one week's wages. Cubans have free access to an intranet service that operates within the island. This allows Cubans to send e-mails from many post offices and other computer centers, but only within the island. Those Cubans who work for joint venture operations can access internationally sent e-mail and the World Wide Web from their work sites. The dredging and filtering of e-mail entering and leaving the island is a common government practice. Palmer argues that access to the Internet on the island is "prohibitively expensive and . . . [blocks] unsuitable material (roughly defined as any site that doesn't promote Cuban tourism). Only a small minority of state officials [are] allowed limited Internet access" (2005). Cuban authorities confine fax machines to hard-currency accounts and lines, which most Cubans cannot afford. Our recent review of Cuban websites indicates that there are 2 national newspapers, 15 provincial papers, 26 magazines, 3 national TV stations, and

TABLE 6.2. Selected Cuban National Computer Servers (.cu)

Ceniai	Cubamar
Infocom	Cubaciencia
Cubaweb	Cubasi
Isla Grande	Portal del medio ambiente en Cuba
Infomed	Cubarte
Citmatel	

10 national radio stations. It is significant that these are all state owned, monitored, and censored.

Like Communist North Korea and Vietnam, the Cuban government occasionally allows limited public debate on selected issues. These are carefully orchestrated events; as Milner (1979, 18) contended nearly 30 years ago, "communist societies make no pretense of guaranteeing the right to such debate and they do not, even in periods of latitude, allow criticism" (1979, 18). Cubans enlist a variety of sayings that soften what others might call censorship. The French NGO Reporters without Borders noted that

> in 2006, Cuba is still the second biggest prison in the world for journalists after China. Three years ago it was the first, following an unprecedented crackdown which saw the arrest of 27 journalists, speedily tried and sentenced for alleged collaboration with the United States against "Cuba's economy and national independence" under the terms of the 88 law or "gagging law." (2006)

A saying about the distinction between public and private speech is noted in the following remark heard in official circles: "In Cuba there is no culture of criticism" (*En Cuba no hay una cultura de crítica*) or "Within the Revolution, everything; outside the Revolution, nothing" (*dentro de la Revolución todo, fuera de la Revolución, nada*). This conceptual clash surfaced in the controversial interview that U.S. journalist ABC News correspondent Barbara Walters had with Fidel Castro in 1977, when Castro remarked:

> If you ask us whether some periodical against socialism could come out here, I tell you frankly that it could not. Neither the [Cuban Communist P]arty, nor the government, nor the people would permit that. In that sense, we do not have freedom of the press which you have in the United States.... Our mass media work is a function of the revolution. (cited in Milner 1979, 18)

Twenty-five years later, Walters again interviewed Castro, and he emphasized his government's role in health care and education as metrics that define human rights in Cuba. Walters remarked:

> For Castro, freedom starts with education. And if literacy alone were the yardstick, Cuba would rank as one of the freest nations on Earth. The literacy rate is 96 percent. (*The Agitator* 2006)

To be sure, Fidel Castro is media savvy. The Walters interview of 1977 took place over 10 days, during which the famous U.S. journalist traveled in a jeep across the island as a guest of the Cuban leader. World media disseminated images of the virile fatigue-clad revolutionary driving the scarf-adorned Walters over the island's mountains and beaches. His appearance helped to humanize his regime, which, at that time, had been demonized in the U.S. media for nearly 16 years. He learned about the use of the media during the early days of his revolutionary struggle, beginning with the now famous interview he gave to Herbert Matthews of *The New York Times* in 1958, after President Batista's army had allegedly killed the guerrilla fighter. That interview led *The National Review* to its tongue-in-cheek remark that Fidel Castro "got his first job in the New York Times" (1961, p. 44).

THE RHETORICAL CRY OF INDEPENDENCE IN 19TH-CENTURY CUBA

If the contemporary media and landscape of Cuba are steeped in political symbolism, then its wellspring surely derives from the island's long colonial history. The colony of Cuba did not partake in the independence wars that inspired other Central and South American colonies to throw off the yoke of Madrid. By 1830, all Spanish colonies in the New World, except Puerto Rico and Cuba, had broken free of Spanish domination. Spanish rule in Cuba was tightened because of the wealth the island produced for the motherland, mostly in the form of sugar, molasses, rum, and wood products (Moreno Fraginals 1964). The ports of Havana, Nipe, Matanzas, and Santiago served as key refurbishing points for transatlantic fleets journeying to the Spanish port of Cádiz. The Cuban-born creoles, however, launched a series of wars in claiming their independence: 1860–1878, 1882, and 1895–1898. Although the U.S. Army intervened at the end of the Cuban independence wars and snatched victory from the hands of the Cubans, important liberation symbols emerged from the Cuban struggle against Spain.

The first is the machete-wielding Cuban soldiers, the *mambises*, who folded the forward brim of their straw hats that survived, as a sort of "peasant helmet" in contrast to the modern garb of the Spanish colonial army. Humility, perseverance, and valor embody the noble *mambises*. A second nearly ubiquitous feature is a historic figure, the bust of José Martí, the father of Cuba's independence movement. The mass-produced concrete busts are found in schools, clinics, government offices, and parks, among many other locations. A third, but less widely distributed symbol, is the array of civic art that depicts 19th-century war heroes. Carlos

FIGURE 6.2. A political billboard denouncing state-sponsored terror, Rancho Boyeros, Havana City Municipality. The play on words denotes the card game term "full house" by using the Spanish word *ases* (aces), which constitutes the first few letters of "assassins" (*asesinos*). *From left to right:* Adolph Hitler, George W. Bush, Luis Posadas Carriles, and Orlando Bosch. Photography courtesy of Korine Kolivras.

Manuel de Céspedes, Antonio Maceo, and Calixto García are just a few of the heroes most commonly depicted in sculptures, which are found in Havana and nearly every provincial capital. Finally, political billboards—the focus of the rest of this chapter—are distributed throughout the island (Figure 6.2).

THE POLITICAL BILLBOARD

Cuba's cultural revolution in the 1960s strove to bring all aspects of art—poetry, civic art, painting, sculpture, and other forms—to the masses (Kapcia 2000, ch. 2; Block 2001). The Ministry of Culture's Casa de las Américas was created in the early years of the Revolution and continues as a particularly important disseminator of poems, books, short stories, novels, including more than 10,000 original works. It has won international prizes for its publications, which have given it considerable legitimacy (Carty 1990, 155). Not surprisingly, perhaps, foreign ownership of the mass media in Cuba is not permitted.

    The Revolution also introduced new forms of mass communication, such as the street mural on buildings and walls and outdoor advertising (billboards). Political billboards are works of art that carry a political or civic message. As Juraga and Booker show, socialist art and propaganda serve partly to "challenge the hegemony of Western bourgeois aesthetics ... [and] ideology" (2002, 6, 9). Graphic arts—posters, billboards, paintings, and murals—also fostered political education, the values of the socialist revolution, and a chance to exploit "a new commitment and also the population's newly awakened enthusiasm" (Kapcia 2000, 14).

Thousands of political billboards dot the island. They are positioned at major streets and highways to maximize their visibility. Political billboards constitute virtually the only form of public advertising in Cuba, other than signs used to identify buildings, state-run establishments, ports, roads, and tourist facilities. Although a few billboards promote tourist destinations and facilities, such places were off-limits to Cubans who could afford meals or lodgings that are charged in hard currency (Scarpaci 1998); this changed when Raúl Castro authorized it in 2008. Although there is no standardized format for billboards, they usually include a quote from a historical figure, celebrate the virtues of Cuban socialism, or both. Indeed, it is the billboard (12 meters × 5 meters is the norm) whose mark on the Cuban landscape is most pronounced.

The Cuban Revolution of 1959 gradually began phasing out private sector activity, and with that came the end of commercial advertising, including radio and TV spots, print media and, of course, commercial billboards. New messages needed to dominate the media and reinforce to the masses that life in Cuba would be different under the leadership of Fidel Castro and his cadre of guerrilla fighters. By the end of 1961 practically all housing, firms, services, factories, and transportation systems came under state control. Nationalization eliminated private sector advertising. Market economies encouraged the consumption of nonessential consumer items, which are the anathema of a socialist society. Instead, most daily needs were satisfied by the state: Food was procured at the corner grocer (*bodega*) with a ration book (*libreta*), housing was the property of the state, which assigned living areas as based on need and political criteria, and virtually everyone worked in the public sector.

In the frenzy of these early years, public notices became essential in keeping Cubans apprised of the rapidly changing state of political and economic affairs. For instance, the need for volunteer work had to be announced at the national, provincial, and local levels. Word about production quotas at the national level and that of the firm also had to be disseminated. Electronic media (TV and radio) played a key role in providing public information, as did print media in the form of newspapers. And sugar cane harvest amounts—the backbone of the Cuban economy until recently—could be readily posted at the level of state farms, government offices at county (*municipio*) and provincial levels, and the national level. Billboards proved to be the ideal medium for accomplishing these tasks.

Billboards have several functions. First, they are relatively inexpensive; once installed, paint and the labor required for painting them are the only costs. Second, they are large and fixed in place and allow a message to be communicated directly or indirectly over a long period. Moreover, they can be repainted fairly quickly if a timely message must be disseminated. Third, they are a good medium for spreading popular slogans, which can be read and interpreted in a few short seconds. As such, they are ideal for informing commuters on the crowded buses and trucks that haul Cubans to and from work. Finally, they serve as constant reminders that the state is present, promoting welfare, safety, history lessons, and socialist ideology for the masses. We suspect that this is their most powerful use, though we have no empirical evidence to support the claim.

PLACE, LANDSCAPE, AND DISCOURSE

In this section, we define five categories or discourses of messages that pervade political billboards. These messages form part of broader discourses that are widely distributed in town and country, mountain and valley, east and west. The sample we review includes patriotism and socialism, conservation, U.S. hegemony, social justice, and civic participation. Although not a complete list of the many types of messages conveyed by political billboards, they do represent a broad sampling of the prevailing political and civic messages (Table 6.3).

Patriotism and Socialism

To the ire of the exile community, the socialist leadership enlists the images of historical figures in promoting the principles of socialism and a centrally planned economy (Grenier and Pérez 2002). Only men of letters, politicians, statesmen, and soldiers who have figured in the promotion of historical events appear with contemporary political rhetoric. It is interesting to note that the images of neither Fidel[4] nor Raul Castro are widely distributed, because both men are still alive.[5] Linking the historical images of the past with the contemporary socialist struggle provides a historical thread, which is important in forging a national identity that is cast as both bellicose and just. Billboards of this ilk aim to legitimize the state.

TABLE 6.3. Sampling of Cuban Political Billboards and Murals by Category

Category or discourse	Billboard or mural title	English translation	Significance	Selected images
Patriotism and Socialism	*Bolivia: Monumento Nacional.*	Bolivia: National Monument	Attaching image of Argentine-born physician Che Guevara on sign that renamed the Cunagua sugar mill as the Bolivia sugar mill, even before Che was killed in Bolivia.	
	Señores imperialistas, no le tenemos ningún miedo.	Imperialists: We have absolutely no fear of you	Located next to the United States Interest Section in Havana. Portrays an old Uncle Sam facing off against bearded guerrillas.	
	La caña es tradición, cultura, identidad	Sugar care is tradition, culture, identity	Heralds a former economic mainstay. Half of the 156 mills on the island have closed since 2000.	

(cont.)

153

TABLE 6.3. *(cont.)*

Category or discourse	Billboard or mural title	English translation	Significance	Selected images
	Somos de la misma casa	We are all from the same house	All Cubans share a common heritage and therefore share a common responsibility in overcoming challenges.	
	Face of Che (no text).		Famous image of Che based on a photograph by Korda, widely reproduced on posters, postcards, and T-shirts, appears here on a rooftop cistern in Pinar del Río.	
	Los cienfuegueros son firmes, no hay duda.	There are no doubts that cienfuegueros [residents of the city or province of Cienfuegos] are committed [to the revolution]	Spoken by Fidel on the 46th anniversary of the guerrilla attacks on the Moncada army barracks. Fidel praises residents of *cienfuegos* for the commitment to the revolutionary struggle. In revolutionary circles, this is a badge of honor. The billboard is located in the city of Cienfuegueros.	

Cuba sí! 150 aniversario del natalicio de José Martí. "Será inmortal quien merezca serlo."

Cuba yes! 150th anniversary of the birth of José Martí, who is quoted: "Those who will be immortal are the ones who deserve it."

2003 marked the 150th anniversary of the island's "greatest martyr," José Martí, 1853–1895. Pictured (left to right) are his birthplace in Havana, a portrait, another portrait, mausoleum (in Santiago, close to where he died in combat, fighting against the Spanish), book cover, and monument to him (in Havana).

La Revolución es intocable.

The revolution is untouchable

Heralding the steadfast course that the state has charted.

Una Asociación de Patria o Muerte.

An association of Homeland or Death

"Homeland or Death" is the conventional way of ending a speech, often followed by "venceremos," or "we will prevail." The billboard is sponsored by a veterans association.

(cont.)

155

TABLE 6.3. (*cont.*)

Category or discourse	Billboard or mural title	English translation	Significance	Selected images
	Ellos señalaron el camino de seguir adelante.	They showed the road to keep going forward	Located in the populous suburb of eastern Havana, the billboard shows 19th- and 20th-century statesmen and soldiers; left to right: Máximo Gómez, Manuel de Céspedes, unknown, José Martí, José Antonio Echevarría, Camilo Cienfuegos, and Che Guevara. The billboard underscores the historical thread that connects 19th-century struggles against Spain with struggles against Batista and the United States in the 20th century.	
Conservation	*No al desplifarlo. ¡Ahorrala!*	[Say] No to wasting it [water]. Save it!	Fresh water is a concern in Cuba. Although the island receives more than 54 inches of rain in most parts, the high evapotranspiration rate and short river lengths make conserving water an ongoing challenge.	
	Te presto mi mar, mis ríos, y mis peces. ¡Cuídalos!	I lend you my sea, my rivers, and my fish. Take care of them!	Ecotourism promises income potential in future years. However, not even Havana has a primary water treatment facility. Havana Bay is one of the dirtiest bodies of water in the Americas.	

156

(cont.)

U.S. hegemony	*Liberen a nuestros heroes.*	Free our heroes	Five Cubans are incarcerated in a U.S. federal penitentiary for spying for the U.S. government while residing in Florida. The Cuban government maintains that even though they were gathering intelligence, they committed no crimes. Their imprisonment has become a cause celebre since 2001, replacing the saga of Elián González, which prevailed in 1999 and 2000.
Social justice	*En Cuba, una vejez digna …*	In Cuba, a dignified old age …	Everyone will have some social security payment as well as free medical care.
	El futuro está en tus manos.	The future is in your hands	Billboard shows a child drawing. The "your" in the phrase "your hands" refers to the child. The message is directed to children and recognizes the importance of laying a good educational and welfare foundation for children.
	El valor de toda la tierra del hombre más rico del mundo no vale más de la vida de un ser humano.—Fidel	The value of all the land [owned] by the richest man in the world is not worth more than the life of a single human being.— Fidel	Presumably, an axiom that few would dispute. It is notable that it is located on the medical school grounds of the University of Havana, not far from a tourist district.

157

TABLE 6.3. *(cont.)*

Category or discourse	Billboard or mural title	English translation	Significance	Selected images
Civic participation	CDRs: Una revolución en cada barrio. "¡Mientras existan en el hombre ansias de progreso, de superación de perfeccionamiento, tendrán una tarea los CDR!"—Fidel	CDRs [Committees for the Defense of the Revolution]: A revolution in every neighborhood. "As long as men strive from progress, betterment, and perfection, the CDRs will always have work!"—Fidel	Originally formed in 1961 as a defense unit against U.S. military aggression, the CDRs now monitor community behavior (antirevolutionary behavior), neighborhood watch functions, and the normal array of planning functions such as waste removal, police patrolling, youth and elderly citizen monitoring, among others.	
	Queremos que sean como el Che.—Fidel	We want [the students] to be like Che.—Fidel	Fidel exhorting the youth to dedicate themselves to the revolution.	
	Si Uds. triunfan, habrá milicias en Cuba.—Fidel	If you are victorious, there will be militias in Cuba.—Fidel	Praising the efforts of voluntary local militias.	
	No hay oxígeno para la contrarrevolución.	There is no oxygen for the counterrevolution	Volunteerism and loyalty will be rewarded. The picture of the fist that crushes the worm refers to the state and "traitors" (worms, Cuban exiles, or *gusanos*), respectively.	

Conservation

Cuba is a small island with limited resources. It is also a developing nation with less than 1% of the population of China. Cubans are keenly aware that many essential materials cannot be produced on the island but must be imported and paid for in hard currency (Aranda 1968). Aside from nickel and some oil, it is relatively resource poor. However, since the collapse of the Soviet Union in 1989, economic necessity has forced Cuba to increase crude oil production (high in sulfur) from just 15% of national consumption to practically 100%. The soils in parts of the country produce some of the world's finest tobacco and indicated a rich agricultural history where sugar cane (now in steep decline) figured prominently. Fresh water for both irrigation and drinking is a major concern. The capital loses as much as 55% of its fresh water supplies through leakage in the pipelines drawing on two aquifers south of Havana. Therefore, water conservation is paramount. One of the few political protests that took place under the socialist regime happened in the heat of August 1994 when power blackouts impeded the distribution of water to parts of Habana Vieja and Centro Habana. Another conservation practice is the promotion of recycling. However, there is no domestic (e.g., household pickup) recycling in place anywhere on the island (Díaz-Briquets and Pérez-López 2000; Scarpaci et al. 2002).

U.S. Hegemony

The predominance of the United States in Cuba's political, economic, and social history dates back to the island's colonial period. From snatching political victory from the Cuban colonial forces in 1898, to supporting a series of corrupt regimes that were sympathetic to the United States in the 20th century, to the coordination of the Bay of Pigs invasion in 1961—the record of fact provides the socialist leadership with myriad examples of U.S. imperialism and domination. These political messages remind those who pass by the billboards of the nefarious record of Cuba's northern neighbor while deflecting blame from the government because of a menacing bully just 90 miles away.

Social Justice

Universal health care, education, free housing, and guaranteed levels of retirement have long been hallmarks of the Revolution. Although the news media often reports the high cost of medical care in the United

States, it is at once keen on promoting the plethora of free social services to the masses in Cuba (Feinsilver 1993). This socialist security net is likely the sine qua non of Castro's socialist government (Chaffee and Prevost 1992). Homelessness, costly universities, poor inner-city schools, and the expensive real estate market in the United States contrast with a modicum of welfare state services in socialist Cuba. Billboards that carry these messages remind Cubans of the stability they enjoy under a centrally planned economy, though the conditions of the schools, hospitals, and clinics are very different from what they should be.

Civic Participation

The fundamental premises of socialism prioritize collective versus individual actions. Social solidarity is built on the collective social action that benefits society at large. Voluntarism is central to these notions. It is a civic duty in which altruism surpasses private material rewards (August 1999). Cuba's social history between 1965 and 1985 is replete with examples that showcase the accomplishments of the socialist economy; people had life expectancies comparable to those of the capitalist industrial economies of the North Atlantic, and their basic needs were satisfied. Food has always been plain, but scarcity was not a serious problem until the 1990s. Raúl Castro's statement in December 2006 was one of the frankest assessments of food shortages and other structural problems:

> In this Revolution we are tired of excuses.... The Revolution cannot lie.... This isn't saying that there have been comrades who have lied, but the imprecision, inexact data, consciously or unconsciously masked, can no longer continue. (Prima News Agency 2006)

Leading the list of top issues are public transportation problems, poor housing, insufficient food, and salaries that cannot cover a modicum of expenses (Snow 2006).

Whether these remarks signal a new departure with Raúl Castro as leader, mass organization participation in such bodies as the Cuban Federation of Women, student associations, and the Committees for the Defense of the Revolution were encouraged because the state had been generous in satisfying minimum material needs. Today, however, material rewards are surpassing certain moral incentives that encouraged voluntarism in the past. The legalization of the dollar in 1993 and the subsequent creation of a two-tier dollar-and-peso economy have contributed to this material and moral schism. Nonetheless, social and occupational mobility in state enterprises is still premised on the comportment of a good socialist citizen. Voluntarism forms a key part of that civic participation, and the neighborhood CDR (Committee for the Defense of the Revolution) is the most widely distributed grassroots organization of this kind. Its seal is seen on at least one door in each neighborhood, which signifies the residence of the block leader. This carving up of the nation's political map into smaller jurisdictions can be traced back to 1976 when planning authorities increased the number of provinces from 6 to 13, ostensibly to cater to the local geographic nuances that were not captured by the larger jurisdictions (Slater 1982). Critics contend that such a territorial reorganization was more a way to impose social control than to enhance planning mandates (Jatar-Hausman 1999).

BEYOND THE INFORMATION LANDSCAPE

We have outlined just a few aspects of political space in Cuba. A complex and varied array of representations herald the triumphs of the Revolution, praise martyrs who have sacrificed their lives in a variety of historical struggles against imperialism, and encourage environmental sensitivity. These civic and political messages form a key part of we call the island's political landscape; they stand out in a country where the market economy advertisements for consumer products, fast-food dining, and other nonessential goods do not exist. In some fashion, these billboards create a sense of place unique to the island, much like a low-tech communist version of Times Square in Manhattan. To what extent these messages tether civil society to the state cannot be known, but it is clear that they form a distinct element of place. We concur with Lefebvre's (1991) phenomenological view that power and social space consist of something beyond ordered diagrams (billboards) and their static distribution. This medium is subtle and ever-present, silent yet imposing.

The exercise of authority in Cuba is striking to us, if only because during our research and living on the island we have seen very little any antigovernment graffiti[6] or the destruction or vandalism of any political billboards. At the surface, this may suggest unquestionable allegiance and the pervasive authority of the state, a disciplined civil society, a great fear of countering these billboards because of harsh recriminations, or some combination of these elements. Indeed, this is remarkable if we consider Allen's assessment:

There is something rather odd about the claim that the whole weight of government, in both its state and non-state appearances, rests upon the exercise of authority, when seduction, manipulation or inducement, even coercion, would all seem to have a part to play in what it takes for people to bring themselves "into line." (Allen 2003, 143)

Globally, alternatives to the marketplace have surfaced as a visible counterforce to the pressures of neoliberal development strategies. For example, Von Blum (1982) shows how resistance art in Los Angeles provides an important social, political, and ethnic-based voice for the poor and non-Anglo groups. The art movement there emerged from the Mexican mural renaissance between the 1920s and 1940s, the migrant labor and civil rights movements of the 1960s and 1970s, and the gangs of the 1980s and beyond. Blacks, Chicanos, Latinos of all stripes, gays and lesbians, Asians and other cultural minorities have found an expression in resistance art whose aim is to "cause passing viewers to rethink traditional attitudes about consumption and refocus on contemporary political controversies.... Billboards, after all, are supposed to sell products and services, not criticize American foreign policy" (Von Blum 1982, 195). Graffiti artists may also employ guerrilla tactics to disspell prevailing norms and "provide alternatives to ... governmental dogma" (Von Blum 1982, 195). A recent review of modern architecture and modernity in Latin America suggests that the use of public spaces and advertising in southern California are increasingly showing up in the literature on Latin American urbanism (Scarpaci 2003). However, these forms of expression and uses of public space are uncommon in Cuba.[7]

Many argue that the notion of community around the globe has been eclipsed by a crass commercialism that erodes the traditional bonds that linked households with local merchants, local farmers, and domestic manufacturers. Marxist theory has had a "tendency to absolutize the power of commodification. The universalization of capitalism thus undermines the social significance of place" (Agnew and Duncan 1989, 4–5). In the case of Cuba, this is both accurate and misleading. At one level, there is no doubt that advertising nonessential goods is anathema to centralized planning. At another level, although commodification is absent in the case of Cuba, there is an imposition of state media that disallows alternative discourses. In other words, only the state can advertise, and political billboards are a pervasive form of the information landscape.

CONCLUSIONS

Power is an amorphous concept, and in this sense we share Weber (1978) and Arendt's (1951) argument that there is no "thing" we can identify as "power." Despite its ambiguity, many individuals and nation-states operate as if there exists such an entity. The ability to define the use of public space in Cuba accounts for the lack of consumer messages that dominate places in market economies. Although multinational logos such as those of McDonald's, Burger King, Taco Bell, Gap, Old Navy, Coca-Cola, and other icons of capitalism can be seen on (used) clothing worn by Cubans, they do not appear on marquees, storefront displays, or billboards.[8] Some Cuban landscape architects, architects, and planners have commented that many of the billboards are of poor or brash design and deface the natural landscape in the countryside much the way a billboard of a commercial nature does in the United States and Europe. Nonetheless, for nearly a half century the state has invested in a wide distribution of thousands of political billboards whose markers extol a variety of political, ecological, civic, and historic messages that serve as an extension of state power.

Cuba's information landscape—especially political billboards—reveals at least four types of discourse that reflect state power in a variety of places: patriotism and socialism, conservation, U.S. hegemony, social justice, and civic participation. In keeping with much of the literature on how place is created, this chapter identifies a regularity and ordering in how the socialist leadership defines place, controls information technology, and uses political billboards, providing a "spatial vocabulary" for broadcasting state-sanctioned ideology on the virtues of socialism. Cuba's tightly scripted information landscape is part of a spatial expression of ideas whose mark on the island is both powerful and distinctive.

NOTES

1. We are grateful for comments on an earlier draft of this chapter by Orestes del Castillo Jr. However, all errors and omissions are ours alone.

2. One website monitoring these *actos de repudios* in Cuba defines the term as "official acts of public intimidation and repression against individuals and their families because of their views, through the use of trained mobs and violence, akin to those employed by Nazi Germany and the Ku Klux Klan as practiced by the Cuban regime" (Cuba Verdad 2006). In 2006, in response to awarding the Sahkarov Prize for Freedom of Thought to the Cuban group Damas de Blanco (Women of White, a group that peacefully demonstrates against the detention

of their husbands, held for several years in jail for opposing the government and, allegedly, conspiring with the United States government), the European Union justified the prize because of the "recognition of their action in favour of the political prisoners in Cuba" (European Union 2006).

3. We base this statement on 48 research trips to the island since 1990 (J. L. S.) and hundreds of photographs taken of billboards and public spaces. It also derives from a long residency on the island of nearly 40 years (A. P.).

4. Although the Cuban American exile community largely believes that Fidel Castro is an egomaniac, our sense is that those on the island believe that his lack of self-promotion in the form of civic art is a genuine sign of modesty. Even since his major surgery in July 2006 and the turning over of powers to his brother Raúl, there has been no public display or grieving. It is unlikely that any large monuments will be constructed until he dies, and then only after burial in his hometown of Santiago, near the gravesite of José Martí.

5. Unlike the practice in China, North Korea, and the former USSR and Soviet bloc nations, only dead heroes are promoted in civic art and political billboards in socialist Cuba. There are, for instance, no large public sculptures or billboards of the leader as there were of leaders in the former USSR or as there are now of leaders in China and North Korea. However, his image does appear on several denominations of paper currency and he is often on TV.

6. Though rare, we have seen graffiti in the form of "abajo Fidel" (down with Fidel) scratched in small letters into the backs of bus seats several times in various buses in Havana, Santa Clara, and Santiago. There are also brief spray paintings of "Fidel Asesino" (Fidel, Assassin), "8A" (for Ochoa, when the general was executed by firing squad in 1989), and even "Viva Gorbachov" in about 1990, when there was some hope that Cuban-style perestroika might unfold.

7. A common protest graffiti message is "abajo Fidel" (down with Fidel), but such messages are erased by participants of mass organizations like the Committees for the Defense of the Revolution. In the 1980s there were murals in Old Havana that conveyed a challenging message, but in an artistic fashion (versus text). Defacing government property through the use of "enemy propaganda" carries a jail sentence of up to 20 years.

8. There are times and places which advertisements for consumer items appear. During the 1991 Pan American Games, for instance, ads for *Tu Cola* (a soft drink) appeared on Cuban television. Billboards for consumer products can be found around the immediate confines of airports and hotels—places where foreigners are likely to be found. These billboards promote cell phones, car rentals, alcoholic products, and even foreign-brand (mostly Asian) consumer durables. For an amusing account of a consumer promotional campaign for cigarettes, see Corbett (2002, 134–138).

CHAPTER 7

▼★

CONCLUSIONS

Whither Cuban Landscapes?

> The best way to avoid working with the ... community
> isolate is not to insist that the Caribbean is no longer
> made up of islands ... but to explore the ways in which
> Caribbean islands are constructed and given meaning
> in regional and global, as well as local contexts.
> —KAREN FOG OLWIG (2007, 260–270)

Landscape is inextricably bound to the study of places. It is paramount in fields of study ranging from cultural geography, biology, and landscape architecture, to the fine arts and urban planning. Our book shows how human activity and the forces of nature have modified parts of the Cuban landscape. We argue that the allure of the island's landscape, however, is that it has not been restricted to academe. Far from it. Cuba is so remarkable that it has been widely portrayed in Hollywood Productions, music, television, popular music, leisurely pursuits (travel, cigar smoking, rum sipping), and political analysis. Like John Gillis's (2004) contention about islands in general, we believe that the less Cuba has been occupied and dominated by non-Cubans, the more it has fascinated others.

We developed this argument in Chapter 1, where we noted that European landscape painters were struck by the island's beauty, which also surfaced in travelers' diaries, newspaper reports, and personal letters. Readers of the United States who are familiar with the Hudson River School of landscape painting in the 19th century will find parallel trends in Cuba's nonphotographic representation of itself. Whereas the U.S. painters

165

responded to modernity and industrialization, Cuban painters like Esteban Chartrand, in his 1877 work, *Marine Landscape (Paisaje Marino)*, and
Valentín Sanz Carta in *The Malangas (Las Malangas)*, captured the colonial countryside in ways that represented the humblest of Cuban society
(*lo cubano*). Gone were the European trappings of elite peninsular lifestyles
(ornate carriages, palaces, manicured gardens). Instead, the common folk
figured centrally in these new Cuban paintings, as did interesting uses of
tropical and insular sunlight.

A growing body of scholars focus on threaded conversations related
to "islandness," whose meaning differs over time and from place to place.
In a physical sense, one can argue that the traditional differences between
continents and islands—once clearly a part of the geographic imagination
and cartographic reality of the world—have become dubious or muted,
especially in a electronic age where territoriality has made the

> entire world ... archipelagic, with islands appearing everywhere, inland as
> well as offshore.... Islandness is no longer associated only with water-bound
> places. The planet itself is now perceived as Earth island. (Gills and Lowen-
> thal 2007, iii)

No longer are islands associated with backwardness and remoteness,
thanks to electronic media and jet travel for the masses of rich nations.
What is distinct, though, is how islands elicit a medley of responses: They
are places of recreation and refuge, punishment and pilgrimage, as well
as the popular stereotype of places that contain the sea, sand, sun, and
sex. These "four-S" paradisiacal images certainly encompass the "demand"
dimension of island Cuba (Figure 7.1), but clearly there is more. Islandness and pleasure appear to go hand in hand, especially when representing
Cuba's historic places (Figure 7.2). We argue that the multiple approaches
to understanding the island of Cuba necessarily engage the conjunction of
art and science.

If, as Godfrey Baldacchino (2007) claims, islands truly are "novelty
sites," it behooves us to consider why Cuba figures into this niche. This
book has shown that the island's representations have been serious and
avant garde, yet also platforms for fancy and whim. To be sure, Cuba has
been "on the edge" throughout its 500 years of European occupation, first
as a marginal player in Spain's colonial empire but then as a key supplier
of wealth and sustenance for the motherland. It has been coveted as *tabula
rasa* by corsairs, exiled French Haitian plantation farmers, and U.S. expansionists alarmed by Humboldt's writings on slavery in Cuba (see Chapter
2). Its marginality eroded soon after the American occupation in 1898.

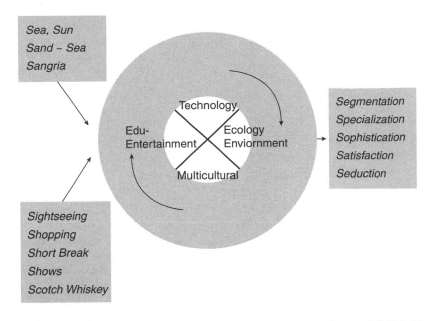

FIGURE 7.1. Demand trends in the tourist experience. From Scarpaci (2006, 10; after Buhalis 2000, 70).

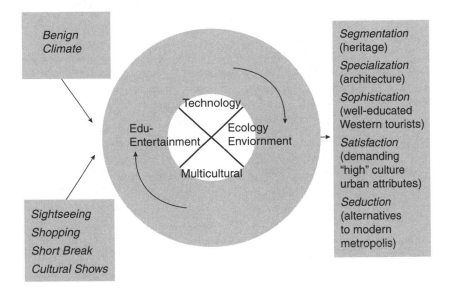

FIGURE 7.2. Dynamic heritage tourism trends in Cuban tourism. From Scarpaci (2007, 11; after Buhalis 2000, 70).

Later, it drifted back to its exotic "novelty" status, only to take world stage again in 1959 with the overthrow of the Batista government. The island of Cuba has thus propelled itself and its Cubanness as a place of innovative conceptualizations (hedonistic and communist, remote yet dangerously close to the United States). It is a frontline zone for celebrating budding yet stifled entrepreneurship under socialist rule, yet in some regards serves as a model for higher education, primary health care, and biotechnology. Cuban representations, ranging from landscape paintings to UNESCO World Heritage Sites, have gained extraordinary and extrainsular importance. Culturally, we have seen how Cuba can use a sort of "in-betweenity" in time and space; aspects of Africa, Spain, and even South Florida crop up in quotidian life. *Cubanidad*, and its myriad landscapes of the past and present, truly offers a conceptual place for experimentation.

To guide our inquiry into *cubanidad*, we enlist the perspective of a "new cultural geography, " which has added social and cultural theory to interpret changes in landscape. In emphasizing political and sociocultural processes, this new cultural geography also assesses how landscape shapes political and sociocultural processes in a particular place. We make the case that no single theoretical lens consistently informs the study of landscape. In line with the work of other geographers (Duncan and Duncan 1988; Price and Lewis 1993), we show how landscape is a central ingredient in cultural, political and social systems.

This book has shown how Cuba's landscape has been shaped by distinct stop-and-goes that have "frozen" and even retarded the evolution of the island's change. Whether the Independence Wars (1868–1878; 1895–1898), which thwarted investment in modernizing infrastructure, or the socialist period (1959–), which tended to ignore efforts at historic preservation until it became a necessary dollar generator, these have been distinctive period markers. Together, these sweeping historical events have given an uneven ebb and flow to the quality of the island's built environment. Mother Nature too—especially in the form of hurricanes—has lent a hand in reshaping shorelines, keys and islands, and river courses. Whether social networks and social solidarity increased in 19th-century Cuba as neighbors helped each other during the hurricane season remains to be studied further. Nevertheless, Cuba's insularity and vulnerability to these forces has been a defining feature of the island's physical, political, and social fabric.

Cuba's developing sugar industry in the late 18th and early 19th century provoked considerable interest by the European elite because of the potential wealth it promised. Thanks in part to the observations by Alexander von Humboldt, it also revealed the evils of slavery. Humboldt,

Cuba's "second discoverer," provided accurate descriptions of daily life that cast the economy of this "island of sugar and slaves" in noneconomic terms that, perhaps in some small measure, helped end slavery, albeit eight decades after his initial visit. Yet this notion of Cuba's being "safe yet exotic" led Fernando Ortíz, the "third discoverer of Cuba," to document the rich tapestry woven by African culture. Together, both "discoverers" carried forth an important ideological theme that would be picked up by the socialist government: Cuba need not be saved by outsiders. To be sure, Cuba was American Creole, but it was also shaped by centuries of Spanish rule. Its allure today in the burgeoning tourist and heritage industries is that it is at once Cuban, African, Spanish, American, and Soviet in intricate yet visible ways. We have argued that many iconic attractions, writings, and paintings portraying Cuba (tropical landscapes, powdery beaches and aquamarine waters, cigar-filled bars, Spanish military architecture, "fiery" mulattas) became important symbols in the island's tourist economy and remain so today despite the socialist turn in Cuba's political economy. Such place depictions, rightly or wrongly, bring international visitors who explore these landscapes.

Cuba's symbolic landscapes portray the values and power of those agents that finance and modify them. In socialist Cuba, the state is the only actor to invoke symbolic values, and, naturally, its intentions are largely political and represent the ideology of the Cuban leadership and the Cuban Communist Party. Chapter 6's review of the information landscape argues that in a globalized world of mass marketing, the Cuban landscape lacks commodity and service advertising. Instead, the state has made astute use of certain symbolic landscapes that dominate contemporary Cuba, because the state has replaced the market as the principal source of information dissemination. Our review of heritage in Chapter 4 shows that there does not appear to be a politicization of national landmarks that were forged during the socialist era. In fact, one might argue that Cuba's heritage sites are relatively less "politicized" than those of other socialist nations (e.g., the former USSR, Communist China, the former Eastern European Soviet bloc countries). Among the striking vernacular and symbolic elements today are the uniformed students walking to and from school and the thick web of health care facilities. These are in no way unique to Cuba, but they do underscore one of the social welfare badges of honor (universal education and health care) that the Castro government touts.

Without referring to the philosophy of environmental determinism (e.g., that climate, resources, and location determine a nation's destiny), there is a good case to be made that Cuba's insularity has played a key role in the nation's political geography; we are not the first to make this point (see Martínez-Fernández 2004, for example). Although Spain preferred to interpret Cuba's lingering 19th-century colonial status as a sign of the island's loyalty to the Spanish Crown, the Spanish American liberators' lack of a navy impeded the ability of Cuba and Puerto Rico to resist Spanish domination. The insularity of a place not much bigger than Tennessee is not such a unique feature. However, the diversity of landscape has inspired scholars and visitors alike. Insularity made the Cuban Missile Crisis possible and has made it easier for Washington to impose a trade embargo for almost half a century. The island nation also boasts a rich stock of about 7,000 plant species, most of which are endemic to the island. Its one-time connection to the North American and South American land masses contributed to such biological diversity, and this will be a powerful ecotourism attraction in the years ahead. To paraphrase Linden (2003), Cuba is, by default or design, one of the best-kept wildland secrets in the Caribbean. Despite such natural variety, we have pointed out how deforestation, massive river damming, and soil erosion forever changed the landscape in Cuba. About one-fourth of total water resources in Cuba are controlled, and salinization hinders the natural productivity of portions of the island's soils. Had the expansion of arable lands for increasing cultivation been carried out fully in the 1960s and 1970s, we shudder to think what the irreversible consequences might have been. Insularity, then, has conditioned Cuba's geopolitical fortunes in undeniable ways.

Our historical analysis in Chapter 2 draws upon Alexander von Humboldt's *The Island of Cuba*. Humboldt's description of Havana, racism, slavery, and sugar production has been invaluable in understanding the unequal social class pyramid noted in that chapter. In turn, the Humboldt discourse has given socialist leaders an internationally recognized Renaissance man-scholar to justify the historical grounding of the island's social, economic, and political history. His belief in manumission may have hastened abolition in 1886. Moreover, Humboldt's description of the economic geography of slavery—conveniently omitted by the American annexationist John Thrasher—helped to combat slavery on the humanitarian, economic, and political fronts.

As in many Caribbean nations, the demand for sugar has been the most deleterious landscape modifier in Cuba. The small network of sugar mills around Havana in the 18th century spread far and wide once the Independence Wars ended, and American investors capitalized on this. Although Humboldt never anticipated the spread of American investment in the sugar industry, he has been virtually canonized in contemporary Cuba because of his naturalist contributions and his avant garde and progressive views on the injustices of slavery. As the Castro government copes with under- and unemployment, there are global market signals that indicate that a growing demand for ethanol may revive the centuries-long production of sugar in Cuba. Since the new millennium, however, sugar has not reigned over the island's landscape, as half of its mills have closed in recent years.

Our brief review of the sugar landscape allowed us to incorporate salient economic and political events that shaped the island's environmental history. If underdevelopment is characterized by limited ways to employ locals, especially with monoculture and commodities that are susceptible to the vicissitudes of the world market, then perhaps no crop reflects this weakness as does sugar. The popular saying "Without sugar, there is no country" (*Sin azúcar, no hay país*) prevailed until the 1990s, when state inefficiencies made it cheaper to subsidize the unemployed than to pay three times the amount needed to produce sugar than the product fetched on the world market. No single economic, political, or cultural practice— not even the 1959 Revolution—has changed Cuba's landscape as much as sugar production. Reopening the United States to Cuban sugar could transform the rural landscape of the island, as sugar would once again become king. A post-Fidel era, with cooler heads in both Washington and Havana, may effect a return to the old days (pre-1959) when trade agreements and tariff restrictions favored Cuba. Reaching that accord will mean that the U.S. cane sugar, sugar beet, and fructose corn syrup producers will allow this to happen.

Regardless of political developments, the forces of nature continue to shape the subtropics in profound ways. As noted in Chapter 1, tropical storms have been especially formative, and Cuba has suffered a series of hurricanes in recent years. The devastation in September 2008 wreaked by Hurricane Ike in northeastern Cuba was particularly cruel (Grogg 2008). Rather than elaborate on the impact island-wide, we focus on the community level—the municipality of Jesús Menéndez—to illustrate how disaster and opportunity form a thread throughout Cuba's landscape history.

Located in Las Tunas province, the municipality is a mostly flat and rural place (Figure 7.3). It has been devoted to sugar cane cultivation since the early 20th century. The Cuban American Sugar Company (CASCo) built it between 1899 and 1901 as the Chaparra mill, and it remained one of the largest in Cuba. Its first harvest was in 1902. In the 1950s it had the capacity to grind 6,800 metric tons of sugar cane per day, in 1952 the mill scored its pre-Castro production record high at 150,188 tons, and in 1960 it was nationalized and renamed Jesús Menéndez. In 2004 the mills had a grinding capacity of 8,500 tons of sugar cane per day, but the following

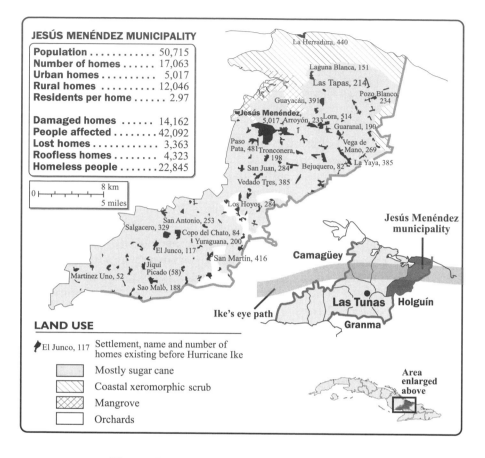

JESÚS MENÉNDEZ MUNICIPALITY

Population	50,715
Number of homes	17,063
Urban homes	5,017
Rural homes	12,046
Residents per home	2.97
Damaged homes	14,162
People affected	42,092
Lost homes	3,363
Roofless homes	4,323
Homeless people	22,845

LAND USE

$\nearrow$ El Junco, 117   Settlement, name and number of
homes existing before Hurricane Ike

Mostly sugar cane

Coastal xeromorphic scrub

Mangrove

Orchards

FIGURE 7.3. The municipality of Jesús Menéndez. Oficina Nacional de Estdadísticas (2007) and *Granma* (*www.granma.cu*).

year all production was halted because of low agricultural yields and poor quality cane. The mill has a bagasse board factory on-site with a capacity to produce 60,000 cubic meters per year (2.119 million cubic feet or 78,477 cubic yards). However, output has dropped drastically in tandem with regional sugar production (Portela 2007).

A share of the housing stock was updated after the Revolution, which left a large stock of fragile houses, poor infrastructure, and unpaved roads. Agricultural settlements are sparsely distributed and range in size from a few dozen to hundreds of homes. They stretch over broad sugar cane plantations that are linked by dirt roads or narrow-gauge railroads.

Hurricane Ike struck in the early hours of September 8, 2008, as a formidable category-3 storm. In this municipality alone, it knocked down one-fifth of the housing stock: 3,363 homes. More than four of every five houses (83%) suffered serious damage among the existing 17,063 homes. In its wake were lumber and thatch roofs intermixed with soaked personal belongings. Winds tore the roofs off 4,323 houses, one-quarter of the total.

The human dimension of the tragedy meant that 42,092 people—four of every five residents–lost some part of their homes. About half had no place to go other than to government shelters or perhaps the less damaged homes of relatives and neighbors. Some of the villages are gone. La Herradura on the northern shore, with 440 houses, nearly disappeared that fatal night.

Although the scars left on agricultural production will last only a year or so (the time it takes to grow one crop of cane), the blow to the housing stock will last longer because of the current economic conditions. An outpouring of international aid will partially mitigate the storm's devastation, yet, Jesús Menéndez may be transformed into a post-sugar economy regardless of the way its population geography has been altered. The scene at Jesús Menéndez is but a microcosm of the devastation felt elsewhere along Hurricane Ike's path. And even though the government will likely manage the scarcity of food in the months ahead, it will be daunting to provide shelter for tens of thousands of homeless people across the island, let alone gainful employment. In one century, the community—carved out of scrub and pasture—has risen and fallen, like scores of others across the island.

Social forces compound those of nature. We have seen how cultural globalization and the forces of modernity homogenize a given area quickly. However, unique places like Cuba afford a new wave of international tourists with a cultural focus. Cuba has been able to graft this niche tourism to its well-endowed beaches, mountains, and wildlife reserves. The socialist government understands that heritage allows it to use the past as an economic resource for the present. The island's eight UNESCO World Heritage Sites and scores of national historic sites serve two purposes. First, they help forge national identity, develop ideologies, and "ground" abstract notions of history and heritage in visible form. The Cuban government identifies, safeguards, and maintains these national heritage sites and monuments in ways that make it difficult to determine whether this is a market economy or a centrally planned economy. Second, these heritage landscapes generate hard currency, and this has proven invaluable in the post-Soviet trading bloc setting. A key question in regard to Cuba's heritage industry is the extent to which locals are benefiting. On one hand, Old Havana's Habaguanex (state corporation) is creating millions of dollars for the national treasury, but it is difficult to tease out the direct local benefit (though clearly there is some). On the other hand, the UNESCO site of Trinidad, Cuba, focuses only on residential housing in the poorer parts of town. These examples indicate that there is some decentralization in managing heritage landscapes despite rhetoric to the contrary. Whether the example is Che Guevara or Ernest Hemingway in Havana, or the fight against the "bandits" of the Escambray in Trinidad, both heritage landscapes legitimize local history and portray positive images of the past, much as Lowenthal (1985) pointed out in other Caribbean settings. And although debates within Cuba have avoided the neoliberal economic polemics that afflict the rest of Latin America, there has yet to be an open discussion on the island: Who wins and who loses in cashing in on heritage landscapes?

Economic difficulties, macroeconomic mismanagement, rising energy prices, the U.S. trade embargo, and theft from state firms have hindered rehabilitation projects. Cuba's endangered heritage landscapes have recently included the Escuelas de Arte, agroindustrial sites (mainly sugar mills), wooden buildings, and some Art Nouveau, Art Deco, and eclectic-style buildings. Nonetheless, the Cuban government is aware of these endangered sites and manages to administer 289 museums. Although no single individual has been more closely affiliated with heritage preservation than Dr. Eusebio Leal, it appears that the locus of control is shifting to a new generation.

An impending polemic will be how to recover Cuban heritage that has allegedly been sold abroad, and how the expatriot community in exile—if given a chance—will respond to this displacement or loss of heritage. To be sure, revolutions cannot be easily compartmentalized, and Cuba's is no exception. We believe that matters of compensating for and repatriating items of Cuban heritage located abroad (or even on the island) will not be easy, given the experience of the Eastern European countries and the former Soviet Union in indemnifying previous owners of heritage items. That controversy notwithstanding, we may anticipate new landmarks in Cuba's heritage landscape that include the U.S. Naval Base in Guantánamo, Cuba, especially Camp X-ray. And once the Castro brothers die, we can expect tributes to these revolutionaries to appear, despite the ire of the exile community.

Tourism, an ally of the heritage sector, is increasing in Cuba. Can Cuba succeed in this new market even though (according to the Heritage Foundation's Index of Economic Freedom) it is a country with scant political, economic, and social liberties? We have shown that the absence of Americans makes Cuba appealing to some tourists. The Cuban landscape remains largely unexplored by international tourists, whose visions of palm trees, blue waters, and live music—reinforced with electronic and print media—prime the world's demand for such places. The island's low population density and narrow width make it eminently appealing even if some argue that it is becoming the "brothel of the Caribbean" (Robaina 2004).

As discussed in Chapter 4, new transportation amenities await the island, which will increase its connectivity with the rest of the world. Cruise line travel emanating from Galveston, New Orleans, Biloxi, Tampa-St. Petersburg, Miami, Key West, Jacksonville, Baltimore, Philadelphia, New York, and Boston may soon become a reality again. A challenge, however, will be avoiding the trappings of vice, narcotics, and prostitution. Sustainable tourism will require Havana and other tourist destinations to implement costly waste and water treatment facilities if the current (2005) level of 2.3 million visitors is surpassed, and if Cuba's portion of the Caribbean market will exceed 10% or so. Revoking the U.S. travel ban to the island would unleash the arrival of 1 million visitors (roughly half of the 2006 market) in its first years and could prove devastating; a small and poor infrastructure might spoil repeat visits, which have always been a hallmark of the Caribbean tourism market. Alternatively, will Cuba eschew mass tourism and focus on niche markets? Its relative location between the third (United States) and seventh (Mexico) largest tourist destinations in the world is fortuitous. We concur that even if 10% of Florida's 40 million annual visitors visited the island, it would overwhelm the current infrastructure. In addition, a Disneyworld–Key West–Havana–Key West circuit, connected by air, rail, and ship transport, would likely be extremely popular. In this regard, it would be wise to recall what the Victorian era Irish writer Anthony Trollope predicted back in 1859: "Havana will soon become as much American as New Orleans" (Trollope 1859, cited in Pérez 1999, 1). As precursors to what we now recognize as globalization, these are just a few scenarios suggesting the tourist map of tomorrow.

Sustainability is already being combined with heritage projects and other aspects of the built environment. Heritage, however, changes often, and who is to say that the bland public housing units built throughout the Revolution will not be celebrated, upgraded, and enhanced? A number of Cuban architects have taken up the task to beautify, modify, and enhance the rather monotonous and dreary public housing "projects" that prevail across the island (Figure 7.4). Moreover, repeated poundings by tropical

FIGURE 7.4. El Vallecito, a public housing complex in Guanahacabibes Peninsula, extreme western Pinar del Río Province, 2007. Shown here is the GP-4 (*Gran Panel*) design commonly used during the socialist period. Thousands of units were built across the island. The photograph (top) shows clotheslines, few trees, solid concrete balconies, and even tobacco leaf drying (upper left balconies). Computer-aided design (CAD) proposal (bottom) remedies some of these issues (e.g., visual clutter), but mainly provides more shade and improves air circulation by using trees and new eaves and balconies. Wood and stone materials come from the local area. Photograph and CAD courtesy Mabel Matamoros Tuma.

storms take a toll on the housing stock; Hurricane Gustav in 2008 damaged an estimated 90,000 houses in Havana and Pinar del Río provinces (Franks 2008).

One sustainability and beautification project by architect Mabel Matamoros and colleagues envisions adding eaves, shutters, shaded entrances, bus stops, public telephones, and modest landscaping to enhance both public and residential spaces (Matamoros, González, Rodrigues, and Claro 2006; Figure 7.5). A whole host of such projects exists on the island, yet it takes financial resources and a growing economy to transform these designs into reality.

Across the Florida Straits, there are many in the exile community who have also proposed sustainable redevelopment projects but in a post-Castro Cuba. Cuban American architect Nicolás Quintana and landscape architect Juan Antonio Bueno of Florida International University have proposed a redevelopment plan for Havana that, if someday desired by the Cuban people and government, would leave a unique imprint on the capital. They propose an approach for policy makers and investors in a market economy to meld heritage, services, and functionality into a postsocialist Cuba.

> Under a political and economic transition that could provide strong incentives for investment, Havana will face the challenge of preserving the city's remarkable architecture and cultural integrity in an environmentally conscious way while also addressing the pressing needs of residents, such as housing and infrastructure.... [The authors use] technical documentation to simulate future growth, taking into account Havana's unique urban, rural and natural landscapes. The objective of [the project] is to visualize future development of the city in an environmentally sustainable way, recognizing historic values and at the same time providing for the needs and aspirations of society. (Woodrow Wilson Center 2008)

Figure 7.6 illustrates a high-density proposal for the Vedado district of Havana. The concept shown, an urban activity center (UAC), attempts to counter the "sprawling suburbia anti-urban development" common in the United States, in which open-air parking surrounds intensively used spaces that are occupied only at certain times of the day (business hours) and year (Christmas holiday shopping). This proposal encourages high-density land use while promoting pedestrian activities. Endowed with lush tropical landscaping and integrated into a public transportation corridor, UACs use a relatively small "footprint" (i.e., the perimeter of the building's base on the ground). Lower floors would attract commercial uses (offices, shops, restaurants, entertainment areas, service facilities) and indoor parking, with residential apartments on the higher levels. If Havana is to retain

FIGURE 7.5. Architectural model that aims to sustainably enhance the quality of life at a public housing project, El Vallecito, in Pinar del Río Province. The proposal includes adding eaves over windows, planting trees around the complex for beautifying the site and creating more shade, developing more community gardens (right center, to the right of baseball diamond), and rimming the rooftops with a facade to hide cisterns. Courtesy Mabel Matamoros Tuma.

its pedestrian-friendly setting, an element like a UAC would help to ensure this essential component of the Cuban landscape.

As tourism continues to increase, leisure and recreational facilities will no doubt spread to more remote and literally "darker" corners of the island. Electrification has long been the bane of stargazers, who are disturbed by the artificial luminosity the lighting brings to the night sky (Ekirch 2005). Remotely sensed images of luminosity in the Caribbean, taken over the past decades, illustrate how modernity has crept into what were once rural areas (Table 7.1). By calculating a ratio of bright-to-dark pixels, as measured by satellite images in the years 1993 and 2000, Sforza and Scarpaci (2008) calibrated how these ratios changed between the time when Cuba was in the worst of its Special Period and the recent time when it was expanding into tourism aggressively. The data show that although there were more lighted evening spaces in Cuba in the new millennium, especially along the northern archipelago, it was still relatively "underlighted" as compared with the Dominican Republic and Puerto Rico, even though it did surpass neighboring Haiti (Figure 7.7). For instance, Table 7.1 shows that there were more than 5 times as many bright pixels (equalsized segments of the island's surface) as dark pixels in Cuba, whereas in Puerto Rico that ratio reached 184, and the island of Hispaniola was almost twice as illuminated at nighttime than Cuba (i.e., 9.491 vs. 5.365

FIGURE 7.6. Architectural scale model of a possible urban activity center proposed for Vedado, in Havana. The model (top view, aerial; bottom, lateral) was designed by Florida International University architecture students Jorge Garciga, Gilbert Atick, Andrea Rodríguez, and Yanina Corbea.

TABLE 7.1. Brightness-to-Darkness Ratios:
Cuba, Hispaniola (Haiti and the Dominican Republic),
Haiti, the Dominican Republic, and Puerto Rico

Country	Brightness-to-darkness ratio
Cuba	5.365
Hispaniola	9.491
Haiti	2.378
Dominican Republic	11.914
Puerto Rico	184.745

Note. Data from Sforza and Scarpaci (2008).

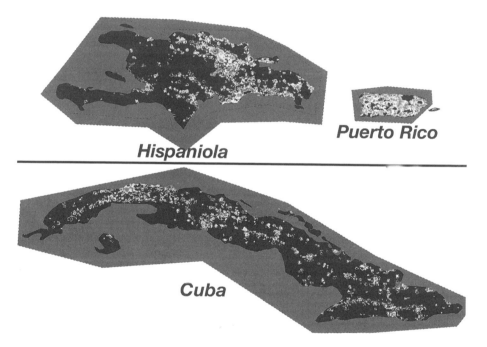

FIGURE 7.7. Generalized brightness-to-darkness ratios, 1992–1994. Although lacking a scale in black and white, the maps show the nighttime "light pollution" in Hispaniola and Puerto Rico (top panel) and Cuba (bottom) based on calculations of luminosity from nighttime satellite images of the Caribbean. From Sforza and Scarpaci (2008).

pixels). An opening of Cuba to increased modernization portends changing rhythms, rituals, work and, most of all, landscapes in the years ahead.

If an expected rise in tourism is on the horizon, then surely the island
will experience new energy demands. Cuba is aggressively searching for
new and alternative energy sources. To assist the island, several multinational energy and mining firms have mapped and staked out a partnership
with the Cuban government in order to tap into to new hydrocarbons.
Figure 7.8 identifies several of the fields Cuba has identified for oil exploration. These fields lie within Cuba's internationally recognized maritime
resources. Although it is unlikely that a tourist in, say, Key West, Florida,
will actually see an oil drilling platform, any spills would no doubt be carried quickly northbound by the Gulf Stream and could surface on Florida
beaches. As in any oil exploration, there will be a risk to flora and fauna
should these Vietnamese, Canadian, Malaysian, or Spanish drilling operations go awry.

Chapter 6 examines the information landscape, a melding of politics,
ideology, media, and semiotics. Information technology, particularly in the
form of simple roadside billboards, creates a unique landscape in a country
where mass consumer culture is absent. To illustrate this, we examined
several discourses of political billboards and representation: patriotism and

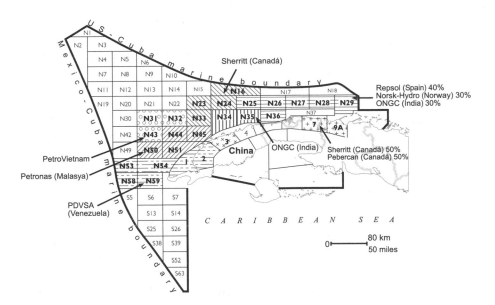

FIGURE 7.8. Cuban-approved international offshore drilling concessions, 2008.

socialism, U.S. hegemony, conservation, social justice, and civic participation. We reviewed how ideology, landscape, and the social construction of space give Cuba a distinctive mark. In particular, historic events, slogans and rallying cries, and historical political figures are widely disseminated by the socialist government. The Cuban landscape displays these ideological messages through advertisements, special protest plazas, mass organizations, and political art. The contemporary manifestation is evidenced by the diplomatic cat-and-mouse game between the United States consulate building on Havana's Malecón and the Cuban government. This entails the Cuban government's use of black flags (called "mourning flags") to block an electronic bulletin board on the U.S. consulate building. If we use Jurgen Habermas's (1975) three broad subsystems operating in society—work as formulated in an economic system, language as a sociocultural system, and domination as a political system—we can assess part of Cuba's "truth claims" about its Revolution. The single-party system monopolizes discourses to deliver its messages to the masses, which, in turn, form a powerful "spatial vocabulary of power." Related information landscapes include comics, declarations, harangues, public shaming, mass rallies, and other forums. Our argument, then, is that place serves as an observable part of power and political processes, and those outcomes are well marked in Cuba. Borrowing Appadurai's (1986) term, Cuba has a unique "ideascape" that champions the Revolution, celebrates martyrs, and victimizes the island in David-and-Goliath fashion. Civil society is particularly constrained in the new electronic media markets, largely because Internet access is highly restricted. We posit that the defining feature of the modern nation-state is its relationship to the media. Like North Korea, China, and Vietnam, the Cuban government constrains public debate on issues that jeopardize the government's status quo.

The current leadership is media savvy. It is steeped in political symbolism whose wellspring derives from the island's colonial history. Cuba's cultural revolution in the 1960s brought poetry, civic art, painting, and sculpture to the masses. A new information landscape includes street art and billboards; the latter decidedly not for dishwashing detergent, facial creams, or automobiles. Instead, these billboards carry political and civic messages steeped in the virtues of what a "new" Cuba should be. They constitute the only kind of public advertising in Cuba and serve as a constant reminder that the state provides welfare, safety, history lessons, and socialist ideology for all. Our review of political billboard messages includes patriotism and socialism, social justice, civic participation, and conservation. This information landscape clarifies the rules of citizenship. Simply stated, the state will do its share if citizens do theirs. Taking these precepts together, the state would argue that this is why Cuba is a "different America." Given the state's total control of information, it is perhaps not surprising that there is little, if any, antigovernment graffiti. In a society where nonessential consumer goods and services are virtually absent, thousands of political billboards stare down on regular pedestrians, bus passengers, and drivers. They became passive, perhaps subconscious reminders, of what is allowed and what is not. In keeping with the literature on how place is created, we trace in Chapter 6 a regularity and ordering in how the socialist government creates place, controls information technology, and enlists political billboards as part of its strict "spatial vocabulary" that disseminates state-approved ideology.

Although the informatics issues are important, it appears that the island's geopolitical reality looms increasingly important on the world stage. As one conservative geopolitical consulting company argues, Cuba's geographic and insular aspect will continue to place it at odds with the U.S. government unless there is a fundamental change in Washington, DC, or Havana, Cuba.

> From the U.S. standpoint, Cuba is always a geographical threat. If the Mississippi River is the great highway of American agriculture and New Orleans its great port to the world, then Cuba sits directly athwart New Orleans' access to the world. There is no way for ships from New Orleans to exit the Gulf of Mexico into the Atlantic Ocean but to traverse two narrow channels on either side of Cuba—the Yucatan channel, between Cuba's western coast and the Yucatan; or the Straits of Florida, between the island's northern coast and Florida. If these two channels were closed, U.S. agricultural and mineral exports and imports would crumble. Not only New Orleans, but also all of the Gulf Coast ports like Houston, would be shut in.
>
> Cuba does not have the size or strength in and of itself to close those channels. But should another superpower control Cuba, the threat would become real and intolerable. The occupation of Cuba by a foreign power—whether Spain, Germany, Russia or others—would pose a direct geopolitical threat to the United States. Add to that the possibility that missiles could be fired from Cuba to the United States, and we can see what Washington sees there. It is not Cuba that is a threat, but rather a Cuba that is allied with or dominated by a foreign power challenging the United States globally. Therefore, the Americans don't much care who runs Cuba, so long as Cuba is not in a politico-military alliance with another power. (Friedman 2006)

We are left with the question about the extent to which *cubanidad*, and the condition of Cuban landscapes, in part framed insularity (or, "islecentricity," as Olwig 2007, calls it), define this place called Cuba. At the risk of flirting with environmental determinism, we confront this question: To what extent does insularity make up the nonmaterial culture of Cuba (as a parallel component to its many phases and landscapes)? Philip Conkling (2007) poses this question in an essay about islanders and "islandness." He draws on the works of George Putz (1984), who in an amusing listing of attributes (Table 7.2) of Maine islanders and their fishing communities has unwittingly touched on features of what we may call the "Cuban personality."

Although the comparison between Anglo-Saxon islanders off the coast of Maine and the Afro-Cuban-Spanish souls of Cuba may be seem a far reach, the accuracy of the traits in Table 7.2 is uncanny. "Islanders share

TABLE 7.2. Maine Islander Personal and Cultural Traits Adapted to Cuba(ns)

Independence—small boats and social circles demand it if a personality is to survive. (Although the small fishing village of Cuba is largely a relic of the past, Cubans' resourcefulness and self-assertiveness are defining features of *lo cubano*.)

Loyalty—ultimate mutual care and generosity; even between ostensible enemies. (Despite a half century of hostility between the United States and Cuba, the Cuban diaspora rarely relinquishes its ties to the island.)

A strong sense of *honor*, easily betrayed. (Nationalism in the 19th, 20th, and 21st centuries was, and remains, widely prevalent.)

Polydextrous and multifaceted competence, or what islanders call *handiness*. (Problem-solving talents include the ability to *resolver* or *solucionar* [to make ends meet] when confronted by problems on the island.)

A belligerent sense of *competition*. (Sports landscapes have been a defining feature of the Cuban Revolution, and the island of just 11 million residents competes often and successfully in Olympic and Pan American Games.)

Earthy *common sense*. (Cubans are practical and realistic in quotidian activities; there is a social stigma associated with being unrealistic or ignoring harsh realities [*hacer el bobo*].)

Opinionated *machismo* in both the male and female mode. (The former requires little comment; the latter is well portrayed in the Cuban film *Lucía*, produced in 1968 by Humberto Solas; it shows the lives of three women at different times in Cuban history: 1895, 1933, and the early years of the Revolution in the 1960s.)

Fragile discretion within a welter of *gossip*. (City and country folk rely heavily on rumor, which is popularly called *radio bemba*—[literally, "lip radio"].)

Highly individualized blends of *spirituality* and *superstition*. (Although traditionally the island is nominally Catholic, church attendance has always been low, even after the liberalization of freedom of religion in the constitutional reforms of 1992. Although many Cubans are nonbelievers, these individuals may have crucifixes or small altars in their homes devoted to a particular *orisha*, as part of the syncretism that *santería* brings in merging Catholicism with African belief systems.)

And, finally, a canny *literacy* and *intelligence*. (One might argue whether the state media outlets permit an impartial view of world events, but Cubans of all occupations have opinions and are well informed about sports, world culture, and politics.)

Note. Adapted from Putz (1984, 26).

a common sense with other islanders worldwide, in much the same way that scientists share a common sense worldwide on such things as denotation, logic, control, and proof," argues Putz (1984, 27).

A final consideration to which we turn our attention addresses a "landscape" that is internal and out of view; certainly it is unseen by most foreigners and is perhaps all too familiar to many residents (Figure 7.9). Drawing on Putz's notion of the commonsense approach that islanders seem to display universally, we highlight the creativeness of the Cuban population in carving out living spaces at a time when resources are limited. We refer to the *barbacoa*, a platform or mezzanine built inside a house to create an extra room. Wooden beams serve as the framing, and planks cross over the framing as a series of joists. Cubans usually build these improvised bedroom and apartment lofts in towns and cities to redress the problems of crowding. Wood is used most commonly, but there are examples of tubular and steel beams throughout the island. Almost all of these materials are taken from collapsed buildings to erect the *barbacoas* (De Real and Scarpaci forthcoming).

FIGURE 7.9. *Barbacoa*, exterior. Lamparilla and San Ignacio streets, Habana Vieja. Courtesy Sergio Valdés.

Cuban author José Antonio Ponte wrote a short story, "*Arte de Nuevo Hacer Ruinas*," in which he describes the vertical generosity provided by the high ceilings of many colonial homes. The character in his fictitious account remarks:

> When you need to add to the size of your house and there's no courtyard in which to build anything more, no garden, not even a balcony; when you need more room and you live with your family in an interior apartment, the only thing left to do is to lift your eyes and discover that the ceiling is high enough so another level could be fitted in, a loft. In short, you discover the vertical generosity of your space, which allows the raising of another house inside. (2002, 21)

Ponte's ideas are the focus of a recent documentary, *Habana: Arte Nuevo de Hacer Ruinas* (*Havana: The New Art of Making Ruins* 2006), produced and directed by German filmmakers Florian Borchmeyer and Matthias Hentschler. The film examines the lives of Havana residents who toil inside the decaying buildings of a ruined city. Once elegant works of eclectic architecture from the beginning of the 20th century now reflect the tattered lives of the people living inside them. Antonio José Ponte serves as guide and interpreter of the devastated landscape of Havana by enlisting the personal narratives of common people. He lends political meaning to the everyday narratives of average Cubans.

Ponte poignantly observes in one scene of the ruined urban landscape:

> If in your private space you cannot rebuild what has fallen down, then you cannot do it any place else. That is why the rulers of the country have a purpose about these ruins: to show their subjects that they cannot change anything. If you cannot renovate your house, you cannot renovate the kingdom. This private failure precedes public failure.... Let the buildings collapse, but you cannot change anything. And I think that has been the most important contribution of the revolution to urban thinking. The idea that nothing can be restored. Nothing can be repared [*sic*]. Then the country cannot be repared [*sic*]. Let it be.[1]

This astute and controversial interpretation of the built environment challenges the power of the state by allowing individuals to create their own landscapes. Ponte's description of Havana emphasizes the Revolution's distrust of the capital which, in many ways, has been seen as more cosmopolitan than Cuban. Its rundown condition becomes the punishment for its prerevolutionary success on the international stage of world cities. This discourse in the film is emphasized by including black-and-white footage of Havana of the 1950s and early 1960s. The decadent images of bars, beautiful women, and crowded streets in the early years of the Revolution portray a landscape—in the eyes of socialist leaders—as a moral ruin. However, the film uses these images to create a cosmopolitan city of loveliness, uneven wealth, and carefree living that contrasts with the present material ruin of Havana. In the end, the ruined become a metaphor for the ruined political subject, which as Ponte claims, is powerless to change anything. Contemporary Havana is but a metaphor of the ruined lives of its inhabitants, ruined not because they lived in and among ruins, but because they are unable to rebuild themselves, except for the *barbacoa*.

Barbacoas, therefore, represent a new type of *cubanidad* in light of the historic evolution we have traced thus far. They capture creativity, and their distribution is significant; in 2004, there were more than 17,000 in Habana Vieja municipality alone. We argue that these lofts constitute a new frontier in Cuba. They represent how households conquer unclaimed spaces in a real estate market that is restrictive, and in a distribution system that makes it difficult to acquire home building supplies. As capital and labor become available, these high ceilings are transformed incrementally to accommodate residents in crowded housing (Figure 7.10). In line with Ponte's story, in which the protagonist returns to the ruins of his dwelling, *barbacoas* represent a sort of Phoenix rising out of the rundown buildings in Cuba. Drawing on historian Frederick Jackson Turner's "frontier thesis," used to explain the pioneer mentality of the United States in the 19th century, we believe this activity captures the spirit and entrepreneurship of the contemporary Cuban faced with limited options. The internal spatial growth of Havana and other cities represents the image of another possible city, of new spaces in which Cubans can aspire to satisfy part of their dreams. Unlike the construction of the 19th-century settlers of the American West, pioneers of the Argentinean pampas, or the early *bandeirantes* of Brazil who created a myth about that nation's frontier, these Cuban spaces are vertical and do not expand to the horizon. Thus, in Ponte's narrative, the builders turn inward, to the only expansive space left to them.

As national and joint venture hotel and recreational companies snatch up selected sites in Cuba, options for expressing this new frontier are limited. The lack of a formal real estate market in socialist Cuba forces islanders to swap homes (*permutarse*), attempting to colocate work and home with as little separation as possible. As a result, the only spaces available for many are the vertical dimensions in cities, where rugged individualism surfaces in creative ways. Cubanologists know that islander ingenuity

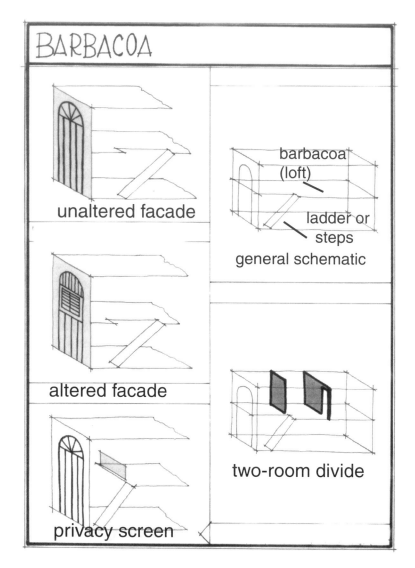

BARBACOA

unaltered facade

altered facade

privacy screen

barbacoa
(loft)

ladder or
steps

general schematic

two-room divide

FIGURE 7.10. Cuban loft options. Adapted and used courtesy of Luis Valdés.

in solving daily problems has a long history. Pérez (2001b) explains how 19th-century Cubans joined forces to handle the devastation of hurricanes. These civic efforts did much to forge a cultural and national identity as well as a broader sense of community; it did as much as the revolutionary movement in that same century. A century later, with the demise of the USSR and the Special Period in a Time of Peace, a new form of Cuban resourcefulness is apparent in "making ends meet" and providing for family. This is how the closed spaces of the *barbacoa* represent a rational, creative, and indelible landscape of the new Cuban frontier.

Beyond such resilience, this book has aimed to show how natural and social history has left its mark across Cuba. The island's landscapes offer a road map for traversing many historical contours. Cuba's natural, historical, sugar, heritage, tourist, and information landscapes create a distinct spatial expression. These patterns have been aided by unique and long historical periods: a colonial era in the context of Spanish America, the prevalence of monocultural sugar exports for nearly three centuries, and a socialist government that interrupted a well-defined period of market capitalism. If market capitalism offers a "landscape of persuasion" where desires are created by a culture of cluttered marketing and advertising, one can only hope that in the near future the most basic needs (food and shelter) are quickly satisfied and that the attributes that have made this island so special will not be lost. Cuba will continue to capture the geographic imagination of future observers by creating a powerful web of landscapes that reveal from where it has come, its present course, and where it might be tomorrow.

NOTE

1. Quoted in the 2006 film, *Habana: Arte Nuevo de Hacer Ruinas*, by German filmmakers Florian Borchmeyer and Matthias Heutscher. (This English translation is provided in the subtitles.)

References

Aber, J. S. 2003. *Baron Friedrich W. K. H. Alexander von Humboldt. History of Geology.* Retrieved September 29, 2003, from *academic.emporia.edu/aberjame/histgeol/ humboldt/humboldt/html.*

Abu-Lughod, J. 1984. Culture, modes of production and the changing nature of cities in the Arab world. In J. Agnew, D. Mercer, and D. Sopher, eds., *The City in Cultural Context.* Boston: Allen & Unwin, pp. 94–119.

Agitator, The. 2006. Bush Bashing. Retrieved July 1, 2006, from *www.theagitator.com/ archives/2003_01.php.*

Agnew, J. A. 1987. *Place and Politics: The Geographical Mediation of State and Society.* Boston: Allen & Unwin.

Agnew, J. A., and Duncan, J. S. 1989. Introduction. In J. A. Agnew and J. S. Duncan, eds., *The Power of Place: Bringing Together Geographical and Sociological Imaginations.* London: Unwin Hyman, pp. 1–8.

Allen, J. 2003. *Lost Geographies of Power.* Malden, MA: Blackwell.

Alongi, T. 2007. *The Dynamics of Tropical Mangrove Forests.* New York: Springer.

American Sugar Alliance. 2008. *World Sugar Price Myth Exposed.* Retrieved June 3, 2008, from *www.sugaralliance.org/desktopdefault.aspx?page_id=139.*

Anuario Estadístico de Cuba, various years. Havana: Oficina Nacional de Estadísticas, Republic of Cuba.

Appadurai, A. 1986. *Social Life of Things: Commodities in Cultural Perspective.* New York: Cambridge University Press.

Appadurai, A. 1996. *Modernity at Large: Cultural Dimensions of Globalization.* Minneapolis: University of Minnesota Press.

Aranda, S. 1968. *La Revolución Agraria Cubana.* Mexico: Siglo XXI.

Arcia Rodriguez, M. 1989. Medio Ambiente. Influencia de la Actividad Agropecuaria. XXIII.1.4.3. *Nuevo Atlas Nacional de Cuba,* La Habana.

Arenas, R. 1991. *El Asalto.* Miami: Ediciones Universal.

Arenas, R. 1993. *Before Night Falls.* New York: Penguin.

Arendt, H. 1951. *The Origins of Totalitarianism.* New York: Harcourt Brace.

Arnaz, D. 1976. *A Book.* New York: Morrow.

Aruca, L. 1996. The Cristóbal Colón Cemetery in Havana. *Journal of Decorative and Propaganda Arts* **22**: 36–55.

Ashworth, G., and Tunbridge, J. 1990. *The Tourist-Historic City*. London: Belhaven Press.

Ashworth, G. J. 2002. Holocaust Tourism: The Experience of Krakow–Kazimierz. *International Research in Geographical Environmental Education* **11**: 363–368.

Atlas de Cuba. 1978. Havana: Instituto de Geodesía y Cartografía.

August, A. 1999. *Democracy in Cuba and the 1997–98 Elections*. Havana: Editorial José Martí.

Back, D. W., Kunze, D., and Pickles, J. 1989. *Commonplaces: Essays on the Nature of Place*. New York: University Press of America.

Baker, C. 2004. *Cuba Classics: A Celebration of Vintage American Automobiles*. London: Moon Handbooks.

Baldacchino, G. 2007. Islands as Novelty Sites. *The Geographical Review* **97**: 165–174.

Barba, R., and Avella, A. E. 1996. Cuba's Environmental Law. *Association for the Study of the Cuban Economy Newsletter*, Winter, pp. 35–36.

Barberia, L. G. 2002. The Caribbean: Tourism as Development or Development for Tourism? *ReVista: Harvard Review of Latin America*, Winter, pp. 72–75.

Barby, P. 1996. *Bright Paradise: Victorian Scientific Travelers*. Princeton, NJ: Princeton University Press.

Barredo, 2003. Cuban Coat of Arms. In L. Martínez-Fernández, D. H. Figueredo, and L. A. Pérez, eds., *Encyclopedia of Cuba* (Vol. 1). Westport, CT, and London: Greenwood Press, pp. 21–22.

Block, H. 2001. *Art Cuba: The New Generation*. New York: Harry N. Abrams.

Boadle, A. 2007. *Cuba Says Not Ready for an Influx of U.S. Tourists*. Reuters. Wednesday, March 7, 4:39 P.M.

Breglia, L. 2006. *Monumental Ambivalence: The Politics of Heritage*. Austin: University of Texas Press.

British Broadcasting Corporation. 2007. *What the World Thinks about America? Poll Results*. Retrieved March 7, 2007, from *news.bbc.co.uk/2/shared/spl/hi/programmes/wtwta/poll/html/political/general.stm*.

Brown, C., and Lagos, A. 1991. *The Politics of Psychiatry in Revolutionary Cuba*. New York: Freedom House.

Burke, L., and Maidens, J. 2005. *Reefs at Risk in the Caribbean*. Washington, DC: World Resources Institute.

Burtner, J. 2006. Boycotting Pleasure and Violence in the Land of Eternal Springtime. *ReVista: Harvard Review of Latin America*, Winter, pp. 52–55.

Bustamante, A. S. 2001. Mensaje del Chairman of the Board, Cuba and Its Heritage/2001. *Herencia* 7(1, verano): 3–4.

Bustamante, A. S. n.d. *Art Lost: Cuban Artistic Patrimony and Its Restitution*. Retrieved July 19, 2006, from *www.futurodecuba.org/ART%20LOST.htm*.

Caribbean Tourism Organization. 2006, September 26. Latest statistics. Retrieved March 21, 2007, from www.onecaribbean.org/information/documentview.php?rowid=4423.

Carty, J. W. 1990. Mass Media in Cuba. In S. H. Surlin and W. C. Soderlund, eds., *Caribbean Studies: Vol. 6. Mass Media and the Caribbean*. New York: Gordon and Breach, pp. 131–148.

Castellanos Romeu, R. J. 2001. *Evolución Histórica de la Distribución Territorial de la Producción Azucarera*. La Habana: Instituto de Planificación Física, Departamento de Investigaciones.

Central Intelligence Agency. 2007. *The World Factbook 2007.* Retrieved January 13, 2007, from *www.cia.gov/cia/publications/factbook/index.html.*

Cepero, E., and Lawrence, A. 2006. Before and after the Cayo Coco Causeway, Cuba: A Critical View from Space. In J. Pérez-López, ed., *Cuba in Transition* (Vol. 16). Washington, DC: Association for the Study of the Cuban Economy, pp. 212–220.

Chaffee, W., and Prevost, G. 1992. *Cuba: A Different America.* Totowa, NJ: Rowman and Littlefield.

Colantonio, A. 2004. Tourism in Havana during the Special Period: Impacts, Residents' Perceptions and Planning Issues. *Cuba in Transition* **14**: 20–43. Washington, DC: Association for the Study of the Cuban Economy.

Colantonio, A. 2005. *Urban Tourism and Development in the Socialist State: The Case of Havana in the Special Period.* Doctoral dissertation, University of Reading, UK.

Colantonio, A., and Potter, R. 2006a. City Profile: Havana. *Cities* **23**: 63–78.

Colantonio, A., and Potter, R. 2006b. *Urban Tourism and Development in the Socialist State: Havana during the "Special Period."* Burlington, VT: Ashgate.

Conkling, P. 2007. On Islanders and Islandness. *Geographical Review* **97**: 191–201.

Consejo Nacional de Patrimonio Cultural. 2008. *Cuadro Estadístico.* Retrived July 11, 2006, from *www.cnpc.cult.cu/cnpc/monumen/Pag005.htm.*

Conway, D. 2006, April. *Yachting and Marina Development in Trinidad: Successful Multiplier Effects for an Alternative Tourism Initiative.* Paper presented at the Association of American Geographers annual meeting, Chicago, IL.

Coons, L., and Verias, A. 2003. *Tourist Third Cabin: Steamship Travel in the Interwar Years.* New York: Palgrave Macmillan.

Corbett, B. 2002. *This Is Cuba: An Outlaw Culture Survives.* Cambridge, MA: Westview/Perseus.

Cosgrove, D. 1998. *Social Formation and Symbolic Landscape.* Madison: University of Wisconsin Press.

Cosgrove, D. 2005. [Review of the book *Islands of the Mind: How the Human Imagination Created the Atlantic World*]. *Human Geography* **87**: 302–303.

Council on Hemispheric Affairs. 2006. Cuba's Oil and Ethanol Could Prosper in Havana's Hunt for Energy Supplies. Retrieved July 13, 2007, from *www.coha.org/2006/11/17/cuban-oil-and-ethanol-could-prosper-in-havana's-hunt-for-energy-supplies/.*

Creswell, T. 2004. *Place: A Short Introduction.* Oxford, UK: Blackwell.

Cuba Verdad. 2006. *Acto de Repudio Newsfeed.* Retrieved December 26, 2006, from *www.cubaverdad.net/themefeeds/acto_de_repudio.php.*

Dana, R. H. 1996. Preface. In J. Miller and S. Clark, *Havana: Tales of the City.* San Francisco: Chronicle Books, pp. ix–xi.

Daniels, S., and Cosgrove, D. 1988. Introduction: Iconography and Landscape. In D. Cosgrove and S. Daniels, eds. *The Iconography of Landscape.* Cambridge, UK: Cambridge University Press.

de la Fuente, A., García del Pino, C., and Iglesias Delgado, B. 1996. Havana and the Fleet System: Trade and Growth in the Periphery of the Spanish Empire, 1550–1610. *Colonial Latin American Review* **5**: 1.

de León, C. 1995. *Ernesto Lecuona: El Maestro.* Havana: Editorial Musical de Cuba.

Dening, G. 2007. Sea People of the West. *Geographical Review* **97**: 288–301.

De Real, P., and Scarpaci, J. (forthcoming). Barbacoas: Havana's New Inward Frontier. In E. Whitfield, ed., *Reading Havana.* New York: Duke University Press.

Díaz-Briquets, S., and Pérez-López, J. 2000. *Conquering Nature: The Legacy of Environmentalism in Socialist Cuba*. Pittsburgh: University of Pittsburgh Press.

Diccionario Geográfico de Cuba. 2000. La Habana: Comisión Nacional de Nombres Geográficos.

Doubleday, G. 2006. *World Heritage Committee to inscribe new sites on UNESCO's World Heritage List*. Retrieved July 7, 2006, from *whc.unesco.org/en/news/261*.

Duany, A., Plater-Zyberk, E., and Speck, J. 2000. *Suburban Nation: The Rise of Sprawl and the Decline of the American Dream*. New York: North Point Press.

Duncan, J., and Duncan, N. 1988. (Re)-reading the landscape. *Environment and Planning D: Society and Space* 6: 117–126.

Duncan, J., and Gregory, D. 1999. Writes of passage: Reading travel writing. In J. Duncan and D. Gregory, eds., *Writes of Passage*. London: Routledge, pp. 1–13.

Dye, A. 1998. *Cuban Sugar in the Age of Mass Production: Technology and the Economics of the Sugar Central, 1899–1929*. Palo Alto, CA: Stanford University Press.

Edge, K., Woofard, H., and Scarpaci, J. 2006. Mapping and Designing Havana: Republican, Socialist, and Global Spaces. *Cities: An International Journal of Urban Policy and Planning* 23(2): 85–98.

Ekirch, R. 2005. *At Day's Close: Night in Times Past*. New York: Norton.

Espino, M. D. 2006, August 3. *International Tourism in Socialist Cuba: A Vehicle for Transition*. Paper presented at the annual meeting of the Association for the Study of the Cuban Economy, Miami, FL.

Ette, O. 2003. *Towards Global Consciousness: Alexander von Humboldt's Conception of Science and the Emerging Ethical "Weltenschauung."* Retrieved September 23, 2003, from www.tavera.com/tavera/revista/abstracts.htm.

European Union. 2006, April. *EU Annual Report of Human Rights: EU Common Position on Cuba: Alternatives and Recommendations. Policy Paper*. Compiled by Jakub Klepal, Prague, Czech Republic.

Feinsilver, J. 1993. *Healing the Masses: Cuban Health Politics at Home and Abroad*. Berkeley and Los Angeles: University of California Press.

Feschback, M., and Friendly, A. 1992. *Ecocide in the USSR*. New York: Basic Books.

Ford, L. 1976. Review of "What Time Is This Place?" *Geographical Review* 65(1): 141–142.

Fors, A. 1956. *Maderas Cubanas*. Havana: Empresora Mundial, Ministerio de Agricultura, República de Cuba.

Franc, M. 2004, December 18. *Cuba Erects Iraq Abuse Billboards near US Mission*. Reuters and Common Dreams News Center. Copyright Reuters Ltd. Retrieved July 1, 2006, from *www.commondreams.org*.

Franks, J. 2008, September 1. *Cuba Says 90,000 Houses Damaged by Gustav*. Reuters Wire Report, 11:39 P.M. BST.

Friedman, C. 2006. *Cuba after Castro*. Stratfor: Strategic Forecasting, Inc. Retrieved May 26, 2008, from *www.stratfor.com/cuba_after_castro*.

Gillis, J. R. 2004. *Islands of the Mind: How the Human Imagination Created the Atlantic World*. New York: Palgrave Macmillan.

Gills, J. R. 2007. Island sojourns. In "Islands," Special Issue. *The Geographical Review* 97: 274–287.

Gillis, J. R., and Lowenthal, D. 2007. Introduction. *Geographical Review* 97(2): iii–vi.

Goldberger, P. 2001. The Future of Cuban Cities. *Herencia* 7(1), 24–31.

Graham, B., Ashworth, G. J., and Turnbridge, J. E. 2000. *A Geography of Heritage: Power, Culture and Economy*. London: Arnold.

Greene, G. 1996. Our Man in Havana. In J. Miller and S. Clark, eds., *Havana*. San Francisco: Chronicle Books, pp. 121–132.

Grenier, G., and Pérez, L. 2002. *The Legacy of Exile: Cubans in the United States*. Boston: Allyn & Bacon.

Grenier, R., Nutley, D., and Cochran, I. 2006. *Underwater Cultural Heritage at Risk: Managing Natural and Human Impacts*. Paris: International Council on Monuments and Sites.

Grogg, P. 2008. Gustav, Ike Leave $5 Billion in Damages as Cubans Struggle to Put Food on Table. *CubaNews* 16(9).

Habermas, J. 1975. *Legitimation Crisis*. Boston: Beacon Press.

Haddock, N. 2002. The Legacy of Human Rights: Touring Chile's Past. *ReVista: Harvard Review of Latin America*, Winter, pp. 58–59.

Hall, S. 1995. New Cultures for Old. In D. Massey and P. Jess, eds., *A Place in the World?: Place, Cultures and Globalization*. Oxford, UK: Open University/Oxford University Press, pp. 175–214.

Hardoy, J. E. 1992. Theory and Practice of Urban Planning in Europe, 1850–1930. In R. Morse and J. E. Hardoy, eds., *Rethinking the Latin American City*. Baltimore and London: Johns Hopkins University Press, pp. 20–49.

Hazard, S. 1871. *Cuba with Pen and Pencil*. Hartford, CT: Hartford Publishing.

Hazard, S. 1872. *Cuba with Pen and Pencil*. Hartford, CT: Hartford Publishing.

Heritage Foundation. *2008 Index of Economic Freedom*. Washington, DC: Heritage Foundation.

Heritage Foundation. 2008. *Index of Economic Freedom*. Retrieved May 26, 2008, from *www.heritage.org/research/features/index/countries.cfm*.

Hermer, C., and May, M. 1996. What to Wear. In J. Miller and S. Clark, eds., *Chronicles Abroad: Havana*, San Francisco: Chronicle Books, pp. 56–73.

Herrera, A., and Seco, R. 1986. La Agricultura y el Medio Ambiente en Cuba. *Acta Universitatis Carolinae, Geographica #2*, Praga.

Herring, H. 1960. *A History of Latin America*. New York: Knopf.

Hewison, R. 1987. *The Heritage Industry: Britain in a Climate of Decline*. London: Methuen.

Hobsbawm, E. J. 1990. *Nations and Nationalism since 1789: Programme, Myth, Reality*. Cambridge, UK: Cambridge University Press.

Holm, D. 1991. *Art and Ideology in Revolutionary China*. Oxford, UK: Clarendon Press.

Humboldt, A. von 1851. *Equinoctial Regions of America During the Years 1799–1804* (Vol. 1). (T. Ross, Trans.). London and New York: Routledge.

Humboldt, A. von 2001. *The Island of Cuba*. Princeton, NJ: Markus Wiener.

Humboldt, A. von, and Bonpland, A. 1849. *Personal Narrative of Travels to the Equinoctial Regions of America, During the Years 1799–1804* (T. Ross, ed. and trans.), Vol. 3). London: Henry G. Bohn

Iñiguez-Rojas, L. 1989. Paisajes. Modificación Antrópica. XII.2.2–3, *Nuevo Atlas Nacional de Cuba*, La Habana.

International Center for Tropical Agriculture. 2003. Retrieved November 1, 2007, from *gisweb.ciat.cgiar.org/metadata/pop/population.html*.

International Commission on Monuments and Sites. 2001–2002. *Heritage at Risk: Cuba*. Retrieved July 11, 2006, from *www.international.icomos.org/risk/2001/cuba2001.htm*.

Isenberg, R. 2007. *The Law Says You Can't Go*. MSN Travel Articles. Retrieved March 7, 2007, from *travel.msn.com/Guides/article.aspx?cp-documentid=384862&GT1=9237*.

Iturralde-Vinent, M. A. 1998. Sinopsis de la constitución geológica de Cuba. *Acta Geológica Hispana* **33**(1–4): 9–56.

Jatar-Hausman, J. 1999. *The Cuban Way: Capitalism, Communism and Confrontation*. West Hartford, CT: Kurmarian Press.

Jenks, L. H. 1928. *Our Cuban Colony: A Study in Sugar*. New York: Vanguard Press.

Johnston, R. J. 1991. *A Question of Place: Exploring the Practice of Geography*. Oxford, UK: Blackwell.

Juraga, D., and Booker, M. K., eds. 2002. *Socialist Cultures: East and West. A Post-Cold War Reassessment*. New York: Praeger.

Juventud Rebelde. 2009. Record number of visitors arrived in Cuba in 2008. *Juventud Rebelde.co.cu, The Newspaper of Cuban Youth*. Retrieved February 2, 2009, from *www.juventudrebelde.co.cu/cuba/2009-02-02/record-number-of-visitors-arrived-in-cuba-in-2008*.

Kapcia, A. 2000. *Cuba: Island of Dreams*. London: Berg.

Kapcia, A. 2005. *Havana: The Making of Cuban Culture*. London: Berg.

Karasik, G. Y. 1989. Recursos hídricos. Módulo de escurrimiento sólido. VII.1.4.10. *Nuevo Atlas Nacional de Cuba*, La Habana.

Karnes, T. 1978. *Tropical Enterprise: The Standard Fruit and Steamship Company in Latin America*. Baton Rouge: Louisiana State University Press.

Kellner, L. 1963. *Alexander von Humboldt*. London: Oxford University Press.

Kiple, K., and Ornelas, K. 2000. *The Cambridge World History of Food*. London: Cambridge University Press.

Kirby, A. 1982. *The Politics of Location: An Introduction*. London and New York: Methuen.

Kirby, A. 1993. *Power/resistance and the Chaotic State: Local Politics*. Bloomington: Indiana University Press.

Knight, F. W. 1970. *Slave Society in Cuba during the Nineteenth Century*. Madison: University of Wisconsin Press.

Kubik, J. 1994. *The Power of Symbols against the Symbols of Power: The Rise of Solidarity and the Fall of State Socialism in Poland*. University Park: Pennsylvania State University Press.

Leavey, J. 2007. *My First Trip to Cuba*. Retrieved March 5, 2007, from *www.forces.org/writers/james/files/cuba.htm*.

Lebedeva, I. M. 1970. Escurrimiento Superficial. *Atlas Nacional de Cuba*. La Habana-Moscú.

Lefebvre, H. 1991. *The Production of Space*. Oxford, UK: Blackwell.

León Moya, A. 2001. Parque Nacional Alejandro de Humboldt, Joya Ecológica del Mundo. *Granma*, December 26, p. 4.

Levi, V., and Heller, S. 2002. *Cuba Style: Graphics from the Golden Age of Design*. Princeton, NJ: Princeton Architectural Press.

Linden, E. 2003. The Nature of Cuba. *Smithsonian*, May, pp. 94–106.

Lipset, S. 1960. *Political Man: The Social Bases of Politics*. Garden City, NY: Doubleday.

Longest List. 2006. The Longest List Conga Line. Retrieved June 3, 2007, from *thelongestlistofthelongeststuffatthelongestdomainnameatlonglast.com/long25.html*.

Loomis, J. 1989. *Revolution of Forms: Cuba's Forgotten Arts Schools*. Princeton, NJ: Princeton Architectural Press.

Lowenthal, D. 1985. *The Past Is a Foreign Country*. Cambridge, UK: Cambridge University Press.

Lowenthal, D. 2007. Islands, Lovers, and Others. *Geographical Review* **97**: 202–229.

Lynch, K. 1972. *What Time Is This Place?* Cambridge, MA: MIT Press.

Mahieux, V. 2002. Rio de Janeiro's Favela Tourism. *ReVista: Harvard Review of Latin America*, Winter, pp. 44–45.

Maiello, M. 2002, December 19. The Godfather Returns. *Forbes.com*. Retrieved March 7, 2007, from *www.forbes.com/2002/12/19/cz_mm_1219godfather.html*.

Mañach, J. 1969. *Indagación del choteo.* Miami, FL: Mnemosyne.

Mandela, N. R. 1994. *Long Walk to Freedom: An Autobiography of Nelson Mandela.* New York: Little, Brown.

Marrero, L. 1950. *Geografía de Cuba.* Havana: Alfa.

Marrero, L. 1957. *Geografía de Cuba* (3rd ed.). Havana: Editorial Selecta.

Marrero, L. 1972. *Cuba: Sociedad y Economía.* San Juan, Puerto Rico: Editorial San Juan.

Martí, J. 1968. *The America of José Martí.* New York: Funk & Wagnalls.

Martínez-Fernández, L. 2001. Introduction. The Many Lives and Times of Humboldt's Political Essay on the Island of Cuba. In A. von Humboldt, *The Island of Cuba.* Princeton, NJ: Markus Wiener, pp. 3–18.

Martínez Fernández, L. 2003. Santiago de Cuba. In L. Martínez-Fernández, D. H. Figueredo, and L. A. Pérez, eds., *Encyclopedia of Cuba* (Vol. 1). Westport, CT, and London: Greenwood Press, pp. 45–46.

Martínez-Fernández, L. 2004. Geography, Will It Absolve Cuba? *History Compass* **2**(1). Retrieved July 12, 2007, from *www.blackwell-synergy.com/toc/hico/2/1?cookieSet=1*.

Matamoros, M., González, G., Rodríguez, J., and Claro, A. 2006, July 6. *Proyecto "El Vallecito": Memoria descriptiva.* Unpublished manuscript.

Matsuda, M. K. 2007. This Territory Was Not Empty: Pacific Possibilities. *Geographical Review* **97**: 230–243.

Matthews, H. 1961. *The Cuba Story.* New York: Braziller.

MBA (Museo de Bellas Artes). 2001. *The National Museum of Cuba Painting.* Havana: Letras Cubanas.

McCook, S. 2002. *States of Nature: Science, Agriculture, and Environment in the Spanish Caribbean, 1760–1940.* Austin: University of Texas Press.

McLuhan, M. 1967. *The Medium is the Message: An Inventory.* London: Penguin.

Meinig, D. W., ed. 1979. *The Interpretation of Ordinary Landscapes.* New York: Oxford University Press.

Menocal, N. G. 1996. An Overriding Passion: The Quest for a National Identity in Painting. *Journal of Decorative and Propaganda Arts* **22**: 186–219.

Milner, J. O. 1979. Fidel Castro and the Cuban Media. In J. Herd, ed., *Mass Media in/ on Cuba and the Caribbean Area: The Role of Television, Radio, and the Press.* Monograph 10, September. Northwestern Pennsylvania Institute of Latin American Studies, pp. 16–26.

Ministerio de Turismo. 2007. Ministerio de Turismo. Retrieved March 6, 2007, from *www.cubagob.cu/des_eco/turismo.htm*.

Mitchell, W. J. 1994. Imperial Landscape. In W. J. T. Mitchel, ed., *Landscape and Power.* Chicago: University of Chicago Press, pp. 5–34.

Montaner, C. A. 2007. Communism Has Failed Cuba. *Foreign Policy*, January/February, pp. 56–58.

Moreno Fraginals, M. 1964. *El Ingenio: El Complejo Económico Social Cubano del Azúcar, Vol. 1. 1760–1860.* Havana: Comisión Nacional Cubana de la UNESCO.

Moreno Fraginals, M. 1976. *The Sugarmill: The Socioeconomic Complex of Sugar in Cuba, 1760–1860* (C. Belfrage, trans.). New York: Monthly Review Press.

Morris, A. 1981. *Latin America: Economic Development and Regional Differentiation.* Totowa, NJ: Barnes and Noble.

Mosquera, G. 1994. Hustling the Tourist in Cuba. *Poliester* (London) **3**(10): 3–6.

Mosquera, G. 1999. The Infinite Island. In M. Zeitlin, ed., *Contemporary Cuban Art*. New York: Arizona State University Art Museum, pp. 23–29.

Muir, R. 1999. *Approaches to Landscape*. London: Macmillan.

Mumford, L. 1986. "What Is A City." In D. L. Miller, ed., *The Lewis Mumford Reader*. New York: Pantheon Books, pp. 104–107. (Original work published 1938)

Murray, D. 1980. *Odious Commerce: Britain, Spain, and the Abolition of the Cuban Slave Trade*. New York: Cambridge University Press.

Naranjo, F. 2003. *Humboldt in Cuba: Reformism and Abolition*. Retrieved September 23, 2003, from *www.tavera.com/tavera/revista/abstracts.htm*.

National Public Radio. 2006, June 15. Cuba Uses Power Play, Literally, on U.S. Station. Retrieved July 2, 2006, from *www.npr.org/templates/story/story. php?storyId=5488800*.

Nemeth, D. 2006. Ideology. In B. Ward, ed., *Encyclopedia of Human Geography*. Thousand Oaks and London: Sage, pp. 241–243.

Nichols, B. 1981. *Ideology and the Image: Social Representation in the Cinema and Other Media*. Bloomington: Indiana University Press.

Nicolson, A. 2007. The Islands. *Geographical Review* **97**: 153–164.

Numbers, The. 2007. Buena Vista Social Club. Retrieved March 5, 2007, from *www. the-numbers.com/movies/1999/0BVSC.php*.

Oficina Nacional de Estdadisticas. 2007. Nomenclador Nacional de Asentamientos Humanos, por Provincias. Edición 2007. Las Tunas, Municipio Jesús Menéndez.

Oficina del Historiador de la Ciudad de la Habana. 2006. *Habana Patrimonial*. Retrieved July 11, 2006, from *www.ohch.cu*.

Olwig, K. F. 2007. Islands as places of being and belonging. *Geographical Review* **97**: 260–273.

Ortiz, F. 1947. *Cuban Counterpoint: Tobacco and Sugar*. New York: Knopf.

Ortiz, F. 1975. *Los Negros Esclavos*. Havana: Editorial de Ciencias Sociales. (Original work published 1916)

Ortiz, F. 2004. Transculturation and Cuba. In *The Cuba Reader: History, Culture Politics*. A. Chomsky, B. Carr, and P. Smorkaloff, eds., Durham, NC: Duke University Press, pp. 26–27.

Overpopulation.com. 2007. Population Density: Latin America. Retrieved March 5, 2007, from *www.overpopulation.com/faq/basic_information/population_density/ latin_america.html*.

Palero, C., and Geldof, L. 2004. Waiting tables in Havana. In A. Chomsky, B. Carr, and P. Smorkaloff, eds., *The Cuba Reader: History, Culture, Politics*. Durham, NC: Duke University Press, pp. 254–258.

Palmer, K. 2005. Contrabandwidth. *Foreign Policy*, March/April. Retrieved June 6, 2007, from *www.foreignpolicy.com/story/cms.php?story-id=2187*.

Patton, D. 2006. High Sugar Prices Favor Corn-Based Sweeteners. Retrieved June 28, 2006, from *Foodnavigator.com*. *www.foodnavigator.com/news/ng.asp?id=67102-sugar-prices-sweeteners*.

Pattullo, P. 1996. *Last Resorts: The Cost of Tourism in the Caribbean*. London: Casell.

Pérez, L. A. 2001a. *On Becoming Cuban: Identity, Nationality and Culture*. Chapel Hill: University of North Carolina Press.

Pérez, L. A. 2001b. *Winds of Change: Hurricanes and the Transformation of Nineteenth Century Cuba*. Chapel Hill: University of North Carolina Press.

Peters, P. 2003. *Cutting Losses: Cuba Downsizes Its Sugar Industry*. Arlington, VA: Lexington Institute.

Peters, P., and Scarpaci, J. 1998. *Five Years of Small-Scale Capitalism in Cuba*. Arlington, VA: Alexis de Tocqueville Institute.

Piqueras Arenas, J. 2003. Slavery. In L. Martínez-Fernández, D. H. Fugeredo, L. A. Pérez, and L. González, eds., *Encyclopedia of Cuba: People, History, Culture* (Vol. 1). Westport, CT: Greenwood Press, p. 114.

Ponte, A. J. 2002. A Knack for Making Ruins. *Tales from the Cuban Empire* (C. Franzen, trans.). San Francisco: City Lights Books.

Portela, A. 2003. Santiago de Cuba Province. In L. Martínez-Fernández, D. H. Figueredo, and L. A. Pérez, eds., *Encyclopedia of Cuba* (Vol. 1). Westport, CT, and London: Greenwood Press, pp. 46–48.

Portela, A. 2007, October. Forgotten Las Tunas Is among Cuba's Least Known Provinces. *CubaNews* 15(10): 6.

Portela, A., and Aguirre, B. 2000. Environmental Degradation and Vulnerability in Cuba. *Natural Hazards Review* 1: 171–179.

Pratt, M. L. 1992. *Through Imperial Eyes: Studies in Travel Writing and Transculturation*. New York: Routledge.

Pratt, M. L. 2003. The Ultimate "Other": Post-Colonialism and Alexander von Humboldt's Ecological Relationships with Nature. *History and Theory* 42: 111–113.

Préstamo, F. 1995. *Cuba y Su Arquitectura*. Miami: Ediciones Universales.

Price, M., and Lewis, M. 1993. The reinvention of cultural geography. *Annals of the Association of American Geographers* 83: 1–17.

Prima News Agency. 2006, December 24. Raul Castro fights corruption. Retrieved July 5, 2007, from *www.idee.org/prima_cuba_no.27news.html*.

Primeras Villas. 2006. Sitio de Prensa Latina Dedicado a las Primeras Villas Fundadas por el Adelantado Diego Velázquez. Retrieved July 5, 2006, from *www.fenix. islagrande.cu/villa/Vttesoro.htm*.

Putz, G. 1984. On islanders. *Island Journal* 1: 26–29.

Puzo, M., and Coppola, F. 1996. The Godfather II. In J. Miller and S. Clark, eds., *Chronicles Abroad: Havana*. San Francisco: Chronicle Books, pp. 98–113.

Raby, P. 1996. *Bright Paradise: Victorian Scientific Travelers*. Princeton, NJ: University of Princeton Press.

Ramonet, I. 2007. Cuba's Future Is Now. *Foreign Policy*, January/February, pp. 58–59.

Ramos, J. M. 2003. *Alejandro de Humboldt: Un Naturalista Antiesclavista*. Retrieved September 29, 2003, from *wekker.seagull.net/bolivar/a_de_humboldt.html*.

Relph, E. 1976. *Place and Placelessness*. London: Pion.

Reporters without Borders. 2006. *Updated Information on Imprisoned Cuban Journalists*. Retrieved December 26, 2006, from *www.rsf.org/rubrique.php3?id_rubrique=367*.

Richardson, B. 1992. *The Caribbean in the Wider World, 1492–1992: A Regional Geography*. Cambridge, UK: Cambridge University Press.

Rippy, J. F. 1958. *Latin America: A Modern History*. Ann Arbor: University of Michigan Press.

Robaina, T. F. 2004. The Brothel of the Caribbean. In A. Chomsky, B. Carr, and P. Smorkaloff, eds., *The Cuba Reader: History, Culture Politics*. Durham, NC: Duke University Press, pp. 257–259.

Robinson, D. J. 1989. The Language and Significance of Place in Latin America. In J. A. Agnew and J. S. Duncan, eds., *The Power of Place: Bringing Together Geographical and Sociological Imaginations*. London: Unwin Hyman, pp. 157–184.

Robles, F., and Bachelet, P. 2006, June 14. Electricity Restored to U.S. Interests Section. *Miami Herald*, p. 9A.

Rogozinski, J. 1999. *A Brief History of the Caribbean: From the Arawak and Carib to the Present*. New York: Facts on File.

Rose, G. 1992. Geography as a Science of Observation: The Landscape, the Gaze and Masculinity. In F. Driver and G. Rose, eds., *Nature and Science: Essays in the History of Geographical Knowledge*. London: Institute of British Geographers, pp. 8–18.

Rössler, M. 2004a. Tongariro: First Cultural Landscape on the World Heritage List. *World Heritage Newsletter* **4**: 15.

Rössler, M. 2004b. *World Heritage—Linking Cultural and Biological Diversity*. Paper presented at the US/ICOMOS Symposium: Learning from World Heritage, Paris.

Santamaría García, A. 2003. Sugar Industry. In L. Martínez-Fernández, D. H. Figueredo, L. A. Pérez, and L. González, eds., *Encyclopedia of Cuba: People, History, Culture* (Vol. 1). Westport, CT: Greenwood Press, p. 304.

Sauer, C. O. 1963. The morphology of landscape. In J. Leighley, ed., *Land and Life: Selections for the Writings of Carl Ortwin Sauer*. Berkeley: University of California Press, 315–350.

Scarpaci, J. L. 1998. Tourism Planning during Cuba's "Special Period." In F. Costa, R. Kent, A. Dutt, and A. Noble, eds., *Regional Planning and Development Practices and Policies*. Aldershot, UK: Ashgate Publishing, pp. 225–244.

Scarpaci, J. L. 2000. Reshaping *Habana Vieja*: Revitalization, Historic Preservation, and Restructuring in the Socialist City. *Urban Geography* **21**: 724–744.

Scarpaci, J. L. 2003. Architecture, Design, and Planning: Recent Scholarship on Modernity and Public Spaces in Latin America. *Latin American Research Review* **38**: 236–250.

Scarpaci, J. L. 2005. *Plazas and Barrios: Heritage Tourism and Globalization in the Latin American Centro Histórico*. Tucson: University of Arizona Press.

Scarpaci, J. L. 2006. Environmental Planning and Heritage Tourism in Cuba during the Special Period: Challenges and Opportunities. In J. Pugh and J. Momsen, eds., *Environmental Planning in the Caribbean*. Burlington, VT: Ashgate, pp. 73–92.

Scarpaci, J. L., and Frazier, L. J. 1993. State terror: Ideology, Protest, and the Gendering of Landscapes. *Progress in Human Geography* **17**: 1–21.

Scarpaci, J. L., and Portela, A. H. 2005. The Historical Geography of Cuba's Sugar Landscape. In J. F. Pérez-Lopez and J. Alvarez, eds., *Reinventing the Cuban Sugar Agroindustry*. Greenwood, CT: Greenwood Press, pp. 11–25.

Scarpaci, J. L., Segre, R., and Coyula, M. 2002. *Havana: Two Faces of the Antillean Metropolis*. Chapel Hill, NC, and London: University of North Carolina Press.

Schein, R. H. 1997. Representing Urban America: 19th-Century Views of Landscape, Space, and Power. *Annals of the Association of American Geographers* **87**: 660–680.

Schlüter, R. G. 2000. The Immigrants' Heritage in South America: Food and Culture as a New Sustainable Tourism Product. *ReVista: Harvard Review of Latin America*, Winter, pp. 46–48.

Schwartz, R. 1989. *Lawless Liberators: Political Banditry and Cuban Independence*. Durham, NC: Duke University Press.

Schwartz, R. 1997. *Pleasure Island: Tourism and Temptation in Cuba*. Lincoln, NE, and London: University of Nebraska Press.

Schwartz, R. 2004. The Invasion of the Tourists. In A. Chomsky, B. Carr, and P. Smorkaloff, eds., *The Cuba Reader: History, Culture, Politics*. Durham, NC: Duke University Press, pp. 244–252.

Schweid, R. 2004. *Che's Chevrolet, Fidel's Oldsmobile: On the Road in Cuba.* Chapel Hill, NC, and London: University of North Carolina Press.

Seamon, D. 1979. *A Geography of the Life-World.* London: Croom Helm.

Seamon, D., and Mugerauer, R. 1985. *Dwelling, Place and Environment: Towards a Phenomenology of Person and World.* Dordrecht, The Netherlands: Martinus Nijhoff.

Segre, R., Coyula, M., and Scarpaci, J. L. 1997. *Havana: Two Faces of the Antillean Metropolis.* Chichester, UK: Wiley.

Seguin, D. 2007, February 12. Viva la Revolución. *Canadian Business,* pp. 63–67.

Sforza, P., and Scarpaci, J. 2008. *Brightness–Darkness Ratio Changes over Time in the Greater Antilles.* Unpublished manuscript.

Shanks, C. 2002. Nine Quandaries of Tourism: Artificial Authenticity and Beyond. *ReVista: Harvard Review of Latin America,* Winter, pp. 16–19.

Silva, S. 1997. *Tropical Mariculture.* New York: Academic Press.

Slater, D. 1982. State and Territory in Post-Revolutionary Cuba: Some Critical Reflections on the Development of Spatial Policy. *International Journal of Urban and Regional Research* **6:** 1–33.

Sloppyjoes, 2007. *Sloppy Joes Bar.* Retrieved March 5, 2007, from *www.sloppyjoesonthebeach.com/history.htm.*

Snow, A. 2006. Raul Castro Speaks about Cuba Food Woes. Associated Press. December 23, 2:34 P.M. ET.

Soja, E. 1996. *Thirdspace: Journey to Los Angeles and Other Real-and-Imagined Places.* Cambridge, MA: Blackwell.

Soroa, P., and Merencio, J. L. 2003. Parque Nacional Alejandro de Humboldt. Retrieved September 29, 2003, from *www.cubasolar.cu/Biblioteca/Reportajes/humboldt.htm.*

Sunday Times, The. 2006, May 14. Thank You My Foolish Friends in the West. Retrieved June 5, 2006, from *www.timesonline.co.uk/tol/news/article717720.ece.*

Szulc, T. 1986. *Fidel: A Critical Portrait.* New York: Morrow.

Tannenbaum, F. 1992. *Slave and Citizen in the Americas.* Boston: Beacon Press. (Original work published 1946)

Thomas, M. Z. 1960. *Alexander von Humboldt: Scientist, Explorer, Adventurer.* London: Constable.

Time. 1992, January 6. Prince of the Global Village. Retrieved July 15, 2007, from *www.time.com/time/magazine/article/0,9171,974617,00.html?promoid=googlep.*

Trollope, A. 1859. *The West Indies and the Spanish Main.* London: Chapman.

Tung, A. 2001. *Preserving the World's Great Cities: The Destruction and Renewal of the Historic Metropolis.* New York: Potter.

United Nations Educational, Scientific and Cultural Organization. 1999. Final Report of the Convention Concerning the Protection of the World Cultural and Natural Heritage, World Heritage Committee. Twenty-third session, Marrakesh, Morocco, November 29–December 4.

United Nations Educational, Scientific and Cultural Organization. World Heritage Sites. 2006a. Retrieved July 7, 2006, from *whc.unesco.org/en/criteria.*

United Nations Educational, Scientific and Cultural Organization. World Heritage Sites. 2006b. Retrieved July 15, 2006, from *whc.unesco.org/en/decisions/&id_decision=518.*

United Nations Educational, Scientific and Cultural Organization. World Heritage. 2006c. *Cultural Landscapes.* Retrieved July 13, 2006, from *whc.unesco.org/exhibits/cultland/landscape.htm.*

United Nations Educational, Scientific and Cultural Organization. World Heritage. 2007. Retrieved July 14, 2007, from *whc.unesco.org/en/list*.

United Nations Educational, Scientific and Cultural Organization. 2008. Alejandro de Humboldt National Park. Retrieved May 28, 2008, from *www.worldheritagesite. org/sites/humboldt.html*.

Urban Design and Planning in Havana, Cuba. 2002. DVD Produced and directed by J. L. Scarpaci. New York: Insight Media.

Urry, J. 2002. *The Tourist Gaze*. Thousand Oaks, CA: Sage.

Valladares A. 1986. *Against All Hope: The Prison Memoirs of Armando Valladares*. New York: Ballantine Books.

Vargas Llosa, M. 2005. *Liberty for Latin America: How to Undo Five Hundred Years of State Oppression*. New York: Farrar, Straus and Giroux.

Vázquez, R. 1994. Prólogo. In R. Vázquez, ed., *Bipolaridad de la Cultura Cubana*. Stockholm: Olof Palme International Center, pp. 7–18.

Village at Tom's Creek, The. 2006. The Village at Tom's Creek: What's Different? Retrieved July 5, 2006, from *www.villageattomscreek.com/whatsdif.htm*.

Von Blum, P. 1982. *The Critical Vision: A History of Social and Political Art in the U.S.* Boston: South End Press.

Von Blum, P. 2002. Resistance Art in Los Angeles. In D. M. Sawhney, ed., *Unmasking L.A.: Third Worlds and the City*. New York: Palgrave, pp. 181–198.

Waters, R. 1985. *Globalisation*. London: Rowman and Littlefield.

Weber, M. 1978. *Economy and Society*. (Vols. 1 and 2). (G. Roth and C. Wittich, eds.). New York: Bedminster Press.

Weiner, R. R. 1981. *Cultural Marxism and Political Sociology*. (Sage Library of Social Research, Vol. 125). Beverly Hills and London: Sage.

West, R., and Augelli, J. 1966. *Middle America: Its Lands and Peoples*. New York: Prentice-Hall.

Woodrow Wilson Center. 2008. *Havana and Its Landscapes: A Vision for Future Reconstruction in Cuba*. Retrieved May 29, 2008, from *www.wilsoncenter.org/index. cfm?topic_id=1410&fuseaction=topics.event_summary&event_id=400004*.

Woolf, S., 1996. *Nationalism in Europe, 1815 to the Present: A Reader*. London: Routledge.

World Resources Institute. 2007. Table A3. Population of the Wider Caribbean. Retrieved March 5, 2007, from *www.wri.org/biodiv/pubs_content_text. cfm?cid=3073*.

World Tourism Organization. 2007. *World's Top Destinations* (Absolute Numbers). Retrieved March 5, 2007, from *www.unwto.org/facts/eng/pdf/indicators/ITA_top25. pdf*.

Zanetti, O., and García, A. 1998. *Sugar and Railroads, A Cuban History, 1837–1959*. Chapel Hill: University of North Carolina Press.

Zelinsky, W. 1973. *The Cultural Geography of the United States*. Englewood Cliffs, NJ: Prentice-Hall.

Zimbalist, A., and Brundenius, C. 1989. *The Cuban Economy: Measurement and Analysis of Socialist Performance*. Baltimore: Johns Hopkins University Press.

INDEX

Page numbers followed by *f* indicate figure; *n*, note; and *t*, table

202

About the Authors

Joseph L. Scarpaci is a broadly trained human geographer who has taught in public health, geography, urban studies, and planning programs at the Inter-American University of Puerto Rico, Rutgers University, the University of Iowa, Virginia Tech, and Virginia Military Institute. He is currently Professor of Marketing in the Department of Economics and Business at the Virginia Military Institute in Lexington. Dr. Scarpaci has been conducting research in Cuba since 1990 and is the author of *Plazas and Barrios* (University of Arizona Press, 2005) and coauthor, with architects Mario Coyula and Roberto Segre, of the Choice Award–winning book *Havana: Two Faces of the Antillean Metropolis* (University of North Carolina Press, 2002).

Armando H. Portela is a physical geographer who worked for 23 years in the Institute of Geography of the Cuban Academy of Sciences. He coauthored the section "Geomorphology (Relief)" in the *Nuevo Atlas Nacional de Cuba* (Institute of Geography of the Academy of Sciences of Cuba, 1989) and produced a number of geomorphologic maps of the island. He currently works at the *Miami Herald* and freelances for the newsletter *CubaNews*, where he regularly publishes on geographical issues of the island.

NUMEROLOGY
KEY TO YOUR INNER SELF

NUMEROLOGY
KEY TO YOUR INNER SELF

HANS DECOZ
WITH TOM MONTE

A PERIGEE BOOK

A Perigee Book
Published by The Berkley Publishing Group
A division of Penguin Putnam Inc.
375 Hudson Street
New York, New York 10014

Cover designer: Anne Vestal
Typesetter: Bonnie Freid
In-house editors: Liza Burby and Karen Hay
Printer: Paragon Press, Honesdale, PA

Avery edition published in 1994
First Perigee edition: February 2002

Perigee trade paperback edition ISBN: 0-399-52732-X

Published simultaneously in Canada.

Visit our website at
www.penguinputnam.com

The Library of Congress has catalogued the Avery edition as follows:

Decoz, Hanz.
Numerology : the key to your inner self / Hans Decoz with Tom Monte.
p.   cm.
Includes index.
ISBN 0-89529-566-0

1. Numerology. I. Monte, Tom. II. Title.

BF1729.N85D43   1994   93-30671
133.3'35—dc20   CIP

Printed in the United States of America

10   9   8   7   6

Contents

For P. Rawat
and
Willy van Eck

*The most important question all of us must answer
is whether the universe is a friendly place or not.*

—Albert Einstein

Preface

Numerology is a language that allows you to expand the horizon of your spiritual awareness. It opens doors in your psyche that you did not know existed.

In fact, this is the case with all language. Before there were words, there were only the most simple and basic thoughts, most of which were confined to survival. But with language came more complex relationships, more possibilities, and vastly more creativity.

Take the word relativity. This word means that there is something other than absolute values in the universe. The word also means that what is true for you may not be true for someone else. Before Albert Einstein introduced his concept of relativity, the world was guided by a belief in absolutes—that things were as they seemed to be, not only for you, but for everyone. But with the emergence of the term relativity, and the far-reaching concepts that Einstein attached to it, humanity was now awakened to new ideas, possibilities, and relationships that shaped our view of life. Our spiritual horizon had been expanded by the introduction of a word that symbolized a large and complex meaning.

That same kind of expansion occurs when one is introduced to the language of numbers. Suddenly, the universe seems far greater and more complex, yet easier to grasp. Now you can think about things that previously were impossible to consider.

Symbols reveal relationships. They are the images that define the arrangement of multiple, often abstract, ideas. Symbols show us how important characteristics are related to each other. They reveal how things are related by their very nature.

For instance, let's consider a set of characteristics that may be within you. If we try to consider one particular talent or trait, we get no picture whatsoever. Let's say that trait is will. This abstract idea exists like a cloud in the sky, seeming separated from other clouds. But now introduce the symbol 1. It serves as an organizing principle for our minds, which attracts certain qualities that naturally belong together, and are related to each other, as if they were family members. The number 1 symbolizes will, as well as beginning, courage, determination, originality, independence, and individuality.

Why are these characteristics united? Because human life has taught us that the beginning of anything is naturally associated with other characteristics, such as resistance—bringing forth the need for will, determination, courage, originality, creativity, independence, and individuality. The 1, or beginning, now opens us up to relationships that are inherent in life—relationships that were in fact always there, but existed in the abstract, and hence appeared separate. Their natural relationship perhaps existed outside of our grasp.

In the end, it's impossible to talk about patterns in life without symbols. Symbols serve to draw upon themselves the vast amount of knowledge that exists in the archetypal world. Archetypes are unique bundles of information, stored in the psyche until we have the means to attract their wealth into our lives. They convey knowledge of things that we previously did not know, or were not conscious of.

The beauty of the use of numbers and human characteristics is that they are naturally and inherently joined. There is nothing arbitrary about joining the number 1 with originality or inventiveness, because 1, no matter what language the number is used in, means the beginning, the origin, the first, the birth.

Because we have these symbols, we have the clarity to ask deep and probing questions about life. For example, were these symbols arbitrarily assigned to specific meanings, or is there an organic pattern behind the numbers and their meanings? Are numbers a reflection of a greater truth that exists beneath the surface of life?

This book, *Numerology: The Key to Your Inner Self,* attempts to answer that question. It will not only serve as a tool for understanding numbers, but it will also help you to better understand your life. However, it's essential to recognize that no tool—no matter how powerful and sophisticated—can approach the vastness of the universe and life itself. Numerology is a springboard to larger realities. But the universe itself is infinite. Numerology opens a window to the vastness of creation. That vastness exists within you. No matter what your numbers may say about you or others, all of us are a part of the infinite universe, and thus way beyond the limits that any tool can convey.

A number of people have been supportive, offered encouragement, or helped in practical ways during the time that I worked on this book. My love and gratitude go out to Wendy Akers, John and Betty Peterson, Nina Gray, Randall and Janice Jamail, Mike Rutledge, David and Debra Mestemaker, and Colin and Carol Gibbins.

Support in the form of encouragement, advice, and practical help of my close friends Niels Lenz and Lee Ann Daruszka, has been especially important to the successful completion of this book.

My very special thanks go to Tom and Toby Monte, without whom *Numerology: The Key to Your Inner Self* most certainly would not have been written.

Hans Decoz
Houston, Texas

Part I
The Inner You

The Western form of numerology, the Pythagorian system, is among the most enduring and popular of all self-help methods ever created.

The Chinese, Japanese, Greek, Hebrews, Egyptians, Phoenicians, early Christians, Mayans, and Incas all employed number systems to gain a deeper understanding of themselves and the universe.

Pythagorian numerology was organized by Greek philosopher and mathematician Pythagoras, who combined the mathematical disciplines of the Arabic, Druid, Phoenician, Egyptian, and Essene sciences. Since then, it has continued to evolve. It formed the spiritual basis for many secret societies, such as the Rosicrusians, Masons, Anthroposophists, and others.

Numerology is used as a practical method of understanding your own deeper nature: your talents and your life goals; your hidden characteristics; your opportunities and challenges. It offers insight into the opportunities that will come to you during the years ahead. It describes the cycles you experience during the course of your life, and offers guidance in career, romance, and prosperity. In short, numerology is a self-help tool, providing meaningful advice for all types of situations.

Today, its popularity continues to grow. Numerology columns now appear regularly in newspapers and magazines. Numerologists are consulted with increasing regularity for everything from personal romance to business decisions. As the industrialized world becomes more computerized and dependent upon numerical systems, the fascination with this ancient spiritual science only grows.

There are many reasons for this system's enduring magic. Simply put, it is highly accurate. People who encounter numerology marvel at the insight and practical advice it offers, as well as its ability to predict future trends and events. Implicit within this spiritual science is an age-old and universal wisdom that people intuitively understand, respect, and respond to. Numerology is very accessible. Anyone who can do simple arithmetic can do a complete numerology chart, and it requires little time to complete.

The charting system used in this book is a combination of traditionally used symbols, and symbols that I have specifically designed. Over the years, I have developed a complete chart that organizes all the numbers and information in a coherent whole. I encourage you to use this chart, at least until you feel comfortable with all the formulas involved, so that no step is omitted. Once you are sufficiently familiar with numerology, you may want to develop your own system.

As I progress through the book, I will introduce the information necessary to produce a full numerology chart.

Symbols are used to differentiate, things like the Life Path number from the Expression or Heart's Desire numbers. The symbol for the Life Path number, for instance, is two concentric circles, with the number within. (See Figure 3.1 on page 111.)

In this section, you will learn about your personality, your strengths, and your weaknesses, and how you can take advantage of this self-knowledge that your numbers provide.

Chapter 1

The Basics and the Benefits of Numerology

At any rate, I am convinced that God does not play dice.

—Albert Einstein

I f you are like most people, you probably dislike math, or perhaps you're intimidated by it. The good news is that numerology is not about math. Yes, some very simple addition and subtraction of small numbers is involved, but that's as complicated as it gets. All the numbers that make up a complete numerology chart are the result of the simpler forms of arithmetic. It is no more complicated, or intimidating, than adding a couple of one- or two-digit numbers.

The art of numerology is based on the personality of numbers, their inner nature and vibration, and how they can be used to better understand yourself and the world around you. You probably never thought of numbers as having a personality, but if you consider them a little, you'll realize that most of us have preferences for some numbers over others. You make these choices because you feel some kind of intuitive attraction to the nature or personality of a particular number or numbers.

But before I discuss the philosophy, there are other aspects of numerology to be considered. Below are some frequently asked questions.

How can I benefit from numerology?

Numerology is primarily a self-help tool. It is a way to gain greater insight and understanding into your inner being and true nature. It reveals aspects of your character and personality in a way that is fresh and inspiring. It gives you a new vantage point from which to look at yourself; one with greater distance and perspective than many other self-help systems. Self-knowledge is the key to success and freedom. Having a greater insight into your strengths and weaknesses will help you in every aspect of life.

Numerology also offers insights into various cycles, opportunities, and challenges that you have already faced, or have yet to experience. In this respect alone, numerology provides you with a greater perspective on life; it helps prepare you for the future. It allows you to cultivate your strengths, and to overcome your weaknesses.

What information do I need to do my chart?

All you need to do your chart is your date of birth (month, day, and year), your full name (first middle, if any, and last names) as it appears on your birth certificate, and the name you go by today. The latter is usually a shortened version of your birth name, or a married name. It's the name you use whenever you introduce yourself.

What is the effect of changing my name?

The effect of changing your name can be considerable, depending upon the other numbers in your chart. While the influence makes itself felt in a subtle way from the day you change your name, the change cannot be considered complete until the new name is fully integrated in your subconscious. Legally changing your name is not as important as how much you use the new name. (For further advice about changing your name, see "The Minor Expression Number" in Chapter 3.)

Can numerology predict health problems, financial difficulties, accidents, and other potential problems?

Numerology can both predict and not predict your future. Certain cycles definitely point to the possibility of painful experiences at certain times in your life, such as accidents, money problems, divorce, and the like. In the same way, numerology foretells many positive events.

However, at such times the person always has the opportunity to turn the course of events in his favor, or to let a beautiful opportunity slide by. Numerology can indicate, for example, that a certain period of your life will be highly rewarding, a kind of payment for years of effort. Numerology can be very accurate in such predictions. However, the rewards are comparable to the effort you have made. Little effort brings small rewards; great effort brings great rewards. In the same way, numerology reveals the sowing and the harvesting cycles of life. If you have sown seeds of selfishness and greed, you will experience a time of loss—financial loss, or the loss of support from others.

Your chart reveals your potential, your strengths, your weaknesses, your challenges, and your lessons to be learned. Every number suggests potential strengths and weaknesses; all things have their light and dark sides. It is your freedom as an individual to draw from your highest potential. A numerologist can have a good idea of which direction a person will likely move in, and how much of his potential he will use or abuse. This is known by considering the balance of a chart, or the spreading of the energies. This is by far the biggest challenge for a numerologist, even after many years of experience. For example, a person with few or no 1s in the overall chart will have a difficult time establishing a strong identity; he will likely lack drive and willpower. On the other hand, he may be a loving, giving, and very cooperative person, but perhaps a bit of a wimp. A person with an excessive number of 1s will have a strong identity, and enormous personal power, ambition, and drive, but will be tempted to become domineering, selfish, aggressive, and perhaps, violent. Both cases are examples of an imbalance within the chart of which the person must be conscious.

Can numerology pinpoint my death?

Numerology cannot predict your death, and neither can any other similar science. I know of one numerologist who claimed to be able to foretell the moment of death; however, the man died at a very inconvenient time in his life, unprepared, and spoiling a perfectly good polo game for everyone else.

Are certain numbers better than others?

No particular number is better than another. All numbers have positive and negative aspects. They can only be considered better than others when they relate to certain demands in their environment, such as their vocational attributes. For example, 4s make excellent accountants, 5s make better salespeople and promoters, 6s make great teachers, and 8s are talented at business matters.

Sometimes we find ourselves attracted to certain numbers. Many people have a favorite number or numbers. Our attraction to a particular number is very much like our preference for certain colors. On the surface, these attractions seem arbitrary, but science has proven that colors influence our mood and behavior. The reverse is also true: Certain colors reflect our inner state. Numbers correspond to our inner state and to our personal preferences in the same way. They, too, reveal much about our nature, and they even influence how we feel.

On a very deep level, each of us understands that a number represents more than just a quantity. The numbers 1 through 9 represent archetypes. Each number has a certain character or personality: the creative 3, the dynamic 5, the responsible 6, the sage-like 7, and so on. Perhaps all of these characteristics are in you, but some are more pronounced than others. It is this link between the character of a particular number, and those same traits within you, that sparks an unconscious recognition or attraction.

Objectively speaking, there is no number that is better than another, so any preference for a certain number, or numbers, is purely subjective.

How do you arrive at the numbers in a chart?

Numerology deals, for the most part, with the single-digit numbers 1 through 9. The only exceptions to this rule are some two-digit numbers that have special meanings, which are explained later on. For this reason, all the arithmetic involved is very basic. Only the simplest addition and subtraction are used to find your personal numbers from your name and date of birth.

The letters of your name correspond to numbers. Each letter is assigned a number by virtue of its position in the alphabet. For example, A is 1, B is 2, C is 3, and so on. Since only the first nine digits are used, the cycle repeats itself. The following shows the letters and their numerical value:

A = 1	H = 8	O = 6	V = 4
B = 2	I = 9	P = 7	W = 5
C = 3	J = 1	Q = 8	X = 6
D = 4	K = 2	R = 9	Y = 7
E = 5	L = 3	S = 1	Z = 8
F = 6	M = 4	T = 2	
G = 7	N = 5	U = 3	

Let's use the name Mary as an example of how these numbers are applied to a name. Using the preceding chart, we can see that Mary is translated into the following numbers:

M = 4
A = 1
R = 9
Y = 7
— 21

You will learn more about the use of the letters in your name in Chapter 3, beginning with the Expression number.

In numerology, there is a standard method of transforming larger numbers into the single-digit numbers. For example, the 21 from Mary becomes a 3 by adding the 2 and the 1. Here are some other examples:

- An 81 becomes a 9 by adding the 8 and the 1.
- A 124 is a 7 (1 + 2 + 4 = 7).
- A 222 is a 6 (2 + 2 + 2 = 6).

Sometimes, you have to do two steps to arrive at a single-digit number. For example:

- A 39 becomes a 3 in two steps.
    Step One: 3 + 9 = 12
    Step Two: 1 + 2 = 3
- An 86 becomes a 5.
    Step One: 8 + 6 = 14
    Step Two: 1 + 4 = 5

This is as complicated as the arithmetic gets!

What is the philosophy behind numerology?

The fundamental premise of numerology is that life, and the universe as a whole, is an orderly system, and that numbers reflect that orderliness. Numbers are by definition orderly.

When we confront the question of numerology, we are facing the same dilemma that we all face with the larger questions of life: Is there meaning and order to life, or is it purely a random and chaotic universe?

There are three possible answers to this question: the universe is ruled by randomness and chaos; the universe is infinitely orderly; or both randomness and orderliness exist.

Randomness is a state in which there is no order or larger meaning. Such a state of affairs would mean that the universe is ruled by chance events, and that there are no orderly laws governing the universe. In fact, we know this premise to be untrue, since the natural sciences, such as physics, mathematics, biology, chemistry, and astronomy are all based on the orderliness, even predictability, of natural law. Moreover, if the universe were ruled by unpredictable events, there would be no sustainable structure to it. On the contrary, the universe not only maintains form and structure, it also changes in precise and orderly ways.

We are continually witnesses to this process of change: Day turns into night, and night turns into day; winter is followed by spring, and summer is followed by fall; and apples grow on apple trees, and figs grow on fig trees, and they never get confused.

Orderliness can be seen in every aspect of existence, from the subatomic world to the world of stars and galaxies. Therefore, we can cancel the first possibility to our original question: There is, at the very least, some orderliness.

But is it all orderly? When we look at the very basics of life—the world of deoxyribonucleic acid (DNA), the molecular world, and the developing child—we see an awesome sequence unfolding. DNA is of such profound orderliness that it has been the template for producing literally billions upon billions of human beings with the same universal characteristics, two eyes, ten fingers, ten toes, et cetera. That no two sets of eyes are alike only shows the remarkable creativity and energy that are contained within this DNA molecule.

The gestation and birth of a child are also examples of remarkable orderliness: It still takes egg and sperm to produce an ovum, and nine months for a child to fully develop and to be born. The growth pattern of humans has remained essentially the same, too: We are born very young, and grow through adolescence, puberty, adulthood, maturity, and old age, at which point we die. The arc of life is consistent and stable. This has been happening for about 2 million years, the length of time humans have inhabited the planet.

If we look up at the stars and see the planets, we see a further example of great orderliness. In creation, there is no randomness, a fact that is the basis for all physical sciences.

Yet, all of us experience events that we perceive as arbitrary or random. How can we reconcile the awareness that beneath our feet and above our heads—indeed, our very bodies—are the products of profound orderliness, while our lives seem permeated by random events of which we can make no sense?

We seem forced to say that, at first glance, both order and randomness exist simultaneously. But wait—doesn't our perception of how much order there is in the universe constantly grow as we learn more? For example, only three decades ago, heart disease and cancer were regarded by most of us as random and terrible events in life. Today we believe that these illnesses are often the result of our daily behavior and eating patterns. Both illnesses have very logical etiologies. Consequently, they are the products of order. The illnesses have not changed; only our understanding of them has.

Many examples of so-called "natural disasters," such as famine, drought, and mud slides, are often perceived as random events. It is only later that the cause is usually discovered to be mankind's ignorance. Specifically, we have not had (and still don't have) a perspective large enough to understand all the variables that come into play when we begin to tamper with the underlying orderliness.

The point here is that our perception of what is random keeps changing as we learn more. Meanwhile, our appreciation of an underlying order grows. However, it is important to keep in mind that the underlying order was always implicit in these events that were previously regarded as random; we simply didn't see the order.

Our growing understanding of order also changes the way we experience space and time. We all have had experiences that we cannot explain that fall into the category of synchronicity or extrasensory perception. These experiences violate our normal perception of space and time. We think of these things as out-of-the-ordinary, but they are really glimpses of the underlying order that our rational minds cannot comprehend, and that we really were not designed to understand.

Nevertheless, this underlying order, which can only be fully appreciated intuitively, is being proven by our most advanced science, quantum physics.

As quantum physicist Fritjof Capra points out in his book *The Tao of Physics,* scientists have now discovered a universal unity among all phenomena. As Capra said, the universe is characterized by the "fundamental interdependence" between all phenomena. And quantum physicist Niels Bohr emphasized that the main consequence of these theories is that we cannot separate any part of the material universe from the rest without making an error. The new vision of reality is a spiritual vision in its very essence.

Progress for the human spirit, as I've come to see it, is an elevation of consciousness to where the individual becomes fully aware of being an integral part of the cosmos as a whole, and of its maker. This mode of consciousness is much, much broader than anything that could possibly develop from a rational thought process. Contrary to the knowledge of the mind, this understanding is rooted in seeing, recognizing, and realizing at a much deeper level. It typically occurs in meditative experiences, but it can also occur in many other settings.

However, science is trying to reach that kind of understanding. As Capra indicated, quantum mechanics is demonstrating that the fundamental reality of the universe—while not immediately apparent to our rational minds—is a vast unity in which all things are related.

In ancient times, this understanding formed the basis for all the natural and spiritual sciences. In fact, natural science was merely the tool that was used to discover the underlying orderliness of the universe, otherwise known as God. Out of this consciousness came such spiritual sciences as numerology.

Numerology is based upon this underlying unity, a unity that manifests itself in a very intimate way in all of our lives. Our names and dates of birth, for example, are connected with our deepest inner being in a way that the rational mind cannot immediately understand. The intuitive mind, however, is capable of perceiving these relationships, and of interpreting them to help us better understand our lives.

The act of giving something a name is not a superficial or intellectual effort, but a reflection of our deep experience of the essence of the thing we are naming. It comes out of our connection, or our intuitive feeling of that thing.

For example, the word storm, with its special combination of vowels and consonants, gives us a feeling of the movement and power of an invisible force. Storm. Say it and you will feel it.

Another example is the word power, which names something, but at the same time gives the experience of the thing we are naming: Power! The biting movement of the jaw makes us feel it.

The word love embraces you gently. It gives you the experience of its meaning.

Every word, in every language, perfectly reflects the feeling and spirit of the thing that is named by the people who use that language. Some will argue that the words used to name things were originally chosen arbitrarily, and then were integrated into our inner feelings. However, our understanding of sound comes from an archetypal and unconscious part of our being. It is intimately connected with our appreciation of music; no matter whether you are tone deaf or have perfect pitch, all of us have an inborn capacity to discern music from chaotic noise. Music is harmony. And music is inside of us.

Nature, too, is filled with events that have trained us to associate certain qualities with sounds: The clap of thunder, the woosh of a river, or the whir of a bird in flight.

From our innate understanding of music and harmony comes the act of naming things according to our perception of their inner natures. This intuitive act is the source of language. All languages emerge from, and represent the natures of the people who use them.

All of this points to a single and incredibly significant fact: Sound and time are both rooted in harmony and universal order.

This is the source of numerology. The numerologist maintains that each of us carries the perfect name that reflects our inner nature or being. That name is a collection of sounds, a melody, that in a very deep and perfect way is you.

What are the specific characteristics of numbers?

Numbers can be seen as archetypes. They represent qualities that all of us possess in greater or lesser quantities. Each number, you might say, is the archetypal quality. The number 1 possesses aggressiveness or dynamism, for example, versus the passiveness and cooperation of number 2. In this sense, numerology has much in common with mythology. Just as each of the Greek gods possessed an absolute set of values, each number has a oneness of being.

To further illustrate, the number 1 embodies masculinity, a strong drive, individuality, and determination. The number 1 could never be confused with the number 2, which has the qualities of sensitivity, femininity, cooperation, and gentleness. Each number is the counterpart, or the opposite, of the number next to it. The personality of the number 1 is the opposite of the 2. In a different, but no less profound way, the 2 is the opposite of the 3, the 3 is the opposite of the 4, the 4 is the opposite of the 5, and so on.

The personality of each number is so clear and defined that once you get to know the numbers, you will be able to predict each number's response to any given situation.

At the same time, each number does possess nuances within its field of characteristics that are enhanced or diminished due to its place in the chart. Also, certain numbers complement other numbers; the right combinations will enhance and support each other. In this way, they may also limit one another's effects. If placed in very prominent positions within the chart, such opposites can be very dynamic, but can also represent internal conflict.

As you read this book, you will note that I have described each number according to its location, taking into account its place in the chart. By reading the information related to the numbers in each section of this book, you will soon become intimately acquainted with their personalities.

Numbers are so much like people that getting to know them is a continuing process. It would be impossible to put down all the characteristics, qualities, and idiosyncracies that each number possesses. For example, 1s like to take John Wayne-size steps—they swing their arms, appear very macho, and seem ready to take control of any situation—and 3s are jovial and have a bounce to their walk. Also, 7s are big readers; 4s know the value of a dollar; but 8s know how to earn large sums, and spend them, too. These are some of the less obvious characteristics with which you will become familiar by studying this book, and you can relate the information to your own life, and to that of others.

Every human characteristic, quality, or idiosyncracy is represented in one of the nine cardinal numbers. Just as the human DNA molecule is made up of four basic nucleic acids that are arranged in a complex, and unique spiralling ladder, so too, do the nine cardinal numbers represent nine archetypal human qualities that are also present in each of us. These nine archetypes are arranged uniquely in us all to form a specific personality with unique strengths and weaknesses.

These nine numbers not only symbolize nine specific archetypes, but also nine stages of development that all of us pass through in order to complete our growth and maturity. As you read this book, you will see how these numbers describe human characteristics, as well as the various cycles through which we all evolve during life's journey.

In one of the nicer examples of symbolic psychology, the shape of the number 9 itself contains a circle on a lead, representing the completion of a cycle, a turning back to the beginning, which is also manifested in the fact that whenever any number is added to the number 9, it comes back to itself. For example, if you add 9 plus 5, you get 14, which if added together (the 1 and the 4 of 14), makes 5 again. An 8 plus 9 is 17, which, if 1 and 7 are added together, gives us 8 again. Aside from this, an important aspect in the nature of the 9 is the fact that it represents completion, and detachment, the final point from which we return to a new beginning. Three different ways of looking at the 9—the shape of the symbol, the mathematical strangeness, and what it represents in numerology—reveal closely related characteristics.

It is interesting to note that the symbols of all numbers reflect their natures. The pillar shape of the number 1 reflects the independence, leadership, and strength of that number. The humble, sensitive, and diplomatic 2 symbolizes its resilient strength: It is easy to depress, and to squash, yet it is flexible, and, like a spring, the 2 rises again, much easier and quicker than does the 1.

The 3 represents self-expression, verbal art, enthusiasm, and inspiration. It is the most imaginative of all numbers, and this is reflected in its open and inviting shape, which is ready to embrace anything in this world and the world above.

The square-shaped 4 is down-to-earth. It sits on the ground, and it is a foundation and a rock of support for other numbers. It represents limitations (often self-imposed) and discipline; it is never a dreamer.

The 5 is the most dynamic of all numbers, and the symbol seems to turn around its central point. The 5 will try anything at least once, and, true to its nature, is open front and back.

The number 6 is the most loving and sacrificing of all numbers. It is the mother/fatherhood number, and it seems pregnant with love.

The 7 is the thinker and the hermit. It is the seeker of truth, and it reminds me of a wise old man with an outstretched arm. In his hand he holds a lamp, shining its light in search of answers.

The 8 represents the balance between the spiritual and the material world, and the symbol reflects heaven and earth in the two circles stacked on top of each other.

The 9 completes the circle. Like the 6, it is a very loving number, but where the 6 sends its love to family, friends, and the community, the 9 gives its love to the world. It is the humanitarian.

As you apply the numbers to specific people and situations, their many nuances will be revealed to you. Soon you will recognize that numbers are not only illuminating, but also fun.

In order to introduce you to the personalities of the numbers, I have provided a short summary of their characteristics, listed below. Also, certain double-digit numbers have specific meanings. These are known as Master numbers (11 and 22), and Karmic Debt numbers (13, 14, 16, and 19). They are also explained below.

The 1 is the most independent, unconventional, and individualistic of all numbers. It represents the beginning, the source, the innovator, the originator, and the uniqueness of the individualist. It is masculine, and it possesses a strong sense of courage and leadership. It is ambitious and goal-oriented. It has direction, and it does not doubt its course of action. It is stubborn, and it has strong opinions about right and wrong. It is a high energy, dynamic force that drives relentlessly towards its destiny. It is the instigator.

The 2 is the most gentle of all numbers, and represents cooperation, diplomacy, and tact. It is the power behind the throne; it is a supportive number, and it often plays the role of advisor. It is very feminine and subtle. The 2 is loving, vulnerable, and humble. It loves music and harmony in any form. It dislikes direct confrontation, is easily hurt, and does not handle criticism well. However, it is extremely resilient. It is the peacemaker.

The 3 is the most playful of all numbers. It is creative, inspirational, and motivating. Self-expression and communication are its central qualities. It is a happy-go-lucky number, and it is both optimistic and enthusiastic. Its energy is expansive and outward moving, and often scattered. It lifts up those around it; it enjoys life and doesn't take things too seriously. It is the sunshine number.

The 4 is the most practical of all numbers, with a sharp eye for details. It is orderly, systematic, methodical, and precise. It is reliable, punctual, and dependable. It does what it says it will do. It is honest, trustworthy, and totally without artifice. It is rigid, and it dislikes changes. It needs predictability, and it likes habits and rituals. It forms the foundation of every enterprise. It is the rock and the cornerstone.

The 5 is the most dynamic of all numbers. It is persuasive; a promoter and a salesperson par-excellence. It is versatile and adaptable. It is the experimenter and the explorer. It is also bright, quick-witted, and a straight-shooter with extraordinary reflexes. It is the juggler of many projects, and it is easily distracted with a love for sensual pleasures and immediate gratification. It is adventurous and courageous; the traveler's number.

The 6 is the most loving of all numbers. It is harmonious with all other numbers, and is committed, caring, sympathetic, protective, and nurturing, as well as responsible, self-sacrificing, and undemanding. It is domestic, marriage- and family-oriented, and community conscious. It is the teacher and the healer. The 6 cares for those who are weaker. It is visually artistic, creative, and a craftsperson. It is also the mother/fatherhood number.

The 7 is the most spiritual of all numbers. It is the seeker of truth, and is mental, analytical, focused, contemplative, and meditative. It is the accumulator of knowledge and wisdom, and the intellectual and abstract thinker. It is insightful and understanding, self-oriented, and often withdrawn. It is an inward, interior journey. It is the scientist, philosopher, preacher, scholar, and sage. It is reflectivity, aloneness, and quiet contentment. It is the hermit's number.

The 8 is the most result-oriented of all numbers. It represents the balance between the material and the spiritual world. It is a powerful, ambitious, and money-conscious number, but it is also generous. It understands money as a tool. It is the leader and the businessperson, with big dreams and big plans. It is the overseer and the manager. It is strength and the perseverance to see things through. It is the gambler. It is understanding, forgiving, and broad-minded. It is the visionary's number.

The 9 is the most humanitarian of all numbers. It is effort and sacrifice without the need for reward. It is giving, sharing, loving, and caring. It is the statesperson, politician, lawyer, writer, philosopher, and above all, the idealist. It is worldwide consciousness, genius, and a synthesizer. It is creative and artistic. It is the architect, landscaper, and designer; a combiner of colors and materials. It is aloof, noble, aristocratic, and a healer of the many.

The numbers 1 through 9 represent the full scope of human characteristics. They are the nine archetypes that, combined in an endless variety, form the basis of each individual's unique personality in much the same way that just three primal colors form the basis of millions of colors found in this universe.

THE MASTER NUMBERS

There are two double-digit numbers that, while they are rooted in the single-digit numbers, require special emphasis and attention. These are 11 and 22. They are called Master numbers because they possess more potential than other numbers. They are highly charged, difficult to handle, and require time, maturity, and great effort to integrate into one's personality.

The 11 is the most intuitive of all numbers. It represents illumination; a channel to the subconscious; insight without rational thought; and sensitivity, nervous energy, shyness, and impracticality. It is a dreamer. The 11 has all the aspects of the 2, enhanced and charged with charisma, leadership, and inspiration. It is a number with inborn duality, which creates dynamism, inner conflict, and other catalyses with its mere presence. It is a number that, when not focused on some goal beyond itself, can be turned inward to create fears and phobias. The 11 walks the edge between greatness and self-destruction. Its potential for growth, stability, and personal power lies in its acceptance of intuitive understanding, and of spiritual truths. For the 11, such peace is not found so much in logic, but in faith. It is the psychic's number.

The 22 is the most powerful of all numbers. It is often called the Master Builder. The 22 can turn the most ambitious of dreams into reality. It is potentially the most successful of all numbers. It has many of the inspirational and intuitive insights of the 11, combined with the practicality and methodical nature of the 4. It is unlimited, yet disciplined. It sees the archetype, and brings it down to earth in some material form. It has big ideas, great plans, idealism, leadership, and enormous self-confidence. If not practical, 22s waste their potential. Like the 11, the 22 can easily shrink from its own ambition, causing difficult interior pressures. Both the 11 and the 22 experience the pressure-cooker effect very strongly, particularly at an early age. It must work toward the realization of goals that are larger than personal ambition. The 22 serves the world in a practical way.

You will learn more about the Master numbers throughout this book.

THE KARMIC DEBT NUMBERS

Numerology is based on the ancient idea that each of us is a spiritual being, or a soul, who incarnates on the earth many times in order to further evolve toward higher states of awareness.

During our long evolutionary path of many incarnations, we have accumulated a wealth of wisdom, and have made many good choices that benefit us in future lifetimes. We have also made mistakes, and have sometimes abused the gifts we have been given. To rectify such errors, we may take on an additional burden in order to learn a particular lesson that we failed to learn in previous lifetimes. In numerology, this burden is called a Karmic Debt.

The numbers that indicate a Karmic Debt are 13, 14, 16, and 19. These double-digit numbers take on great significance when they are found in the core numbers (the most important numbers including Life Path, Expression, Heart's Desire, Personality, and Birth Day), and in the various cycles during the course of your lifetime. Each has its own unique characteristics, and its own particular difficulties.

When you are calculating your chart—especially your core numbers and different cycles—you may encounter the numbers 1, 4, 5, or 7. These single-digit numbers can be arrived at by adding a variety of two-digit numbers. The number 1 can be arrived at, for example, by combining the double-digit numbers of 10 (1 + 0 = 1), 19 (1 + 9 = 10, 1 + 0 = 1), 28, 37, 46—all of which total to 10, and then to 1. However, only in the case of 19 is a Karmic Debt indicated. Karmic Debts are also associated with the numbers 4, 5, and 7. These numbers can be preceded by an array of two-digit numbers, but when the 4 is preceded by a 13; or when the 5 is preceded by a 14; or the 7 by a 16; a Karmic Debt is also read as part of the single-digit interpretation.

A Karmic Debt can be found in different places in the chart, as a result of totals based on your date of birth, for instance, or calculations based on the letters of your name. This means that two people with a 16 Karmic Debt that is located in different places in the chart, express it very differently. Thus, all I can do here is lay out the general characteristics of the Karmic Debt, and some broad guidelines for dealing with it.

13 Karmic Debt

Those with the 13 Karmic Debt will work very hard to accomplish any task. Obstacles stand in their way, and must be overcome time and again. One may often feel burdened and frustrated by the seeming futility of one's efforts. There may be a desire to surrender to the difficulties and simply give up on the goal, believing it was impossible to attain in the first place. Some with the 13 Karmic Debt fall to laziness and negativity. But efforts are not futile, and success is well within reach. One simply must work hard, and persevere in order to reach the goal. Many highly successful people in all walks of life, including business, art, and athletics, have a 13 Karmic Debt.

The key to succeeding with the 13 is focus. Very often, people with the 13 Karmic Debt do not concentrate or direct their energies in one specific direction, or on a single task, but scatter their energies over many projects and jobs, none of which amount to very much. A temptation with the 13 is to take shortcuts for quick success. Too often, that easy success doesn't come, causing regret and the desire to give up. The result is a poor self-image, and the belief that one is incapable of amounting to very much.

In order to focus, you must maintain order in your life. Order is essential to success. You must maintain a schedule, keep appointments, and follow through. Keep your environment neat and under control, and never procrastinate. If you sustain a steady and consistent effort, you will realize much reward.

14 Karmic Debt

The 14 Karmic Debt arises from previous lifetimes during which human freedom has been abused. Those with a 14 Karmic Debt are forced to adapt to ever-changing circumstances and unexpected occurrences. There is an acute danger of falling victim to abuse of drugs, alcohol, and overindulgence in sensual pleasures, such as food and sex. You must put the reins on yourself. Modesty in all affairs is crucial to overcoming this Karmic Debt.

Also important is the need to maintain order in life, and to establish one's own emotional stability. You must also be willing to adapt to the unexpected occurrences of life, all the while maintaining your focus on your goals and dreams. Flexibility and adaptability are at the very core of this struggle.

Orderliness in one's immediate environment is crucial to maintaining clarity and focus. Mental and emotional stability must be attained in order to avoid being thrown about by the changing fortunes in the external environment.

But the key to the 14 Karmic Debt is commitment. Life will resemble a roller coaster ride, but it will always travel in the right direction if one's heart is set on what is true and good. Set yourself a high goal, maintain order wherever possible in your life, avoid excessive sensory indulgence, and maintain faith. Above all, do not give up on your goals and dreams.

Those with the 14 Karmic Debt will experience life to the fullest, and as long as they maintain a high dream, they will achieve success and great spiritual development.

16   Karmic Debt

The 16 Karmic Debt—wherever it shows up on the chart—means destruction of the old and birth of the new. The 16 is about the fall of the ego, and all that it has built for itself. It is a watershed, a cleansing. All that has been constructed, and all that serves to separate the person from the source of life is destroyed. Through the 16, reunion with the great spirit is accomplished.

This can be a painful process, because it usually comes after much ego inflation. This results in a struggle between the ego and the divine will. Life presents challenges to your grand plans, which can be resented and struggled against. It is a lost battle, and you will likely feel humbled in the face of the collapse that follows. This humility is the key to later success, however, because you will learn to follow the intimations of a higher reality. In the destruction of the old, a spiritual rebirth takes place with an entirely new awareness. This rebirth affects every area of your life. It is a life much the better for the fall.

Those with the 16 Karmic Debt must be careful of egotism. Very often, those with the 16 use their highly intuitive and refined intellect to look down upon others, and view the rest of the world as inferior. This causes acute alienation and loneliness. In addition, it invites retribution, for the egotist is humbled more harshly than any other.

When the 16 is in one of the core numbers, this process of destruction and rebirth is a continual cycle that actually serves to bring you into higher consciousness and closer union with the source of life.

The 16 Karmic Debt can be a path of progress and great spiritual growth if it is looked at properly. One develops great faith by placing one's life in the hands of God. Through such faith, gratitude and peace are firmly established.

19 Karmic Debt

The person with the 19 Karmic Debt will learn independence and the proper use of power. You will be forced to stand up for yourself, and often be left to stand alone. Difficulties will be faced and overcome through personal struggle.

One of the central lessons for people with the 19 Karmic Debt is that you stubbornly resist help. Much of your independence is self-imposed; you simply don't want to listen to others, or to accept the help or advice of others. The 19 Karmic Debt can become a self-imposed prison if you do not open up to the reality or interdependence and the mutual need for love.

The most important lesson for the 19 Karmic Debt is: While you seek to stand on your own feet, you are still a human being, deeply connected with others, and in need of the support, assistance, and human understanding that all people need. Those with the 19 Karmic Debt will learn the hard way that "no man is an island," and that we are, indeed, "all bits of the main!"

As you can see, numbers represent both the best and the worst of human nature. Numerology, in its own unique way, helps you to gain insight about your personal make-up, and offers you the opportunity to take advantage of your strengths and overcome your weaknesses.

Numerology deals with "the inner you;" the important part of you that is often hidden behind concepts and expectations that are inaccurate or incomplete. Your perception of yourself is necessarily limited because you cannot help but be subjective in your view of yourself. Numerology enables you to look at yourself from a more objective angle, revealing aspects of your personality that you were not aware of or whose influence and potential you had underestimated. Numerology is a powerful tool to self-discovery and self-improvement, and it enhances the quality of your life.

Chapter 2

Your Date of Birth— A Doorway in Time

We don't do what we want and yet we are responsible for what we are—that is the fact.

—Jean Paul Sartre

I f ever there was a moment of total transformation, it was the moment of your birth. In that instant, you stepped through a door in time into a new reality—the reality of human life. You left behind the memory of what was before, and entered the physical realm in the purest condition: untouched by this world; not yet influenced; not yet inhibited; and free of concepts, expectations, judgments, and self-consciousness. (Small wonder that everybody around you instantly fell in love with you!)

Yet, even at that moment, you were a person with your own unique character, as unique as your DNA. Everything that is you existed in potential, much like a play that is about to begin.

Your life is indeed like a play. Birth is the raising of the curtain; death the curtain's descent. The play has evolved through various stages of preparation, but does not really begin until you are born. When all the players go on stage, they have been prepared for their parts. Their characters are outlined, and the stage is set. At the moment the curtain is raised, the play itself exists as a potential within the characters, the director, the musicians, and the audience.

In the same way, the moment of your birth provides that broad outline for your life. Your entire life exists as a potential that has been prepared for. You have ultimate freedom to do with your life as you like: to fulfill its potential completely, or to make some smaller version of yourself. It all depends upon your effort and commitment. You make the decisions to fulfill, to whatever extent, the potential life that exists within you. That is your choice. In this sense, the possible you is implicit during the moment of your birth.

THE LIFE PATH NUMBER

The most important number in your numerology chart is based on the date of your birth, the moment when the curtain goes up in your life. This number is called the Life Path number. It can be compared to the plot of a potential play. The Life Path number gives us a broad outline of the opportunities, challenges, and lessons we will encounter in this lifetime.

How to Find Your Life Path Number

Your Life Path number is the sum of the month of your birth, plus the day of your birth, plus the year of your birth.

To find your Life Path number, begin by turning the month, day, and year of your birth into single digit numbers. For example, let's say you were born on December 25, 1964. December is the twelfth month of the year. To turn 12 into a single-digit number, add the 1 and the 2 of 12 to get the 3. December is therefore a 3 month.

To turn the twenty-fifth day into a single-digit number, add the 2 and the 5 of 25 to arrive at 7. The number 25 is therefore a 7.

To turn 1964 into a single-digit number, add the $1 + 9 + 6 + 4$ to get 20. Then add the 2 and the 0 of 20 to get 2.

Now, to find your Life Path number, add these three single-digit numbers together. In the example, I add the 3, 7, and 2 $(3 + 7 + 2)$ and arrive at 12. The 12 is reduced to 3 by adding 1 and 2.

Another way to illustrate these steps is as follows:

December = 12 (the twelfth month) = $1 + 2 =$	3
25 (the twenty-fifth day) = $2 + 5 =$	7
$1964 = 1 + 9 + 6 + 4 = 20; 20 = 2 + 0 =$	2
	—
Total	$12 = 1 + 2 = 3$

The Life Path number is 3.

The only correct way of arriving at the Life Path number is by turning the month, day, and year of your birth into single-digit numbers first, and then adding the three single digits together. Never add the three whole numbers $(12 + 25 + 1964)$.

Only by adding single-digit numbers can you accurately arrive at the Master numbers (11 and 22) that may be in your chart. As explained in

Chapter 1, Master numbers are the only two-digit numbers that are not reduced to single-digits when calculating the chart.

For example, let's say you were born on May 29, 1948. Using the correct way of calculating the Life Path number, we would do the following:

May is the 5th month =	5	
29 = 2 + 9 =	11	(Eleven is a Master number, and it is not reduced.)
1948 = 1 + 9 + 4 + 8 =	22	(This is, again a Master number, and thus not reduced.)
	—	
Total	38	38 = 3 + 8 = 11

A Life Path of 11 is a Master number, and it is not reduced.

The wrong method of calculating the Life Path is to total the whole numbers first, and then reduce. This results in an incorrect Life Path number. The example illustrates this point:

May =	5
29 =	29
1948 =	1948
	—
Total	1982

1982 = 1 + 9 + 8 + 2 = 20; 20 is reduced to 2 by adding 2 + 0.

Using this method, the Life Path would be 2, not 11. You would have missed the Master number.

In my lectures, I often encounter people who go to great lengths to manipulate the math in order to place a Master number in their chart. This is based on a misunderstanding of the Master numbers.

Master numbers are extremely challenging for those who have them in their charts. They are highly paradoxical in nature. On one hand, they connote great potential, and the presence of some highly developed ability. On the other hand, they represent a great deal of inner tension, which originates from a deep desire to achieve some high ideal. The presence of a Master number suggests the influence of an archetype, or a highly focused energy, that directs one's life toward a goal.

The term Master number is not given to the 11 and 22 because they are masters in the family of numbers, but because they symbolize the presence of a powerful energy within the psyche of the individual. Because that energy is so powerful, it can easily take control of a person's life. In effect, it becomes the person's master. It is the challenge of the individual with the master number to take charge of that energy, and to use it according to your own choices.

Understanding and using a Master number is a gradual process, and it is usually not until maturity is reached that you take full control of your Master number. It is at this point that the Master number becomes truly rewarding.

1 Life Path

If you have a 1 Life Path, you are a born leader. You insist on your right to make up your own mind, and you demand freedom of thought and action.

You have drive and determination. You don't let anything or anyone stand in your way once you are committed to your goal. You assume your responsibility to be the protector and provider for those you love. You demand respect and attention, and you become irritated and even domineering when important things do not go your way. You need to feel in command of important undertakings, and you resist supportive roles. You seek the foreground and the limelight.

You are exceptionally creative and original, and you possess a touch of the unusual. Your approach to problems is unique, and you have the courage to wander from the beaten path. You can be impatient with your shortcomings and those of others. You are very concerned with your status, and you foster the appearance of success and self-satisfaction. The need to appear well-off propels you to strive for growth, success, and the finer things of life.

You should watch out for selfishness, conceit, and an overconcern with appearance. You must guard against overzealous behavior, anger, and aggressiveness. If these qualities are not brought under control, you could become excessively domineering, vindictive, and even violent.

You perform best when you are left to your own devices. Ideally you should own your own business in construction or crafts, and you should be your own boss. Hold fast to your life's dream, and work with the determination you possess to realize it.

You can become overly stressed by your driven nature. Be careful about the food you eat, and maintain an exercise program you enjoy. Competition sports are often a healthy outlet for a person with your drive, particularly sports that involve running and swimming.

Don't let pride and overconfidence be your masters. Remember, your talents and abilities are a gift from a higher source, which should promote gratitude and humility, rather than pride and conceit.

More often than not, a person with a 1 Life Path will achieve much in life as long as the drive, creativity, originality, and pioneering spirit are fully employed. Your talents are varied and your potential for success is considerable. You may be attracted to business, the military, or governmental institutions, as long as you have a leadership role and the possibility to do things your way.

 Life Path

The key word in your nature is peacemaker. You are extremely sensitive, perceptive, and a bit shy. These qualities are both your strengths and your weaknesses, for while you possess enormous sensitivity to your feelings and those of others, that same sensitivity can cause you to hold back and repress your considerable talents. Sensitivity and perceptiveness are among your many fine qualities.

Because you intuitively know what people want or feel, you can be extremely diplomatic and tactful. You are also patient and cooperative. You work well with groups, and you somehow find a way of creating harmony among diverse opinions.

You enjoy music and poetry, and require a harmonious environment.

You have an eye for beauty, and a fine sense of balance and rhythm. You have healing capabilities, especially in such fields as massage, acupuncture, physical therapy, and counseling. However, your sensitivity can also be your downfall. Your extremely delicate ego bruises easily, and you can make too much of someone else's thoughtless remarks or criticisms.

Because you are easily hurt, you may tend to withhold your own thoughts and contributions to the matter at hand. This can cause you considerable resentment and anger. Too often, you run from confrontation to avoid a battle.

When you employ your considerable inner strength, you will discover your enormous power and abilities to direct difficult situations toward your own goals. It is the awareness of your inner strength that will give you the courage to use your own personal power when it is needed.

You are a sensitive and passionate lover; your perceptiveness makes you aware of your partner's needs and desires, which you are able to fulfill with almost magical delicacy. However, when you feel you have been mistreated or jilted, you can react with devastating power, sometimes using personal criticisms vindictively.

Your awareness, diplomatic skills, and organizational talents give you the ability to bring off difficult tasks. You willingly step out of the limelight to facilitate the success of your endeavor. In truth, you are often the power behind the throne. However, you often do not receive the credit you deserve for the fine work you've done, or your role is underestimated, and your accomplishments overlooked. Rather than brood over your losses, you need to confront those who make less of your contributions, and stand up for your accomplishments.

You need security and comfort, quiet settings, and the company of loved ones. You are a perfectionist when it comes to your home and work environment. You have excellent taste, which is obvious in your private surroundings. You are a fine companion and possess a good sense of humor. Friends seek you out for your calming and peaceful company. You are a safe haven to other sensitive people who recognize your compassion and understanding. When you have found your niche in life, you have all the talents and intelligence for great success. Seek out work that allows your sensitive nature to flourish. Be the glue that binds others together.

Counseling, teaching, and healing are the areas that offer you success and satisfaction. You are also uniquely suited for a career in music, architecture, advertising, agriculture, industrial design, fashion, repairing watches and other fine machinery. Politics and law allow you to use your considerable talents in negotiation and problem solving.

 Life Path

As a 3 Life Path, you possess a great talent for creativity and self-expression. Many writers, poets, actors, and musicians are born under the 3 Life Path. You are witty, possess a gift for gab, and savor the limelight. Your talent for the expressive arts is so abundant that you may well have felt drawn to becoming an artist while still very young. However, your artistic abilities can only be developed through discipline and commitment to the true development of your talent.

Thanks to your gift for self-expression, you can be the life of the party, and the center of attention. However, you could easily squander your talent by becoming a social butterfly.

Your creativity is the gift that can give you the comfort and luxury you desire, but not without continual focus and discipline.

You are optimistic, and you possess the resilience to overcome many setbacks. You are socially active, popular, and inspire people with your sunny happy-go-lucky attitude. You can be generous to a fault. Many people born under the 3 Life Path have difficulty handling money, because they can be disorganized, and not particularly serious about their responsibilities.

You are emotional and vulnerable. When hurt, you withdraw into a cloud of silence, eventually emerging from your reticence with jokes and laughter that cover up your true feelings. You can become moody and cynical when depressed. You can succumb to sarcastic remarks, which can be painful to those around you. When used positively, your talent for self-expression can be a great inspirational force in the world, uplifting others, and bringing much success and happiness to you.

Life Path

The 4 Life Path is practical and down-to-earth, with strong ideas about right and wrong. You are orderly and organized, systematic and controlled, and you are decisive and methodical, employing a step-by-step rational approach to problem solving. Once committed, you do not give up easily.

You are not one for get-rich-quick schemes. Rather, you use hard work and long hours while building a business or career; you seek to establish a solid foundation. Precise, tenacious, and persevering, you have great potential for success, but only after putting out effort, and by overcoming the limitations you so often encounter.

Justice and honesty are sacred to you. You are reliable and dependable, a cornerstone in the community. Though not an idealist, you are willing to work for a better world in a realistic way. However, you can be rigid in your ideas, and sometimes too quick in judging your fellow man.

You are loyal to those you love, and work well with others. It is important that while being part of a team, you have your own responsibility and well-defined task, but you perform better when your responsibilities are not overlapping with those of others.

Your potential for success is particularly good in areas such as banking, accounting, management, organization, building, agriculture, science, and the legal fields.

You have to be careful not to be bossy and rude. You possess rare discipline and perseverance, and not everyone can keep up with you.

You can handle money carefully, and you like the security of a nest egg. Your love of work often leads you into a career early in life. Because of your methodical nature, you can easily become rigid and stuck in convention. You can also be overly cautious when changes are necessary. This can cause you to miss opportunities that present themselves. You must cultivate flexibility in your character.

You are well-suited for marriage, and often become a responsible, loving, parent. However, anything that violates your profound sense of order, such as separation or divorce, can be a shattering experience for you. You easily become obsessed and even vengeful, seeking your own definition of justice. You are courageous and a true survivor. You are a builder and the foundation of any enterprise. Your hard work and practical, traditional values pay off to provide you with the rewards you seek and deserve.

 Life Path

The key to your personality is freedom. You love travel, adventure, variety, and meeting new people. You possess the curiosity of a cat, and you long to experience all of life. You love to be involved in several things at the same time, as long as you are not tied down to any one area.

You like change, new things, and new horizons. You make friends easily, and your personality is upbeat and often inspiring, attracting people from all walks of life.

You have a way with words, and an uncanny ability to motivate others. Highly suitable vocations for you include sales, promotion, entertainment, investment, science, medicine, the occult, public service, and all careers that require travel and verbal skills. A person with a 5 Life Path is often comfortable in front of an audience, particularly as master of ceremonies or in comedy.

You are sensual and you love to taste all of life. Sex, food, and other sensory experiences are essential to the enjoyment of your life. You find it difficult to commit to one relationship, but once committed, you can be as faithful as an old dog.

You likely lack discipline and order. You can also be impulsive, doing or expressing things you regret later. Freedom and a need for adventure sometimes are not properly controlled by those born with this Life Path, which can cause problems with drug abuse, overindulgence in food or sex, or general abuse of the gift of life.

You are multitalented and possess a variety of diverse abilities. However, discipline and focus are the true keys to your success. Without these, many of the tasks you begin will remain unfinished, and you will fail to realize the true fruits of your abilities. With hard work and perseverance, the sky is the limit.

You may have been perceived as a wild child by adults, and as a source of concern by your family. However, do not be obliged to hurry your choice of career. You are often a late bloomer, and you need to experience life before you can truly know and commit to your heart's desire.

Your challenge is to learn the true meaning of freedom. Change is constant in your world, requiring adaptability and courage. Try to maintain an exercise program; keep your body in shape and limber. The flexibility and durability of your body will promote security and confidence within you.

You yearn for freedom, and self-employment attracts you powerfully. Your challenge is to settle into one area in order to cultivate your ability sufficiently to earn a living, and to attain success. Once you find your niche, the motivation and inspiration you supply to others will bring you much in return. You will find your friends and colleagues supporting and promoting you on the road to success.

6   Life Path

You possess great compassion and you seek to be of service to others. You have concern for the weak and the downtrodden. You are a healer and a helper to others. You are capable of giving comfort to those in need, and you frequently offer a shoulder for others to cry on.

Your task in life is to develop the tools necessary to be truly helpful to others, rather than to simply be a sympathetic ear. You must find the balance between help and interference. In the same way, you must learn the delicate art of the counselor who knows when to leave the struggle to others, and when to avoid taking away the necessary experiences and lessons of life. You are naturally balanced. Therefore, you are well-equipped to support and ground others in times of trial.

It is in your nature to take on responsibility—you often fill the void left by others—and you do not turn away from personal sacrifice. At times, you may feel overburdened by the travails of others. However, the love others bestow upon you is your well-deserved reward.

You try to maintain harmony within the family or group, balancing and fusing divergent forces. You seek marriage, and you are often a wonderful parent, offering warmth, protection, and understanding to children.

You are generous, kind, and attractive. You are often admired, even adored, which baffles you. You are humble, and yet you carry a deep pride. You move well and gracefully, but will have to work to stay in shape. Seek out physical exercise, and limit the sweets and dairy you crave to keep yourself from becoming plump and round.

When young, you must be careful not to choose partners for the wrong reasons. Do not let sentimentality influence your decisions, especially those involving the choice of a spouse. You need to be needed, but you must learn to discriminate between those who you can help and others who are made weaker by your care. After all, it is in your nature to be attracted to the weaker brothers and sisters among us.

The temptation and the danger for you is to think of yourself as the savior of the world, carrying the burdens of others on your shoulders.

You are blessed with musical talent, as well as talent in the visual and performing arts. However, your creativity may be suppressed due to your willingness to sacrifice, or your inability to fully appreciate your talents. This is not to say that you cannot excel in these areas; on the contrary, you have the talent, and with effort you can make a success in a number of artistic fields.

You also have enormous talent in business. You are blessed with a great deal of charm and charisma, which you use effectively to attract the people and the support you need.

Other vocations that offer you potential for success are mostly found in the areas of healing, teaching, hospitality, management of apartment complex or government institutions, and anything related to animals.

7   Life Path

The 7 Life Path is the searcher and the seeker of truth. You have a clear and compelling sense of yourself as a spiritual being. As a result, your goal is devoted to investigations into the unknown, and to finding the answers to the mysteries of life.

You are well-equipped to handle your task. You possess a fine mind; you are an analytical thinker who is capable of great concentration and theoretical insight. You enjoy research and putting the pieces of an intellectual puzzle together. Once you have enough pieces in place, you are capable of highly creative insight, and of practical solutions to problems.

You enjoy your solitude, preferring to work alone. You need time to contemplate your ideas without the intrusion of other people's thoughts. You are a lone wolf; a person who lives by your own ideas and methods. As a result, close associations are difficult for you to form and to keep, especially marriage. You need your space and privacy, which, when violated, can cause you great frustration and irritation. When your life is balanced, however, you are both charming and attractive. You can be the life of a party, and you enjoy performing before an audience. You enjoy displaying your wit and knowledge, which makes you attractive to others, especially the opposite sex. But you have distinct limits. While you are generous in social situations, sharing your attention and energy freely, you are keenly aware of the need to come off stage, and to return to the solitude of your lair. You associate peace with the unobtrusive privacy of your world. Therefore, intimacy is difficult for you, because you guard your inner world like a mother lion does her cubs.

However, all this privacy and solitude can cause isolation and loneliness.

You can be aware of an emptiness in your life, a part of you that yearns for company and close companionship that may be unsatisfied.

If isolation is brought to the extreme, you can become cynical and suspicious. You can develop hidden, selfish motives, which people may sense, and this may cause them to be uncomfortable around you. You must guard against becoming too withdrawn and too independent, thus shutting out the love of others, and keeping you from experiencing the true joy of friendship and close companionship.

You must especially watch out for selfishness and egocentricity; thinking of yourself as the center of the universe, the only person who really matters. Social contact gives you perspective on yourself and on life, while too much isolation can make you too narrow, and even shut off from the rest of the world.

Secretly, you may feel jealous of the easy relationships formed by others; you may perceive others as less inhibited than you, or more free to express themselves. You may harshly criticize yourself for not being more gregarious, powerful, or capable of greater leadership.

Your challenge in life is to maintain your independence without feeling isolated or ineffectual. You must hold fast to your unique view of the world, while at the same time being open to others, and to the knowledge they have to offer.

With your abilities to learn, analyze, and seek out answers to life's important questions, you have the potential for enormous growth and success in life. By the time you reach middle age, you will radiate refinement and wisdom. Pythagorus, who lived more than 2,500 years ago and is often called the father of numerology, loved the 7 for its great spiritual potential.

The person with a 7 Life Path often finds success and satisfaction in business, science, religion, insurance, invention, the occult, and anything related to research.

Life Path

Those with the 8 Life Path are gifted with natural leadership and the capacity to accumulate great wealth. You have great talent for management in all areas of life, especially in business and financial matters. You understand the material world; you intuitively know what makes virtually any enterprise work. Your talent lies not with the bookkeeping or petty management, but with the greater vision, its purpose, and its long-range goals.

You are a visionary, and you are a bit reckless. You possess the ability to inspire people to join you in your quest, but often they are incapable of seeing what you see. Therefore, those around you need your continual guidance, inspiration, and encouragement. You must prod them into action, and direct them along the lines of your vision.

You attract financial success more than any other Life Path, but effort is required.

Your challenges in life are to achieve a high degree of detachment, and to understand that power and influence must be used for the benefit of mankind. Those born with the number 8 Life Path who do not understand the real and relative value of money, are bound to suffer the consequences of greed; they run the risk of losing it all. You must learn to bounce back from failures and defeats. You have the character and resilience of a true survivor. It is not uncommon for a person with your Life Path to experience major reverses, including bankruptcy and financial failure, but you also have the talent and the sheer guts to make more than one fortune, and to build many successful enterprises. More than most people, your failures in marriage can be extremely expensive for you.

Despite the difficulties that life presents, you will experience the satisfaction that comes from material wealth, and the power that comes with it.

Business, finance, real estate, law, science (particularly history, archeology, and physics), publishing, and the management of large institutions are among the vocational fields that suit you best. You are naturally attracted to positions of influence and leadership—politics, social work, and teaching are among the many other areas where your abilities can shine. Civil government, sports, and journalism are other areas that require the characteristics of the 8.

You are a good judge of character, which aids you well in attracting the right people to you. Most 8s like large families, and they sometimes tend to keep others dependent longer than necessary. Although jovial in nature, you are not demonstrative in showing your love and affection. The desire for luxury and comfort is especially strong in you. Status is very important. You must be careful to avoid living above your means.

Your Life Path treads that dangerous ground where power lies—and can corrupt. You may become too self-important, arrogant, and domineering, thinking that your way is the only way. This leads inevitably to isolation and conflict.

The people you run the risk of hurting most are those you love: your family and friends.

Be careful of becoming stubborn, intolerant, overbearing, and impatient. These characteristics may be born early in the life of an 8 Life Path, who often learns these negative traits after suffering under a tyrannical parent, or a family burdened by repressive religious or intellectual dogmas. Those with the 8 Life Path usually possess a strong physique, which is a symptom of their inherent strength and resiliency.

9 Life Path

You are philanthropic, humanitarian, socially conscious, and deeply concerned about the state of the world. You have great compassion and idealism. You are a Utopian and will spend your life trying to realize some aspect of your Utopian dream, sacrificing money, time, and energy for a better world. It is in giving that you will find much satisfaction.

You have a broad outlook on life. You tend to see the big picture, rather than minute details.

You naturally attract people from all walks of life who can fit into your larger plans, and who take over the areas you find uninteresting. The person with a 9 Life Path is rarely prejudiced and rarely accepts others' social biases. Instead, you evaluate people on the basis of what they can do for the larger cause. You are the true egalitarian. You are imaginative and creative, especially at harmoniously arranging the beauty that is already potential in the environment. These abilities can lead you into such fields as interior decorating, landscape art, and photography. But because of your strong social consciousness, you can be an effective politician, lawyer, judge, minister, teacher, healer, or environmentalist. Vocations that require self-sacrifice, and that have a clear social impact, are common among 9s.

You are often disappointed by the realities of life: the shortcomings of others or yourself. Somehow you don't want to accept the imperfections of the world, a feeling that drives you constantly to try to improve upon it. But rather than be satisfied with your efforts, and those of others, you relentlessly push on, striving for greater accomplishments. You are often unsatisfied with the results. In short, you lack the perspective that would otherwise make it possible for you to enjoy life more fully, and to accept its natural limitations.

You have a controlled enthusiasm, and the ability to finish what you start.

A key to your personality is the necessity of sacrifice. You have to learn to let go of material possessions and relationships, the inherent lesson being that holding on too tightly to anything causes pain.

Money comes to you through mysterious or unexpected ways: inheritance, the benevolence of someone who was inspired by your work, or a lucky investment. Conversely, if you pursue money for its own sake, after giving up on your larger dreams, you're likely to find yourself empty-handed. The most successful and satisfying road for a 9 is giving, sharing, and sacrificing for a larger goal, without expecting anything in return. Your greatest chance at success is to tie your personal fortunes to an endeavor that makes the world a better place for others. Very often, this turns into a highly successful and lucrative enterprise, providing amply for you and your family. Your life rests on the axiom that the more you give, the bigger will be your reward.

You are romantic, but your love is more impersonal. You tend to be focused on your dreams.

When you are not in harmony with your true nature, you can fall to moodiness, or become aloof and withdrawn. You can become timid, uncertain, and ungrateful, putting the blame for your troubles on others or the world. You have a gift for examining your life objectively and at some distance. Be honest with yourself. By openly facing your shortcomings, as well as your strengths, you develop equilibrium. You are thus able to love, and to better understand yourself and all of life.

11 Life Path

You have the potential to be a source of inspiration and illumination for people. You possess an inordinate amount of energy and intuition. There is so much going on in your psyche that you are often misunderstood early in life, which makes you shy and withdrawn. You have far more potential than you know.

You galvanize every situation you enter. You inspire people, but without your conscious effort. Energy seems to flow through you without your control. This gives you both power, and sometimes, emotional turmoil.

You are a channel for information between the higher and the lower, between the realm of the archetype and the relative world. Ideas, thoughts, understanding, and insight can come to you without your having to go through a rational thought process. There seems to be a bridge, or connection, between your conscious and unconscious realms, that attunes you to a high level of intuition through which even psychic information can flow.

All of this amounts to a great capacity for invention. Many inventors, artists, religious leaders, prophets, and leading figures in history have had the 11 prominent in their chart.

Because you are so highly charged, you experience the consequences of a two-edged sword. You possess great abilities, but indulge in much self-reflection and self-criticism. You often feel highly self-conscious. You are aware on some level that you stand out. Even when you try to blend with your environment, you often feel conspicuous, alien, and out-of-place.

You are blessed with a message, or a specific role to play in life. But you must develop yourself sufficiently to take full advantage of that opportunity. Until that time, your inner development takes precedence over your ability to materialize the great undertaking you were chosen to perform. Consequently, 11s seem to develop slowly, but they simply have more to accomplish in their evolution than the average person. Thus, your real success does not usually begin until maturity, between the ages of thirty-five and forty-five, when you have progressed further along your path.

You may often be frustrated, largely because you have extremely high expectations of yourself. But these expectations can be unrealistic, and can prevent you from accomplishing anything. You can be very impractical, envisioning a skyscraper when all that was necessary was a two-story house.

You may also suffer from bouts of confusion and a lack of direction. This gives rise to loss of confidence, and the onset of deep depression. The cause of these emotional problems is your lack of understanding of your own sensitivity and potential. Your desire to achieve some great ambition is enormous. However, a lack of confidence in your own ability to realize this dream may cause you much frustration. You sense the enormous potential you possess, which requires equally enormous confidence in your ability to materialize your dream. Confidence is the key that unlocks your potential.

On a strictly physical level, you must protect your nervous system, which is inordinately vulnerable to stress, because of your acute sensitivity. Depression is often the result of long periods of stress that have gone unrelieved.

Seek out peaceful and harmonious environments, as well as relaxing music, and follow a healthful diet in order to restore balance and peace.

As an 11 Life Path, you are a highly charged version of the 2, and possess many of the characteristics and talents of that number.

You can be extremely diplomatic and tactful. You are also patient and cooperative. You work well with groups, and somehow find a way of creating harmony among diverse opinions.

You have an eye for beauty, and a fine sense of balance and rhythm. You have healing capabilities, especially in such fields as massage, acupuncture, physical therapy, and counseling. (All vocations noted under the 2 Life Path also suit you.)

Like the 2, you are a sensitive and passionate lover; your perceptiveness makes you aware of your partner's needs and desires, which you are able to fulfill with almost magical delicacy. However, when you feel you have been mistreated or jilted, you can react with devastating power, sometimes using personal criticisms vindictively.

You are a fine companion, and you possess a good sense of humor. When you have found your niche in life, and have begun to realize your true potential, your rewards will more than compensate for your trials earlier in life.

22 Life Path

You were born under the most powerful and potentially most successful of all Life Path numbers. It offers you the extremes of life's possibilities: On one hand, you have the potential to be the Master Builder, the person capable of perceiving something great in the archetypal world, and of manifesting it in the relative world. On the other hand, you can slip into the depths of obscurity, achieving little more than personal support.

Your power is delicate. It exists by virtue of your ideals and vision, which you must use to inspire others to join you in your dream. Only by marshalling collective forces are you able to bring together the necessary elements—people, ideas, resources—that will enable you to realize your goals.

Consequently, your goal is one that requires dramatic evolution. By being able to integrate seemingly conflicting characteristics within yourself—your inspiring vision and your natural tendency toward practicality, for example—you develop the talent to deal effectively with a great variety of people. This allows you to understand and to unite many differing peoples toward a single goal, melding them into a concerted whole. Your task in life is to unite the dream with the bottom line. In short, you are the visionary with your feet on the ground.

You are good at business and politics. You naturally understand large institutions, and have the ability to think and to act on an international scale. (You also share the vocations of the 4.)

You are gifted with uncommonly sound common sense. You are able to see the beauty and potential in a given idea, but also the practical methods that will bring it to fruition. Somehow, you understand the limitations of ideas—what will work and what will not. This is an intuitive gift that can evaluate possibilities on the basis of their practicality.

While in many aspects the 22 is the most promising number, it is also the most difficult to live up to. You have a great ambition, which can be a most difficult master, driving you to accomplish all that you are capable of.

You are a steady partner in any relationship. You offer sound advice and consistent emotional support. You do not suffer from flights of fancy, and you naturally resist the emotional heights. You are unconventional in thought and action, but tend to be traditional in appearance. You avoid airs and pretensions.

Your challenge is to share your vision, and to allow others to make their personal contributions. That requires flexibility on your part, perhaps your weakest characteristic. You often lack faith in the ability of others. Therefore, you tend to control people and situations, and are sometimes tempted to manipulate.

Your Life Path number is the most important number in your chart.

Whatever your personal history was before you came into this world, it brought you to this moment in time, ready to start on this path. From this point on, you continue your personal evolution within the limitations and opportunities of human existence. There will be experiences of every kind following your progress along this path, all of them reflected in your Life Path number. For this reason, the Life Path is sometimes called the Life Lesson, or the Destiny.

As we continue to explore the relationship between you and the numbers in your chart, you will realize how all the other numbers, those that are derived from your name, as well as those coming from your date of birth, are linked to, and limited by, the Life Path number. You might say that the Life Path number is the pie, and all the other numbers are the ingredients.

THE BIRTH DAY NUMBER

The day you were born bears great significance in understanding who you are and where your talents lie. The day of birth indicates some special talent you possess. It is a gift to you that will help you along your life's path. Your day of birth is one of your five core numbers, as mentioned in Chapter 1. It is the least significant of the core numbers, but perhaps the most finite in that it reveals a specific ability that you possess in a marked degree.

Your Birth Day number is the number of the day you were born, and is examined as both a single- and a double-digit number. The reason for this twofold way of looking at the number is that a double-digit Birth Day number suggests that you possess additional characteristics not directly revealed by the single-digit number. For example, a person born on day 15 can be said to have a 6 Birth Day number, but the double digits, the 1 and the 5, suggest other abilities and character traits not revealed by the 6 alone. The 15 brings very different underlying talents to the 6 than does the 24, which is derived from the 2 and the 4, also a 6, but is quite different in nature. This is particularly important when understanding the Birth Day number, and for that reason all thirty-one Birth Days are described separately below.

The symbol for a Birth Day number is a diamond with the number inside. (See Figure 3.1 on page 111.)

1 **Birth Day**

You are a leader. You have a great ambition and a strong drive for success. You are highly independent, and you dislike the restrictions of having to work with others. You easily become frustrated with the routine. You are a pioneer, a gambler, and an initiator. You are very creative; you possess a keen and rapid mind. You have excellent business instincts, and with the appropriate training, can run large organizations and big businesses.

You use information for a specific purpose. Knowledge is a practical tool in your hands; you dislike information or knowledge for its own sake.

You possess a broad vision and a great capacity for motivating others. You have great willpower. However, your opportunity for accomplishment is enormous. You are generally open to the ideas of others, but you can be extremely stubborn and hard-headed once you become attached to your plans.

Avoid laziness and procrastination. You are given to anger and frustration, and you have a tendency to force the issue at times when things are not developing as rapidly as you would like.

Your determination, willpower, and inventiveness are the keys to your success, and will likely bring you much personal reward and financial gain.

2   Birth Day

You are very sensitive, intuitive, and diplomatic. You are aware of your surroundings, and easily influenced by your environment. You love beauty and attention. Your sensitivity makes you highly emotional and vulnerable to being hurt. You can fall victim to depression and lack of confidence.

Your talents lie in personal relations and diplomatic skills. You are keenly aware of what is on the minds of others, and you can usually adjust to create peace and harmony with others. In the same way, you possess the art of a diplomat, helping others to find the middle ground or area of agreement. You may also possess artistic and musical ability.

You are warm and affectionate, and you need the same from your close friends and loved ones. You want to be hugged and cuddled. There is a tendency to fall into childhood patterns when giving and receiving affection. You like to be made to feel secure and safe.

You are very cooperative, and you work best in partnerships. You enjoy being the power behind the throne, rather than the figure on the stage. You are modest and kind. You have great diplomatic skills. Your intuition allows you to perceive what another wants even before he or she says it.

You can continue a project better than you can start it. You are very attentive to details. You need harmonious and peaceful environments. Without them, you can easily become stressed and high-strung.

You are the glue that keeps important projects and groups together. While you may not get all the credit you deserve, you are indispensable in any endeavor.

3 Birth Day

You have a highly developed creative talent. You are an artist at heart. You could excel in writing, and visual or performing arts. If you are not professionally involved in one of these areas, you should consider taking up art as a hobby.

You are highly imaginative and quick-witted, and you possess the gift of gab. You have great enthusiasm. Others find you inspiring and charming. You are a wonderful salesperson. You are friendly, sociable, affectionate, and loving. You possess a good deal of charisma. You can also be moody and subject to rapid ups and downs. You have a fine sense of harmony and art in everything that you do, from your dress to the way you decorate your home. You have a gift with plants and flower arranging. Be careful not to waste time and energy on trivial matters. Keep your long-term priorities in perspective.

4 Birth Day

You are a hard worker and a conscientious person. You are precise and take great care at what you do. You are highly principled, disciplined, and responsible. You take your obligations very seriously. You are highly ethical. You can be proud and upright, but, conversely, you are not particularly arrogant. You have compassion for people. You tend to persevere in the face of an obstacle or personality problem.

You love your family, and make a wonderful mate. Yet, you are not overly emotional, or very demonstrative of your love. You tend to understate your affections. You are constantly focused on the foundations of your life; whether they are in business, career, or family matters, you take care of the basics. You are highly rational. You are not one for pie-in-the-sky solutions to problems. Nor are you given to get-rich-quick schemes.

Yours is the slow, patient approach; sound and secure. You are a natural organizer and manager. People, especially relatives and co-workers, tend to rely on you. You are perceived as the rock of any endeavor. You can be stubborn and rigid. Your nature is to dig in and wait. This can close you off from solutions or creative ideas. You must work at being more flexible. You often experience frustrations and repression. You are not an emotional person, and perhaps you don't fully understand the emotional realm. This is the reason you can be rather tactless at times.

Be careful to avoid excess work, and to miss out at smelling life's roses. After all, you love to commune with nature.

 Birth Day

You love change, travel, and adventure. You are a bit of a rolling stone. You have enormous curiosity, and you yearn to see far-off places, and to meet exotic people. Your arena is the world itself, and it is just a matter of time before you are off once again on another excursion.

You are highly adaptable, and you need excitement. You relate well to others, and you have an easy way with words. In fact, you have a talent for promotion, public relations, and, for some, writing. Your social skills are highly refined. Your ability to communicate and promote a product or event makes you a natural salesperson. You work well with others as long as there are not too many restrictions. You have trouble being bound to a desk or within an office. You can easily feel cooped up or trapped unless there is much variety and change in your life. You become bored and restless easily.

You may be a little irresponsible, and you therefore need to learn discipline and orderliness.

You have a quick and analytical mind. You may be over-confident and headstrong. However, you are highly creative, and you can usually come up with a remarkably workable solution to most problems—either your own or those of others.

You can be impatient and impulsive. You can also overindulge your senses in food, alcohol, sex, and drugs. You must be careful to protect your health from the excesses of your tastes.

6   Birth Day

You are family-oriented, and have a talent for settling disputes between people to the satisfaction of both sides. You somehow know the middle ground.

Your lesson in life is to work with the whole subject of balance. You must come to truly understand the ancient and fundamental principle of opposites that seek harmony. Whether the realm is the emotions, caring for others, finances, work, or play, you must learn where you can be of service, exactly what you can do, and what your limits are. You have a considerable amount of artistic talent. You have a deep appreciation of beauty and art. You are highly responsible, and will do without in order to fulfill a debt. Your focus is on relationships. You want to help others. You have a talent as a healer, and could make a profession of the healing arts, either as a nutritionist, an alternative health therapist (acupuncture or massage, for example), or a doctor.

You need to know you are appreciated. You are given to flattery and vulnerable to praise. Criticism, on the other hand, leaves a very damaging impression on you. You take it deeply to heart.

You will sacrifice your own comfort to support and help others. You are generous, kind, and understanding.

You can be very emotional and given to extremes in sympathy and sentimentality. You must learn to provide more than merely a shoulder to cry on. Study and development of your healing skills bring you great rewards in life.

 ## 7 Birth Day

You possess a highly developed mind. It is your instrument for investigating the world and all of its subjects. You are philosophically and spiritually oriented. You can, and should, specialize in one given field in order to make full use of your abilities and your natural intellectual gifts.

You tend to be analytical and rational in your approach to relationships. Emotions are a cloudy and uncertain realm for you, which, very often, you do not trust. Emotional people are sometimes viewed by you as a bit immature or unpredictable.

You have excellent intuition. You should meditate and do some type of spiritual exercise in order to develop your intuitive talents. Once you have begun to trust your intuition, you will develop a sound faith.

You should avoid taking anything at face value. Nor should you take excessive chances or gamble. You are not the type who should be given to reckless living. It tends to backfire quickly for you.

You prefer to work alone, and set your own pace. You tend to finish projects once started. Your interests lean to the scientific, technical, and metaphysical.

You are very sensitive and feel deeply, but you don't share your feelings easily, or communicate them well. You like to spend time alone, but have to be careful not to become too withdrawn.

You can be opinionated and stubborn. You must guard against becoming too analytical, coldhearted, and cynical. You can be highly critical and self-centered, traits that can lead to much unhappiness, especially in marriage, if you are not careful. However, once married you tend to be loyal and faithful.

Make the most of your gifts of mind without losing your heart in the process. Share your emotions with those you trust, and maintain long-lasting, close relationships. This will balance your mental life, and will be a source of great support.

 Birth Day

You have a talent for business, and a good sense of money. Your approach to business is original, creative, and daring. You have sound judgment, and need the freedom to exercise it, lest you become bitter and tyrannical elsewhere in your life. It is advisable to avoid partnerships wherever possible. You are highly competitive, and close partnerships, especially when power is divided equally, can lead you to indulge in intrigue and manipulation.

You are efficient, and can handle large projects. If you do not already run your department or own business, you are destined for such a position. Leadership is your gift. In the same way, you have a great talent for organization. You can manage large groups of people, and guide them along the lines of your vision.

You are realistic, self-confident, practical, ambitious, and goal-oriented. Others respect you and your judgment. They know that you can be depended upon; you come through. You enjoy a challenge. The expectations of others stimulate you, especially if they doubt you can pull it off. You tend to be dramatic with money. You have a need for status, and you may show off the fruits of your labor with an impressive car or house.

You are proud of your family, and you like to be complimented. You have strong character, but you may be domineering and bossy. You have little patience with weakness, be it your own or someone else's. You do not express your feelings much.

You must develop the qualities of perseverance and survival. You will meet many obstacles, which must be viewed as challenges that in fact make you stronger. Your attitude toward the difficulties in life will be the difference between success and failure.

9 Birth Day

You are broad-minded, idealistic, and compassionate. You should obtain a varied education, especially in the arts. You are highly creative. Many great artists are found under this number.

You must come to truly understand life to be of greater service to society. You have a greater social role to play that will require a blend of the practical and the humanitarian. You must have a keen sense of what will work, but at the same time, direct those efforts toward some greater good.

Your challenge is to find a place for yourself that has some direct benefit to others. The more you can be of service to humanity, the greater will be your personal reward on all levels, from the material to the spiritual.

Children born on day 9 usually take their time before choosing a profession. You are socially oriented, and you have the gift of charm. You are well-liked and even admired by others. You can relate to people in all walks of life. You have a broad vision of the world, and you can see the grand scheme of things, including international politics and great social movements.

You express your feelings well, but sometimes can be a bit dramatic. You have a strong interest in philosophy and metaphysics.

The 9s tend to attract money from other sources, such as inheritance or a stroke of luck.

There is an element of sacrifice in the number 9 that demands that you learn forgiveness and unconditional love. You must avoid negative attachments. Do not hold onto people or situations because you feel that justice has not yet been done, or that someone still owes you something. Your task in life is to truly let the universe judge such situations, and to rely on your own forward-moving life path to bring you the necessities and rewards you deserve.

10 Birth Day

You are highly ambitious, and yearn for independence. You possess leadership abilities, and a strong drive for success. Your test in life is to live according to your dream: to have the courage and the stamina to overcome obstacles, and win the independence you so deeply want. You possess a sharp mind and fine analytical skills. You have excellent managerial skills. You plan well, and you can organize people to carry out your plan.

You are often frustrated by routine activities. You can become dull and even depressed if you are bound too tightly to the smaller details of life. In order to rescue yourself from such a fate, it will be necessary to take prudent risks. You must learn to assert yourself. You are a pioneer at heart. You must live up to such a charge.

You can be stubborn and rigid when it comes to ideas that you feel strongly about. Yet, you are a loyal and devoted friend, and can be demonstrative of your affections. Conversely, you are highly competitive, and can suffer from jealousy when it comes to the success of others, especially colleagues or friends.

By using the determination and creativity you possess, you can achieve much success.

11   Birth Day

You are very idealistic and possess a great deal of intuition. In fact, your intuition is so keen that you would make a fine counselor and/or healer. You seem to understand people before they reveal their inner being themselves. In general, you also have an appreciation for what motivates people. You are highly sensitive, emotional, and reactive. You bruise easily from the criticism of others, and can take some time recovering from such slights. You can be very inspiring. You possess the qualities of a visionary, and are often able to excite others with your ideas for a better world. Your intuition and sensitivity lead you inevitably toward philosophical and idealistic pursuits.

You tend to inspire people to move in a specific direction, or adopt new methods of living. Your presence is galvanizing. You have a good deal of leadership ability, as well. But your life stands more as an example for others, rather than for sustained or orderly leadership. You prefer to let people take up their own struggles once you have helped point the way, rather than be directly involved in the day to day activities of leadership.

You have a great deal of determination. Once you set your mind on your goal, you will devote yourself entirely to it. Your sensitivity, however, makes your life a bit bumpy at times. You are highly aware of what others think, and, whether you care to admit it or not, the thoughts of others matter to you. You must work hard to maintain your own center in the emotional storms you encounter. You work well with others, often inspiring them by your example and your idealism.

You do not do well in the business world, except perhaps in the role of advisor. Your mind works intuitively, rather than rationally. Your thoughts and actions tend to be dramatic. You explore and solve problems mainly through intuition.

You are more dreamer than doer. You experience quite a bit of nervous tension, and you must use proper dietary practices—especially the avoidance of too much fat and sugar and the inclusion of minerals in the diet—in order to maintain the health of your nervous system. You are concerned with the well-being of mankind, and seek to make the world a better place.

12   Birth Day

You possess a high degree of artistic talent that emerges in virtually everything you take seriously, from your home and cooking, to the way you express yourself, to any artistic endeavor you commit to. You are highly imaginative and quick-witted. You can be the life of a party, entertaining people with stories, jokes, or witty remarks. You have plenty of vitality; your body heals quicker than most people's.

You are especially talented in verbal and writing skills. These areas, as well as acting and other performing arts, should be cultivated.

You have a great deal of enthusiasm, and make an excellent salesperson. You can make the best out of a given situation, and are easily satisfied.

You are emotional, friendly, sociable, and affectionate. You can also be moody and given to self-indulgence, especially when it comes to feelings of depression or self-pity.

Be careful to keep your priorities in perspective, and to not waste time and energy on trivial matters. The keys to your success are commitment and discipline. You must learn to focus your considerable creativity in a given area or field. This will keep from scattering your energies in an endless number of areas.

13   Birth Day

You have a great love of family, tradition, and community. You are the foundation of any enterprise you commit to; you do your work with determination and precision.

You love things that are solid and grounded in the practical. Yet, you possess a considerable amount of artistic talent that is searching for concrete forms of expression. Not surprisingly, you love nature—the ultimate union of beauty, form, and function.

You are a natural organizer and manager with an eye for detail. You can work hard, long, and conscientiously. As long as you are taking good care of yourself, you have excellent concentration. Your co-workers recognize your discipline and come to rely upon you. You have to be careful not to become overworked to the point that you no longer take time to play and smell the roses.

Ironically, you may feel that you have yet to find the work you truly love or were meant to do. There may be a feeling that your talents are buried too deep for you to find them. This can lead you to try many different vocations without a feeling that you have truly found your place.

Your challenge is to make the most of what you are doing right now. You must raise the work you are currently responsible for to a high degree of art. Make the most of what is right in front of you. The universe is guiding you always. You need to cultivate faith and a willingness to apply yourself to the matter at hand. If you refuse to develop such an attitude, you may wander from job to job, or relationship to relationship.

Use your considerable perseverance and determination. You can be stubborn and rigid, refusing to allow new and creative ideas to penetrate your strict adherence to established methods. This can, and often does, lead to frustration and repression for you. Things seem to take forever, especially when you resist bringing fresh approaches into your very tidy and comfortable way of doing things.

The keys to your success are your willingness to maintain order and discipline in your life, and your willingness to make the most of every opportunity that comes your way.

14 Birth Day

You love change, excitement, and travel. You easily become bored, and you need the new and the exotic to feel stimulated and alive. You are highly adaptable, which makes change easy for you.

You have a gift with words and likely possess much talent as a writer or an editor. You are highly social, and you work well with others as long as there are not too many restrictions to bind you. You get restless easily, a characteristic that can make you change vocations or relationships much too quickly. Major changes in your life should be studied well before you make them.

You can be overconfident and headstrong, but you also tend to be lucky and a natural gambler.

Underlying your love of change is much insecurity. Beneath an exterior of calm and coolness lies much emotional turbulence, which reflects itself in your life as rapid change and mercurial mood swings. Your challenge is to ground in a particular profession or life style that will provide limits and form for your considerable creativity. You are exceedingly versatile and talented. There are few things you cannot do. You are also industrious once you have made a commitment to a specific task. The key to your success is balance. You must avoid making major changes just to escape the routine, or as a means of avoiding responsibility for difficult situations.

You have a quick and analytical mind. You are original and practical, but can be erratic. You have to force yourself to finish projects once they are started.

You must avoid the pitfalls of overindulgence, such as sex, alcohol, drugs, and food.

By grounding in a particular field, and by committing your considerable talents to your work, you can make a great success of your life.

15 Birth Day

You are highly creative and artistic. You also have a gift for languages. No matter what you do as a profession, your love tends to be the arts, especially the visual arts, such as painting, calligraphy, or sculpture.

There is yearning within you to ground within the family or community structure, but there is a hint of wanderlust, too, which makes grounding difficult. You want the best in your life, and you strive for it.

Commitment to relationships, especially home and marriage, is a central issue in your life. You must be willing to bring out the best in your partner, or the place you live. In the same way, you must truly commit to your own abilities; make the most of them! Honor your talent, and cultivate it with hard work and refinement.

You are very sensitive. Criticism has a very negative effect on you. For this reason, you tend to support others to the point of denying yourself. You want to live according to the golden rule; you treat others as you would want to be treated. You are generous and understanding. As a parent, you are devoted to your children, and you can maintain stability and love within the family. You tend to be demonstrative in your affections. You must beware of becoming too soft in relationships. People can see you as an easy mark, or abuse your well-worn shoulder, upon which many tears have been shed. Be more than a willing ear. You are responsible, but you keep your own counsel and make your own decisions. You probably look young for your age.

In addition to your artistic talent, you possess sound business and financial instincts. You tend to be thorough and conscientious in your approach to business, these traits pay off in the long run.

You have considerable talent as a healer, but need to develop the actual tools of the healing vocation in order to truly help others.

You are multitalented, and with focus and determination, you have great potential for success.

16 Birth Day

Your overpowering orientation is toward the philosophical and spiritual aspects of life. You are driven to understand the unseen world. On some level, you feel like a foreigner on planet Earth. Your realm is the world of spirit. Your challenge is to find a way to ground that desire and understanding in practical terms so that it can effectively be shared with others.

You have a fine analytical mind that is capable of penetrating beneath the surface of the subject at hand. You also have the capacity for excellent concentration. You must use that mind to your greatest advantage. Investigate the subjects you love, and gain a depth of knowledge in these fields. Specialize; become an expert in a given area. This will give you a means of earning a living and personal power to share your wisdom.

The great pitfall you face is the possibility of becoming aloof, mental, and critical. This will result in alienation, and even bitterness. You can easily lift off the ground, becoming impractical and dreamy. If you indulge too much in flight of fancy, you may drift from reality, and give up the possibility of earning an adequate living.

You have excellent intuition, and may even possess psychic ability. Trust your intuition, and use it as a guide in life. But at all times, be practical in your application of your insights. Find concrete means of expressing yourself. Pick a field that suits you—science, metaphysics, philosophy, psychology, or teaching, for example—and deepen yourself in its understanding. But beware of becoming overly dogmatic and shut off from the truths of others.

You prefer to work alone, rather than in a group. However, you can easily lose interest in your projects, and must work hard to finish what you start. You have to have faith and let opportunities come your way. You may miss out if you reach and seek.

You are very sensitive and feel deeply, but you don't share your feelings easily; nor do you communicate them well. The realm of the heart troubles you for its shifting, nebulous qualities. You must work hard to understand this area of life.

You like to spend time alone to contemplate and to meditate, but you have to be careful not to withdraw too much. Long-term relationships are not easily established. You must work at maintaining them.

17 Birth Day

You are highly ambitious, and you are blessed with excellent business and financial instincts. Your approach to business is original, creative, and daring. You are very independent.

You have very sound judgment. You are an excellent manager and organizer. You are gifted with the ability to see the larger picture, and, remarkably, how the details come into play. You are efficient, and can handle large projects.

Your challenge is to avoid becoming obsessed with your own judgment and power to the point that you refuse to delegate authority or responsibility to others. You can easily slip into the role of dictator—benevolent or otherwise—feeling that you, and only you, have sufficiently sound judgment to guide the ship.

You are self-confident and have high expectations of yourself. Interestingly, the expectations of others stimulate you, especially if they doubt you can pull off what you intend to do.

You tend to be dramatic, especially with money. Like the 8 Birth Day, you have a need for status, and are likely to make purchases that indicate how much money you are earning.

Whether it is business or socially oriented, you have a big dream. Your ambitions spread out far and wide, and you will not rest until you have placed your mark on the world.

You love your home and family, and like to be complimented. Avoid becoming domineering or possessive of your enterprise. Sharing the fruits of your labors with others will multiply your pleasure manifold.

18 Birth Day

You are a born leader, and an efficient manager who is capable of organizing and inspiring others. You are especially talented in the areas of politics, religion, art, and law. You are highly creative, and have an excellent understanding of people.

You are broadminded, and should be educated in several different fields, particularly the arts. Many great artists are found under this number.

You tend to be a late bloomer, and must be willing to take your time in choosing a profession. You need experience and exposure to many different types of people before you find the one area in which you will specialize. You can relate to people in all walks of life. You will do quite a bit of traveling and go through many changes.

At bottom, you have a great dream for humanity. You want to improve the conditions of people, whether they are in your community, state, country, or the world at large. There is where your deepest satisfaction liesæwith performing some task that will benefit others.

You are able to express your feelings well, though a bit dramatically at times. You have a calm and even aristocratic appearance. However, beneath it there is a sense of frustration with not having received your due in life, either from parents, co-workers, or your community. Your challenge is to learn acceptance and forgiveness. There is an element of sacrifice in your life. You need to let go of all negative attachments. Any thoughts of revenge will backfire badly against you. You need to apply your spiritual and philosophical outlook in all matters in which the balance seems to have been struck against you.

You attract money from all work that is service-oriented. The more you do for others, the more you receive—spiritually and materially—in return.

19 Birth Day

You are highly determined, and yearn for independence. You tend to struggle to achieve the degree of self-sufficiency you desire, and you may endure considerable frustration in your struggle for independence. The reason is that your desire for independence is so strong that it eclipses so many other balancing perspectives. This is a central lesson in your life: to learn the difference between the dream of independence and the reality of interdependence.

Your challenge is to achieve a wider degree of perspective on yourself and others. Exchange ideas with others, lest you become insulated and isolated by your own views. This can become a kind of prison for you. You can be very stubborn, which emanates from fear. Try to see that all of life is but an ecosystem, a life cycle delicately balanced in such a way that everyone should be supported.

You are highly ambitious and have a strong drive for success and power. Although self-confident, you like to be encouraged. You are a hard worker, and an important fixture in any enterprise in which you are involved. People are attracted to your deep commitment to your work, and the steadiness with which you do it.

You are a pioneer at heart; you are willing to take risks to get what you desire. As such, you are willing to change your environment often, and even enjoy doing so. You are demonstrative in your affections, and willing to sacrifice for others. You are highly idealistic, but if your ideals fail, you can become bitter and negative.

You are very sensitive, with many emotional ups and downs. You tend to find yourself in dramatic situations, yet you like to control your emotions in public and come off as if everything is under control.

With your determination, and your inventive and creative mind, you have the potential for achievement and financial reward.

20 Birth Day

You are highly sensitive and very impressionable. You possess great awareness, and you can sense the feelings of others, even when they try to hide their inner thoughts. Consequently, you are easily influenced by your environment.

You are very emotional, as well, which makes you all the more subject to the changing winds within your surroundings.

All of this creates a great need to develop and maintain your own center. Once you have accomplished this task, life will become more manageable and less threatening.

You are especially moved by beauty, harmony, and love. You give affection, and you need much in return. You especially need physical affection; that is, plenty of hugs and warmth. You like to spend time with family and friends. You are a cooperative partner, and you hate to be alone.

Your talent lies in your keen insight and your willingness to act as an advisor to those who are able to wield power. You operate best as the power behind the throne.

You are less an initiator than one who sees a project through to completion. You are good with details; not much escapes your attention. You are modest, diplomatic, and polite. You have the ability to persuade others to your point of view by using gentle means. You are brilliant at making others think they are brilliant, which makes you a gifted counselor, salesperson, lawyer, or politician. Your high sensitivity makes you aware of other people's feelings. You also act considerately. You must develop the ability to truly see how necessary you are the success of any enterprise you enter. You are the glue that binds projects together. Speak up for yourself when necessary, but learn to quietly go about your business, confident in the fact that you are fundamental to any success.

21 Birth Day

You are very creative, with a strong will to succeed. You have a social gift. You get along well with others, and you generally enjoy people immensely.

Your imagination is highly charged. It reveals itself in everything you do, from your sparkling conversation to your most prized projects. You are quick-witted, and you can think on your feet. Both your mind and body are vital and seemingly radiating with life. You are talented in writing and verbal skills. You can succeed as an artist, writer, or editor. You are inspiring and enthusiastic. You are uplifting at social gatherings, and often serve as the life of the party. You are an excellent salesperson.

Your challenge is to ground and focus your energies deeply in a specific field or endeavor. You must develop yourself and your talents in order to make the most of your life. Otherwise, you can easily let charm and wit pass for outstanding work, thus wasting your talents.

You can be given to paranoia, especially when you are nervous or your imagination runs out of control.

Your love runs deep, and you can be passionate. More often than not, however, you are on the receiving end of affection, simply because people are charmed by you or attracted to your charismatic personality.

22   Birth Day

You have great potential as a leader, organizer, or builder of an institution or business. You have a vision and the capability to materialize it. You possess the capacity for great strength, but conversely you can be deeply afraid of the dimensions of your ambitions. You may secretly feel that nothing will measure up to your original dream. Consequently, you can turn away from your ambitions. This can result in enormous disappointment to you should you sacrifice your dream because of fear of failure.

Your challenge is to be willing to start your enterprise small, and take practical steps toward enlarging it to its full scope.

You have a gift for seeing both the details of a plan and how it should unfold. You are orderly and patient. You can approach a problem methodically and systematically. Your solutions tend to be unique. You keep your own counsel, and you have much inner strength. Conversely, you can be nervous and suffer grave doubts about yourself, which you also tend to hide.

You have unusual perception. Your intuition is very good, and you should rely on your first impressions.

You are both practical and idealistic. You tend to want to ground your ideals in realistic methods. You are not one to indulge too much in grandiose plans for their own sake.

You have enormous potential for success. Many who have left a permanent stamp on humanity—inventors, Nobel Prize winners, leading artists, and statespeople—have had the 22 prominent in their charts.

23   Birth Day

You love change and excitement, and you need both to feel truly alive. For you, life is an adventure to be lived to the fullest. You don't want to be cheated from having your share of experience.

You are highly adaptable, which makes change a great deal easier for you than for others. You have an easy way with relationships, and you generally get along well with most people you meet.

You have a gift for communication and promoting yourself. You possess talent in verbal and writing skills, and would make an excellent writer, editor, or salesperson.

You are quite affectionate and sensitive. You work well with others as long as there are not too many restrictions placed on you. You do not like to be cooped up in the same place for long; you get restless and bored easily.

You are versatile and talented, and there are few things you cannot do. You have a very sharp mind and a fine understanding of the body, which makes careers in medicine or health both possible and rewarding.

You are very creative and witty. But you can shirk responsibility, and then let your gift of gab get you through the tight spots. There can be a tendency toward sensorial indulgence, especially in food, alcohol, and sex. You need to learn to focus your considerable energies. Discipline and order are necessities for you to be successful in life.

24 Birth Day

You are family-oriented with a gift for restoring and maintaining balance and harmony in relationships. You are emotional and sensitive, and like to demonstrate your love. You can be overly emotional and even melodramatic. You have a tendency to magnify your emotional issues, especially when they involve some kind of criticism of you.

You are willing to sacrifice much to maintain harmony in important relationships. You willingly provide a soft shoulder to cry on or a ready ear to hear out someone's travail.

You are energetic, responsible, and helpful, but your sympathetic nature may cause you to interfere in relationships and get you into trouble. Know your limits. At the same time, you must avoid being taken advantage of.

You have a gift for both the healing and the cultural arts. Your artistic talent goes in many directions, but you are likely gifted in acting and drama. However, you generally do well in business, because you are systematic, careful, and patient in your approach to business issues. You can be a bit impractical, however, and you need others to give you sound advice. You are a good friend and a faithful companion. You attract practical people to you, who gladly advance you along the lines of your talents.

25 Birth Day

You possess a sound, rational mind, and keen insight. You are logical and intellectual in your approach to life. At the same time, you have fine intuition, which, if you are able to listen to it, will guide you well through life.

You are capable of investigating and researching subjects deeply. Your analytical skills force you to avoid taking anything at face value. This is where you are at your best: using your intellect to ferret out facts and information to deeply understand the matter at hand, and then making sound decisions.

You would fare well in the sciences, teaching, philosophy, metaphysics, and psychology.

Your challenge is that while you are using your mind to analyze life's issues, you must not neglect the heart. You can become easily imbalanced in favor of the intellectual, which can make you aloof, critical, and—at the very worst—cynical. Do not let your intellect rule your life to the point that it obscures the fundamental human qualities of understanding, compassion, and love.

You prefer to work alone, and to set your own pace. You tend to finish projects once started. You may possess artistic talent, especially in sculpture.

You are very sensitive and feel deeply, but you don't share your feelings easily, and you do not communicate them well. Work hard to develop and to maintain deep and important relationships. Learn to share your emotions and deeper thoughts about life. Trust is the key to your emotional happiness.

26 Birth Day

You have a good sense of money and a talent for business. Your approach to business is original, creative, and daring. You possess sound judgment, and you need to be in charge of whatever you are doing. You are a good manager and organizer. You have a gift for seeing the larger view, but you may neglect the details. You are efficient, and you can handle large projects, enterprises, or businesses. You are realistic, self-confident, practical, and highly ambitious.

Your challenge is to maintain a balance between your material goals and the fundamental human qualities of understanding, compassion, and love. Your business life can cause you to become callous and jaded towards others. Do not let the dog-eat-dog attitude become your only means of looking at life. All people have talents and karmic burdens. Maintain gratitude for all that you have been given, and share it with others to the extent that you are able.

You can be very diplomatic and tactful. You prefer to get things done by persuasion rather than by force. You are dependable, and have high expectations of yourself. You can easily overdo ostentation, and may appear showy in the eyes of others. You are proud of all you possess, and you like to be complimented.

You have a strong character, but you may be domineering and bossy. You have little patience with weakness, be it your own or someone else's. You have to be careful not to be discouraged too easily. Life will test your resolve and your willingness to get up off the floor after being knocked down. But you possess the strength and courage to succeed over any difficulty. You do not express your feelings much. It is hard for you to give up the past.

You are generous and willing to help in a crisis. You can be philanthropic and a pillar of your community.

27 Birth Day

You are a born leader and an efficient manager, capable of organizing and inspiring others. You are especially talented in the areas of politics, religion, art, and law. You are highly creative, and you have an excellent understanding of people.

You are broadminded, and should be educated in several different fields, particularly the arts. Many great artists are found under this number.

You tend to be a late bloomer, and must be willing to take your time in choosing a profession. You need experience and exposure to many different types of people before you find the one area in which you will specialize. You can relate to people in all walks of life. You will do quite a bit of traveling, and you will go through many changes.

At bottom, you have a great dream for humanity. You want to improve the conditions of people, whether they are in your community, state, country, or the world at large. This is where your deepest satisfaction lies, with performing some task that will benefit others.

You are able to express your feelings well, though a bit dramatically at times. You have a calm and even aristocratic appearance. However, like the 18, beneath it there is a sense of frustration with not having received your due in life—either from parents, co-workers, or your community.

Your challenge is to learn acceptance and forgiveness. There is an element of sacrifice in your life. You need to let go of all negative attachments. Any thoughts of revenge will backfire badly against you. You need to apply your spiritual and philosophical outlook in all matters in which the balance seems to have been struck against you.

You attract money from all work that is service-oriented. The more you do for others, the more you receive—spiritually and materially—in return.

28 Birth Day

You possess a gift for leadership, but it is employed best through cooperative effort. Your means are generally gentle persuasion, rather than overt displays of power. You are unconventional, idealistic, and independent. You are extremely ambitious. You possess much self-confidence, but need much encouragement.

You have an exceptionally analytical and rational mind. You are an excellent planner, with a talent for directing and managing groups of people. You easily become frustrated with routine activities. You're willing to take risks. There is pioneer spirit in you. You like to be on the frontier of whatever you are doing. Once a project is started, however, you prefer to turn it over to others to run and maintain. You are a great starter, but you are not much interested in keeping the show going.

You can be very stubborn and rigid once you have committed to an idea, something you do more than you realize. You tend to identify with your ideas, and you do not like them changed; you have a powerful ego bond with most of what you do, which makes compromise difficult for you.

You are highly emotional, and enjoy demonstrating your love. On the other hand, you can become irritated and angry easily, and given to tantrums.

You are very creative, and you have a great mind for marshalling facts in order to sell ideas. You make a wonderful debater and salesperson.

With your determination and inventive mind, you have the potential for achievement and much financial success.

29 Birth Day

You are very intuitive and creative; your mind thinks in pictures. You seem to draw information and ideas from out of the sky.

Your intuition is your gift, along with a powerful drive to know the oneness of all things. You are so driven by spiritual pursuits that no matter what you do in life, the worlds of spirit and philosophy will be central to your daily behavior. You feel linked with the larger universal forces, and nothing will change that.

You have a fine mind and keen insights, but these do not come as a result of logic or rational thought. You are more likely to direct your life by inspiration, rather than by calculated reflections.

On some level, you know that you are in the hands of destiny, and that you must surrender to the higher powers that shape your life. You are usually a late bloomer. Your early and middle thirties tend to be years spent in apprenticeship and slow development. During this period, you can become frustrated with your progress, or the apparent lack of it.

You need to develop faith. You are a highly charged person with much to do, but you must develop character and sound judgment before you begin to tap your true potential.

Just as a tree needs roots to grow tall, so, too, do you need to develop depth of character in order to begin to expand in the ways you desire and ultimately envision. Your highly developed intuition makes you a wonderful counselor, healer, or health practitioner. You have a gift for inspiring people. Many people admire you without your knowing it. You are a visionary, and others sense your wisdom.

You are acutely sensitive and easily influenced by your surroundings. You love beauty and harmony. You crave social interaction and much attention. You can be very emotional, often experiencing extremes of happiness and sadness. You are usually too easily hurt. You get depressed easily, and feel the lack of confidence during times you are in a dark mood.

Despite your sensitivity, you possess leadership abilities. You are modest, diplomatic, and polite. You have the ability to persuade, and can be quite forceful.

Your high sensitivity of others makes you compassionate, kind, and gentle. You have an opportunity for fame and success as long as you do not pursue either as your gods. Look for ways to help others and to convey a larger message of harmony and insight with which you were blessed. This will bring you the material and social fruits you desire.

30   Birth Day

You have a highly developed creative talent. You are an artist at heart. You could excel in writing, or visual or performing arts. If you are not professionally involved in one of these areas, you should consider taking up art as a hobby.

You are very imaginative and quick-witted, and possess the gift of gab. You have great enthusiasm. Others find you inspiring, charming, and charismatic. You are a wonderful salesperson.

You are friendly and sociable, affectionate and loving. You can also be moody and subject to rapid ups and downs.

You have a fine sense of harmony and art in everything that you do, from your dress to the way you decorate your home. You have a gift with plants and flower arranging. You can make a wonderful interior designer and a fine cook.

However, you can waste your talent in too much socializing and not enough focus and discipline. Be careful not to waste time and energy on trivial matters. Keep your long-term priorities in perspective.

31   Birth Day

You have a great love of family, tradition, and community. You are the foundation of any enterprise you commit to, doing your work with determination and precision.

You love things that are solid and grounded in the practical. Yet, you possess a considerable amount of artistic talent that is searching for concrete forms of expression. Not surprisingly, you love nature—the ultimate union of beauty, form, and function.

You are a natural organizer and manager with an eye for detail. You can work hard, long, and conscientiously. As long as you are taking good care of yourself, you have excellent concentration. Be careful not to become so overworked that you no longer take the time to relax.

Your co-workers recognize your discipline and come to rely upon you. Ironically, you may feel that you have yet to find the work you truly love or were meant to do. There may be a feeling that your talents are buried too deep for you to find them. This can lead you to try many different vocations without a feeling that you have truly found your place. Your challenge is to make the most of what you are doing right now. You must raise the work you are currently responsible for to a high degree of art. The universe is guiding you always. You need to cultivate faith and a willingness to apply yourself to the matter at hand. If you do not develop such an attitude, you will find little stability in your career or personal life. Use your considerable perseverance and determination.

You can be stubborn and rigid, refusing to allow new and creative ideas to penetrate your rigid adherence to established methods. This can, and often does, lead to frustration and repression for you. Things seem to take forever, especially when you resist bringing fresh approaches into your very tidy and comfortable way of doing things.

The keys to your success are the willingness to maintain order and discipline in your life, and to make the most of every opportunity that comes your way.

Within the full scope of your chart, your Birth Day number is linked to your Life Path number closer than any other number. Your Birth Day number not only indicates specific talents and abilities, it also reflects your attitude towards the challenges and opportunities that are hidden in your Life Path number.

An interesting, and perhaps illuminating, aspect of the Birth Day number is, that if you put ten people with the same Life Path number in one room, you will find it difficult to recognize common denominators among them. There are simply too many other numbers in their charts causing an unlimited number of variations in appearance and behavior. However, if you put ten people with the same Birth Day number in one room, you easily recognize a certain alikeness in the way they carry themselves.

THE CHALLENGE NUMBERS

Each of us is born with both strengths and weaknesses. Numerology looks at life as if it were an educational process that is meant to bring out and enhance our talents, and turn our weaknesses into strengths. This serves to complete our being.

There are four Challenges to be faced during our lives. For many of us, the same challenge is repeated, while others have four distinctly different lessons to learn.

The job of becoming whole is one in which you must face your weaknesses, and consciously work to improve yourself. The Challenges on your life path provide specific lessons that you must attend to, and, in order to inspire and help you, life will place you in situations that require the specific characteristics of your Challenge numbers.

The four Challenges you are required to overcome during the course of this lifetime will influence you during different periods of your life, except for the Third or Main Challenge, which lasts from birth until death.

The Challenges are fluid periods of your life, not confined to specific years so much as general periods. All of your Challenges are present at birth, like actors standing in the wings.

Your First Challenge moves to the foreground in the early part of your life, and often endures to early mid-life, by which time you will have overcome this obstacle.

Before you conclude your First Challenge, the Second Challenge will be influencing you. Your Second Challenge will be felt most intensely in the middle part of your life.

The Third or Main Challenge is unique. It will be felt during your entire life, and is more strongly felt than the other Challenges.

The Fourth and last Challenge begins in late mid-life, and endures throughout the rest of your life.

How to Find Your Challenge Number

The Challenge number is one of the few areas of numerology in which subtraction is used. It is derived from your date of birth, using the month, day, and year, in that order. (The European style of using first the day, then the month, then the year should not be used.)

To find your Challenges, use the following formula. I will use an example to make the steps easier to understand. Let's find the Challenges for the Birth Date, May 29, 1950.

1. Reduce the month, day, and year of birth into single-digit numbers, like you did to find your Life Path number. *But in this case, Master numbers are reduced.*

2. Taking the above example, May becomes 5; 29 becomes 2 (2 + 9 = 11, 1 + 1 = 2); and 1950 becomes 6 (1 + 9 + 5 + 0 = 15, 1 + 5 = 6). Now, the Birth Date has been reduced to the numbers 5, 2, and 6.

3. Take the digits for the month and day (5 and 2), subtract the smaller from the larger (i.e., find the difference). In this case, 5 − 2 = 3.

    This person's First Challenge is 3.

4. Take the digits for the day and the year (2 and 6), subtract the smaller from the larger. Using the example, subtract 6 − 2 = 4.

    This person's Second Challenge is 4.

5. The Third and Main Challenge is arrived at by taking the First and Second Challenge and subtracting the smaller from the larger. For the example, 3 is the First Challenge, and 4 is the Second Challenge. Therefore, the Third and Main Challenge is found by subtracting 3 from 4 and arriving at 1.

    This person's Third and Main Challenge is 1.

6. Taking the digits of your month and year of birth (5 and 6), subtract the smaller from the larger to find the Fourth and last Challenge. Using the example 6 − 5 = 1.

    This person's Fourth and final Challenge is 1.

Sometimes, as in the example, Challenges are repeated. In this case, the Third and Fourth Challenges are the same.

Figure 2.1, shown on page 59, is an illustration of the charting system and symbols, used for the Life Path number, Birth Day number, and challenges for a person born May 29, 1950.

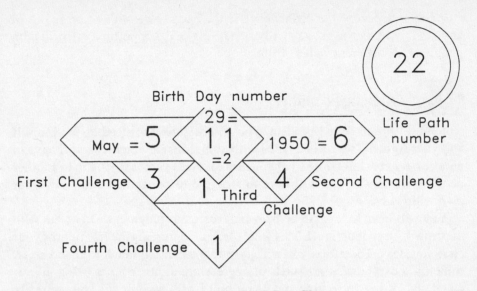

Figure 2.1 The Birth Day Chart

The Challenge numbers are one of the few places in the chart where a 0 can appear. This occurs in the case when two of the digits are the same (for example, the First Challenge for a person born on May 5 is 5 – 5 = 0). Also, the number 9 cannot appear in the Challenges. The largest difference possible between two single-digit numbers is 8 (9 – 1 = 8). Therefore, with the Challenges, the 0 takes on the characteristic of the 9. The 0 Challenge is actually the 9 Challenge.

Below is a description of the meaning of the Challenge numbers.

0   Challenge Number

You are not personally involved enough with the betterment of mankind. You are intellectually aware of the problems and pain that is endured by those of us who are poor, sick, victims of famine, or other natural disasters, but you do not allow yourself to share in the experience.

You will be offered numerous opportunities to serve selflessly for good causes, and you should accept as many of these opportunities as you can realistically handle. Selfless service offers its rewards in intensely satisfying feelings of personal gratitude. Your happiness is closely connected to the experience of devotion to something larger than you. Only through service to humanity will you be able to feel connected and part of the whole of the human race.

Another aspect of the 0 Challenge is the need to be without prejudice of any kind. For this reason, you will often be given the opportunity to deal with people of all different walks of life.

1 Challenge Number

You must learn to be independent. You will be forced to stand up for yourself and your rights. You will be faced with situations in which you will have to choose between defending what you think is right versus giving in to another person's demands. You will have to struggle to strengthen and know your own willpower.

You will have to learn to be firm and trust your judgment. Don't run with the crowd; be an individual. This whole lesson represents the frontiers of your consciousness. Therefore, you will have to experience much trial and error, sometimes exploding with bursts of aggression; at other times being intimidated and letting frustration and anger build within you until you are ready to act on your deepest instincts.

You will learn your own set of values; you will develop into an individual with original and innovative ideas.

2 Challenge Number

You are overly sensitive and too aware of other people's expectations. You suppress yourself to avoid feeling conspicuous. You can be overwhelmed by self-consciousness. You fear gossip about you. As a result, you become inhibited. All of this results in a suppression of your own individuality and uniqueness. You yearn to blend into the crowd.

You let your own feelings and emotions play too big a role. Your hypersensitivity causes fear, timidity, and lack of self-confidence. You experience unnecessary fear and emotional turmoil.

Little things seem disproportionately difficult to overcome, and they sometimes have a paralyzing effect. Jealousy can cause much pain and misunderstanding.

These negative aspects of the challenge actually spring in part from positive characteristics you possess, especially your acute awareness and intuition. You are an antenna for other people's feelings; you know before a word is spoken how they feel.

You lack the inner strength to maintain your own center, and you try to conform to the prevailing emotional atmosphere. This challenge makes you understanding and compassionate; you have an enormous empathy for the inner turmoil of others, and you can do much good for people with emotional problems.

3 Challenge Number

You are your own worst critic. You suppress your individuality and creativity. Each time you want to make an impression, you doubt yourself beforehand, and you criticize yourself ruthlessly afterward. Your criticism of yourself is far more severe than anyone else's.

As a result, you tend to play it safe by staying on the surface, indulging in superficialities. You rarely express what goes on deep inside of you; instead, you cover up your feelings with humor or perfunctory remarks.

You often feel alone and lonely. Your fear of social interaction causes you to strain conversation by making too many jokes and forced joviality. It may help you to find a creative outlet for your imagination, possibly through writing, painting, singing, or dancing.

You must make an effort to bring out your true self. You will learn to truly value your own creative talents above anyone else's judgments. This must be viewed as a process of individuation in which you become a whole human being, independent and free of the need to conform to others.

4 Challenge Number

You tend to be disorderly and disorganized. You are impractical and tend to fantasize about projects or possibilities that have little value or future. You must learn to discriminate between iron balloons and those that will fly.

You have difficulty finishing projects, because your vision becomes chaotic and loses track of the path ahead. You have to learn to be aware of the details. Keep your environment clean and orderly. Be efficient.

You have the ability to be practical and organized, but you must learn the value of these characteristics. This will cause you to incorporate them into your daily life and to give you the basis for success.

This is the Challenge of building a lasting foundation for your life. You will need perseverance and repeated effort. Get-rich-quick schemes will likely backfire; persistent effort is the key to your future happiness.

5 Challenge Number

You are in danger of becoming a rolling stone. Your desire to experience and enjoy life can overwhelm every other priority you have. Your need to freedom dominates you. You want to try everything and go everywhere. You must guard against overindulgence, and even dependence, upon alcohol, food, drugs, and sex.

You must work at establishing and maintaining long-lasting relationships. Be tolerant and understanding. This will enable you to have people in your life who are more than mere company.

You need to discipline your urge to change every situation that does not immediately suit you. Stick with projects; maintain your friendships; and don't abandon people or situations the minute they become the slightest bit difficult.

If few 5s are in the chart, you have a fear of change and cannot let go of people and situations. This holds you in the past, restricting your growth. Learn to take prudent risks and to be more adventurous.

6   Challenge Number

Your Challenge deals with distorted idealism. Your ideals are unrealistically high, making life difficult for you and others. You have a hard time being satisfied with anything you do, or with what others do for you. You lack gratitude. This prevents you from seeing the beauty in your life. You may also suffer from rigid thinking, which keeps you from having a clear perspective that would otherwise awaken you to the many good things you have received.

At bottom, this Challenge is about having blinders on. You are unable to see a broader view, which makes you think you have all the answers. This keeps away information and perspectives that would be helpful to you.

Your desire to be of service to others is sincere. However, it may be blocking you from seeing the necessity of working on your own inner development.

You can be domineering and righteous, often telling others what is right and what is wrong. You often feel a lack of appreciation from others.

There is an opportunity to be of service, to teach and to heal, but you will have to achieve a balanced perspective between your idealism and your resistance to personal transformation.

7   Challenge Number

You are highly skeptical of anything that cannot be proven to you. You are particularly doubtful of anything having to do with spiritual matters. Therefore, it is difficult for you to find a personal philosophy that would give you peace of mind and insight into the purpose of your life.

You repress many of your natural inclinations, because they do not fit into your intellectual or rational thinking. You are in need of the part of your being that you are now repressing: the child within.

All the characteristics that have to do with the irrational and holistic side of life—spirit, humor, playfulness, and intuition—are being shut out. Your challenge is to find some philosophy, and, ideally, a community that will give you additional perspectives, and force you to bring out the many other characteristics that are a fundamental part of you. Otherwise, you risk loneliness and isolation.

You have to learn faith. When you consider that most of life is made up of the invisible world—thoughts, emotions, insight, and love—you can begin to appreciate that only a small part of life is within the domain of your senses.

You may have too much pride. You may experience a deep and humbling transformation that will set free the inner being you are keeping trapped within you.

8 Challenge Number

You risk making money and power the main priority in your life. Your desire for financial wealth threatens to obscure your other human characteristics and spiritual well-being.

This challenge causes financial concerns to overwhelm all other needs, and influences everything you do. You risk the fate of Midas, turning everything into gold, yet isolating yourself from other parts of life.

For many with this Challenge, there is a danger of becoming so obsessed with materialism that they may be tempted to ruthless and unscrupulous business practices, possibly crossing the borders of the law, and causing themselves and others much misery.

You are facing a very real spiritual test in which you must realize that "man does not live by bread alone." If you overcome this hurdle, you will achieve real spiritual and material balance. You can make yourself a powerful river, bringing an inexhaustible supply of nourishment to all, rather than a lake, whose nature is limited and can easily grow stagnant, and can no longer support life.

The Challenges are important because they represent very specific shortcomings. When you become aware of a particular weakness in your make-up, you can work on overcoming it. Without this awareness, you continue to be a victim. Your shortcomings stand between you and a fuller, more satisfying experience of this life.

Your Life Path number, your Birth Day number, and your Challenge numbers are all based on your date of birth. They are connected to that one moment in time when you stepped into this world and became a human being in your own right. These numbers relate to each other and should be understood together as one package of information.

Perhaps the most challenging aspect of numerology is the connection between the different numbers in a chart and how they influence each other. However, with practice and an open mind you will soon be able to understand yourself and others with greater depth and clarity.

Chapter 3

Your Name Is Not an Accident

Lead me from the unreal to the real!
Lead me from darkness to light!
Lead me from death to immortality!

—Brihadaranyaha Upanishad

I call the moment of your birth a door in time. Your name is your true vibration, the melody of your soul as it passed through that door in time and entered this world. Your name can be seen as a musical score, rich in vibration and nuance. This vibration and nuance are not arbitrarily connected to you, but are an exact reflection, in every detail, to the vibrational entity that is you.

Also, your name represents the inheritance of your personal history up to the moment of your birth. Whatever that history is, it has shaped you into what you are.

There is much speculation throughout history of reincarnation and the transmigration of souls, but whatever the actual truth may be, you entered this life as a unique entity with shape and form that was the result of some kind of evolution. That is you.

Many people argue that they were named by their parents, and that their names are arbitrarily chosen for them. But I believe that our parents chose names for us by subconsciously picking up on our vibration, and then naming us accordingly. They gave sound to the vibration that they recognized as us. Misspellings or last-minute changes of mind are part of the fine-tuning process the result of which is that you receive the name most fitting to you.

You may have noticed that a name very often fits the person perfectly, sometimes even in humorous ways. The name Herb is a very distinct personality type. So is Mary or Bob.

Another indication of how names fit personality types can be seen in the names authors give their fictional characters. I am often impressed by their choices.

These names almost always work out numerologically to fit the character and his or her place in the plot. In other words, the author is intuitively tuned into "real characters" that people his or her book, and names them in a way that is similar to a parent naming a child. Intuition is the guiding force in both cases.

Not only is your name an exact musical vibration of you in your current state, it also represents all the accumulated knowledge and experience of your evolutionary inheritance.

All things begin in the vibrational world. Your name is an outward sound, or a melody, that radiates from your soul. Numerology is the method of unveiling the hidden information in your name.

Now, let's take a close look at your name by examining the Expression number, the Minor Expression number, the Heart's Desire number, the Minor Heart's Desire number, the Personality number, and the Minor Personality number.

THE EXPRESSION NUMBER

Your Expression number reveals your physical and mental constitution, the orientation or goal of your life. Some numerologists refer to this number as the Destiny, because it represents a lifelong target at which you are aiming. You work at fulfilling this potential every day of your life. Thus, the Expression number reveals your inner goal, the person you aim to be.

Your Expression number also reveals your talents, abilities, characteristics, and shortcomings. The extent to which you learn to use these abilities and to tap into your inner potential defines who you are.

To the numerologist, your individual talents and characteristics are represented by each letter in your name, and its corresponding number. Like a mosaic, these combine to form a totality, a picture that reveals the real you. Your name at birth can be seen as a blueprint of your potential. The key word here is potential.

The Expression number is derived from your full name at birth, meaning your first, middle (if you have one), and last names. Typically, it is the name that appears on your birth certificate. Occasionally, there are questions about exactly what name is used. A few examples, and how to decide which name to use, are listed below. These examples also apply to the Heart's Desire and other core numbers.

When clerical errors occur on a birth certificate, if the mistake is accepted by the parents, and from that point onward is the acknowledged name, this name on the birth certificate, with the spelling error, is used to find the Expression number.

If the mistake is not accepted by your parents, and you grow up using the original name given by your parents—ignoring the clerical error—that original name is used to provide the Expression number, as opposed to the name with the error that appears on the birth certificate.

If you have been adopted, and you have been provided a new name by your adopting parents, use the original name given to you before the adoption.

If you were adopted, and never knew your original name, use the name that is the earliest remembered name. However, without the original name, a complete chart may not be possible.

Even if you have never used your original name, that name still represents the blueprint of your life, and is used to find the Expression number.

Names given at confirmation, by a spiritual teacher or guru, or at some other religious ceremony, are not used for the Expression number, but can be used additionally to give further insight into the personality. (See Minor Expression, Minor Heart's Desire, and Minor Personality in this chapter.)

If you received more than one middle (or last) name at birth, use all the middle (or last) names.

If there is a junior, senior, the third, et cetera in your name, always discard such additions. They are too general to bear any significance to your name.

How to Find Your Expression Number

The individual letters of your name are all assigned a specific single-digit number, as I explained in Chapter 1.

Each letter is given a number according to the place it falls in the alphabet: The letter A, being the first letter, is a 1; B is a 2; C is a 3; and so on. Letters that come after I (the ninth letter of the alphabet) and have double-digits, such as M, the thirteenth letter, are reduced to single digit numbers in the same way as described earlier; that is, by adding the two digits. The letter M, therefore, becomes a 4.

For the numerical value of each letter, see the listing below.

1	2	3	4	5	6	7	8	9
A	B	C	D	E	F	G	H	I
J	K	L	M	N	O	P	Q	R
S	T	U	V	W	X	Y	Z	

To find your Expression number, write out your full name, and place the appropriate numerical value beneath each letter. Add the numbers of your first name, and then reduce it to a single digit. Do the same for your second and last names. Now, add the three single-digit numbers, and reduce them to another single-digit number to find your Expression number. If at any time you encounter a Master number, 11 or 22, do not reduce it to a single-digit number.

Throughout the book, we will use the name Thomas John Hancock as an example:

T	h	o	m	a	s		
2	8	6	4	1	1		Total: 22

J	o	h	n				
1	6	8	5				20 = 2

H	a	n	c	o	c	k	
8	1	5	3	6	3	2	28 = 2 + 8 = 10 = 1

The numbers in Thomas total 22 (Master numbers are not reduced!).
The numbers in John total 2.
The numbers in Hancock total 1.
His full name at birth totals 25.
John Hancock's Expression number is 2 + 5 = 7.

After doing the same simple addition, you can find the text that provides the information related to your own Expression number.

The symbol used for the Expression number is a triangle with the number inside. (See Figure 3.1 on page 111.)

Expression Number

You are a natural leader, independent, and individualistic. You are extremely ambitious, original, and courageous. You employ new and unproven methods. You are an explorer and an innovator. Openness to too many peripheral influences limits and frustrates you. You are self-reliant, confident, and energetic.

You possess executive abilities, and are most successful at owning or independently managing a business. You need the freedom to make your own decisions based on your own ideas. You can be an astute politician. You also possess the ability to influence the opinions of your milieu. The number 1 symbolizes the front-runner, pioneer, warrior, risk-taker, and daredevil. Generals, top politicians, successful business people, self-made millionaires, religious leaders, inventors, activists, and avant-garde artists are often born with a 1 Expression. Strength and perseverance are central to your success. You must be willing to travel the frontiers of life, away from the beaten path. You possess a great reserve of willpower that must be directed at your goals. You do not give up, but relentlessly pursue your aims.

You are quite opinionated. People tend to be inspired or repelled by your strong personality. You have great powers of concentration and the ability to visualize your goals, thus making them more attainable. You stand up for your convictions, and hold your ground. All of these abilities, enhance your chances of success in life. There is a tendency to be self-centered. You can be domineering and, in the extreme, a bully. You can be highly critical of others, complaining that people lack the industry or determination you possess. But this lack of understanding can alienate friends and family members from you. You must learn to control this tendency if you are to maintain harmony in relationships.

Once you are convinced of the inherent correctness of your ideas, you stubbornly, and sometimes rigidly, defend and propagate them. Avoid obstinacy and antagonism. You must cultivate balance, compassion, and perseverance. You easily assume the role of protector. You spring into action when leadership is needed.

Pride can be your downfall. You so powerfully identify with your goals and ambitions that you sometimes refuse to see a potential flaw or weakness in your well-laid plans. You possess strength and determination, which, when applied to any endeavor you are committed to, will lead you to great success in life.

2 Expression Number

You have a great talent for working with others; you possess tact and refinement. You have a highly developed intuition, which provides you with insight into personalities and situations. Therefore, you act with tact and subtle persuasion. You possess a kind of radar, avoiding the landmines within another's personality, yet bringing out goodwill. These abilities make you the perfect diplomat.

Your abilities are better expressed while working with others than by working alone. In the same way, you perform better in a partnership than in a leadership role. People with the 2 Expression are often found in politics, medicine, learning institutions, laboratories, secretarial services, multilevel marketing, and entertainment (although rarely seeking the limelight).

You seek balance and peace in all relationships and situations. The key to your personality is sensitivity, but there are two sides to the coin: You have the ability to perceive the thoughts and emotions of others, and can work gently with others for a mutually shared goal. This makes you a great asset in any group endeavor.

However, your sensitivity makes you vulnerable. You can be thrown off balance by an unkind word, a conflict, or by hostile conditions at work. You are far more upset by these conditions than people without your sensitivity. While others appear to be enduring troubled times with a modicum of turmoil, you suffer the turbulence of life as if your very survival were at stake.

In difficulties, you tend to persevere and steadily erode the resistance. You are like a gentle wind that shapes a rock.

You are friendly and open-minded. You are a great support person, pulling the best out of those around you. You are the power behind the throne. You are indispensable to the leadership of another, providing insight and advice that are essential. Yet, despite the invaluable service you provide, you often do not get the credit and recognition you deserve, which can be frustrating. Your natural modesty, and the enjoyment you get from being an important asset, are usually satisfaction enough for you.

Close relationships are essential to your happiness. When single, you dream of finding your soul mate. When married, you are concerned with your spouse's needs, emotions, and thoughts. You are an outstanding marriage partner, giving, thoughtful, and conscious of meeting the needs of your loved one. You provide great support for your spouse's career. You are a passionate lover.

Parenthood is not an easy role for you, probably because you lack the will to enforce discipline, and need a tranquil, delicate, and harmonious environment.

You are blessed with a high degree of musical talent. You have a good sense of rhythm and harmony. You are also a good counselor with an inborn talent for psychology and finely tuned intuition.

3   Expression Number

You are optimistic, inspiring, outgoing, and expressive. People see you as cheerful, positive, and charming; your personality has a certain bounce and verve that so powerfully affects others that you can inspire people without effort.

All of this upward energy is a symptom of your tremendous creativity. Your verbal skills may well lead you into the fields of writing, comedy, theater, and music. Yours is the number of self-expression, rich in imagination and spirit. But you have to be careful not to scatter your talents. Your bane is that you often lack discipline and order in your life. Avoid becoming a happy-go-lucky spendthrift, escaping responsibility and commitment. You must learn to concentrate and focus. These are the keys to your success. You have great potential in the arts and areas that require creative solutions to problems. You are able to perform leaps of imagination, providing unconventional ideas as if they have suddenly descended from above. Hard work and focus, however, are the foundation for a successful future. Though you possess great verbal skills, your mind tends to see life in pictures rather than in words. Yet, you have the ability to think abstractly. Creativity is a sensitive faculty that is often suppressed in childhood. If you lack the confidence to pursue your ideas, you may divert your abilities into a scattering of trivial pursuits.

To overcome this problem, you must make a choice. You have to limit your field of vision and the number of activities you engage in, and bundle your energies into a single thrust. Focus your life; choose the area that you love the most, and commit. There, you will find success, and a great deal of happiness.

Love, romance, and money are within your reach. You are aided by your friends and admirers. Often people appear out of nowhere to help you in key situations. You have to learn to accept the involvement of others in your life. You are not a loner, nor are you particularly independent. You are social; you need an audience and the support of others to fully realize your abilities.

On the down side, you can be superficial, moody, and intolerant. You are emotional and sensitive, sometimes presuming criticism where none was intended. You can also be jealous and gossipy. Beware of becoming cynical and sarcastic. These traits can suppress your natural creativity.

Be goal-oriented. This is a practical, step-by-step approach to your larger ambitions. You possess the natural abilities to attain a high degree of excellence.

4 Expression Number

You are the bedrock of society, the foundation of any enterprise. You are an organizer and manager. Your approach to life and problems is methodical and systematic. You are a builder and a doer. You turn dreams into reality.

You possess a highly developed sense of structure. You enjoy management systems, and can carry out your well-laid plans. You are not the type to embark on any trip without a map.

You take your obligations and those of your family quite seriously. As a result, you are reliable and responsible. You enjoy seeing a project through from start to finish, but can become too narrowly focused. You put your nose to the grindstone, and have a tendency to become a workaholic. You are driven by a contempt for all that is unstable, insecure, and unpredictable. You distrust the unconventional, preferring instead the tried-and-true. But this can make your endeavors move slowly and cause you much frustration, especially with the apparent limitations of your resources. At the same time, concern for these limitations causes you to be careful and cautious, shutting you out from possible shortcuts and creative solutions provided by more daring people around you.

It is important that you recognize restrictions for what they are: guiding forces that are testing you and directing you toward your goals.

Your challenge is to be more imaginative, and to attract more creative people into your life who can advise and inspire you.

In relationships, you need to be somewhat moralistic. You are extremely honest and sincere. You have integrity and are trustworthy, but you can also be rigid and stubborn. Don't let your strong likes and dislikes overrule your common sense and compassion. Be more understanding of others' shortcomings. Because you tend to focus on details you can fall into a rut and become a little dull and overly serious. Often, people born with the 4 Expression need to lighten up and have more fun.

In your conservative and careful way, you are good with money. You are very conscious of the balance between income and expenditures. You can limit your expenditures; saving money is important to you.

You are a surprisingly good parent, and love to be involved with children. Somehow, you relate a little more than others to the innocence of children, perhaps seeing a good deal of yourself in them. You, too, are idealistic and respect the simplicity of children.

Many accountants, bookkeepers, government officials, managers, and lawyers are born under the 4 Expression. You can be attracted to the arts and music, but will likely bring your love of structure and order to any artistic field. Classical music and opera are particularly appealing and inspiring for you. You have a keen eye for detail. You have great stamina, and can work conscientiously and persistently toward your goals. This eventually brings you success and standing in your community.

5   Expression Number

You are a free spirit. You love change, adventure, and excitement. You love your freedom. Like a bird that needs its wings to live, you cannot exist without it. Freedom is the nucleus around which your life revolves. You need it for your very survival. By using freedom properly, you are able to explore and develop all of your varied talents. You will meet many types of people, and you will travel great distances. Freedom is the atmosphere necessary for you to bring forth your many talents.

You are capable of doing almost anything, and probably of doing it quite well. Only by avoiding the imprisonment of illusory security are you able to bring forth your abilities.

You are unusually adaptable. In fact, change is a blessing for you. In the same way, you need challenge and variety. You hate the routine of life; being stuck is a catastrophe for you. You become miserable when you are held back or held down.

The taste, texture, and color of life have an overpowering allure for you. From childhood, you dream of seeing foreign lands, experiencing the sensual and the exotic. You want to try everything at least once in life.

All of life is a playground for your senses. But this can get you into trouble. You may fail to respect your natural limits, either biologically or socially. Any sort of boundary is an anathema to you, which can blind you to your natural limits, and may cause you to overindulge your desire for food, sweets, alcohol, sex, and drugs. You are gifted in your ability to communicate. Your facility with words is almost limitless. You can be a salesperson, politician, lawyer, public relations person, or minister. You also possess the talent to share and advance new ideas. You are talented with your hands. You love the new and untried. Your field is the frontier. You are a bit of a gambler, and often play for very high stakes. All of this combines to give you a youthful enthusiasm, which others find infectious and attractive.

You like to work with others, but need to perform your task unincumbered by the restraints of others. You are a clever and quick thinker, but your thought processes, like your life in general, can be unorganized and scattered. You must stay grounded and focused if you want to be successful. You fall in and out of love frequently, especially early in life. You are naturally sensual and commonly have a strong sex drive. These characteristics usually make for a lively and exciting love life, but you must guard against shallow feelings in relationships. Your challenge is to develop mature and lasting relationships. Self-discipline and setting healthy limits is the key to your success in virtually every area of your life. Ironically, you will find that as you learn to set appropriate limits for yourself, you will develop more self-mastery, and you will realize even greater freedom. This is especially true when it comes to finishing what you start. Your tendency is to give up once you have a project or job under control; you grow bored quickly. You start to fantasize about a new challenge, or the rewards of your great accomplishment, long before the work is finished.

The 5 Expression desires the whole world. You are aware that you have many talents that can bring much success. But that success depends on your willingness to choose certain areas to concentrate on, and to bring them to perfection.

6   Expression Number

You are a loving and caring individual with a tendency to put the needs of others before those of yourself. You are responsible and trustworthy, with a high regard for justice and honesty. Duty will follow you all your life, and sometimes it will feel a little too much of a burden. You are artistic. Harmony and beauty are high on your list of priorities. You have a musical talent, but the creative talents of a 6 are sometimes left undeveloped or suppressed as a result of your tendency to sacrifice your time and pleasure to the service of others. You are highly creative in all areas of life, particularly in the visual. You are also a talented business person, and can work methodically toward the realization of your goals. You have a natural gift with flowers, gardens, and animals. Your love of children has caused numerologists to dub you the cosmic mother or cosmic father. The very shape of a 6 resembles and symbolizes "pregnant with love."

You are a natural counselor and healer, but you must be careful not to interfere with the freedom of others. You are recognized as an idealist, mainly regarding marriage, friendships, and humanity.

The 6 is the most balanced of all numbers, but also contains within itself the greatest paradoxes. It is as if opposite tendencies were tenuously poised. Because of its gift for harmonizing these opposites, you are uniquely qualified to handle and to integrate contradictions within yourself. It is for this reason that 6s so frequently find themselves in the role of healers or counselors, creating a peace between opposing points of view, or internal conflicts within the self.

While you can be very idealistic, there may also be a temptation to acquire beautiful objects by improper means. You must also guard against other meddlesome behavior and domestic tyranny, or always having to have your own way in a family dispute. Conversely, you have it within yourself to understand another person's dilemma, and to come up with a creative solution. Your natural ability to give comfort and warmth can smooth over hurt feelings like a healing balm. You attract love and appreciation, and rightly so, because you give the same in return.

You make an outstanding teacher (especially with young children or special education students), healer, counselor, social worker, psychologist, artist, designer, gardener, florist, and farmer. You can be successful in business, particularly one that involves dealing with people.

7 Expression Number

You are gifted with an analytical mind and an enormous appetite for the answers to life's hidden questions. You have a strong interest in exploring scientific matters, philosophy, and even mysticism. You possess clarity and persistence in your search for truth. You can be a great researcher, educator, and philosopher.

You are driven by a desire for knowledge and truth. You must learn to discriminate between illusion and reality, but you are well-equipped for this task. Your fine mind offers you insight into the veiled mysteries of life. You also possess a considerable amount of perspective. Somewhere inside you, you are aware of a peaceful place that you call upon during difficult times. You need time to be by yourself. Too much social interaction causes you stress. You need your privacy and a place that can be shut off from the hustle and bustle of life. You tend to keep your thoughts to yourself, and be secretive. Unless your 7 Expression is balanced by extrovert characteristics (usually revealed by the numbers 1, 3, 5, and 8), your introversion may pull you deeply within yourself, and even cut you off from others.

You have a strong dislike of the superficial and mundane. You are often surprised by the lack of understanding or depth of knowledge of others, many of whom do not take the search for knowledge as seriously as you do.

This can cause you to be critical of others, and even cynical about life in general. The more cut off from others you become, the more hidden are your motives. Once you develop understanding of people and life, your advice and counsel will be sought by those around you who need your wisdom.

You love to specialize your knowledge and to develop great depth within your field. You are a perfectionist. You should complete your studies early in life, and not be driven too hard by a desire to be successful. Let things come at their own pace and be open to opportunity, but remember that your rewards, satisfaction, and contentment come from a higher source.

A 7 can be distant and aloof. When dominated by their darker characteristics, you can be unfaithful, dishonest, and cruel. Contemplation, meditation, and the softer, finer vibrations of life, can restore your sense of harmony, and keep you on the path to peace and balance. You have a logical mind. Your analytical skills cause you to approach a problem in a detached, surgical kind of way. Researchers, analysts, investigators, inventors, technicians, scholars, lawyers, bankers, watchmakers, priests, philosophers, theologians, and administrators in some scientific or technical fields are among the vocations 7s are drawn to.

8   Expression Number

You have the power and potential to achieve great things. It is both your challenge and your birthright to gain dominion over a small part of the earth. Whatever your enterprise, you strive to be the best, and the most successful in your field. You are highly competitive, and will not rest until you are satisfied that you have bypassed the opposition. You enjoy challenges and rivalry.

You are a realist and a visionary planner. Money and authority are available to you if you are willing to discipline yourself—generally an inborn talent— and persevere in the face of the considerable obstacles in your path.

You are dynamic, and have a talent for efficiency. You understand the larger picture, see the broader challenges, and know how to marshal your collective resources to address problems. You delegate responsibility well; it is best for you to leave many of the details to others.

You are a great leader of people and an outstanding judge of character. You are demanding of those who work for you, often putting things in no uncertain terms: Do it my way or don't do it at all! At the same time, you don't hesitate to reward the faithful and hardworking employee. You are not a particularly tolerant leader; too much tolerance violates your sense of efficiency. You go directly after your goal with courage and tenacity.

You have a natural understanding of money, authority, and power. You are able to struggle consistently after your goals. Eventually power falls to you. Within you lies an innate balance between the higher and the lower characteristics of man. Your challenge in life is to balance your higher ideals, and your understanding of the hard realities of the earth.

Much effort will have to be put out, and many ups and downs experienced, before you reach the level of success you desire. Life will probably test you many times with obstacles that seem insurmountable. But, in reality, these are merely opportunities for you to learn how to use power and authority in the face of difficulties, and to find out just how much power lies within you.

It is crucial for your success that you balance the material and the spiritual. You have chosen a path that requires balance between giving and taking, reward and punishment, action and reaction. Despite the obstacles on your path, you are a true survivor.

When focused exclusively on your desire for results and success, you can become stubborn and intolerant; you can be driven and overambitious, causing you to be exacting and without perspective.

Be careful of your alcohol consumption, a danger-zone for you. You can be a social drinker, mixing business with pleasure—a hazardous cocktail.

As an excellent manager, organizer, and administrator, you have talents in many careers, including entrepreneur, executive, banker, broker, negotiator, gambler, coach, collector, head of an institution, builder, art dealer, manufacturer, promoter, military officer, police detective, smuggler, engineer, pilot, or sea captain.

You have been entrusted with special gifts, the use or abuse of which has an immediate and often physical effect upon you and those around you. Use these gifts for the good of mankind, and accept your own good fortune with gratitude. This is your rewarding stage in your evolution. Yours is a lifetime of harvest.

9 Expression Number

You are the humanitarian. You are attracted to a cause or movement whose purpose is to make a better world. You are extremely idealistic, sometimes to the point of being naive about people or methods. You have great compassion, and seek to create a more humane society. You are drawn to those who suffer physically or at the hands of injustice. You are the righter of wrongs. Your deepest intention is to transform the world.

You are willing to sacrifice in order to advance your cause. Indeed, this seems to be a theme in your life. From time to time, you find yourself involved in a project whose very life depends upon your willingness to sacrifice something that relates directly to your ego. You are highly idealistic. You are also a visionary with the ability to influence and direct the masses. Deep inside, you long for the love and approval of the many, and you seek fame. Part of your hunger for fame has to do with your need for validation; you are your own harshest critic. You realize your greatest satisfaction when you are involved in some activity that directly benefits the public good. Politics, law, protection of the environment, teaching, and healing are areas in which you would succeed.

You have a broad view of humanity, and you are not shackled with prejudice. You should have friends and associates from all walks of life, all colors, and all religious backgrounds. People fascinate and enrich you. A wide diversity of people and experiences stimulate and bring forth qualities within you that would otherwise lay dormant.

You have an abundance of artistic talent. Many with your Expression number find themselves in the arts, especially in literature, painting, and visual and performing arts.

The number 9 indicates the completion of a cycle or a block of learning.

The 9 Expression suggests that you have reached the point at which a breakthrough can occur; during this lifetime you can apply all that you have learned along your evolutionary path and complete a major stage in your development. This is why many geniuses have the 9 Expression.

You have the ability to synthesize many diverse bits of knowledge into a unified whole. Your appearance is important. You are keenly aware of how others perceive you. As a result, they see you as a person with a great deal of control. Conversely, you are charismatic. Despite the cool and distant personality you project, people are attracted to you.

You tend to express your love somewhat impersonally. You also tend to be preoccupied with your vision or cause, and sometimes overlook the needs of those closest to you. You need to be reminded to give your love more personally and more openly. Ironically, you are a very loving and sincere person, but you often neglect to express what you truly feel. In the same way, you can overlook your own needs. You can avoid sharing your deeper feelings, creating a reservoir of emotion. You tend to postpone your personal satisfaction in favor of some larger work. Try to be more spontaneous and courageous about showing your real self, including your vulnerability.

Your basic belief in the goodness of humanity is unshakeable. This causes you to encourage the best in people, but occasionally makes you vulnerable to being taken advantage of. You are not a very good judge of character. The surest way to personal satisfaction is for you to become part of some larger social cause. Your nature is to serve. You are happiest when you feel you are helping to advance the human race.

11   Expression Number

Your is the most highly charged Expression number of all.

You are like a lightning rod, attracting powerful ideas, intuitions, and even psychic information like unpredictable bolts. You are a powerful presence without any awareness on your part of having personal power. You are a channel for higher vibrations. But in order to be emotionally and psychologically at peace, you must learn to control that flow of energy. You possess a bridge between the unconscious and the conscious. The trouble is that the unconscious is an infinite resource, while the conscious, by definition, is a limited arena. The two are therefore at odds until they can learn to live in harmony with each other. This is where control comes in. Until you are able to control the flow of energy from this infinite source, you may feel like a victim of its whimsy, thrown about by emotional turmoil and nervous tensions.

You have always sensed that you are different, but it is an undefinable feeling. You are enormously sensitive and aware, especially as a child. This makes you vulnerable to all conflicts and painful situations. For most of your upbringing, however, you did not realize that other people did not possess the same sensitivity, or see the same things you were seeing. This caused a great reservoir of emotion that was dammed up behind an inability to express your feelings, even to yourself. For this reason, most 11 Expressions have a difficult childhood. Your extreme sensitivity made you very shy as a child. This usually manifests in adulthood as hesitation and acute vulnerability. You are very careful about sharing your feelings with others, and about choosing your friends. You compensated for your sense of separation in childhood by creating an elaborate fantasy world. You daydreamed more than other children. You have a lively imagination, and even in adulthood have a hard time separating reality from fantasy.

Your challenge is to bring forth your primitive, earthy strength. You need to be grounded in order to deal with your lightning bolts. The more you are able to call upon your inherent human strength, the greater is your capacity to take advantage of your extremely sensitive awareness. Once this is accomplished, your antagonist becomes your benefactor.

You are highly emotional and dependent upon relationships. Emotionally, you go up and down with the fortunes of your love life.

You are idealistic, impractical, and at times disorderly. You are often unrealistic in your expectations. Your reasons for doing things are usually born of a mixture of logic, emotion, and intuition, which can rarely be explained satisfactorily to your more rational associates. The 11 Expression is the number most dependent upon other core numbers in your chart for insight into your vocation. The 11 charges every area it enters, but it needs a grounding vocation and discipline to be effective. A balanced 11 is one of the most unique and impressive of all people. It is gifted with insight and illumination, which it can transmit to others. This makes you a natural teacher in whatever area you enter.

22   Expression Number

You are the Master Builder. You possess a unique gift for perceiving something in the archetypal world—infinite and divine—and for making some semblance of it manifest on earth.

You dream big. Every goal you have is enormous in scope. You dream of creating something that will last for centuries. Your desire is to change history. You want to make your mark on human civilization. There is no limit to what you are capable of, nor to what you dream of doing. Of all the numbers, yours possesses the greatest potential for accomplishment. At the same time, you possess the greatest liability. What it will require of you to fulfill your potential is nothing less than your entire life.

Even as a child, you have a vague sense of what you must do, and you have always been deeply intimidated by the awesomeness of your task. You have felt the intimations of your power. But these feelings have caused you to be paralyzed by doubt.

You must advance well into adulthood before you can begin to make use of your power, and truly commit to your destiny. The promise and reward of your Expression is equalled only by the degree of difficulty and struggle necessary to realize its potential.

The number 22 offers those who fully realize it a chance to jump into another dimension in which your day is expanded, your capacity to create and inspire multiplied, and your ability to perform lasting service to mankind extended beyond the normal limits of one life.

You may turn away from the challenge you face for the safety of limitations and practical considerations of the 4 (22 reduces to a 4 Expression). You may not want to take the great risks that the 22 presents. Instead, you may try to content yourself with limited achievements, telling yourself that your big dreams are unrealistic fantasies. This can cause some frustration, because on some level you feel called to greater things. Nevertheless, your chances to be successful, even when you limit your efforts, are still good.

You have great leadership abilities. You are persistent. You also refuse to back down in the face of a challenge. You like to work in large enterprises and on an international scale. Borders or racial identities mean little to you. You see yourself as a world citizen, playing on the planet, and refuse to be limited by petty conventions.

You should marry someone who does not depend on you for entertainment; rather, choose a spouse who can participate with you, but can also provide an independent contribution to your goals.

You are blessed with a farsighted vision. Your efforts are directed toward great accomplishments and long-standing progress. You deeply want to create a great edifice that will make a lasting contribution, and you have all the tools necessary to do just that. In choosing a career direction, there are no real limitations for the 22 Expression; the field is wide open.

Your Expression number is you. Your full name at birth contains all aspects of your personality, down to your deepest desires, and your most hidden fears. Your full name also shows your true potential, including those talents and abilities you have not yet had the opportunity to use, and may not even be aware of. You might say that your Life Path number, and all the other numbers based on your date of birth, represent the path you will walk during this life. However, your Expression number, more than any other number in your chart, shows the person walking this path. In addition, the Expression number is the number that indicates your career options more than any other number in your chart.

THE MINOR EXPRESSION NUMBER

The influence of the short name is minor in comparison to your full name. Interestingly, the short name often compensates in some way for numbers (and their related characteristics) that are missing or out of balance in the full name.

For instance, a number missing in the full name may show up prominently in the short name; or a number (or numbers) that appears in excess in the full name can be compensated for in the short name. If a name change takes place later in life through marriage or for professional reasons, it adds or subtracts certain qualities. It can also focus and intensify existing characteristics or talents that may be latent.

As a rule, I recommend that you don't change your name on impulse. Marriage, of course, does not leave much room for choice, although more and more women are hyphenating their names or staying with their maiden names. However, if you must change your name (for professional reasons, for example), try to choose a name already in your family, and thus connected to you through your ancestors. Those characteristics are already present in your lineage, which makes the new name easier to assimilate into your personality.

Whenever you consider changing your name, the best guide is your own intuition. Discussing name changes or various names for a newborn child with a numerologist can be helpful. But never allow someone else—including a numerologist—to design a name for you.

In answer to some commonly asked questions when it comes to short names:

- The short name is the name you feel closest to in relaxed and social settings.
- The short name is the name you would use when thinking about yourself, including your last name. Who are you? What name best describes the inner you?
- When figuring out the Minor Expression number, never use the middle initial, unless you introduce yourself with that initial, such as, "Hi, I'm Tom J. Hancock."
- Names you have used in the past reveal inner feelings and characteristics

that were prominent during that period of your life. If you are no longer using that name, it bears no resemblance to your current identity.

To find your Minor Expression number, use the same formula used to find the Expression number. Add the numbers of your first name and reduce them to a single digit. Do the same with your last name, then add the two digits together and reduce them to a single digit to arrive at your Minor Expression number.

For example, Thomas John Hancock usually introduces himself as Tom Hancock. This results in the following:

T	o	m					
2	6	4					12 = 3

H	a	n	c	o	c	k	
8	1	5	3	6	3	2	28 = 10 = 1

Tom Hancock's Minor Expression number is 3 + 1 = 4.

The symbol for the Minor Expression number is a triangle, somewhat smaller than that for Expression. (See Figure 3.1 on page 111.)

Minor Expression Number

This number makes you better equipped for the daily struggle of life. This is a powerful number with good leadership abilities. It is independent, individualistic, original, and innovative. It adds courage and a willingness to take risks. The 1 Minor Expression number makes you more determined and goal-oriented.

2 Minor Expression Number

Your shortened name adds sensitivity and awareness of other people's needs and feelings. It makes it easier for you to work with others using tact and diplomacy. Your abilities as a peacemaker and counselor are heightened. Because you are more sensitive now, you should be conscious of making your environment—both at home and at work—more harmonious and peaceful. Your short name makes you a good deal more honest; you are now able to remain in the background, and to direct and influence people more indirectly. The 2 is often called the power behind the throne.

The 2 also possesses musical abilities.

3   Minor Expression Number

Your short name increases your capacity to enjoy life. It boosts your optimism, cheerfulness, good taste, and interest in sports.

You communicate more easily, and your sense of humor is enhanced. You are inspiring company, often motivating and uplifting others. Your artistic ability, especially your facility with words, is increased. The three is a happy-go-lucky number, which, on the negative side, can make you avoid difficulties, and to try to find the easy way out of challenges.

4   Minor Expression Number

Your short name makes you more practical, orderly, efficient, and dependable. You will feel more principled, honest, and determined. You will be a little more organized and capable of putting ideas into reality.

You are better able to work with details. Your conscientiousness will be enhanced, as will your ability to work diligently and consistently over a long period of time. Discipline increases under the 4. Your short name enhances your ability to be the pillar of society. Family and friends rely on your judgment more. However, you could become too rigid and inflexible.

5   Minor Expression Number

Your short name adds considerable flexibility and versatility to your personality. You now enjoy more travel and adventure. You are more curious about people and new places, and you seek out more excitement in life.

You are more dynamic and alive. New and original ideas come quicker to you. You are a good deal more creative. Your verbal skills are increased, and your ability as a salesperson or as a promoter are enhanced.

You suffer more when confined by restricted spaces or rigid rules. You yearn for greater freedom of movement and expression. You are more likely to strike out on your own with your own ideas or methods.

6   Minor Expression Number

Your short name adds love, warmth, generosity, and genuine concern for others. It increases your concern for family and those less fortunate than you.

You are better equipped to deal with duty and responsibility, and even find greater satisfaction in it. You want to do good in the world. You become more socially conscious, and seek ways to better the plight of others.

Your artistic abilities are enhanced. You are more concerned with beautifying your home, or engaging in healing and teaching.

7   Minor Expression Number

Your short name stimulates your desire for knowledge. It helps you to specialize and deepen your understanding of a particular subject. It helps you to focus. Your 7 Minor Expression number encourages you to accumulate knowledge regarding the mysteries of life. It makes you a more analytical thinker. You are better able to look below the surface of things. You don't take things at face value. You may desire more time for private contemplation and meditation. This is a pull to spend more time alone.

8   Minor Expression Number

Your short name provides you with more leadership abilities and business sense. It encourages you to use more power in your relationships, and directs you to higher standards of success.

Your Minor Expression number makes you a better judge of character. You are more realistic in your evaluation of others and their potential. You are not easily fooled.

You must be willing to apply more effort toward all of your endeavors. You likely demand more of yourself.

Your abilities as a manager, organizer, and administrator are enhanced. You are competitive and determined. You are more likely to initiate your grander plans and visions.

9   Minor Expression Number

The influence of this number makes you more concerned with the well-being of others. Your Minor Expression number increases your sensitivity to the needs of society. You feel an urge to serve humanity in a more direct way.

The number 9 helps you to better communicate and understand all types of people.

You are more aware of your artistic talent and the need to express yourself. Your name opens you up to a larger view of life. It attunes you to political movements, philosophical theories, and spiritual practices. You are more sensitive to the larger patterns of humanity.

11   Minor Expression Number

Your short name increases your sensitivity, intuition, and perceptiveness. It leads you toward deeper investigation of the mysteries of life. You are attracted to religion, philosophy, and spiritual understanding. It may awaken your intuitive, and even psychic abilities. At the same time, your Minor Expression number makes you more sensitive to your own shortcomings. It encourages you to work on yourself. You cannot avoid personal transformation under this influence.

Your increased sensitivity will encourage you to seek out harmonious and peaceful environments. This will balance the nervous tension that the 11 can stimulate.

Your capacity to work with others is also improved. You are now more humble and modest, and seek ways to avoid conflict and maintain harmonious relationships. Your heightened intuitive powers bring highly creative ideas, sudden insights, and realizations.

22   Minor Expression Number

Your short name increases your ambition, orderliness, and capacity to complete large undertakings significantly. Your ability to manage people and direct them toward some difficult and ambitious goal is greatly enhanced. Your understanding of systems and organization is also strengthened.

At the same time, you feel the burden of such lofty ambitions. High demands can cause you much self-doubt. You may be aware of more inner tension, resulting from an inner drive to manifest your ideals in reality.

As a result of your Minor Expression number, your efforts are more likely to be directed toward endeavors that are truly great in scope and have a lasting impact.

Your Minor Expression number, as with all other numbers derived from the name you use on a daily basis, reveals a more superficial you.

THE HEART'S DESIRE NUMBER

The Heart's Desire number (sometimes called the Soul Urge number), is just what the name implies: your innermost yearning; the dreams closest to your heart. Consequently, it shows your underlying motivation, or the general intention behind many of your actions. It dramatically influences the choices you make in life. Its influence is everywhere in your life—your career, your environment, friendships, and life style.

Your Heart's Desire is derived from the vowels of your name. Note that vowels are pronounced from free-flowing breath: Aaaaa; Eeeee; Iiiii; Ooooo; and Uuuuu. Consonants, on the other hand, have a distinct beginning or end. They are sharply begun or sharply finished. For example: B, D, K, P, S, T, and X.

There is a distinction in consonants, a harder edge than the soft and flowing vowels. The vowels reveal the tender you, your love, caring, and vulnerability. Consonants reveal certain of your characteristics that, among other things, shield your more vulnerable parts. Your public personality, which is revealed by the consonants, is a fundamental aspect of who you are, but these characteristics tend to be those aspects that you willingly show the world.

The vowels are A, E, I, O, and U. All other letters are consonants, except, in some cases, the letter Y.

The letter Y is inherently vacillating in its nature and usage, and consequently is sometimes a vowel, sometimes a consonant, depending upon how it is used in the name.

When determining if the Y is a vowel or a consonant, the basic rule is this: When the letter serves as a vowel, and in fact sounds like one, it is a vowel. The same is true when the Y serves as the only vowel sound in the syllable. Examples of both of these cases are such names as Lynn, Yvonne, Mary, Betty, Elly, and Bryan.

However, if the Y does not provide a separate vowel sound, as when it is coupled with another vowel, it is considered a consonant. In names such as Maloney or Murray, the Y is a consonant, because the vowel sound depends upon the long E in Maloney and the long A in Murray.

In general, the Y is a consonant when the syllable already has a vowel. Also, the Y is considered a consonant when it is used in place of the soft J sound, such as in the name Yolanda or Yoda.

In the names Bryan and Wyatt, the Y is a vowel, because it provides the only vowel sound for the first syllable of both names. For both of these names, the letter A is part of the second syllable, and therefore does not influence the nature of the Y.

How to Find your Heart's Desire Number

To find your Heart's Desire number, add the numerical value of the vowels of each of your names; reduce them to single digits; add the single digits; and reduce them again to a single-digit number, which is your Heart's Desire number. Just as with the Expression number, do not reduce Master numbers to single digits.

(Always place the numbers for the Heart's Desire above the name. The space below the name is used for the Personality number, as you will learn later.)

For example:

$$\frac{7}{6\ 1} + \frac{6}{6} + \frac{7}{1\ 6}$$

vowels:

THOMAS   JOHN   HANCOCK

The name Thomas has two vowels (6 and 1), which total 7.

The name John has one vowel, which is 6.

The name Hancock has two vowels (1 and 6), which total 7.

Thomas John Hancock's Heart's Desire number is therefore 7 + 6 + 7 = 20, which reduces to 2.

The symbol for the Heart's Desire number is a circle with the number inside. (See Figure 3.1 on page 111.)

1   Heart's Desire Number

Your overpowering need is to be independent, and to direct your own life according to what you believe. Your dream is to become the leader of whatever field you enter. Whether it is in business, community, or in your general area of expertise, you are driven to be the reigning figure. You have the courage and the confidence to lead others. You believe firmly that your judgment is preeminent over all others. This gives you the confidence to make bold decisions, and to carry them out, even when other lives are greatly affected by what you do. You rarely look back once you have made a decision.

You possess intelligence and wit. You are keenly insightful, and you are good at evaluating the abilities of others.

You are supremely individualistic. You like to project your own unique persona in your manner and dress. Consequently, you don't mind being controversial, and you can even enjoy the attention and impact you have made on your surroundings.

You dislike routines, or anything that limits your freedom and independence.

Whenever you commit to something you truly love, you are absolutely tenacious in your ability to endure difficulties and overcome obstacles. You are highly responsible; you hate passing the buck. You possess remarkable willpower and a strong drive to succeed.

You are always looking for innovative ways of doing things. Because you seek to be the boss in any endeavor, you have a tendency to dominate others. If you are not careful, especially in dealing with your subordinates and family, you may become ruthless in your decisions and behavior. You can also fall victim to impatience and intolerance, particularly if you grow conceited.

You are the pioneer and the ground-breaker. You love the foreground, the hot-seat of responsibility. You have all the talents to succeed. As long as you maintain balance in your life, allowing others full expression of their thoughts and abilities, you will easily rise to the top of your chosen field and realize your ambitions.

2   Heart's Desire Number

You want peace and harmony in all aspects of your life. You want to devote your life to someone or something. You fall in love easily. You are extremely sensitive and emotional. You can be sentimental, and you cry at sad stories. You need friends and society. You appreciate the refinements of life. You desire comfort and security. You have refined taste, and you can be a connoisseur. You love music, and you possess a good deal of musical talent.

Your sensitivity is actually a symptom of your highly developed intuition. But you must learn to trust it. You are a gentle soul, and shy away from confrontation as long as possible. You experience a battle within when you do not believe you can handle a situation; this may have a paralyzing effect on you.

You prefer to give in when you should assert yourself. You must learn to be more decisive. Very often, you are afraid to use your own power in the face of someone else's aggressiveness. You incorrectly perceive yourself to be in a weaker position; you may ultimately give in merely to avoid a fight.

Conversely, you are extremely diplomatic and tactful. You like to accomplish things through quiet persuasion. You dislike force.

You have to fight uncertainty and doubt. You need to develop confidence and a willingness to stand up for what you believe to be right.

You function best in a supportive role, guiding the more public person in quiet, unobtrusive, yet essential ways.

3 Heart's Desire Number

You love a good time. You are generally happy, friendly, and outgoing. You have a gift for gab. You are very witty, creative, and playful. You inspire and entertain people. You are considered by many to be a great companion. Many outstanding comedians have this Heart's Desire. You have a good mental and emotional balance, and there is little that gets you down.

You have a gift for self-expression, and you are drawn to the verbal arts—writing, acting, singing, and creating poetry. You may have a great talent in one of these areas. If your creativity is blocked or suppressed, you tend to daydream and fantasize. Your imagination needs a constructive outlet; otherwise, it may run away with you. At the same time, you have great difficulty expressing your deeper feelings and important personal thoughts. You prefer to stay on the surface, entertaining people with your wit.

If you fail to deal honestly with your inner nature, you may succumb to compulsive talking. Such behavior may be merely a way of siphoning off emotional energy that is building beneath your surface. Your deeply felt emotional life cannot be avoided or suppressed. But you possess the talent to channel these feelings into a highly creative and artistic form. Art and self-expression are your outlets. You need discipline to make full use of your abilities. Too often, you may scatter your energies in many directions, beginning projects that are never finished, and you may never really succeed in anything.

Your success depends on your ability to commit to your work, and to see it through to completion. You have so much creativity and inspiring upward energy that you are in desperate need of an anchor. Hard work and discipline serve this purpose and bring out the best in you. Because you are gifted with such a sparkling personality, you are tempted to stay on the surface and play with life. You are confident, and you love the attention others give you, but these characteristics can lead to vanity and self-absorption. You have the potential to live a very full and successful life thanks to your talent for artistic self-expression. The key to your success is a balance between the creative forces and self-discipline.

4 Heart's Desire Number

You like to live a stable, well-organized life. You dislike sudden changes. You prefer orderliness in all things. You have a systematic mind that is reflected in everything you do. You can establish and maintain a routine. You are exacting with details and quite thorough.

You like to carefully analyze a problem, and then tackle it in a logical and practical approach. You want to be dependable, a rock of strength, and an example of discipline for others.

Work is central to your life, but you may have a tendency to overdo it; you can easily become a workaholic if you're not careful. You have a great deal of energy and can accomplish a lot.

You want a family, and you are a good parent. You may carry the discipline and the need for orderliness too far, especially in your family, making your children and your spouse feel oppressed and limited. Flexibility is your key to harmony and balance in life. For you, structure is more important than freedom, which you tend to interpret as chaos. But others do not have your need for well-defined systems. In fact, they may feel deeply inhibited and uncomfortable with it. The peace you get from orderliness may represent a prison to someone else.

You need and want much love, but you are not very demonstrative. You can be a little rigid and stubborn.

You are honest and unpretentious. You detest liars and affectations.

You can be very determined and tenacious. You are the bedrock of any enterprise. You have the courage to go into the nitty-gritty of a problem and come up with a solution. But try not to lose sight of the larger picture while you plumb the depths of the bottom line.

5 Heart's Desire Number

Freedom is essential for your happiness. You love change, new experiences, meeting new people, adventure, and travel. You love exotic and far away places. Variety is more than merely the spice of life—you thrive on it. You are extremely flexible and adaptable. You have more curiosity than the proverbial cat. You have a sharp mind and a natural ability with words. You are a born communicator: clear, fluent, and imaginative in every area that interests you, of which there are many!

Your Heart's Desire makes you very well-equipped for life. Change, the only constant in life, doesn't threaten you as it does other people. You are highly resourceful. Generally, you can think clearly in a crisis; you have good mental and physical reflexes. Whenever you fall, you tend to land on your feet. You are highly enthusiastic. You get excited easily over a new idea or opportunity. Your nature is unconventional. You are a bit of a gambler, taking risks whenever you think the rewards are worth it.

You are very socially oriented, and rarely, if ever, dull or boring. You are, of course, drawn to those people who, like yourself, are original thinkers, and who have exciting personalities.

You enjoy being involved in several projects at the same time. You need continual stimulation by the new and fascinating. You tend to discard boring pastimes quickly. Your love of freedom and change can have numerous consequences. You can be irresponsible, especially when it comes to finishing tasks. You have a hard time persevering at a given project and bringing it to completion. You must be careful that your love of sensory pleasure doesn't lead you to excessive indulgence in alcohol, food, sex, and even drugs.

You are a bit of a hero, and you want to save the world. This causes you to make promises you often cannot keep. Down deep, you long to please everyone, an impossible goal. Many 5s can be emotionally superficial. They feel love passionately, but fear making deep and lasting commitments. As a result, they resist the depths of emotional attachments, and remain on the surface where it is safe.

You will experience many changes and unusual events, but you learn best through experience. Therefore, your life will be full, and you will make great strides in personal growth.

6 Heart's Desire Number

Your attention is directed to helping and caring for those you love. You are exceedingly domestic. You love your home and family, and you work hard to make both comfortable and secure. Your love for family and friends is a major source of your happiness, and sometimes unhappiness.

Your desire to help others is so strong that you often find yourself sacrificing your own personal needs for someone else's. You can overdo it, becoming too deeply involved in other people's lives. You risk interfering in personal matters, and/or smothering those you love in too much affection. This can be especially weakening to children, who never experience their own personal strength if an adult is too protective.

You are extremely loyal and rarely let anyone down. You need to feel appreciation for your giving and caring. You want to know that you are needed.

You are generous and very forgiving. You are somehow able to overlook the worst mistakes in another, and to find enough good in that person to continue the relationship.

You are patient and warm, sympathetic, sometimes to the point of sentimentality.

You have a natural ability as a counselor and healer. You are an excellent listener, both compassionate and understanding. You are able to both sympathize and to empathize with a person's dilemma. Your challenge as a counselor is to be adequately educated so that you can do more than provide a sympathetic ear or shoulder.

You possess a great deal of artistic talent, though you may not have a lot of confidence in your ability. Art gives you a great deal of pleasure and satisfaction. You are especially sensitive to your environment, and you have a knack for creating an artistic, healing, and harmonious atmosphere in your home or work space.

Your deepest intention is to love those around you, and to be loved in return. The 6 is the most loving of all numbers, especially in a one-to-one relationship. Your instincts are toward your family and friends. You envision a beautiful and harmonious life with love as the basis for all social interaction. Your love is returned manifold; people appreciate you and the love you give, and they are willing to go to great lengths to keep you close at hand.

7   Heart's Desire Number

You love knowledge, study, and insight. You value the gifts of your mind, which you use to great advantage to penetrate the mysteries of life. You study things in-depth. You search beneath the surface of things. You abhor shallow judgments or opinions.

You have a natural gift for analysis and research. Once you have grasped the facts of a subject, your creativity and abstract approach lift your thinking beyond the rudimentary to the philosophical. You have a theoretical mind, but rather than indulge in fantasies or idle thought, you prefer to base your theories upon scientific facts.

You enjoy mental and physical puzzles: figuring them out, taking them apart, and putting them back together. Some people may perceive you as cool or aloof. You are somewhat introverted; you may feel slightly removed and even a little different from others. The fantasy of the hermit or monk engaged in a life of study and meditation appeals to you. In relationships, you tend to keep things business-like and impersonal. You prefer to talk about the facts of a given situation, rather than the cloudier issues of emotions and personal feelings. You distrust feelings, both your own and those of others. The whole emotional realm strikes you as unreliable, and a bit unnecessary.

Your inability to fully understand the emotional aspect of life is your Achilles heel. You are so rational that the unpredictability of the heart frightens and surprises you. Your challenge is to trust. You need to share your heart with someone. This is a courageous step for you, but it will result in enormous growth and satisfaction.

The advice here is to make a true connection with another human being. Without it, you may marry out of convenience or to fulfill social expectations, but it will not lead you out of loneliness. The more removed you are from people, the more you risk isolation, bitterness, and a cynical attitude toward life. This choice represents a true crossroads in your development. By sharing yourself with others (without compromising your independence and your need for privacy), you can cultivate your enormous charm, and share your understanding of life. You are a natural teacher and advisor, and the wealth of knowledge you will accumulate in life is meant to be shared with others.

This is not to say that you must compromise your need for privacy or time spent alone to contemplate life. These are natural aspects of your personality, which are essential to your growth. These characteristics should not be threatening to your spouse, but must be understood as fundamental to your being.

You are blessed with a great reserve of intuition, which can be cultivated by regular meditation and contemplation. Your "inner voice" is your greatest guide and friend.

You are idealistic and have high expectations for yourself. Learn to balance your serious nature with regular doses of fun. Your intelligence and refinement make you charming and distinguished in appearance. As you get older and more comfortable with your identity, people are naturally attracted to you. They see your wisdom, your deep understanding of life, and the refinement you radiate.

8 Heart's Desire Number

You want success in its fullest meaning—wealth, power, and material comforts. You have an enormous ambition. You dream of big projects, great undertakings, and vast rewards. You are a visionary. You see the horizon and the promise. In general, you also see the methods necessary to fulfill that promise. But you are not especially good with details; you need others to help you deal with the smaller parts of the picture. Your challenge is to make full use of the complete spectrum of your abilities, as indicated by your other core numbers. In the same way, you must bring forth the best from others and orchestrate their talents toward the realization of your vision. In short, you must lead by example, demonstrating the standard for commitment, determination, and excellence.

All of this requires effort on your part. You will meet with obstacles and difficulties. Your determination and commitment will be tested. But you have the power to overcome every obstacle you face, and accomplish the goals you've set for yourself.

Your task in life is to learn to use power in refined and elevated ways. The expression and use of power is directly related to one's personal evolution. The more primitive uses of power rest with violence and the threat of deprivation. The higher expressions depend upon your capacity to care for, and nourish, the people and projects in your charge, giving each exactly what is needed at the appropriate time and in appropriate amounts.

You have a creative mind and an unusual approach to business and problem solving.

You need to refine your ability to evaluate others. It is essential for you to be involved in a project that both challenges you and offers the potential for rewards. When you are uninvolved or unoccupied with a worthwhile task, you can become deeply despondent, depressed, and frustrated. Without a challenge, you can lose balance in life, and become selfish, cruel, and even self-destructive. You are the perfect example of the old cliche, "Idle hands do the devil's work."

Disappointments become shattering, causing terrible consequences in self-image and self-love. You can reflect this negative power upon everyone around you. Perspective is everything for you. You have a natural talent for balancing the spiritual and material planes. You need to cultivate courage and stamina. Courage is a choice. You need to decide to be brave in the face of fear. A balanced 8 is among the most powerful and satisfying of numbers. It is the spirit of the true survivor, able to bounce back and achieve a greater victory.

9 Heart's Desire Number

You want to be of service to the world. Your deepest satisfaction comes from knowing that you have advanced the cause of humanity.

Your ideals are of the highest order. You are a perfectionist. You strive to make the world a Utopia; to make each person's lot in life better; to become perfect yourself. One of your challenges in life is to strive toward your lofty goals, and at the same time to recognize the good you are doing.

You like, and are fascinated by, people from all walks of life. Human nature is a lifelong study for you. You are highly intuitive, but not an especially good judge of character. You are a bit naive, as well, thinking perhaps that all people have the same values as you. You dream of having the resources to immediately relieve the suffering of others, whether it is economic, physical, or psychological.

You are gifted with a good mind and a great deal of wisdom, which makes you a natural teacher, counselor, or healer. As much as you desire to be of service to others, you also crave fame and the approval of the masses. Much of the energy you expend in life is directed toward putting yourself before an audience, most often as a salesperson whose product provides some social good; as a philanthropist or an artist.

You are attracted to the arts as a vocation, especially as an actor, photographer, or writer. But whatever your profession, any involvement in the arts, even as a hobby, will provide you with a deep and lasting satisfaction. Secretly, you dream of having a big impact on the world. Others may see this as egotism, especially when you are still young. But your concern for others is genuine. You must apply yourself in this direction in order to become psychologically whole and personally satisfied.

Your vision is on the crowds of people, which can cause you to overlook the needs of those closest to you. You need personal love, as well, but have a tendency to put your needs in the background. Still, you are a loving person, and need only be reminded to direct and demonstrate that love to those nearby. If, however, you are focused exclusively on the masses, people will perceive you as distant and a bit aloof.

You are emotional and sensitive. You can also be moody and critical. You have high expectations for yourself and others. This can cause you much anger when your expectations are unfulfilled. One of your most important life lessons is to forgive.

Because you are striving hard to attain high ideals, you may think of yourself as superior to others. Arrogance is a trap many 9s fall into. The danger is that arrogance cuts you off from the thing you love the most: people. Your happiness and contentment are therefore highly dependent on the ease with which you are able to serve and to influence mankind.

It is the paradox of your Heart's Desire that you receive by giving. Both your material success and your spiritual satisfaction are made possible through service and sacrifice to others.

11 Heart's Desire Number

You have a wisdom beyond your years. Even as a child, your understanding of life was considerable, though it likely went unrecognized by others.

You are a born peacemaker. You are driven by a desire to settle conflicts and create harmony. You are a healer and a visionary. You long to make the world a better place, and cannot rest until you have dedicated your life to some worthwhile cause.

Your realm is ideas and philosophy. You are attracted to the world of energy more than to the mechanical or material planes. Philosophy, religion, and less traditional forms of healing are among your specialties.

You are obsessed with the quest for enlightenment. You are extremely sensitive, and possess a high degree of intuition. Subtle messages and the feelings of others do not escape your attention. You are powerfully aware of the thoughts and feelings of others. Unless you are well-grounded, this can throw you about emotionally. Your awareness can be both a gift as well as a problem, because you so deeply desire to please others and keep harmony in your environment.

Many 11s were born into extremely hostile or turbulent families. This often results in psychological pain, lack of confidence, and shyness during childhood. Somehow, the child with an 11 Heart's Desire recognizes the sources of his family's problem. This creates an internal conflict for the child, who naturally loves the troubled parent, but cannot cope with that parent's behavior. Therefore, many 11s are scarred early in life. They understand the sufferings of others, and they seek to be of service in some way.

You understand the importance of close, loving relationships. Therefore, you are selective in choosing your friends and spouse. You are a romantic, idealistic, but somewhat impractical person. Unless you have other balancing characteristics (as indicated by 1s, 4s, and 8s in your chart), it is wise to team up with a more practical and realistic partner. This is, in fact, the easiest way for you to heal yourself and to find your greatest satisfaction.

You have a magnetic and charismatic personality. You like pondering abstract matters. Your intelligence is electric. Ideas, solutions to problems, and inventions seem to come to you as if out of the blue. You are highly charged and intense. This can cause nervous tension. You need to care for your nervous system with ample amounts of rest, a peaceful environment, and proper diet by avoiding extreme foods and drugs.

You are often more concerned with universal justice than with the individual.

The 11 is a Master number, possessing great potential. It has been entrusted to you as a gift that you are worthy of. The key is to maintain a hold on your ideals, and seek ways to practically implement them.

You have a specific role and gift to give to the world. This requires time and maturity to fully comprehend. But with patience and perseverance, you will discover why you felt different, and even unique as a child. At that time, you will discover that what made you feel weak as a child will make you feel strong and confident as a mature adult.

22 Heart's Desire Number

Deep inside, you long to create something that will have a lasting impact on the world. Whether it is a political movement, a business, or a philosophy, you have a strong inner drive to manifest something of major importance. Like the 11, yours is a Master number, possessing all the intelligence, sensitivity, and electric creativity that such a power would suggest. You have the inventiveness of the 11, and the down-to-earth practicality of the 4. This combination can make you supremely capable of making your ambitions a reality.

The demands of this Heart's Desire are as enormous as its potential. What will be required from you to fulfill your noble ambitions is nothing less than a commitment of your entire being.

The path you have chosen is not an easy one. You need time to develop, and you are unlikely to begin to fulfill your ambitions until after you have reached a certain level of maturity.

Whether you know it or not, you possess great power within your being. You were born with this power in a latent state, but on some level you were aware of it. Early in life, this power manifested as an awkwardness and a discomfort inside of you. Your self-image has always been one of contradictory extremes: on one hand you sensed your uniqueness and potential; on the other you may have felt insecure, and perhaps even inferior.

This paradox has caused waves of self-doubt and lack of confidence. But it is also a powerful generator of energy that, when combined with the higher characteristics of the 22, can become a dynamic and unrelenting force. In order to channel such great power, you need a noble goal for which to aim.

You will probably try your hand at several different kinds of work before you rise to the challenge of your true ambitions.

You can be a great leader, inspiring and motivating with your vision and work ethic. Your ideas are so creative and superior that they inspire enthusiasm, and sometimes even devotion, among your co-workers.

You should be involved in large enterprises or governmental institutions. You have the organizational and diplomatic skills sufficient to keep difficult and delicate projects on track.

Once you come into possession of your full power, there are many psychological and spiritual pitfalls to be faced. You can become arrogant. You can become deluded into thinking that your judgment is beyond question, and that the advice and support of others is unnecessary. You may seek to control all power in a given enterprise. This dangerous and egocentric attitude is sometimes even extended to family members whom you may seek to keep under your thumb.

Your challenge, once you have begun to use your true gifts, is to remain humble in the face of your significant accomplishments.

You perform best when your domestic foundation is stable and supportive; it is very important to have a partner who shares your dreams, and who has a high degree of strength and independence to keep up with your drive.

Challenges somehow draw the best out of you. Your human qualities—creativity, humility, understanding, and compassion—increase with the level of your performance. Therefore, commitment to excellence is central to your success and inner development.

Once you become thoroughly acquainted with the complex, archetypal personalities of the numbers and their relationship to the locations in your chart, you are able to recognize other bits of valuable information. For example, you will be able to see how the Heart's Desire number in particular influences your choice of surroundings, the kind of environment you like to live in, and the kind of people you attract. Therefore, a good understanding of your Heart's Desire number can result in some practical and positive changes in your life.

THE MINOR HEART'S DESIRE NUMBER

The Minor Heart's Desire number is derived from the vowels of your short name. The short name is a refinement of the more complex qualities of your longer name. It sharpens and bundles the energies that are reflected by your full name. It intensifies certain aspects of your being, and deemphasizes others. For this reason, the short name often provides insight into what you truly want in life. It also often reveals the extent of your understanding of what you want from this life. It reveals both your strong desires, and the limits you place upon your potential.

To find your Minor Heart's Desire number, add the sum total of the vowels in your short name in the same manner as that described under Heart's Desire. Remember, do not reduce Master numbers to single digits.

(As with the Heart's Desire, place the numbers above the name.)

For example:

```
   6                7
   6              1   6
 T o m         H a n c o c k
```

The name Tom has one vowel with a value of 6.
The vowels in Hancock total 7.
Tom Hancock's Minor Heart's Desire is 4 (6 + 7 = 13, 1 + 3 = 4).

The symbol for the Minor Heart's Desire is a circle, smaller than that for the Heart's Desire. (See Figure 3.1 on page 111.)

1   Minor Heart's Desire Number

With a 1 Minor Heart's Desire, you draw from yourself more strength and determination. You try to be more original, innovative, and independent. You value courage and the will to meet adversity head on.

You are willing to lead, and less willing to follow. You are less easily influenced and intimidated. You are willing to stand alone, and are better able to fight for what you think is right. (Check your Hidden Passion, described in Chapter Four, to see if there is an overabundance of 1's, five or more, which can make you selfish, stubborn, and domineering.)

2   Minor Heart's Desire Number

Your shortened name has a calming effect on your mind. It makes you more tactful and diplomatic. You are more sensitive and aware with this name. Any musical ability you may have will be enhanced.

You will be more refined and gentle. You could become a little less willing to step into the foreground, or to do things strictly on your own. The 2 is a supportive number, and enjoys working with others.

3   Minor Heart's Desire Number

Your shortened name adds enthusiasm, creativity, and liveliness to your personality. You have a great facility with words, and a deep appreciation for the arts. Writing, singing, acting, and dancing all come easier, especially if you already have talent in any of these areas. Your Minor Heart's Desire encourages you to be more social, more flexible, and more fun-loving. It makes you less serious.

You are more witty, and much more inspiring. The 3 provides you with uplifting energy, which can motivate others.

4   Minor Heart's Desire Number

Your 4 Minor Heart's Desire adds orderliness and practicality to your personality. It makes you more serious, responsible, and practical. Your short name encourages you to pay close attention to details, the nuts and bolts of business. You are less irritated by the routines of life. Your shortened name inspires you to become more grounded, and to think about your basic security and that of your loved ones.

You are more likely to be a perfectionist, and less interested in a varied social life.

You also have strong ideas concerning right and wrong.

.5   Minor Heart's Desire Number

Your shortened name encourages you to seek more freedom and adventure in your life. You want to become less conventional, and more individualistic. Your native intelligence and imagination are enhanced. You are more dynamic, enthusiastic, and flexible. You attract more excitement into your life. It is easier to adapt to changes with this Minor Heart's Desire.

6   Minor Heart's Desire Number

Your short name increases your capacity to radiate warmth, solicitude, and kindness. You are more patient with others, and a far better listener. Your willingness to carry the burden of others is increased.

Your Minor Heart's Desire increases your creativity and your domestic instincts. Women with a 6 feel better at home; men feel more comfortable in the roles of husband, father, and provider.

Your sense of harmony and social consciousness are enhanced. You are better able to settle disputes. The 6 is the most balanced of all numbers, and is in harmony with all other numbers. Very few people with 6s in prominent places stray far from their true natures.

7   Minor Heart's Desire Number

Your shortened name increases your desire to study, focus, and specialize in one particular field. It increases your need for privacy, contemplation, and meditation. You turn inward and reflect on your inner nature. You are also more likely to ponder the deeper questions of life.

Your Minor Heart's Desire enhances your intelligence and ability to deal with abstract information. You may find yourself expressing a kind of off-beat humor, as well. The 7s are highly refined and intuitive. They do not take things at face value, but seek the depths of understanding.

8   Minor Heart's Desire Number

Your Minor Heart's Desire increases your ambition and inner strength. Your ability to deal with business, managerial, and organizational matters is enhanced. You are able to focus on your goals, and to apply the necessary determination and effort to realize them.

Your shortened name increases your capacity for leadership and personal power. It makes you more conscious of material wealth. You are more willing to work hard to improve your status or financial position.

Your shortened name makes you more aware of being a good judge of character, and you are willing to work on this talent. This results in becoming a shrewd judge of others, and a better negotiator.

9   Minor Heart's Desire Number

The shortened version of your name broadens your outlook on life. It makes you more compassionate, socially oriented, and concerned for the welfare of humanity. Your Minor Heart's Desire indicates your idealism and capacity for self-sacrifice toward a higher goal. You want to make a difference in life.

You may be more likely to hold yourself aloof, and thereby make it harder to find the personal love you need. Your appreciation for the arts is increased, and any artistic talent you may have is enhanced. You may want to become more of a teacher, and are attracted to knowledge that will further this ambition.

11   Minor Heart's Desire Number

Your short name increases your sensitivity, intuition, and perceptiveness. It inspires you to deepen your investigation of the mysteries of life. You are more attracted to religion, philosophy, and spiritual understanding. It may awaken your intuitive, and even your psychic abilities.

At the same time, your Minor Heart's Desire number makes you more sensitive to your own shortcomings. It encourages you to work on yourself.

Your increased sensitivity will encourage you to seek out harmonious and peaceful environments. This will balance the nervous tension that the 11 can stimulate.

Your desire to work with others is also improved. You are likely to feel more humble and modest, and to seek ways to avoid conflict and to maintain harmonious relationships. Your heightened intuitive powers bring highly creative ideas, sudden insights, and realizations.

22   Minor Heart's Desire Number

Your short name increases your ambition, orderliness, and capacity to complete large undertakings significantly. You develop your managerial skills, and seek to direct people toward some ambitious undertaking. You will feel more attracted to the study of organizational methods. You are more concerned with your fellow man, and you want to create something that will improve the well-being of others. Your practical nature is joined with your more idealistic and spiritual values.

At the same time, you may feel burdened by new and lofty ambitions.

High demands can cause you self-doubt. You may be aware of more inner tension, resulting from an inner drive to manifest your ideals in reality. As a result of your Minor Heart's Desire number, your efforts are more likely to be directed toward endeavors that are truly great in scope, and have a lasting impact.

Your Minor Heart's Desire number is significant in more ways than one. In order to fully understand the meaning of your Minor Heart's Desire number, a certain amount of honesty is required. It is a challenge to analyze your Heart's Desire number next to your Minor Heart's Desire number, and, without cutting yourself any slack, try to recognize what you are trying to hide, or what you are avoiding.

THE PERSONALITY NUMBER

Your Personality number is derived from the consonants of your full name. Your Personality is like a narrow entrance hall to the great room that is your true nature. It is those aspects that you feel comfortable sharing with people at the outset of a relationship. With time and trust, you invite others into the deeper aspects of your nature; you reveal more of who you really are, in effect, your Heart's Desire, Expression, and so on.

Your Personality number often serves as a censoring device, both in terms of what you send out, as well as what you allow to approach. It discriminates in the kinds of people and information you let enter your heart and mind. For this reason, your Personality is usually much more narrow and protective in its definition than the real you. It can screen out some of what you do not want to deal with—people or situations—but it also welcomes those things that immediately relate to your inner nature.

Fortunately or unfortunately, this narrow entrance is the first impression people get of you. It either welcomes and intrigues them, or it causes them to lose interest.

How to Find Your Personality Number

To find your Personality number, add the numerical value of the consonants of each of your names in the same manner as described earlier in the Expression and Heart's Desire. Note: Do not reduce Master numbers when calculating the Personality number.

Example: Thomas John Hancock

T	h	o	m	a	s		$15 = 1 + 5 = 6$
2	8		4		1		

J	o	h	n				$14 = 1 + 4 = 5$
1		8	5				

H	a	n	c	o	c	k	$21 = 2 + 1 = 3$
8		5	3		3	2	

The name Thomas has four consonants (2, 8, 4, and 1), which total 6.

The name John has three consonants with a combined value of 5.

The name Hancock has five consonants, which total 3.

Thomas John Hancock's Personality number, therefore, is $6 + 5 + 3 = 14$, which reduces to 5.

The symbol used for the Personality number is a square with the number inside. (See Figure 3.1 on page 111.)

THE MINOR PERSONALITY NUMBER

The Minor Personality number is based on the consonants of your short name, and it gives additional information about how you present yourself to the outer world. This number reveals in particular those aspects of your personality that you are, or have become, most comfortable with.

A name change that occurs later in life, such as through marriage or for professional reasons, can have a significant impact on your approach and your attitude in dealing with others, and this is reflected in your Minor Personality number. For this reason, name changes are not recommended and should be considered carefully, perhaps with the guidance of a numerologist. With a marriage, for instance, a hyphenated name is suggested, to add traits without changing your attitude entirely.

To find your Minor Personality number, add the numerical value of the consonants of your short name, and reduce them to a single digit. Do not reduce Master numbers.

In the example:

T	o	m	H	a	n	c	o	c	k
2		4 +	8		5	3		3	2
	6			21 = 2 + 1 = 3					

Tom Hancock's Minor Personality number is (6 + 3) = 9.

The symbol for the Minor Personality is a smaller version than the one for the Personality. (See Figure 3.1 on page 111.)

The following descriptions can apply to the Personality as well as the Minor Personality, but keep in mind that the influence of the Minor Personality is far overshadowed by that of the Personality number, which is based on the full name at birth.

1   Personality and Minor Personality Number

You radiate with a dynamic and efficient energy. You appear controlled and capable. You value courage and effort in the face of difficulties, and these qualities show. Others can sense that you will not be pushed around. You should dress in a dignified manner, caring for the details of your appearance. While you may spend most of your time in staid business dress or suits, bright and cheerful colors work well for you. You are fashionable, but have your own style.

Your appearance suffers more than most people's when you are overweight. Overweight directly contradicts the type of personality you are trying to project. Straight lines and square corners accent your good physique and enhance your appearance as a leader.

You are recognized as a pioneer; you have your own ideas of how to do things. You are a risk-taker, original, and highly creative.

You should be wary of appearing too aggressive or unreceptive. You can intimidate people if you don't soften your exterior somewhat. By doing this, you will attract less confident people who will be more willing to approach you with their thoughts and suggestions.

2   Personality and Minor Personality Number

You appear friendly and unpretentious. You have a soft and warm exterior. Others perceive you as a gentle, safe harbor. People are drawn to you, because, among other reasons, you appear warm and unthreatening.

Your dress is neat and clean. Your clothing should be comfortable, soft, and flowing. You should avoid plain and understated clothes. Make an effort to be a little more daring and exciting in your appearance. This will balance nicely with your perceptive and open personality. The opposite sex is attracted to your gentle and attentive nature, yet senses the passion beneath your surface. You have sex appeal.

Exercise is important to your appearance, and to promoting the level of strength you radiate. You are very patient and understanding, and you are a wonderful listener. You make others feel important and loved.

You are sensitive and become tense in a disharmonious atmosphere. You experienced quite a bit of negative criticism as a child, which made you shy growing up. Though you may be well past that shyness, a bit of the vulnerability has remained with you, and is often sensed by others.

You are a peacemaker. Arguments leave you drained. People sense your desire for harmony. But you must avoid being the blank tablet for others' projections. People may underestimate your strength, but this is a mistake. You are strong. You bend, but don't break.

You have a fine sense of beauty and excellent taste. There is a grace in your movements, reflecting your keen sense of harmony and refinement.

3   Personality and Minor Personality Number

You are highly attractive. Many men with a 3 Personality are very handsome; women are often strikingly beautiful.

Your vibration is full of life. You are uplifting, inspiring, and charming. You are a fun person to be around. Your wit and sparkling personality make you the life of a party. You are extroverted and optimistic. You appreciate fine clothing and jewelry, and enjoy dressing up a bit. You like glamour, and are sought after by the opposite sex. You are a romantic. You fall in and out of love rather quickly. You are affectionate and giving.

Do not let your charm be an incentive to play too much. Work at developing deep and lasting relationships. You have to avoid scattering your attention for popularity. You can be flippant about commitments, and may dramatize or exaggerate. Your wit can cause you to rely too much on superficial, humorous conversation.

You have a distinct lucky streak that attracts many opportunities throughout your life. You also have a knack for promoting yourself, as well as for inspiring others. When backed up by hard work and self-discipline, these qualities almost ensure your success.

4   Personality and Minor Personality Number

You radiate reliability and consistency. People trust you and feel secure with your judgment. You are seen as a cornerstone of a business, and are relied upon to do your work efficiently and expertly.

You have strength and respectability. You tend to dress in a utilitarian manner, concerned mostly with convention, practicality, durability, and price. You present yourself as someone who values correctness, control, and precision. All of this stems from the fact that your most prized characteristic is your work. You want to be judged on the basis of your performance, rather than on your appearance. You are frugal and have learned to respect the dollar. You are concerned about the security of your future and those you love; however, this may appear to others as a bit too austere.

You tend to wear earth colors and conventional attire. You could benefit by putting a little flair in your dress. Wear more uplifting colors. Loosen your dress with less severe lines. If you wear a brown suit, include a bright tie or some jewelry.

You are a family person. You love the intimacy, consistency, and the security a family provides. You are a good provider and protector. But family members may take your efforts for granted.

You are a true patriot. You love your country and are an integral part of your community. Your consistency and adherence to your well-laid plans usually pay off in a comfortable and secure future.

5   Personality and Minor Personality Number

You are a stimulating person. You brighten social gatherings with your fresh and original ideas. Your conversation tends to be sprinkled with novelty and wit. You have a quick tongue and charisma. You are probably an excellent salesperson. There is a lot of nervous energy within you that is looking for an outlet.

You love your freedom, and you see this life as an ongoing adventure. You are upbeat and optimistic. This is infectious for those you meet. As a result, you inspire others.

You have a strong and attractive body, with good muscle tone. Your movements are supple, graceful, and athletic. Your bane is that you love to indulge your senses with food and drink, and you can easily gain weight. You have an appetite for anything that stimulates the senses—sex, food, alcohol, and drugs. Discipline is a necessity for you. The negative side of a 5 Personality number can give rise to an addictive personality. You like to dress fashionably and can get away with more colorful clothes. However, you should be aware of the value of quality, and of the power of modesty.

You are a little irresponsible, and quick in satisfying your sensual urges. You are attractive, and that, coupled with your innate ability to promote yourself, makes it easy for you to satisfy your desire for new and exciting relationships.

You have a kind of swashbuckling personality. People see you as the adventurer that you are. They expect the unexpected from you, and when they don't, you often surprise them.

You have a quick and eclectic mind. You attract information from all directions, but you can be a bit superficial, skimming over the surface of a wide diversity of subjects. This may cause you to be a bit of a dilettante. You can get away with it much of the time, but for your own success and happiness, you should try to ground knowledge, and to deepen your understanding.

Your versatility and adaptability make you capable of getting the most out of virtually every opportunity in life. You decide quickly on a course of action, and your timing is usually good. You radiate the potential for success, which attracts others who can further you along your path.

6   Personality and Minor Personality Number

You exude understanding and compassion. People sense your warmth and fairness. For this reason, you attract many people who are in need of comfort, including the disadvantaged. People tend to come to you to unload their burdens. You inspire confidence.

You have a fine sense of justice. You do everything in your power to keep harmony, and you are even willing to sacrifice your personal desires for the good of others.

You can take this too far, however, sometimes playing the role of the martyr. You have to guard against being taken advantage of. You are not always a very good judge of character. You tend to see the best in people.

You can also become too involved in the lives of others, to your own detriment. (This aspect can be balanced by other numbers in your chart.) You are hospitable and domestic. You love children, and you are a good parent. You are romantic, faithful, and very protective.

You are artistic. You love music, flowers, and gardening. You are a natural interior designer. You have an excellent sense of color and taste.

You are more concerned with the content of your personality than your appearance, which causes you to be less conscious of the style of your clothes. You are more interested in comfort and the utility of clothing than the statement it makes.

Those who are 6 Personality numbers are exceedingly generous. You are not particularly logical when it comes to finances. You are very vulnerable to praise and criticism. You tend to worry a lot, which causes you stomach problems.

People see you as a maternal or paternal figure. They want to relax in your presence and unburden themselves. You are the safe port in the crowd.

7   Personality and Minor Personality Number

You seem mysterious and different. People see you as serious and studious. You are highly independent and self-sufficient. Your exceptional intelligence and wisdom are quickly noticed; people respect you. You are not one to attract people on the basis of your warmth or compassion, though you may be loaded with both, but on the basis of your obvious insight into life's mysteries.

You are hard to get to know. You are often withdrawn. It is common for people to see your focus turn inside of yourself in the middle of a conversation.

You have the makings of an intellectual and an aristocrat, but you have to guard against arrogance and an attitude of, "I've got it all figured out." There are periods in your life when you have little concern for your clothing or fashion, while at other times you are very aware of your clothing and use it to make a specific impression. You appear dignified no matter how you dress, but a well-groomed 7 with a touch of dash definitely has an advantage. Your confidence increases when you know you are well-dressed.

You are recognized as spiritual and religious, with your very own ideas regarding the purpose of life and the Creator.

You are an inspired speaker, but only when discussing subjects that really interest you. Otherwise, you are not one for chatter.

Your love of knowledge and wisdom shows.

8 Personality and Minor Personality Number

You appear strong and powerful. You have an impressive personality, and can influence, and even intimidate through sheer force. You have natural authority. Your competence and enthusiasm attract people with resources. You radiate confidence. People defer to you because they sense your sureness and effectiveness. You also exude a kind of controlled benevolence. People sense that you are generous, once you are convinced of the worthiness of the cause.

It is important for you to dress well. You radiate a kind of raw power and ableness, which needs to be refined and enhanced by your clothing. You may even dress a bit flashy, but that will not harm you. Quality is among your highest priorities, and should be reflected in your clothing. Although most 8s have a strong constitution, they can be prone to indigestion, ulcers, and heart disease due to their reckless eating and drinking habits, and their propensity to be workaholics.

Your Achilles heel is your capacity for an egocentric attitude. The negative side of your personality can cause you to be ruthless, greedy, and intensely lonely. Conversely, you can be spontaneous and excited. You are essentially warm and jovial. In your heart of hearts, you want everyone to be as excited and as happy as you. Those who are around you often sense this. Your co-workers and employees usually like you.

9 Personality and Minor Personality Number

You have an impressive and aristocratic bearing. No matter how tall you are, you appear noble and upright. You are very much in control of the image you send out to others.

Many actors, dancers, and other performers have a 9 Personality number. You are elegant, graceful, and charismatic. Many admire you.

You have the kind of stature that pulls people to you or repels them intensely. Some are jealous of you, and may seek to belittle you.

You may encourage this to some extent by the amount of arrogance you radiate. This is a caution for all 9 Personalities. They are sometimes aloof and hold themselves above the world.

Your challenge is to come down to earth with your fellow man. Conversely, you have a great compassion for humanity, and you want to dedicate yourself to improving the lot of others.

You are better when dealing with the trials of the many than the troubles of a single person. You are more capable of working on the grand scale, addressing the needs of society, than on a one-to-one basis.

You are kind, sympathetic, helpful, and compassionate. Behind the controlled and calm facade, you are sensitive, vulnerable, and emotional.

You have excellent taste. There is a good deal of artistic talent in you that shows in your home environment and in your clothing.

You tend to see yourself as a guardian of society; a benevolent leader, guiding and directing your community toward a better world.

11   Personality and Minor Personality Number

The 11 Personality is similar to a 2 Personality, but with even more sensitivity and nervous energy. You are often too vulnerable, and even minor criticism directed at you can have a devastating effect. Those with an 11 Personality or Minor Personality should consciously develop and express more primal strength.

Those with an 11 Personality have an extraordinary understanding of the human psyche and are consequently gifted counselors. However, they tend to have difficulty maintaining stability in their personal lives, and often lack confidence. They are easy prey to hardcore salespeople, and learning to say no can be a considerable challenge. There is also a tendency to attract the wrong kind of relationships, particularly at an early age.

Later in life, your 11 Personality has the potential to become a major asset. Your perceptive awareness and talent for diplomacy give you an edge over others that allows you to influence and even manipulate them.

22   Personality and Minor Personality Number

The 22 Personality is similar to the 4 Personality, but with the ability to reach for higher goals. You make a distinct impression on others, which either makes them your fans or causes them to turn away. People notice you when you step into a room.

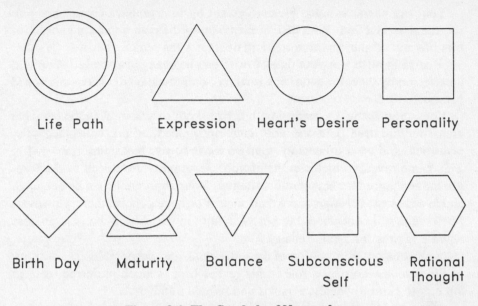

Life Path   Expression   Heart's Desire   Personality

Birth Day   Maturity   Balance   Subconscious   Rational
                                     Self   Thought

Figure 3.1 The Symbols of Numerology

Like the 11 Personality, you also have the ability to influence others, but for very different reasons. You have considerable strength and self-confidence and you are quite willing to apply this in dealing with others. You can be overbearing, and many a weaker Personality will try to move out of your range for safer ground. Your challenge is to become more aware of the feelings that may motivate another person and to respect these feelings.

Men with a 22 Personality are powerful and impressive individuals who have an easier time than others applying for loans, negotiating contracts, or demanding promotions. Women with a 22 Personality are no less powerful, but within this society they often have to overcome obstacles related to society's expectations as to what a woman's role should be. They may scare men, or make them feel less confident, which in turn can cause these men to be hostile. For this reason, it may be even more important for a woman with a 22 Personality to be more sensitive.

Your Personality and Minor Personality number give you an indication of how others perceive you. After all, it shows what aspects of your personality you feel comfortable with and are willing to expose to the outer world.

You are able to learn much about yourself if you contemplate your Personality and Minor Personality number in relation to the other core numbers. How much of yourself do you reveal? What aspects of your make-up do you try to hide?

Your full name, as it was given to you at birth, reveals your true personality; the potential you. Your date of birth shows the path you have chosen for this life and all the opportunities and obstacles that come your way. Neither your name at birth, nor your date of birth can be changed or erased. You will be affected by them for better or for worse, until the day you leave this world behind.

Your short name, the name you use to introduce yourself, indicates what areas of your true potential you have recognized, where you place your priorities, and what aspects of your personality you feel comfortable with. This name reveals which aspects of your personality are drawn to the foreground, enhanced, or sometimes softened. Your short name can be changed, and in many cases changes more than once. You have a choice there. However, I believe that it is beneficial to put your faith in the natural, holistic process when it is time for a name change.

In most cases, the intuition of the individual, and the combined sensitivity of the people who play a role in his or her life, is much preferred over an attempt to carefully analyze names and related numbers.

I have seen numerous cases in which a name change as a result of marriage proved to be beneficial in ways that were not immediately obvious. I have seen cases in which nicknames, even used during a short time, enhanced positive qualities and eliminated shortcomings in the individual. I have seen cases in which an individual stubbornly persisted with a name change that made no sense to anyone, but felt important, without logic or reason, to the individual, and these name changes also proved to be beneficial. But I have also seen name changes as a result of whimsical impulses, or in an effort to portray something one is not, and these changes rarely have a positive effect on the person. More often than not, they result in confusion and instability.

I do not pretend to understand the reasons or the infinitely complex processes that make us who we are and that continue to support this life in all its variations, I sincerely doubt that the mind is capable of ever understanding something of such magnitude. However, I believe that life is a supportive and orderly system, and consequently, that your given name and date of birth are never a coincidence. You were born at the precise moment, and given the perfect name, to continue your personal evolution towards greater fulfillment and contentment.

Chapter 4

More About Your Name

Know thyself.

—Inscription at the Delphic Oracle

S o far, we've talked about the strongest, and usually the most obvious, aspects of a person's character. But now we enter into the more hidden realms, where people are driven by desires or ambitions that even they may not be aware of. In order to become free human beings, we must make these subtle, unconscious traits conscious. We must become aware of ourselves in our deepest recesses in order to take control of our lives. Otherwise, we are slaves to our unconscious desires. Illuminating these hidden traits is what this part of the book helps us to do.

THE KARMIC LESSON CHART

Numerology is based on the understanding that we enter life with certain strengths and weaknesses. Karmic Lessons are areas that we are currently weak in, and that we must face and work on in this life. There can be more than one Karmic Lesson. As we have already seen, each letter in your name corresponds to a specific number. Certain numbers repeat within your name, while others may be missing. Karmic Lessons are indicated when one or more of the nine single-digit numbers are missing in your name. A Karmic strength is suggested when a number is represented two or more times. (See Hidden Passion in this chapter.)

The letters and numbers of your name point to talents and abilities that you possess. These characteristics can be compared to a workshop in which certain tools are available to you. Missing numbers, those that are not represented in the letters of your name, imply tools that are unavailable, and that must be learned and mastered during this lifetime.

Generally, long names—eighteen or more letters—with eight or all nine numbers represented, indicate capable people who can deal with almost any situation. Their personalities are well-formed; their interests are widespread; and their capacities to overcome obstacles are well-defined.

Short names—up to fifteen letters—that also contain within them as many as eight or more of the nine single-digit numbers, suggest powerful people with a strong need to lead or to shine in a crowd. They are multitalented, and tend to be survivors. They are resilient, and they bounce back from adversity sooner and easier than do others.

People with long names who have very few numbers represented, six or less, confront a powerful paradox in their lives. On one hand, they tend to deal with many obstacles in their personal lives, facing intense and often tumultuous relationships. Also, they often lack the phoenix-like ability to rise again from adversity in these areas.

On the other hand, such a person is often extremely talented in a specific area, and has the ability to direct all of his or her resources to obtain a very high level of success in that particular area. (After all, when a long name contains only six or fewer different numbers, at least some of these numbers must be represented several times.)

Many outstanding actors, singers, scientists, military strategists, television personalities, craftspeople, and artists have names with various numbers missing, and they have the kind of focus this type of name implies.

For people with three or more numbers missing, it is supremely important to focus on your career and talents, and to persevere in the face of any difficulty or obstacle. The kind of keyhole energy suggested by such a name gives you the ability to achieve great success in a specific part of life; but before such a success can be achieved, adversity must be overcome. Perseverance, therefore, becomes the key to your happiness.

It is not uncommon to have a name with six numbers represented, but five numbers in a name is rare, and four numbers in a name of average length is extremely uncommon. I know of one lady with a name of sixteen letters, which translates into three different numbers (ten 5s, two 4s, and four 3s; in other words, she has six numbers missing). For obvious reasons, I will not mention her name. Suffice it to say that, although she has known many difficult times, and faced challenges many of us might have found almost impossible to conquer, she persevered, and is today an extremely talented singer and dancer.

How to Find Your Karmic Lessons

Let's use Thomas John Hancock again to find the Karmic Lessons.

```
T h o m a s   J o h n   H a n c o c k
2 8 6 4 1 1   1 6 8 5   5 8 1 5 3 6 3 2
```

We can see that Thomas John Hancock has the following arrangement of numbers: 1 four times; 2 two times; 3 two times; 4 one time; 5 two times; 6 three times; 7 missing; 8 three times; and 9 missing.

Thomas John Hancock has two Karmic Lessons; the numbers 7 and 9 are missing in his name, which, in a name of 17 letters, is average. He would therefore look at the numbers 7 and 9 below to see the meaning of these two Karmic Lessons.

See Figure 4.1, shown below, for an illustration of the Karmic Lesson Chart as used in our charting system.

Figure 4.1 The Karmic Lesson and Hidden Passion Chart
The Karmic Lesson and Hidden Passion chart shown here, is based on the name Thomas John Hancock.

The 7 and the 9 are missing in his name and so 7 and 9 are his Karmic Lessons.

The 1 is represented in his name more than any other number, and is his Hidden Passion.

4 1	2 2	2 3
1 4	2 5	3 6
0 7	3 8	0 9

1 Karmic Lesson Number

You need to show more initiative in your life. You must learn to be more determined. Your will needs to be strengthened. You will be forced to stand up for what you believe to be right. You will need to make your own decisions. You must learn to be more independent. You will encounter many strong-willed people in your life with whom you will struggle. You will have to learn to assert yourself or to be suppressed by these forceful people.

This is happening so that you can learn to become more forceful and dynamic. Learn not to concern yourself too much with what others think. You may be too meek and timid. Learn to promote yourself. Work on your self-confidence, and have more faith in your judgment and abilities. Overcome any tendency to procrastinate.

The effect of this Karmic Lesson is diminished if you have at least one 1 among your core numbers.

2   Karmic Lesson Number

You must learn to be more diplomatic and tactful; to stay in the background when necessary; and sometimes to accomplish something without the need to be praised and rewarded. Learn to be part of a team. You must learn to be more sensitive to other people's needs and feelings. You will regularly find yourself in a situation in which the only road to success is through patience and attention, requiring you to work closely with others.

The effect of this Karmic Lesson is diminished if you have at least one 2 among your core numbers.

3   Karmic Lesson Number

You are highly self-critical. Every time you find yourself at the center of attention, you manage to find something in your performance to be entirely inadequate or embarrassing. You have established an impossible standard of perfection as the only measure of your actions.

You need to lighten up on yourself. Realize that you have within you a critical faculty that must be contained and controlled. Otherwise, it can prevent you from doing what you truly enjoy in life.

You're too serious. Be more optimistic and cheerful; enjoy life as it was meant to be and share this joy with others. Life will put you in situations that require imagination and communication. You will be tested in these areas. You will be forced to face the challenge.

Missing 3s often produce artists, but their success requires much work and perseverance. The effect of the Karmic Lesson is diminished if you have at least one 3 among your core numbers.

4 Karmic Lesson Number

You feel confusion about your life's direction. You will have to establish a methodical and disciplined approach. You need to create a foundation for your life. Otherwise, you will feel lost and tossed about by change. You have trouble finding the work you do best. You tend to be somewhat impractical and disorganized. You look for the answers to life's problems outside yourself, rather than within. New jobs start off as the answer, but do not have the same glamour for long. You quickly discover that the new work requires the same effort and perseverance, without the excitement you expected, which may cause you to give up too soon. Concentration and application need to be strengthened.

The effects of this Karmic Lesson are diminished if you have at least one 4 among your core numbers.

5 Karmic Lesson Number

You need to be more adventurous. You must overcome your fear of living. Take every opportunity to experience life. Travel, see strange and exotic lands, meet new people, and have many new experiences. Broaden your vision, and be more social. You must learn to embrace change. You will be required to adapt to new circumstances. Overcome your tendency to be rigid and inflexible. Your lesson in life is to learn to have faith. You will learn to flow with life, to adapt with the changes, and to grow. You will learn a great deal through experience.

The effects of this Karmic Lesson are diminished if you have at least one 5 among your core numbers.

6 Karmic Lesson Number

You have a major issue with commitment and responsibility to others. You have a hard time committing to marriage and to other important personal relationships. You have to learn to show true emotion.

You may feel isolated and alone, but do not understand why. The reason is that you very often form relationships, yet remain heavily guarded, putting up a show of emotion without truly communicating affection or care. This can make the bond between you and others superficial. You must learn to establish sincere relationships.

You will learn the importance of close friends and lasting relationships. You will learn to give, and, when necessary, to sacrifice. This is the one certain way to true friendship and lasting love.

The effects of this Karmic Lesson are diminished if you have at least one 6 among your core numbers.

7   Karmic Lesson Number

You need to deepen your knowledge and talents in a specific discipline. You lack the will or the determination to perfect yourself or a specific talent you possess. You must learn to be your own critic, without self-condemnation, in order to bring your abilities to their full development. You will learn not to take things at face value. A superficial understanding of important matters will prevent you from experiencing the satisfaction of your true potential.

The effects of this Karmic Lesson are diminished if you have at least one 7 among your core numbers.

8   Karmic Lesson Number

You can attract a considerable amount of money, and even be a good business person, but you experience major ups and downs in your financial affairs due largely to your lack of caution in handling your resources.

You are highly independent, and you do not want to be told how to do things. You have great problems with authority figures. This stems from a know-it-all attitude, and a stubborn behavior that prevents you from knowing your limits.

You will have to work at learning how to handle money. In all likelihood, you will attract enough of it, but it has a tendency to slip through your fingers. This Karmic Lesson forces you to learn your limitations, and the limitations of your resources. Learn to be efficient.

The effects of this Karmic Lesson are diminished if you have at least one 8 among your core numbers.

9   Karmic Lesson Number

You must learn to be more compassionate, tolerant, and understanding. You have to learn to identify with the trials of others. There will be times when you will have to sacrifice some egocentric ambition for the good of a particular project or some larger goal.

You must learn to broaden your view of life. You have to see things on a larger scale. You do not realize the enormous potential you have in influencing your own destiny and that of others. Therefore, you hold back your efforts to help people, or further a particular social cause. You have an issue with commitment to community or mankind.

The effects of this Karmic Lesson are diminished if you have at least one 9 among your core numbers.

The Karmic Lesson number that is found more often than any other number in Western names is the 7. This reflects the fact that, although (or perhaps because) organized religion is a major force in the West, the individual's personal search for spiritual enlightenment, through aloneness and contemplation, is not encouraged. It is interesting to notice that names found in the East, in particular Chinese, Japanese, and Eastern Europe, almost always include the number 7.

THE HIDDEN PASSION NUMBER

As I mentioned in the text on Karmic Lessons, numbers that appear two or more times in your name represent a particular strength or ability. The number that is most often repeated in your name represents your specific field of expertise, or a concentrated talent.

Metaphorically, this talent can be seen as having a power all its own to shape your life. Its existence gives you a strong desire to develop and to express that particular ability. Having the talent demands that you express it, that you experience this part of you, and that you live according to its nature. In this way, the Hidden Passion shapes your personality, and guides your life.

How to Find Your Hidden Passion Number

Find the number or numbers that are most often represented in your name. For example, Thomas John Hancock's Hidden Passion is 1, which is repeated four times in his name, more than any other number (see Karmic Lessons).

It is interesting to note that in Northern European names (based on Germanic languages, including English), which dominate American society, the letters representing the number 5 (E, N, and W) are found more often than other letters. The result is that the Hidden Passion 5 predominates all other numbers. This is reflected in the fact that for American (and Northern

European) people, freedom is the highest priority. (The terms U.S.A. and America also have a 5 Expression.)

On the other hand, Southern European names, which are based on Latin languages, predominate with letters representing the number 1, particularly the letters A and S. This, in turn, is reflected in the individualism and tolerance for unconventionality, which is found among these peoples.

You can have more than one Hidden Passion. (See Figure 4.1 on page 115, which also shows the Hidden Passion(s) in a chart.)

Because the Hidden Passion is based on the number value of each letter found in your name, and these range from 1 through 9, the 11 and 22 Hidden Passions do not exist.

1 Hidden Passion Number

You have a strong drive to stand out. You have a great ambition, and a desire to accomplish. You are highly competitive, and you want to be the best and the first in everything you do. You are highly energetic and creative. You are capable of influencing, and even of dominating others. You have highly developed political skills, and you can succumb to manipulation unless your ideals are high. Ironically, there are times when you lack confidence, especially at an earlier age, but you have the strength to overcome this obstacle.

You are a survivor, a warrior, and a leader. Many great athletes and politicians have this number as a Hidden Passion. Too many 1s (6 or more in a name of average length) can make a person bullish, aggressive, violent, and even tyrannical.

2 Hidden Passion Number

You are highly considerate, sensitive, and intuitive. You seek peaceful and pleasant environments. You work hard to establish harmony among your peers and co-workers. You work well in groups, often serving as the peace-maker. You may appear shy and timid, and although you like people, there is an inner fear. You dislike noise and roughness.

You are committed to your work, and you perform your job with a high degree of competency, patience, and persistence. You are a magnet for information. You are often one of the pillars of any organization. People naturally rely upon you.

You have a tendency to worry too much about trivial details, and can waste time on petty affairs. You may be too sensitive and easily hurt; your feelings can get in the way of your sound judgment.

You have a good ear for music and rhythm, and an appreciation for the arts. You love beauty in your environment. You have fine and delicate taste.

3 Hidden Passion Number

You are highly social, and have a gift for self-expression. You love to entertain and to attend parties.

You are exceedingly popular, and you are a good friend. You are highly talented in one or more of the arts—writing, acting, music, or painting. You need excitement. When things are dull, you tend to fantasize, and sometimes to exaggerate. You are very inspiring and motivating to others. You are blessed with a considerable amount of charm and charisma. You are highly optimistic, which can make you a bit of a rolling stone. You think that the grass is always going to be greener on the other side of the hill.

You need discipline and focus to make the most of your talents. You can fall victim to scattering your energies. You have to guard against being selfish and indulging in too much sensory gratification.

4 Hidden Passion Number

The 4 Hidden Passion is systematic and organized, and there are few goals out of your reach. You have determination, perseverance, and self-discipline.

You are perceived as solid as a rock and just as reliable. Your family and friends have faith in you and your ability to care for them.

You identify with work, and can be very unhappy if you are in a job you do not love. You have a sharp eye for details. You enjoy the security and steadiness of schedules. You do not like the unexpected.

You are practical and realistic. You are also concerned about the welfare of your community.

You love nature and the beauty and efficiency that characterizes natural law.

You have sound judgment and understanding when it comes to estimating the value of a plan or the feasibility of an enterprise.

You have good concentration.

Your family and home are very important to you. Your love runs deep and is extremely loyal and protective. Those who have many 4s—four or more—in their names or in prominent places in their chart must guard against becoming obsessed with details, and becoming rigid, narrow-minded, and boring.

5   Hidden Passion Number

You love travel, change, and new challenges. You are highly adaptable and versatile. You have a talent for languages, and you are generally good with words. Writing, promotion, and public relations work suit you perfectly. You are sensual, and a bit impulsive. You love to satisfy your senses, which can get you into trouble.

Overindulgence in food, drink, sex, and drugs are common among people with too many 5s (six or more). You are resourceful and original. You have a good sense of humor and a quick tongue. Your desire for freedom is extremely strong, and it will take effort and discipline to stick with whatever it is you start. There is a tendency to give up a project or situation prematurely.

You may be interested in too many things, which can make it hard for you to apply yourself to one area successfully. You are very unconventional.

Commitment in relationships and your work is fundamental to your happiness. You may have a tendency to wander from person to person, or job to job, making depth of relationship or deep expertise difficult.

6   Hidden Passion Number

You have a dream to be of service to those you love and to your community. You have the ability to be a healer, counselor, or teacher.

You are a highly responsible person who is willing to sacrifice much. You must be careful not to become a doormat for those who do not appreciate you, or those who seek to take advantage of you.

You are idealistic and have strong opinions. You also have a tendency to become self-righteous. You are generous and a humanitarian.

You are an excellent parent and marriage partner. You are helpful and forever willing to listen to someone else's troubles, but must be careful not to interfere.

7   Hidden Passion Number

You have a highly developed mind, and a fine intuition. You are intellectual, and you deal well with abstract ideas. You like to be alone to contemplate, meditate, and study.

You are drawn to the philosophical and metaphysical. Nevertheless, you can be highly skeptical and even cynical of things you cannot prove.

You are a deep thinker with unusual understanding and insight. You do not like to waste time on trivial and petty matters. You are a specialist and a perfectionist. You come up with unique solutions to problems, and you can be very convincing when the subject interests you.

You can be self-centered, melancholic, and depressed. Loneliness is quite common among people with many 7s; they have to learn to be alone without being lonely. Faith in the order and balance of nature is a must. You may seem different, alien, and hard to get to know to others, but once they "know" you, they love and respect you. Even though you tend to keep to yourself, you are generous with your love, and you are genuinely concerned with the happiness of those around you, but you are not demonstrative.

8   Hidden Passion Number

Success and material rewards are important motivations for your actions. You believe in effort, and you are very goal-oriented. You can dominate and impress others with your vision and common business sense. You are a born manager and organizer; your subordinates usually like you. Leadership and authority are obvious, but it is wise not to be too forceful, demanding, and dominant.

You are a good judge of character with an uncanny ability to sense other people's strengths and weaknesses. There may be a tendency to abuse this talent. All 8s have to be wary of greed and ruthlessness. Your ability to sense where someone else is coming from is much better served with your natural counselor's instinct.

Many 8s in a name are an advantage in the business world and a considerable help in the quest for success. However, they can also be the cause for hardships. Many tests and frustrations have to be overcome, and, most important, the proper balance and perspective regarding spirit and matter have to be attained.

You need a family to be proud of and status to feel rewarded. You may have a tendency to show off your wealth and success.

9   Hidden Passion Number

As a warm, generous, and compassionate person, you would do well and be quite happy in any undertaking that not only supplies you with a decent living, but is also for the good of all.

You are artistic; the 9 is responsible for many creative geniuses. However, these talents are often suppressed, sometimes coming to the surface at middle or old age.

You have a strong desire for insight and universal knowledge.

You are emotional; your feelings are not always sensible, and they too are often suppressed.

You can get caught up in dreams and ideals without being practical, but you have enough fire and enthusiasm to attract support. Your oratorical abilities save many a situation.

You are driven to do your own thing, and you are quite independent.

The Hidden Passion numbers found most often in Western names are 5, 1, 3, and 9 respectively. It is interesting to note that the four most common Hidden Passion numbers based on Western names are idealistic as opposed to practical.

THE SUBCONSCIOUS SELF NUMBER

The Subconscious Self reflects the confidence you have in your personal power and competence, as well as in your ability to deal with sudden events and situations. It shows your capacity to correctly assess a situation and to respond appropriately.

The Subconscious Self is derived from your Karmic Lesson Chart, in which it is possible to have all nine numbers represented in your name, or fewer than nine; in fact as few as five, or as many as eight. For example, you may be missing a 6 or a 7. This means that when you encounter a situation that requires the characteristics of a 6 or a 7, there will be some feeling of inadequacy, or uncertainty as to how to properly deal with the demands of the situation.

On the other hand, you still have the other seven or eight numbers represented in your name, which means your ability to deal with situations that require any of those numbers is well-developed. You possess a certain confidence or assurance that makes you feel familiar with the situation, and able to deal with it effectively. Hence, a person with eight numbers represented in their name will tend to be more confident in most situations than a person with only five numbers.

In general, someone with eight numbers in his name is quite capable of dealing with most situations.

Paradoxically, a person with all nine numbers represented tends to be aloof or overly complacent when dealing with sudden events.

How to Find Your Subconscious Self Number

To find your Subconscious Self number, simply count the amount of numbers represented in your name, as revealed in the Karmic Lesson Chart; or subtract the number of Karmic Lessons in your chart from 9, and arrive at your Subconscious Self number.

For example, in the case of Thomas John Hancock, as we saw in his Karmic Lesson Chart (Figure 4.1 on page 115), the 7 and the 9 are missing in his name. His Subconscious Self there is 9 – 2 = 7. Or, since he has seven numbers represented in his name, his Subconscious Self is 7.

The Subconscious Self numbers range from 3 through 9. A name consisting of two or less numbers is never found.

The symbol for the Subconscious Self is an arched doorway. (See Figure 3.1 on page 111.)

3   Subconscious Self Number

You respond to emergencies by looking for support from friends and family. However, life will force you to confront these occurrences until you learn to use your own power. You will search early in life for a lover and a partner to depend on. You may marry an older person who can offer you some security and protection. You have to guard against extreme depressions, and control your tendency to blow emotional experiences out of proportion. You have to discriminate more in your choice of friends. The key to your success lies in your finding a well-defined goal to focus on. This has the effect of bundling and directing your energy, making it impossible for you to achieve impressive results.

4   Subconscious Self Number

You may have a tendency to lose yourself in trivial details, causing confusion and indecisiveness, and even paralyzing your ability to react quickly and forcefully.

You have to learn to trust your instincts, and to act quickly. Hesitation and procrastination have to be avoided. You need a solid foundation in your life. You need a family and work environment in which you have responsibility, dependents, and the rewards that come with completing specific tasks.

Subconscious Self Number

You tend to scatter your energies far and wide, making it difficult for you to complete projects and tasks. You need discipline and organization in your life. You have a strong urge to escape difficulties by forcing change, instead of trying to work out the problem. However, you learn quickly, and you adapt well to change. Your success in life depends on your ability to ground yourself and accept responsibilities. A family and career do much to anchor your life.

 Subconscious Self Number

You like to help others, sometimes to the extent that you do not pay enough attention to your own needs. You are primarily concerned with your home and your family. Everything else comes second. You radiate love and genuine concern for others. During times of distress, you turn to your family and friends. You are responsible and willing to sacrifice for others.

 Subconscious Self Number

You can appear indifferent to your surroundings and somewhat aloof. You are well-balanced and can survive many a stormy time. In times of trial, you withdraw within yourself, finding solace and answers in your creative and analytical mind. You may be a bit of a loner, and you do not easily share your feelings with others.

 Subconscious Self Number

You handle unexpected situations in an efficient manner, and often manage to get the best out of them. You learn quickly, and you usually do not repeat the same mistakes. You want to be rewarded for your efforts, and to relate your success to the material aspects. You are dependable and solid in almost any kind of situation. You do not panic or scare easily. You have a business-like attitude to problems, and you realize quickly what needs to be done. You have a good understanding of money and the physical world. You are a survivor. You show leadership and organization, and are physically coura-geous and competent.

9   Subconscious Self Number

You have every number represented in your name, which gives you the ability to deal with all types of situations. Paradoxically, you can be aloof, and, perhaps, indifferent and arrogant. Although you may think of yourself as considerate of others—even to the extreme—you may, in fact, be too self-conscious to perceive the messages others are sending out.

The ability to read situations or people properly requires that you become less self-conscious, and less inhibited. You may fail to see the need to be alert to the possible pitfalls of a situation. You may have trouble with relationships simply because you misread others. Perhaps too much of yourself is being projected upon situations or people.

There are certain aspects to the Subconscious Self number that require careful consideration. As a rule of thumb, a low Subconscious Self number indicates a difficult life. However, the length of your name should be taken into account. A short name with a low Subconscious Self number is indicative of an ability to bundle and focus one's energy. This usually results in a successful career. A long name with a low Subconscious Self number often indicates difficulties in many areas of life, including your career. However, these conclusions should be drawn very carefully, and always after considering other areas of the chart. Keep in mind that numerology is not an exact science, and that it is easy to draw the wrong conclusion. When such a conclusion is of a negative nature, much damage can be done.

THE BALANCE NUMBER

People experience different internal responses to life's challenges. Some withdraw from difficult situations to think them through; others withdraw from their emotions, to try and keep themselves from feeling anything. Some explode with emotions, but allow the explosion to pass quickly. Others linger with their feelings, holding on to them well past the time they should have let them go.

Very often, these are conditioned or emotional responses that emerge without thought or analysis. We have been influenced to respond in this way. Maturity and self-development help us to learn new and more effective methods of handling our world and the problems we confront. Your Balance number provides you with the guidance on how best to deal with difficult or threatening situations.

The symbol for the Balance number is an inverted triangle. (See Figure 3.1 on page 111.)

How to Find Your Balance Number

To find your Balance number, add the numerical value of the initials of your full name, and reduce them to a single-digit number. When you calculate your Balance number, always reduce the Master numbers. Master numbers do not apply to the Balance number, because the Balance number indicates an approach or an attitude, rather than a talent or special ability.

In the case of Thomas John Hancock, whose initials are T, J, and H, you can add the values for the T (2), J (1), and H (8), which give a Balance number of 11, which is reduced to 2.

Mr. Hancock would look below for the 2 Balance number to find how he can most effectively deal with the "off" balance situations.

1 Balance Number

Draw strength from yourself, but be more willing to share your troubles with family and friends. You can be a loner in the face of problems. This can isolate you during troubled times. Be open to the advice of others. This will widen your perspective on the problem, and will give you new information on which to base your approach. Strength, creativity, and courage are the arms with which you will win the war.

2 Balance Number

Use tact and diplomacy. Be less emotional. Be courageous in your approach to the solution you seek, rather than backing away from a problem because you fear confrontation. Work hard to defuse tension; your innate talent is to find a solution mutually satisfying to all.

You are willing to compromise. Be more optimistic and lighthearted. Try not to blow problems out of proportion. You are overly sensitive, and you have to work to be more balanced.

Balance and harmony are there for you the minute you apply yourself to any problem. You can be the peacemaker.

3 Balance Number

Be more lighthearted and optimistic in your approach to problems. Try to work with others toward a mutually satisfying solution. Use your considerable charm to influence the situation.

You can be extremely emotional when faced with a problem. Try to control this tendency; you need a degree of objectivity. You may become too personally attached to the solution you seek, thus failing to see that the outcome can be beneficial to all concerned.

4 Balance Number

Try to have perspective and a more laid-back attitude toward emotionally charged issues. Control your anger. Discipline is your strength. Also, look at the larger picture and the need for compromise. Your sense of justice must be elevated to another level at which such virtues as forgiveness, compassion, and deep understanding are the guiding lights. A practical approach to these ideas is to try to put yourself in the shoes of the person with whom you are in conflict. There are always more angles to a problem than you tend to acknowledge.

5 Balance Number

Try to focus on your problem, rather than avoiding it. You may try to escape the issue by indulging your senses to keep from feeling the pain of a conflict. Be careful not to do this with food, alcohol, and drugs.

You are capable of finding a highly creative solution to any situation the minute you put your mind to it. The answer lies well within your grasp.

6 Balance Number

Your strength lies with understanding people and the underlying conditions of a conflict. But you can rely too heavily on friends and family to provide you solace instead of handling the situation directly and responsibly. You may be too likely to retreat to the good feelings provided by people not involved in your situation.

Responsibility is the issue here. You helped create the situation in the first place, and you are an essential part of the solution. Accept your role.

7 Balance Number

You retreat into some safe haven within yourself, and you hope you will not have to deal with the issue at hand. Yet, the clarity and analytical abilities of your mind are sufficient to provide you with insight into the problem, and a clear path to its solution.

You can be engulfed in the emotional aspects of an issue, which cloud your mind and prevent you from using your clarity to find an answer. You have to work at confronting yourself and the issues you face unemotionally and calmly. Get past the emotion and you will find an answer.

8   Balance Number

Use your considerable power in a balanced way. You may tend to use power in a manipulative way, rather than confront people on principal. Use it by accepting personal responsibility for the issue and its solution. You have enormous creativity, and you have the leadership to find an answer to almost any problem.

Try not to force your own solution upon groups, but include their concerns and ideas in the larger solution that you can bring about. Learn to use power for the good of all.

9   Balance Number

You will find your solutions by empathizing with the concerns of others. You have a gift for understanding a wide variety of people and for seeing the broader picture. But too often you retreat into aloofness, a kind of ivory tower, in which you regard yourself as an aristocrat. You will find your solutions by coming down to the practical reality at which people live. It is in giving that you will receive.

Your Balance number is not considered one of the core numbers. However, during times that you experience emotional turmoil in your life, your Balance number becomes considerably more important. When an emotional upset dominates your life completely, the influence of your Balance number, at least for a short period, overshadows even the core numbers.

SPECIAL LETTERS IN YOUR NAME

Each letter in your name represents your characteristics, but the location of the letters can determine their impact.

For instance, the first letter of your name (use your first name at birth) is called the Cornerstone. It gives you an indication of your character, particularly in the way you approach opportunities and obstacles.

The last letter of your first name reveals your ability and attitude toward finishing projects that you start. This letter is called your Capstone. Together, your Cornerstone and Capstone can tell you much about your capacity to start and finish a project successfully.

The first vowel of your first name reveals something of your deeper self. As I explained in Chapter 3, the Heart's Desire is a somewhat hidden, but strongly represented, core number in your chart. It is a big part of yourself that you do not reveal easily or indiscriminately, and it is usually recognized only by your relatives and friends. The first vowel of your name is the little window through which you allow the uninitiated a glimpse at your deeper self.

It is interesting to note that a person who uses a first name with a different first vowel as the original birth name is particularly apprehensive of revealing his or her deeper self.

For example, Thomas's first vowel is the letter O. He goes by Tom, allowing another person, the first time they meet, a limited view of his deeper nature through the little window of the first vowel.

Albert, who introduces himself as Bert, is more protective of his vulnerable Heart's Desire, and he does not reveal his true first vowel. Only those who know him to have the birth name Albert are allowed to look through the little window into Bert's heart.

I have described a general meaning of the letters of the alphabet below. However, keep in mind their location in the chart, and adjust the description accordingly.

Special Letter

You are ambitious and independent, and possess great drive. You are not easily influenced. You are direct, and can be opinionated. You want to take charge. You have willpower, and are resolute and purposeful. While you are courageous and bold, you are also stubborn and willful. You must work on becoming more flexible and more willing to listen to others.

 Special Letter

You are emotional, sensitive, and a bit shy. You are friendly and understanding. Peace and harmony are essential to you. You are loyal and firm in your beliefs, and you often cling to ideas after they have outlived their usefulness. You must learn to change more with the times, and to become more independent in thought.

Special Letter

You are intuitive and demonstrative of your feelings. You possess good self-expression, and a strong sense of humor. You are inspiring, cheerful, melodramatic, and even extravagant at times. You are outspoken and spontaneous, lighthearted, and optimistic. However, you are often scattered, and you lack focus.

 Special Letter

You are down-to-earth, practical, efficient, orderly, and systematic. You are also shrewd and determined. You can concentrate and overcome many difficulties. You have a natural authority, but you can also be stubborn and rigid.

 Special Letter

The E needs plenty of freedom. Because you are physical and passionate, you will probably be married more than once. You like to be social and to entertain. You are highly perceptive, and not easily fooled. You are original and versatile. You are also capable of looking at a situation from different perspectives. You must learn discipline.

 Special Letter

You are responsible, self-sacrificing, loving, hospitable, and friendly. You possess a warm heart, and you are very compassionate. You feel the pain of others, and you are considerate. You are helpful, but you must be careful not to interfere in the lives of others. You have to guard against a tendency to indulge in melancholy and depression.

G **Special Letter**

You are a thinker, and have strong willpower and determination. Your vision and imagination may bring wealth. You are methodical, disciplined, and orderly, but you can also act quickly when opportunities arise. You may well be clairvoyant.

H Special Letter

You are creative and original. You make and lose money easily, but you will probably do well financially in the long run. You are independent, and rely on your own judgment. You are sometimes a loner. Skepticism and self-doubt are your greatest enemies. You need time in nature to feel your true self, and to reestablish direction and clarity.

I Special Letter

You are emotional, considerate, and understanding. You are artistic, and you have good taste. Without balance and steadfastness, there can be nervous tension and accident-proneness. You have to try not to switch from one extreme to another; look for balance.

J Special Letter

J is for justice. You are honest, loyal, reliable, and sincere. You want to improve the lives of others. You may try too hard to please everyone. You have a clever mind, and you are very talented. However, you have to work at motivation to make use of your talents.

K Special Letter

Illumination, intuition, and revelation are the key words for the K, the eleventh letter of the alphabet. You are emotional and creative, with a strong drive to succeed. You can be quite forceful and multifaceted. Nervous tension, fear, and hesitation are the negative aspects of this high-strung and idealistic letter.

L Special Letter

The L tends to intellectualize experience, which can result in your being slow to react or to make decisions. You are honest and sincere. You give easily, and you have a good-natured disposition. You move quite often, and travel more than most. You tend to be prone to minor accidents during times of emotional stress. It is very important for the letter L to maintain equilibrium in all aspects of life.

Special Letter

You are energetic and hardworking with a touch of the workaholic. You are efficient, and you do not tire easily. You probably have a strong physical constitution. You are domestic, and want financial security. You are tolerant, and can endure hardships. You have to learn to be more patient with others.

 Special Letter

You are intuitive, creative, original, and unconventional. You are opinionated, and change your mind only after much discussion. You like to keep track of life by writing in a diary. You are sensual, and you may be involved in many love affairs during your life's course.

 Special Letter

Willpower, religious convictions, and high moral standards are the basis of the O. You are patient and thorough when preparing for some new venture. You respect rules and regulations. You are emotional, and you have to guard against jealousy. You have a tendency to spells of brooding and imaginings.

 Special Letter

You are intelligent and knowledgeable in many areas. You give an impressive and commanding first impression. You can be aloof, overly secretive, and distant. You possess common sense and level headedness, but you are frequently impatient. You can be too attached to possessions, and not very generous with your time.

Q **Special Letter**

The Q attracts money, but it can be erratic and unstable, causing you sudden losses. You have natural authority, and you can influence others. You are not easily understood. You appear mysterious, and you may quite often be the victim of gossip. You are direct and outspoken with a talent for oration. Negative Qs can become boring and compulsive talkers.

Special Letter

You are gentle, kind, and helpful, but also highly emotional, and you carry an intense inner power. You are lively, and you can work hard. You must try to stay balanced and even-tempered. You must also learn to be less critical and more tolerant. You have a willingness to sacrifice time and energy for a good cause. You also tend to lose things, and you may have a bad memory.

 Special Letter

The S is charming and charismatic, as well as warm and devoted. You have mood swings, which is perhaps the result of a sad childhood. You are intense, and you may react in an extreme manner. You are often too impulsive; you must learn to take time before making a decision, and carefully sort out your emotions. You are passionate and loving, and you will experience many emotional ups and downs.

 Special Letter

You are dynamic, and you live a hustle-bustle kind of life. You may have to force yourself to slow down sometimes. You like to expand and enlarge your world continuously. You are extremely protective of others. You can be aggressive when committed to an undertaking or relationship. You are often too sensitive and quickly hurt, which may cloud usually good judgment and a sense of morality.

U **Special Letter**

You experience accumulation and loss, especially of money. Indecisiveness and selfishness are at the root of the problem. Learn to size up situations more quickly, and then be read to give energy and commitment. You are very creative, intuitive, and intelligent. You have a knack for showing up at the right time and the right place. You tend to be lucky! You are attractive and charming, and you can be quite glamorous.

Special Letter

You are intuitive and insightful. You are inspired and may be prophetic, but your imagination is equally strong and can cloud your objectivity. You have big plans and ideas, and you possess the ability to manifest them. You are efficient and want to see results. You may be eccentric, which does not always work in your favor. You are sincere, loyal, and dependable; however, you can also be quite unpredictable and overly possessive, especially in relationships with the opposite sex.

 Special Letter

Intuition, determination, and a strong sense of purpose are W's trademarks. You like to be involved in many activities. You need change, and you like to meet new people. You have charisma. You provide stimulating company. You express yourself very well, and you are very creative. There is, however, a tendency to procrastinate and to cut corners. You can be superficial.

 Special Letter

You are very sensual and artistic, as well as responsive and perceptive. You learn easily. You love excitement, and you may have to guard against indulgence in sexual excesses. You are also temperamental, and you have an addictive personality.

 Special Letter

The Y is freedom loving. You have a strong dislike of limitations and restrictions. You are ambitious, courageous, and independent. You have a refined and stylish personality. However, you often vacillate, and you are slow to make decisions. You have good intuition, and you are very perceptive.

 Special Letter

You are optimistic and dynamic. You tend to look at the bright side of life. You have high expectations, but also have common sense. You are understanding, compassionate, and kind. You have a sharp mind, and can respond quickly when necessary. You have good reflexes, both physical and mental. You have wisdom and an ability to be a mediator of opposing parties. You have to guard against impulsive and impatient behavior. You can be stubborn.

The letters of your name reveal the strengths and weaknesses that have been part of your make-up since the day you came into this world. Through careful analysis of your chart, particularly the letters of your name, and the order in which they appear, you have the opportunity to recognize and to overcome your weaknesses, as well as to take full advantage of your strengths.

Study the descriptions of the letters, then write your name in large print on a piece of cardboard, and contemplate each letter and the position where it is found. You will be amazed how much insight can be gained through this method.

THE PLANES OF EXPRESSION

Each of us experiences life on four different levels: with our physical body; our mental faculty; our emotional make-up; and our intuition. Each of these areas has a specific means of perceiving information. The physical body is capable of touch, taste, pleasure, and pain. It provides us with a sense of the physical world. The mental body, like the emotional and intuitive natures, perceives the invisible worlds. Our minds deal with the world of thought.

The heart, of course, is preoccupied exclusively with the world of emotion. Our feelings teach us many things about ourselves and about others. Finally, we have the capacity for direct contact with the higher realms by way of intuition. Intuitive insight comes in a flash. It is not rational—that is the world of the Mental Plane—but comes as if it were placed at the doorstep of our minds. Intuition, therefore, bypasses all efforts save that of perception.

These four faculties exist in all of us. But each of us depends more on one or two of them for the bulk of our knowledge. Some of us are possessed by our senses, while others live almost exclusively in their hearts, or in their minds. Numerology indicates how we as individuals function on each plane.

The letters of the alphabet are divided into four categories: Physical, Mental, Emotional, and Intuitive. The proportion of each category in your name gives a good indication of which Planes of Expression are strongest in you, and which ones are weaker. These Planes of Expression can greatly help you to understand your talents and abilities.

The letters of the alphabet are also considered to be either creative, vacillating (wavering), or grounded (practical).

The chart below shows the status of the letters in the alphabet according to these categories:

	Creative	Vacillating	Grounded
Physical	E	W	D M
Mental	A	H J N P	G L
Emotional	I O R Z	B S T X	
Intuitive	K	F Q U Y	C V

(Notice that no letter in the alphabet is both grounded and emotional.)

The Planes of Expression Chart is one of the more complex systems in numerology; however, a good understanding of the Planes of Expression rewards you with considerable insight.

How to Find Your Planes of Expression

To find your Planes of Expression, copy the scheme in Figure 4.2, then place the letters of your name on this chart according to their category. Count the number of letters on the horizontal rows to find which of the Planes is most strongly represented in your chart.

Next, add the numerical value of the letters together in their different fields, and reduce the total to single digits. Add the fields together on the horizontal

	CREATIVE		VACILLATING		GROUNDED		TOTAL	
	Number of letters	Value	Number of letters	Value	Number of letters	Value	Number of letters	Value
Physical					M	4	1	4
Mental	AA	2	HJHNHN	8			8	1
Emotional	OOO	9	TS	3			5	3
Intuitive	K	2			CC	6	3	8
	6	4	8	11	3	1	17	7

Figure 4.2 The Planes of Expression Chart

rows as well as vertical, and reduce the total to single digits. The Master number 11 is not reduced. However, the 22 Master number is extremely rare and its attributes do not fit the Planes of Expression. For that reason, the 22 is reduced to 4. You may wish to use Tom Hancock's Plane of Expression Chart below as a guide.

Study Thomas John Hancock's Planes of Expression. After some contemplation, your conclusions include that: Tom is more creative than practical, but his creativity is of a practical nature. It is functional, without frills and unnecessary decorations (the 4 value in the creative field).

He likes to work with his hands, and he expresses his creativity in a visual form, rather than in music or writing (six letters in this field).

The eight vacillating numbers reveal his concern with the financial side of his endeavors. He is not impulsive, and he takes his time before making a decision. He would do well to rely heavily on his intuitive understanding of the situation (11), and to be a little more daring; to take a chance rather than to wait too long and miss an opportunity.

He has a tendency to be taken advantage of by glib salespeople (8 in the vacillating field), and should, in such circumstances, trust his feelings; if it doesn't feel right, it probably isn't (again the 11, truly an asset).

His intuitive powers are strongly represented by the three letters in the Intuitive Plane (the average number of intuitive letters in a name of this length is one or two), which also reveal a talent in healing and counseling, with a practical and result-oriented approach (the 2 value of the letter K, and the 6 value of the two Cs, which total 8).

On the Emotional Plane, we see that Tom's imagination may, at times, cause turmoil (three creative and emotional letters), but he is also very concerned with the well-being of his relatives and friends (the letter O is represented three times), as well as people at large (9 value). He is not pursuing this in a serious manner, but rather with optimism, motivation, and inspiration (3 in the Emotional Plane and vacillating field). He is protective (the letter T), and willing to be flexible (the letter S).

Five letters on the Emotional, compared to eight letters on the Mental Plane, show Tom to be much more inclined to approach his experiences from a mental point of view; however, he likes to be involved and to express his ideas when someone is in need of advice and comfort (5 and 3). In such circumstances, he is quick-witted, a good problem-solver, and original in his approach. At the same time, he does not allow his heart to become involved if it does not really concern him (again the combination 3 and 5).

Tom, with the larger number of letters in the Mental Plane, is in the first place a thinking person; however, he is not decisive (six letters in the Mental and vacillating field). He relies more on his mental faculties than any of the others, and he is always aware of the possible pay-off (eight Mental letters).

He is stubborn and does not often ask for advice. He has a tendency to impress, even to dominate, others in discussions. Occasionally, he will throw out an original idea (two As), but his self-doubt as to the practicality of these ideas will prevent him from taking full advantage of these moments of creative originality. He fears he will be thought of as a fool, and this suppresses his desire to express many strange and original ideas (two in the creative field and Mental Plane).

The Physical Plane in his chart reveals that Tom is not interested in physical activities. He is neither an athlete, nor an outdoors person (only one letter); however, he is strong and stocky with most of his physical strength located in the lower part of his body (the letter M, with a value of 4).

He trusts the earth and little else; flying is against his nature, and swimming or boating do not excite him (also the 4). He enjoys lonely walks (1). He has a tendency to rely on his physical strength, and he may wait too long before calling a doctor when becoming ill (also the 1).

There is a rich source of information available through the Planes of Expression chart, and the above analysis is but an example. For a better understanding of the personalities of the individual letters, read in Chapter Six about the Transits, and keep in mind the numerical value of the numbers.

The following is a description of the numbers in your Planes of Expression chart as they appear in the column that shows the total value of all the letters in that particular category.

Accent on the Physical

You have many letters in the Physical Plane indicating a practical and material approach to events and circumstances with an eagerness to be involved, to "do something," in a direct and physical manner.

You are an athlete, and you have the body to prove it. You like to be involved in physical activities. You gain a better understanding of material matters through your sense of touch. You may be a gifted cook, gardener, builder, or any other professional who requires much physical involvement.

Below is a description of the individual Physical numbers.

 Physical Plane

You are active and inspiring; you are daring in business and other areas of life. You have strong likes and dislikes, and you live according to your opinions.

You are charming and witty, but you get bored easily. You work hard, and you are determined and very goal-oriented. You thrive on the combination of enthusiasm and challenge, the lack of which makes you dull and disinterested. You are like a flare, burning brightly for a specific duration, but must move on to other projects in order to sustain your excitement.

Physical Plane

You are highly sensitive, and at various times in your life, you have probably suffered from shyness and a lack of self-confidence. You may feel vulnerable physically, but you are quite tough. Your strength is in persistent, but gentle effort.

You tend to worry too much. You can suffer from bouts of fear, based largely on lack of confidence in your own personal power.

You are good at gathering information, and you have a keen eye for details.

Once you gain some confidence in yourself, you begin to move with a natural grace and sense of rhythm.

Physical Plane

You are highly attractive, whether you know it or not. Something radiates from you that should be cultivated. You possess the potential for charisma.

You are charming and witty. You express your feelings well. You are emotional, but tend to respond in ways that you know will be attractive. In this sense, you often repress your true feelings.

You are highly artistic, imaginative, and dramatic. You express yourself with a certain flair. You dislike hard work. You need to acquire discipline. You are fun-loving, and a great and entertaining companion at social events.

Physical Plane

You have a great deal of energy and determination. You are eminently practical and organized. You are good with details, and you are able to stick to routine procedures.

You have excellent concentration, and you are quite serious. You can be tenacious when confronted with an obstacle or an adversary.

You are loyal, honest, warm, and generous. You dislike changes, and you can be rigid and inflexible. You are a good debater. You must control your desire to dominate people and situations.

You appreciate traditions and well-established routines.

 Physical Plane

You have a natively strong constitution. You are versatile and resourceful. You have a flexible body and quick reactions. You enjoy change, travel, and meeting new people. You have a talent for promoting ideas.

You are attracted to the new and exciting. You seek knowledge and understanding through experience.

You go about life in a unique and innovative way; you avoid the conventional and traditional.

You speak well about many different things, and you are an excellent salesperson if you believe in the product.

 Physical Plane

You combine practicality and artistry. Many successful artists are found to have this number on the Physical Plane. Teaching and healing come naturally to you. Your appreciation of beauty and art is visible in your surroundings.

You are an excellent marriage partner. Parenthood is very satisfying for you, as is the simple act of service to anyone you come in contact with.

You are a loving and emotional person. Also, you are very curious about the lives of others. This can get you into trouble, however, especially if you confuse service with interference.

You are idealistic and imaginative.

7   Physical Plane

You must make a conscious effort to maintain your physical health. Your body will be a major source of education for you in this life. You will learn a great deal about healing. You should study nutrition and other forms of holistic health. You have a talent as a healer. Your refined understanding of the body as an instrument that needs fine-tuning and care can be of benefit to you and to many others. You have good intuition and an ability to understand abstract thoughts. Your mind naturally grasps scientific and technical matters, and you may do extremely well in any of these fields.

You perform best in quiet places. You need peace of mind and time to think and to contemplate. You should specialize in a single area of study. You are a perfectionist, and you do not take anything at face value. You like to probe, to research, and to discover the deeper answers to life's questions.

You have self-control and dignity, but you must guard against becoming too withdrawn.

8   Physical Plane

You are highly ambitious, and you have great talent as a leader and manager. You are competitive and you will not settle for second best in anything. You have a strong sense of justice, and you will fight vehemently to get what you think you deserve.

In all likelihood, you have a strong constitution. Many with an 8 on the Physical Plane have powerful bodies and strong and impressive voices.

You have a vision and a strong direction, and you will work hard to manifest your dreams. You do not realize your vulnerability until forced to.

Money and power are integral parts of your life.

Your challenge is to strike a balance between the material and spiritual values.

You are conscious of your status, sometimes excessively so, and you will occasionally not refrain from making a show of your achievements.

Many respect and admire you for your hard work, vision, and success. You have an excellent chance of being financially successful and secure in your later years.

9   Physical Plane

You have a strong presence. You are charismatic, and you have a dramatic flair in your personality, which may direct you to the theater.

You are also drawn to politics, publishing, promotion, and public service—any career that requires a certain amount of time before the public. You are attracted to doing things on a large scale.

You are a humanitarian. You are concerned about the well-being of society. You have a great deal of compassion, tolerance, and generosity.

You are highly idealistic and a bit of a dreamer. However, you are not particularly practical. Very often, you are not understood by others, and you are sometimes considered indifferent and aloof.

In some way, you want to please everyone, and tend to give promises that may be impossible to keep. If you develop your abilities, you have a significant chance of becoming famous.

11 Physical Plane

You are highly charged and charismatic. You can inspire many with your original ideas and keen insights into life. Despite your obvious strengths, you likely have a sensitive nervous system and constitution.

Your physical body is one of your greatest teachers. You must learn to treat it well by determining what makes it strongest, and how to maintain that strength. Your sensitivity will cause you to have to make adjustments in your diet, exercise, and methods for dealing with stress.

You have good intuition and flashes of insight. You are guided by your faith and your inventive mind.

22 Physical Plane

The 22 on the Physical Plane is similar to the 4, but also indicates a strong desire to prove yourself, if only to yourself. You have enormous potential to make things happen, but there is a fear of failure that, if allowed to become too strong, can paralyze you. A 22 on the Physical Plane can push a person into the limelight.

Accent on the Mental

You have many letters in the Mental Plane, indicating a mental approach to events and circumstances. You think, analyze, decide on your position, try to figure what is best, and then react.

You have an inquisitive mind, and you are always exploring the deeper meaning of things. You have the ability to visualize ideas, and to solve practical problems without putting a pen to paper.

Below is a description of the individual Mental numbers.

1 Mental Plane

Your mind is very sharp and quick, coming up with good and innovative ideas in a flash. You process information quickly, but tend to put it in short-term memory. You use information for a specific purpose, but forget it quickly when it no longer has any relevance to your immediate needs.

You are the proverbial quick study. You pick up information like a vacuum, and you may have a facility with languages.

You are extremely original. You love moving into the frontier of any enterprise to come up with innovative methods. You are a ground-breaker.

You are witty and charming. You get bored easily.

 Mental Plane

You are able to retain much information and knowledge, thanks to your good memory. You are very sensitive to the thoughts of others and to your own feelings, which in turn influences your capacity for clear thinking. Your sensitivity makes you avoid direct confrontations. You work hard at assessing what others want, and you try to conform. You possess a remarkable flexibility, which can be a great gift, but you are something of a chameleon, changing political or social stripes with the prevailing winds.

 Mental Plane

You are extremely artistic, creative, and a bit flamboyant. You are attuned to fashion, and to interior and architectural design. You have a talent for designing office space and landscaping.

However, you can be scattered mentally, having thoughts pop in and out of your mind seemingly at random. You need to develop discipline and focus.

4 Mental Plane

You are a fine planner with a good eye for details. You are very conscientious and practical. However, you can get lost in the details of a project, and you can lose sight of the larger picture.

You must learn tact, and give others—especially family members—room to live according to their own standards. You can be somewhat domineering, especially when you are concerned about their general well-being.

5   Mental Plane

You have a quick and highly versatile mind. You can absorb great quantities of information quickly, and retain the important points.

You are impatient with routine procedures, and will rebel if forced to conform to any existing pattern for very long. You like to be involved in several projects at the same time. You are dynamic and resourceful.

6   Mental Plane

You have the mind of a poet, writer, or actor. You see life in artistic terms. Teaching and healing come naturally to you.

You carry much responsibility, and you are very dependable. You fulfill your obligations. Your appreciation of beauty and art is visible in your surroundings.

Your prospects for success in business are excellent, due to your practical and responsible behavior.

7   Mental Plane

You have a studious and scholarly mind. You may have a genius for one particular field of study. You study a subject in depth, and you abhor a superficial understanding of anything you regard as important.

You analyze things down to the infinitesimal particles. You want to know the inner workings of things, what makes them tick. You may be too occupied with your thoughts, and have a tendency to withdraw, especially when you are emotionally troubled.

You can be extremely critical of yourself and others. You analyze personalities with an eye toward finding out secrets and faults. Your mind can look too much on the dark side of things, as if that were the more fundamental part of a human. Your challenge is to use your fine mind constructively, and to attain faith.

You have an excellent intuition, which serves you well in life.

8   Mental Plane

You have a great talent as a business person. You can manage large corporations and institutions. You understand how to organize people, and to direct them toward some larger common goal.

You are highly ambitious and competitive. Money and power are essential to your sense of identity and self-respect.

You must guard against arrogance and superiority. You can be imperious.

You are demanding of yourself and others. You seek excellence in all things, and you refuse to settle for less.

Mental Plane

Your thinking goes naturally to large-scale endeavors. You are concerned about the general well-being of society, and you have a long-range perspective.

You are highly compassionate, but somewhat impersonal, in your relationships with others. It takes a long time for people to get to know you intimately. At the same time, you give your energy unselfishly to worthy causes, and earn the respect of people for your commitment.

You are romantic, and possess a touch of the dramatic. You are likely attracted to public service or the theater, either as a benefactor, actor, or writer.

You have a broad view of humanity, and you can deal effectively with people from all walks of life. You have little, if any, prejudice.

11 Mental Plane

You have a highly charged mind. You are creative, intuitive, and extremely inspirational. You are not particularly rational or logical in your thinking. Invention is your strength, with new ideas, fresh insights, and unconventional solutions to problems.

You are extremely sensitive, and you have trouble handling criticism. If posed to you in an unthreatening way, you will be open to anything another has to say. You seek the truth in virtually every situation, even if it reflects harshly on you.

You are charismatic, and have interesting ideas on every subject. This makes you attractive to the opposite sex. You have your own style, and you even have a certain degree of class in your dealings with others.

Mental Plane

You have all the aspects of the 4, described above, but in addition to those, you have the ability to plan and to execute truly brilliant visions. This is one

Master number that is very difficult to tap into, because it requires you to overcome many fears relating to the expectations and approval of those around you. Courage and self-confidence are required to live up to the potential of this number.

Accent on the Emotional

You have many letters in the Emotional Plane indicating that your initial reaction to events and circumstances is emotional; you feel, and your heart responds immediately, pointing you in a direction, and inspiring your reaction. Usually the heart rules the head in your case. You are vulnerable to the emotional problems of others, and quick to comfort and to sympathize. You have a tendency to make mountains out of molehills. You fall in love easily and not always with the right person.

Below is a description of the individual Emotional numbers.

1   Emotional Plane

You are very emotional, even mercurial. You experience much nervous tension and can be high-strung. You are roused to love and anger quickly. You can be stubborn and proud. You can become personally and emotionally identified with a particular project or person to the point at which you become deeply attached, and even possessive.

You are demanding in close associations, especially in love and marriage. If not careful, you can easily be domineering. You need a strong-willed, yet flexible person as a spouse.

2   Emotional Plane

You are extremely sensitive and vulnerable. You guard your heart with great care, and you take a while before you fully trust another. You are likely talented in music. You have a great talent for tact and diplomacy. You dislike confrontation. Your strength is in persistent, but gentle persuasion.

You worry too much, and you need much love and understanding. You have to work on your self-confidence.

You are a perfectionist, and you add beauty to everything you do. You like company and companionship; you dislike working alone.

3 Emotional Plane

You are very romantic, as well as creative and imaginative.

You fantasize about your perfect "other": a white knight on a horse, or a beautiful princess. Your response to painful emotional situations, especially in childhood, was to create a fantasy world to which you escaped. You may still be doing that as an adult, perhaps to your detriment. Reality lacks the romance and excitement of your fantasies.

However, you can be disorderly and disorganized. You can also be rather moody.

You likely have much artistic talent, especially in writing, acting, or singing.

4 Emotional Plane

You distrust emotion, and you want to control your own emotions. You love order, which makes you dislike any sort of emotional situation or turbulence. But this repression can cause you much anger and even nervous tension.

There is an unnecessary acceptance to unfavorable circumstances and relationships. This should be avoided.

You can manage and organize; you are good with details.

5 Emotional Plane

You have a powerful curiosity about many people. You love to meet new people, travel, and have many love affairs. Your emotions do not run very deep, however, and long-lasting relationships are hard for you to maintain.

You can be moody and taciturn. You are a born observer, and you do not miss much.

6 Emotional Plane

You are very emotional, yet you possess a rare degree of balance to which you can turn. You love family and close friends as few people are able. You worry too much, and feel responsible for other people's actions.

You take justice and honesty with extreme seriousness; however, you may be too disciplined.

You have artistic talent. You like to help others more than most, and you are willing to sacrifice your own needs.

You have an ability for teaching and healing. You need much love, and you can give the same in return. You are highly idealistic, and you are very committed once you decide upon your soul mate.

7   Emotional Plane

You are emotional and need love, but you have trouble expressing your feelings. You tend to hold back, rather than to risk being hurt. This causes others to think you are a bit cool or withdrawn, but in fact you are more likely to have powerful emotional experiences that build up inside you. You are vulnerable to emotional explosions. You may be inhibited. You need to work on allowing your emotions to show spontaneously. This requires great trust and courage on your part.

You have a very sharp mind and excellent intuition. You perform best in a quiet place. You have self-control and dignity. You may be too occupied with yourself and have a tendency to withdraw, especially when you are emotionally troubled.

8   Emotional Plane

Your emotions are powerful, and you tend to dominate in your personal and business relationships. You are likely to be the controlling partner in any relationship.

You are highly ambitious. You are driven by your competitive instincts. You tend to be status conscious and want to show the world your success.

Money and power are integral parts of your life. You dream of big things in life, heading corporations, building big businesses, and directing large numbers of people.

9   Emotional Plane

You love the many, and you want to dedicate yourself to the service of those less fortunate than yourself. You are willing to make great sacrifices for a worthy cause, and draw enormous satisfaction from knowing that your life has made a positive difference to others. Conversely, you have difficulty in one-to-one relationships, especially relationships with the opposite sex. You are viewed as impersonal, and sometimes a bit aloof. You can also be hard to get to know.

You are a person possessed by your dream, and you have trouble with relationships that are not an integral part of that dream.

You appear to others as self-sufficient, which can make close relationships a little more difficult since people want to be needed.

You have enormous artistic talent, especially in a variety of arts, such as interior design, photography, acting, and writing.

You have great compassion and idealism. In fact, you are so idealistic that you can be a bit impractical, and you can lose touch with the ground. You need a practical, down-to-earth cause to be most effective.

11 Emotional Plane

You are highly emotional, intuitive, and extremely sensitive to your environment. You have a tendency to go up and down emotionally with whatever is the overriding stimulus in your surroundings.

You are overly concerned with the opinions of others. You are highly aware of what others are thinking. You perceive their motivations and hidden feelings.

You enjoy, and even need, beauty and harmony around you. You are very tactful and diplomatic. You have a gift for saying the right thing at the right time.

You are extremely vulnerable to stress. You can experience much nervous tension, and if not properly cared for, can suffer some type of nervous disorder.

You have a subtle mind and talent as a healer and counselor.

22 Emotional Plane

(See 4 Emotional Plane.) Clearly the power and the drive of the Master number 22, its practical, goal-oriented, visionary approach, and its devotion to plans and projects that are more important than the individual's emotional experiences, cause this number to fall outside the realm of the Emotional Plane of Expression. The number 22 simply does not concern itself with emotional affairs. Therefore, the 22, when it is found in the Emotional Plane, is always reduced to 4.

Accent on the Intuitive Plane

You have many letters in the Intuitive Plane, which is extremely rare and makes you intuitive to the point of being psychic. Your experience of, and reaction to, events and circumstances is intuitive; you often act before you think and get away with that. In fact, this usually proves to be the right approach in your case.

You will experience a number of premonitions during your life, and, like all intuitive people, will have to learn to discriminate between fantasy, imagination, and intuition.

Below is a description of the individual Intuitive numbers.

 Intuitive Plane

You are highly intuitive with flashes of insight. You probably attribute most of your thoughts to your mental capabilities, but in fact your insights come from another, higher resource.

 Intuitive Plane

You have a fine intuition. You are extremely sensitive, and you tend to direct your thoughts to spiritual and metaphysical matters. These are intuitive insights you attract.

 Intuitive Plane

You are very original, imaginative, and sometimes have fantastic ideas about spiritual matters. You are very artistic and inspiring. You have a talent with words, and you may be drawn to the pulpit.

Your intuition is above average, but you tend to color and exaggerate your insights.

 **Intuitive Plane**

You are traditional and you like established procedures. You do not feel comfortable with abstract and unproven ideas. You prefer your ideas to be practical and useable. Your religious beliefs tend to be conventional.

5 Intuitive Plane

You are very intuitive, and rely heavily upon your insights. Your knowledge and understanding stretches beyond the limits of the subjects you have studied. You have an intuitive feeling about many different areas of life, but you need to deepen this understanding with discipline, hard work, and focus. You need to ground your many diverse thoughts with study.

6 Intuitive Plane

You are extremely intuitive and spiritual. You take your spiritual ideas and experiences quite personally. There is a danger of too much attachment to your ideas, and thus you may experience delusion.

You have talent as a teacher or minister. You have psychic experiences often related to friends and relatives, and you should take these messages seriously.

7 Intuitive Plane

You have great intuition and insight in abstract and metaphysical matters. You seek a broad perspective on all intuitive matters. You like to provide scientific and rational support to all of your insights.

You have an inventive mind, and likely have a talent as a writer or composer.

8 Intuitive Plane

You have a powerful intuition and much psychic ability. Your intuitive powers lead you to business and organizational matters. You can assess people quickly and accurately. You are an outstanding judge of character.

9 Intuitive Plane

You love the abstract, and you have grandiose ideas concerning the spiritual. You can influence large groups of people.

You are an idealist, and a dreamer, and you are not particularly practical.

You are very impressionable, and you sometimes put your faith in people who do not deserve it, which makes you vulnerable to being taken advantage of.

You must learn to be more discriminating in your dealings with other people.

11 Intuitive Plane

You are extremely intuitive, and perhaps even psychic. You sense things well in advance, like coming events, the changing moods of people, and trends. You must work to ground your life in some practical discipline in order to keep your imagination and intuition from running away with you.

22 Intuitive Plane

(See 4 Intuitive Plane.) The Master number 22, being both grounded and visionary, concerns itself only with what it perceives as reality—the practical, material world, and the world of plans and ideas.

The Master number 22 is driven to turn ideas into reality, to create great things, and to use its power to motivate and to direct others. The number 22 shuns the realm of intuition, its insecurities, and its self-doubt, and is therefore always reduced to a 4 when found in the Intuitive Plane.

The Planes of Expression Chart is perhaps the most complex section of a numerology chart. However, once you have a good understanding of the personality of each letter of the alphabet, you will be able to learn much about a person by studying his or her Planes of Expression.

Your Hidden Passion number, Karmic Lesson number, Subconscious Self number, Balance number, and Planes of Expression numbers, all point to different aspects of your character.

Your Hidden Passion number indicates a desire and aptitude for the aspects of that number. It has a close connection with your Heart's Desire number, because both numbers reveal not only specific talents, but a way to enhance your happiness if an outlet for these talents and desires is found in your career and/or life style.

Your Karmic Lesson number(s) indicates areas you have to work on, and is therefore on a par with your Challenge numbers. When you acquire the aspects of your Karmic Lesson number(s), your ability to overcome obstacles is enhanced; hence, the quality of your life improves.

Your Subconscious Self number can be looked at as the number that most clearly shows how you grade yourself, which in turn reveals how confident and decisive you are in different circumstances. This ties in with your Karmic Lessons, because once you acquire part or all of the aspects of your Karmic Lesson number(s), you also elevate your faith in your own abilities.

Your Balance number comes to the foreground whenever you experience emotional turmoil. Your Balance number is more indicative of approach and attitude, than of abilities and talents. It is the funnel through which your strengths and talents flow with the least friction, to confront whatever problem lies at the core of your turmoil.

Your Planes of Expression show how your energy is divided over the four categories consisting of the Physical Plane, the Mental Plane, the Emotional Plane, and the Intuitive Plane. Once you have gained some insight in your Planes of Expression, you can benefit from this knowledge by relating it to your choice of career, life style, and environment. For example, if you have a large number of letters on the Physical Plane, you would be happier and more successful if your work allowed for hands-on, physical activity. Or, if you have a large number of letters on the Mental Plane, you will be better off in an environment that inspires study and intellectual interaction.

Although these areas of a numerology chart are not as important, nor as easily recognized, as the core numbers, a good understanding of these areas is extremely beneficial.

Self-improvement is a natural, day-by-day process. The guidance that numerology offers helps you to take advantage of all your unique characteristics. It is easier and faster to swim with the flow than it is to swim against it, and you are swimming your own private river, competing only with yourself.

Chapter 5

Connections Between Your Name and Your Date of Birth

The softest things in the world overcome the hardest things in the world.

—Lao-Tzu

The inner you is represented in numerology by your name; your relationship with time and space is represented by your date of birth. We have been examining your name and date of birth individually, but now let's look at what can be learned when we combine these two sources of information. This results in the Bridge numbers, the Maturity numbers, and the Rational Thought numbers.

THE BRIDGE NUMBERS

The Bridge numbers are the numbers that indicate how you can make the relationship between the individual core numbers in your chart easier and more compatible. They are not considered shortcomings, but areas that, when improved upon, make you less inhibited and self-conscious.

Becoming more yourself is a matter of laying bridges between the different core numbers; those parts of your personality that are strongly represented in your chart.

In order to make your talents and abilities (Expression number) easily available to your main lesson and expected direction of growth (Life Path number), you will want to bridge the gap between these two aspects of your being.

You will be more comfortable with yourself when your outer personality (Personality number) merges with your inner needs and desires (Heart's Desire). Merging the core numbers results in becoming whole.

How to Find Your Bridge Numbers

Bridge numbers are arrived at by subtracting the smaller from the larger core numbers. A person with a 7 Expression and a 1 Life Path, has a Bridge number of 6. If that person has an 8 Personality, we find two more Bridge numbers, namely 1 (between the Expression and the Personality), and 7 (between the Personality and Life Path).

When you calculate the Bridge numbers, criss-cross between all the core numbers (all Master numbers among the core numbers should now be reduced to single digits). You may discover that almost all cardinal numbers are represented.

If, for example, someone has a Life Path number of 1, a Birth Day number of 6, an Expression number of 7, a Heart's Desire number of 4, and a Personality number of 8, the following will be the Bridge numbers:

1 (7 minus 6 and 8 minus 7)
2 (6 minus 4 and 9 minus 6)
3 (4 minus 1 and 7 minus 4)
4 (8 minus 4)
5 (6 minus 1)
6 (7 minus 1)
7 (8 minus 1)

Obviously, this makes sense only when you agree that to become truly whole, you must fully absorb the positive characteristics of all cardinal numbers.

However, the more important Bridge numbers are those that close the gaps between the Life Path and the Expression, between the Heart's Desire and the Personality, and between the Expression and the Heart's Desire. In the example, they are 6 (7 Expression minus 1 Life Path), 4 (8 Personality minus 4 Heart's Desire), and 3 (7 Expression minus 4 Heart's Desire). This is one of the few areas in the chart where we can find the number 0. The number 9 is never found, because the largest difference between two single-digit numbers is 8 (9 minus 1).

Below is a description of the Bridge numbers.

 Bridge Number

A 0 bridge number indicates that you have at least two core numbers alike. This is considered fortunate, and an opportunity to make real progress in the areas of life expressed by the repeated number. For example, if you have a 7 Life Path as well as a 7 Expression number, intellectual and spiritual growth are particularly strong in your chart.

However, if you have three or more identical core numbers, the balance may be off. Three 7s for instance, will make a person withdrawn and solitary, someone who has difficulty accepting his feelings or those of others.

The challenge here is to find balance. If you have three or more identical core numbers, study the meaning of this number and ask yourself if you are excessive in its characteristics or—and this is quite common—if you have turned away from this number completely.

The worst possible scenario is of a single number dominating the chart (for example, when 40 percent or more of the letters in the name represent the same number) so that the person absorbs all the negative aspects of the number. I would advise the person to work at embracing the neglected characteristics, or, in the extreme, even to consider a name change.

1 Bridge Number

You should rely more on your own strengths and abilities. Be more decisive; don't beat around the bush; and be straightforward when expressing your thoughts and feelings. You need to take charge more often. Get off the beaten path and find original ways of doing things. Do not try to be conventional, or try so hard to behave according to the expectations of others.

2 Bridge Number

Be more sensitive to the needs and expectations of others. Do not rock the boat too often, but keep the peace and try to make things run smoothly. You have to use your ability to influence others with gentle diplomacy, instead of confrontations. Be more cooperative.

3 Bridge Number

Loosen up a bit. Have fun; recharge your batteries. Be more generous to yourself. Communicate your deeper feelings without fear to those close to you. Be more creative, particularly in the areas of dancing, acting, poetry, or writing. Develop faith in yourself.

4   Bridge Number

Avoid procrastination. Try to be more reliable and punctual. Be practical, methodical, and systematic in your endeavors. Keep track of details; avoid chaos. Work on the basics of life. Physical and outdoor activities bring you closer to yourself, so get out in nature, work in the garden, or build a fence.

5   Bridge Number

Only the combinations 6 minus 1, 7 minus 2, 8 minus 3, and 9 minus 4 can cause this Bridge number to appear in your chart. The need to be more flexible and adaptable is required in all cases. Be willing to go out on a limb; be adventurous and unconventional. However, the combinations indicate rather different requirements, and are therefore listed separately.

6 minus 1

Try to find a balance between the extremes of self-sacrifice and of selfish behavior. Sometimes you take your duties and responsibilities too seriously; other times you turn away from them. Co-dependence may be a problem for you. Be more independent.

7 minus 2

This combination is paradoxical: At the same time it is both disharmonious and potentially gifted. You are sensitive and in need of love and attention, while also very private and inwardly focused. This creates a certain amount of inner conflict. You have a tendency for self-pity, and you tend to withdraw as soon as a relationship shows the slightest bit of turmoil. You take criticism too personally. The high potential comes from the combination of analytical power (7) and intuition (2) represented here.

8 minus 3

The combination of the business-minded, goal-oriented, determined, and visionary 8, and the playful, creative, outgoing, and happy-go-lucky 3 is unstable.

Your strength lies in using your creative talents in a business-oriented manner. Your weakness is your tendency to suppress your creativity in favor of career and business. This can make you overly cautious and slow to make decisions.

9 minus 4

You should probably spend less time on petty details, and direct your attention towards increasing your awareness of world and humanitarian matters, large-scale projects, and political and environmental issues. You have a tendency to waste time and potential. You should learn to delegate more.

Be tolerant and flexible. Accept changes. Rigid ideas and dogmas may keep you from reaching out and following your dreams. Make freedom a high priority in your life.

6   Bridge Number

This Bridge can only be built through service, more involvement with family and community affairs, and a greater sense of responsibility. You should also allow your creativity to flow more freely.

This Bridge number results from the combinations 7 minus 1, 8 minus 2, or 9 minus 3.

7 minus 1

The 7 and 1 mixture is generally harmonious, but the above-mentioned advice is directed to this combination as well. This combination often creates eccentrics—people who are highly inventive and unconventional.

8 minus 2

The 8 and 2 cause similar struggles, but are often recognizable in broken romantic relationships caused in part by over-sensitivity, criticism, a tendency to gossip, and large fluctuations in financial matters. The positive side of this combination is your innate ability to negotiate. You are both the leader and the diplomat.

9 minus 3

This is a very creative combination. You are an artist at heart, and you must live according to that. The difficulty here is in the suppression of talents, and the lack of serious application. The bright side reveals a true gift to inspire and motivate large groups of people.

7   Bridge Number

Coming from either 8 minus 1, or 9 minus 2, this number urges you to spend more time and effort on spiritual matters.

8 minus 1

The 8 minus 1 combination can cause a person to become too interested in material matters. Excessive attachment to money, goods, and status quo can make you vulnerable to the temptations of the material world.

9 minus 2

The 9 minus 2 combination is subtle. The temptation to think that you are spending so much time and effort on the well-being of mankind that you are on your way to sainthood is very strong, and potentially self-deluding.

Righteousness, no matter who you are and what you have accomplished, is always an obstacle; it brings prejudice, arrogance, and indifference.

There are two challenges here that may be particularly problematic for you: the need to be more humble, and the responsibilities you have to yourself. Saving yourself is a lifetime job.

8   Bridge Number

This number can only result from the combination 9 minus 1, and the important theme here is understanding the function of money. Money is a tool for trading, no more and no less. This combination of numbers suggests an idealist. Sometimes the idealism is taken too far and becomes impractical. Often this is expressed in a dislike for money.

Occasionally, the 1 dominates the 9 to such an extent that the person becomes obsessed with personal success. More often though, the 9 and the 1 together reveal the very ambitious humanitarian who has the potential to do very well in the corporate world, or any career that offers international connections and activities.

A good understanding of your Bridge numbers helps you to take better advantage of your talents and abilities. They tell you how to make your core numbers more compatible with each other, and how to avoid some of the internal friction that so often results from contradicting core numbers.

THE MATURITY NUMBER

Your Maturity number indicates an underlying wish or desire that gradually surfaces around age thirty to thirty-five. This underlying goal begins to emerge as you gain a better understanding of yourself. With self-knowledge comes a greater awareness of who you are, what your true goals in life are, and what direction you want to set for your life. This, in a nutshell, is the gift of maturity: You no longer waste time and energy on things that are not within your own special identity.

No matter what your age is at present, your life is being channeled in a specific direction, toward a very specific goal. That goal can be seen as a reward or the fulfillment of a promise that is implicit in your current efforts, often without your knowing it consciously. While the characteristics of this number are usually visible during childhood, we tend to lose sight of these aspects until later in life. But our lives are always being affected by this influence, nonetheless. Your Maturity number begins to have a more profound impact on your life after the age of 35. The influence of the number increases steadily as you grow older.

How to Find Your Maturity Number

Add your Life Path number and your Expression number and reduce the total to a single digit, except in the case of a Master number, to find your Maturity number.

For example, Thomas John Hancock's Expression number is 7. His Life Path number is 5. Now, add his Expression number (7) to his Life Path number (5) and arrive at his Maturity number of 3 (7 + 5 = 12, 1 + 2 = 3).

The symbol for the Maturity number is two concentric circles on a tapered base. (See Figure 3.1 on page 111.)

1   Maturity Number

As you mature, you will find yourself needing an increasing amount of independence and individuality. You will fight harder for the recognition and rewards you feel you deserve, and you will be less willing to accept failure or limitations in any form. Your drive and determination will grow as does your ability to take charge.

If there are already several 1s in your chart, especially among the core numbers, you will have to strive to avoid becoming bossy, rigid, stubborn, and selfish. A person who allows these characteristics to run free will become bullish and lonely later in life.

If there are not many 1s in your chart, the influence of the Maturity number will help you to establish your independence and success. From this foundation, you will be able to build an active, adventurous, and exciting life.

2 Maturity Number

You will discover that you possess a growing talent for understanding and working with other people as you mature. Your ability to influence others through tact and diplomacy will grow. These talents will further you along in your career or business. You will become increasingly shrewd and learn the art of discrimination. Your sensitivity to the needs and desires of others improves dramatically. You will be able to evaluate their motivations with a growing clarity and an uncanny accuracy.

You find you can get more done by persuasion and gentle guidance than by force. You may well have to learn to assume the role as the power behind the throne. Your influence is less public, and you may not always receive the public recognition you deserve. However, your satisfaction comes from having your own ideas come to fruition, which is the result of teamwork and cooperative efforts.

If you already have many 2s in your chart, especially in the core numbers, you may become overly sensitive, a characteristic you will have to keep in check. If you have few 2s in your chart, the influence of your Maturity number will greatly increase your ability to work harmoniously with other people.

3 Maturity Number

As you mature, you will find yourself becoming increasingly extroverted and optimistic about your future. Your self-expression and creativity will improve markedly. You may become inspired to take up some type of artistic endeavor, such as writing, acting, or music, if you are not already involved in one of these areas.

Your ability to communicate will substantially improve. You are naturally more fluent, and you may find yourself dressing with a certain flair. Be careful not to fall victim to superficial appearances, or to chase after glamour and extravagance.

With a 3 Maturity number you can look forward to a pleasant and social later part of life. Your attitude will be increasingly positive, and your popularity will rise.

If you already have several 3s in your chart, especially in your core numbers, you may have a tendency to scatter your energies, and to take your responsibilities less seriously.

If you have few 3s, or are missing 3s entirely, you will experience a great relief from the tension and seriousness of life. You will be more relaxed and capable of enjoying life.

The 3 Maturity number is a blessing in the later part of life. It promises enjoyment, close friendships, and much happiness.

4   Maturity Number

Your maturity will find you increasingly practical, organized, and far more down to earth. You will be capable of putting your ideas into concrete form. Your later life promises to be a time of accomplishment and activity. You become more focused and goal-oriented, and less willing to discard details and cut corners. There is little interest in a quiet retirement. You are too involved in seeing your plans and efforts come to life.

Your family and friends will profit from your 4 Maturity number, because of your increasingly helpful and reliable nature. However, you must guard against becoming rigid, narrow-minded, and opinionated, especially if several 4s are already found in your chart. If you are lacking 4s, or have only one or two of them, you will benefit by your increased understanding of systems, organization, and the rewards of a methodical approach to life.

It will do you good to take time to relax and to enjoy the flowers every day.

5   Maturity Number

There is no slowing you down as you enter maturity. Your influence grows as you become more dynamic and versatile. You now begin to realize your life-long goal of freedom.

There will be travel and adventure, and exciting, unexpected events. Your originality, creativity, and verbal abilities grow stronger.

You will become interested in areas you never before considered. You may have a tendency to become restless and impatient. You may quickly lose interest or become bored with projects that progress slowly. Your perseverance is tested, especially because you may find it easy to abandon things that no longer hold your interest. You will have to work to maintain your concentration, discipline, and focus. Do not scatter your energy over too many interests. This is especially the case with people who have several 5s in their chart, particularly among the core numbers.

For those with few 5s, the increasing ability to adapt to change, and the willingness to take risks, provide much spice to life.

6   Maturity Number

As you mature, you will become increasingly concerned with the well-being of family, friends, and community. You will be drawn to the role as healer, counselor, and teacher. You have a growing ability to give comfort and sound advice to those in need. You naturally assume the role of patriarch or matriarch for those in your care, no matter how old they are. You become more responsible and protective.

You may well become involved in environmental protection, volunteer work, or politics.

You are naturally idealistic, and you strive to realize those ideals as you grow in maturity and in personal resources. Your careful and balanced approach to business and financial matters provides you with sound and secure success later in life. The 6 Maturity number provides an outstanding financial foundation for the future. In addition, the influence of the 6 promises an old age surrounded by loved ones.

For those who have few 6s in the chart, or none at all, this Maturity number promises the close relationships that you have strived for most of your life.

7   Maturity Number

You will become increasingly occupied with the larger questions of life by reading, contemplating, and searching for a deeper understanding of who you are, and what this life is all about.

You may turn to philosophy or religion, but you will likely examine a wide array of ideas, broadening your knowledge in many disciplines.

Your intuition grows stronger, as does your ability to look beneath the surface of every subject you study. You are able to analyze abstract questions and live according to your higher ideals.

You may find yourself needing more time alone; your need for privacy will likely increase. If you already have several 7s in your chart, you will have to guard against becoming withdrawn and alienated. If you have no 7s, you will now have the ability to deepen your understanding of one particular field. You will have the opportunity to become grounded in a particular area of study.

8 Maturity Number

As you mature, you will grow in success and financial reward. You will find yourself deepening your commitment to your work. You will find it easier to overcome difficulties that manifest in your path. Your capacity to use power will grow; you will be recognized as a pillar of influence and dependability within your community. You will have to be strong and self-disciplined to avoid sudden painful material losses. Beware of an inflated ego, the surest symptom of an imminent fall.

The 8 Maturity number requires a certain degree of detachment from material success; otherwise it will rule your personality, and it will make money an obsession. Detachment allows you to remain focused on the higher values of mankind. One of your important motivations should be a desire to build, create, or market in order to enjoy the game of business.

Your wisdom and sheer common sense are recognized by many, and will attract important positions. It is possible that you will be given responsibility for the care and management of other people's property. You may also be asked to guide large institutions.

If you already have several 8s in your chart, especially in the core numbers, you will have to guard against selfishness, accumulation for the sake of status, and greed. If you have few 8s in your chart, or one at all, your opportunity to achieve the success and financial independence is greatly increased.

9 Maturity Number

Your concern for the well-being of society will grow more powerful as you come to maturity. You will be drawn to much public service. The long-term good of your community, and even of the world, will increasingly occupy your thoughts.

As you mature, your appreciation for the arts and beauty in any form will also increase. It is quite possible that you will be actively involved in the arts, if that is not already the case, often as a benefactor.

Service to humanity is fundamental to your life. You will grow in understanding and wisdom. Involvement with international affairs or humanitarian service offers you much satisfaction.

If you already have several 9s in your chart, especially among the core numbers, you will have to guard against arrogance, aloofness, and alienation.

If you have few 9s in your chart, or none at all, you will gain a sense of your personal place among the human race. You will feel you belong, and that you have provided something of lasting value for the future.

11   Maturity Number

(Read the text for the 2 Maturity number first.) The 11 adds considerable intuitive powers. You will experience a number of premonitions and other psychic experiences, particularly as you get older. Your sensitivity will increase, you become more subtle, and will often be surprised by the accuracy of your first impressions. You will become more spiritually inclined, and your understanding of life will be enhanced. You will be able to afford to put faith in your intuition. You will become more discriminating in the process of accepting people into your world. Relationships are of a lasting nature only if you can be tolerant of the other person's idiosyncrasies.

22   Maturity Number

(Read the text for the 4 Maturity number first.) This Maturity number is the result of an 11 Life Path and an 11 Expression. The early part of your life has been difficult. You have often felt you are a stranger in your own life. You were extremely sensitive and vulnerable. With age, you will discover a generous supply of personal power, enabling you to fulfill some of your most daring dreams. You will become much more practical, and learn how to influence others. The key to fulfilling the promise that is inherent in the 22 Maturity number is self-confidence.

When you consider the method in which your Maturity number is calculated, you realize that it is something to look forward to. It is the combination of your Life Path and your Expression numbers. Once the influence of your Maturity number enters your life, you have reached the point at which you are able to direct your strengths (as expressed in your Expression number) towards the path in front of you (your Life Path). Your Maturity number reflects the way in which you merge your strengths and challenges.

THE RATIONAL THOUGHT NUMBER

Your Rational Thought number reveals what can probably best be described as your way of thinking.

Are you a practical, methodical thinker, or a dreamer? Do you frequently allow your imagination to color your perception? Are you unconventional and original in the face of a practical problem, or do you stick to proven methods?

This is the kind of information that is available from your Rational Thought number.

How to Find Your Rational Thought Number

Your Rational Thought is found by adding the sum of the value of all the letters in your first name to your day of birth. For example, let's assume that Thomas was born the twenty-fifth day of the month.

T	h	o	m	a	s
2	8	6	4	1	1

22

The sum of the letters in the name Thomas is 22. (Do not reduce Master numbers when calculating the Rational Thought number.)

His Birth Day number is 25, which reduces to 7. Thomas has an 11 Rational Thought number (22 + 7 = 29, 2 + 9 = 11, which is not reduced).

The symbol for the Rational Thought number is a hexagon with the number inside. (See Figure 3.1 on page 111.)

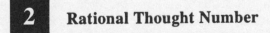 **1**   **Rational Thought Number**

You are an independent thinker, original, and not easily influenced by others. You tend to pursue a line of thought stubbornly, and you can be dominating in intellectual discussions.

2   **Rational Thought Number**

You take the subtle approach. You allow your intuition to be a large part of your intellectual explorations. You are open to the ideas of others, and may be even a little too easily influenced.

Rational Thought Number

You are creative, but your thoughts tend to be scattered. You jump around inside your head without focus. You come up with solutions that reveal an illogical approach, yet they often work.

 Rational Thought Number

You are the practical, methodical thinker. You think things through step by step, and you are almost always well-prepared when others question your reasoning. You may be a little rigid in your approach, and you are uncomfortable with new, unproven ideas.

 Rational Thought Number

You have a flexible and adaptable approach. You are quick with solutions, and you have the cunning of a fox. You can talk yourself out of most tight situations, but your priority is often winning the contest, not being right.

 Rational Thought Number

You are a listener, and you relate everything to the effect it has on others. You notice things that escape others, but when trying to find solutions, you often focus on details, forgetting the larger picture. Justice is a major factor in your thinking, many people in the legal field have this number.

 Rational Thought Number

You are never satisfied with a simple answer. You tend to delve into all the aspects of a question until you feel you understand the problem completely. Then you proceed to solve it without hesitation. Few people are able to compete with you when it comes to finding answers.

8 **Rational Thought Number**

You are the visionary, and you focus on the large picture. You ignore the details in favor of spectacular solutions, and you love to blow someone's mind. You understand the balance between the rational and the irrational, and you have no problem combining the two.

9   Rational Thought Number

You are always aware of the expectations of others, and you hold off on expressing your opinion until everyone has had their say; then you point to the mistakes and the things that were overlooked. Your success in solving problems and in finding answers is the result of a process of elimination, more than it is a matter of stringing together logical answers.

11   Rational Thought Number

The 11 is the illuminator. You have answers and insights based on the proverbial light bulb. Your Rational Thought number is the most magical and difficult to understand (for others). You have the makings of an inventor, or a spiritual guide.

22   Rational Thought Number

A combination of vision and system gives your Rational Thought number the most potential for success. You can switch quickly from the large picture to any minute detail that requires your attention at that time. You dream big, and you have the capacity to lay a foundation for your dream that gives clear directions for each step, each little detail, that needs to be taken care of. A 22 Rational Thought number can only result from the 11 of the name and an 11 or 29 Birth Day. This reveals a strong intuitive side in you. Premonitions and an intuitive assessment of future effects are strong aspects that can be used and strengthened.

The influence of your Rational Thought number increases considerably when you are faced with an intellectual challenge. It is important to keep in mind that this number has almost no impact when the issue at hand is predominantly emotional.

The Bridge number, the Maturity number, and the Rational Thought number require some contemplation to be fully understood. A helpful approach to gaining insight into the effect and influences these numbers have on your life is to take some time to focus on each one of them.

It is difficult, and it takes practice, to understand how each number in your chart (and particularly those that are less obvious, such as the numbers described in this chapter), effect you in very specific areas. A beginning student may have a tendency to merge all the information found in a numerology chart into one big soup, without discriminating between the different areas influenced by each number. The areas described in the chart are deeply hidden, yet influential. They have to be considered in relation to all of the other numbers in a chart, but without losing sight of their specific domain.

The Hierarchy
of the Chart

B y the time you have fully analyzed your name and date of birth, you will notice that virtually every number is represented in your chart. This is true for most people. Naturally, this can be confusing. The reason for this confusion is that we haven't learned to prioritize the relative values of each number and its position in the chart.

The Life Path, for example, carries far more weight than the Maturity and Balance numbers. In addition, each member of the core numbers bears special significance to our personality. The Heart's Desire represents your inner needs and motivations—the more private you—while the Personality number reveals the public you; the face, or the mask, you show the world. It is what people recognize first when they see you. Your closer relationships, however, come in contact with the personal, inner you: your Heart's Desire.

One of the benefits of numerology is to differentiate and to reveal the many aspects of your personality and inner being. It also shows how aspects within you influence each other. What follows is a short course in how to prioritize the numbers of the chart, to discern their individual importance, and to show how each aspect of the chart relates to a specific part of your being.

The Life Path number is by far the most important number in the chart. Next, read the Birth Day number. In order of importance, the Birth Day number belongs in fifth or sixth place, but it is closely related to the Life Path, and should be seen in connection to it. Follow with the Expression number, which reveals your talents, abilities, goals, and is particularly important in relation to career.

Then read the Heart's Desire, and understand it as the motivator behind virtually all of your choices, in particular those related to life style and environment. Also, look at the Minor Expression and Minor Heart's Desire as contributing influences to your overall ambitions and personality. The Personality number completes this picture of the core numbers. Remember, while the Personality number is the last of the core numbers, it is the first impression that people will get. The Personality number is usually what gets you hired, while the Expression number is the greatest influence on how well you perform. The Heart's Desire number influences the type of conditions you like to work under: alone, or with people; in a small non-profit organization, or in a big corporation; in the inner-city or in the country.

The core numbers outline the basic personality. The rest of the chart reflects a closer look at you—your many nuances, individual character traits, and strengths and weaknesses.

The Challenges follow, and are, in my opinion, among the most important sources of information flowing from the chart. The Challenges, more than any other number, point to aspects of your personality that you have to work on. They represent the first and most obvious obstacles that stand between you and success.

Follow with the Maturity number, but keep in mind that it does not enter your life until after the early thirties, after which its influence grows more important with age. The Maturity number is a kind of secondary Life Path number. It adds specific challenges, as well as abilities, to your life.

Next, read the Karmic Lessons, which reveal weaknesses or undeveloped areas. Follow with the Hidden Passion, which reveals what you are good at, and what you love to do. Then go to the Subconscious Self, which shows how confident and secure you are in the use of your talents and abilities.

The Balance number stands somewhat apart, but is very revealing, particularly when you are off-balance as a result of emotional turmoil. The Balance number reveals your strengths in turbulent times.

The remainder of the chart is made up of the Bridge number, Cornerstone, Capstone, First Vowel, Rational Thought number, and Planes of Expression. Each of these areas is well-defined in this book, and is easily identifiable as to the role it plays in your life. Each represents subtle, but important aspects of your personality.

When you study a chart, first look at the individual numbers and their relative positions in the chart. Next, look for numbers that will have a strong impact upon each other. (This is an aspect of numerology that requires practice and takes time.) For example, what happens when a person has a 1 Heart's Desire, an 8 Expression, and a 2 Personality? Or, what does it mean when a person has three 4's among the core numbers, but many letters with the value of 5 in the name? With practice, you will learn to read a chart with confidence and clarity.

You will learn more about the hierarchy of the chart in Part Two.

Part II
Time and Timing

Thus far, we have discussed only those numbers of a numerology chart that concern the personality. These numbers influence a person for the duration of his or her life. Now we will concern ourselves with the cycles; those numbers that influence a person only for a certain period of time.

In order to better understand how these two different parts of the chart (called the personality chart and the progressive chart) relate to each other, always keep in mind that the personality chart shows who you are, and the progressive chart shows where you are in relation to time. Your Life Path number reveals the path you have chosen to walk during this life. The numbers based on your name reflect your character. The numbers that are found in your progressive chart indicate what opportunities, outside influences, and obstacles you will encounter and how you will deal with them. However, even if the cycles of two people would be the same, which is highly unlikely, they would approach these cycles in different ways, according to each person's own unique personality.

It is therefore important to have a clear understanding of the personality chart before attempting to analyze one's cycles.

Chapter 6

Cycles and Patterns

Time, which is the author of authors.

—Francis Bacon

In modern life, we tend to see time as linear. For example, we usually see our lives as a linear progression from birth to death. But in all traditional cultures, in both East and West, time is seen as being circular, or even spiral. This is based on how we really experience time in nature. The seasons, for example, are more cyclical than linear. So, too, are the patterns of the sun and the moon, and the cycles that are at the very foundation of our lives: breathing in and breathing out; waking and sleeping; and even birth and death.

These are some of the cycles that make up our lives. When you think about it, your life is a never-ending pattern of cycles, some of which are so identifiable that you may even recognize certain kinds of experiences, or lessons learned, during their duration. You may have had to learn a certain lesson during a particular time in your life, and then, later on, had to address that same lesson from another point of view.

For example, at various times in your life, you have had to learn how to deal with authority figures. Later, you may have encountered new authorities and your accumulated knowledge had to be put to use. You may even have had to become the authority figure yourself, at which point all your accumulated knowledge—from being both a follower and a leader—had to be utilized. At that point, another cycle had run its course.

Our lives are based upon knowledge and wisdom that is accumulated over many years and many cycles, and that is continually being utilized in the patterns of our development.

In numerology, there are numerous cycles connected to your name and date of birth. Some of these cycles are long-term cycles, as long as twenty-seven years, or even longer, while others are of shorter duration, ranging from nine days to nine years.

Most of these cycles are based upon nine stages of development, and proceed according to the nine cardinal numbers. This is not an arbitrary choice, but actually a recognition of an organic pattern of development in our lives. Let's look briefly at how these nine steps can be understood as a nine-stage cycle.

As anyone who has set out to achieve a goal knows, the initial stages of an endeavor are begun alone. You come up with an idea, or begin a particular project. These initial stages are characterized by individual effort; the need to work hard to get the ball rolling. You must work to understand the nature of your task: the challenges, opportunities, and possible pitfalls that you face. This might be called the first stage of development.

The next stage is ascended to when you get to know people in the field of your endeavor, and you start to attract the support of others. This is a time for diplomacy, tact, and flexibility. Still, you must stay focused on your long-term goals so that the influence of others, though essential, will not cause you to lose yourself. This is the second stage.

Having accumulated energy and support, you are now ready to channel those energies into a focused product. This is a time of creativity. At this stage, you have a product, a creation. You now have your work of art, in whatever form it may be. You have reached the third stage.

The fourth stage is characterized by hard work, ongoing productivity, and the need to refine the product you created in stage three. Having given birth to some entity, you must now give it greater form. Form requires details. You must focus on the particulars of your creation. Form, consistent effort, and careful attention to details characterize the fourth stage.

These qualities create freedom and success. If you work hard enough and long enough, the feelings of being restricted by your labors will eventually give way to a sense of success, accomplishment, and relief. The number 5 stands for the freedom that comes from having accomplished form. Now is a time to express yourself. Do not feel restricted or repressed, but allow your inner nature room to breathe. Give voice to your needs; express your inner feelings; and be free to experience yourself fully.

The sixth stage, of course, brings the need to balance such freedom against the limits of time, energy, and resources.

Unrestricted freedom, while an ideal, leads to lack of focus, then to chaos and decay. Our need for freedom must be balanced by our need to focus and to develop specific opportunities. Otherwise, our lives would become purely wasteful and meaningless. The number 6 symbolizes the stage of development in which one begins to understand nature and the intrinsic limits it imposes on things, in order to make all living things productive. This is a new stage of artistic development in which various energies are brought into balance and harmonized.

Such a stage prepares one for the seventh stage, the stage of refinement and perfection. A 7 is the symbol of humankind's attempt at achieving a higher state of development, expression, and a rarefied understanding of life and the universe. When you attempt to perfect any physical object, or to attain a humanitarian or spiritual ideal, you are feeling the influence of the number 7 in your life.

Sincere efforts at self-development and perfection lead to greater power and self-mastery, as long as they are not carried to extremes of irrelevance or insanity. The 8 is the number that symbolizes the power that comes from having achieved a greater understanding of life, and particularly of a specific aspect of life, whether it is in business, healing, or art. It also suggests a balance between the spiritual and the physical worlds.

The number 8 symbolizes infinity and the spheres of heaven and earth. A person with such an understanding naturally accumulates greater personal power. Having achieved such power, the person is ready for the ninth stage of development, which is service to humanity.

The stage of completion is symbolized by the 9. In this stage, you understand your link with all of humanity, and with the cosmos at large. Having achieved the first eight stages of development, which have varying degrees of personal and social consciousness, one is ready to serve in a much greater and more widespread capacity.

Having completed a cycle, in whatever area of your life, you are now ready to start a new one, perhaps with an even more challenging endeavor.

You have added a certain amount of wisdom and experience to your portfolio of life, and your account in the bank of karma has been credited accordingly.

THE PERSONAL YEAR CYCLE NUMBER

The first and foremost of the several cycles that influence your experience of life is the Personal Year Cycle.

In numerology, each year of your life is part of an evolving pattern that can be described as a nine-year cycle or epicycle. These cycles begin at your birth and progress, one by one, through nine steps that complete an epicycle, and then begin again.

The epicycle starts with a 1 Personal Year, progresses to the 2 Personal Year, and so on to the 9 Personal Year. Each epicycle has a particular tone or character that is distinguished by the opportunities offered, and by the lessons to be learned during that period.

Each numbered year has its own characteristics, as symbolized by the number itself: A 1 Personal Year has all the qualities the number 1 has, just as the 2 Personal Year has the 2 qualities. At the same time, the epicycle is also influenced by other shorter and larger cycles that are at play. These cycles include the Transits, Essence numbers, and long-term cycles. But the influences that are most clearly identifiable are the Personal Year and the Essence numbers.

The Personal Years form the building steps that mark your progress through life. Your maturity and development take place in nine-year stages. Each nine-year period marks the beginning and the end of a particular stage of development. Each has a natural rhythm and flow, as summarized by the nine stages described briefly below:

- The 1 Year: A year of new beginnings, seed-planting, and high energy.
- The 2 Year: A year of relationships, sensitivity, and cooperation.
- The 3 Year: A year of creativity, motivation, and inspiration.
- The 4 Year: A year of hard work, discipline, and opportunities.
- The 5 Year: A year of change, freedom, and unpredictability.
- The 6 Year: A year of responsibility, domestic affairs, and service.
- The 7 Year: A year of contemplation, self-awareness, and spiritual atonement.
- The 8 Year: A year of reward, respect, and recognition.
- The 9 Year: A year of completion, release, and transformation.

While you are personally evolving through your own epicycle, the planet at large is also progressing through a nine-year cycle, which influences you. This planetary cycle is called the Universal Year Cycle. Individual years in that nine-year period are found by reducing the four digits of any particular year to a single-digit number.

For example, the Universal Year for 1992 is arrived at by adding the $1 + 9 + 9 + 2 = 21$, which is reduced to 3 ($2 + 1 = 3$).

How to Find Your Personal Year Number

To find your Personal Year number for any given year, add the month and day of your birth, plus the Universal Year number for that year. For example, someone born on May 15 finds his or her Personal Year number for 1992 by adding 5 (May) plus 6 (the fifteenth) plus 3 (1992) to arrive at a Personal Year number of 14, which is reduced to 5. Your Personal Year number changes each year.

Another way to illustrate this formula is shown below, using November 29 for the year 1996 as an example:

November - (11 = 1 + 1 = 2)	2
29 = (2 + 9 = 11, is 1 + 1 = 2)	2
1996 = (1 + 9 + 9 + 6 = 25, is 7)	7

The Personal Year in this example is 2 + 2 + 7 = 11, which is reduced to 2. Note that your Personal Year for the year of your birth is the same as your Life Path number.

When calculating your Personal Year number, *always reduce* Master numbers 11 and 22 to single-digit numbers because they do not apply to the Personal Year Cycle, but are reduced to 2 and 4, respectively.

The influence of the Personal Year begins in January and ends in December. There is a cusp period of three months on each end of the year. During the first three months of the year, the influence of the previous year is waning, while the present year is still gathering energy. The year's energy and influence peaks around September, after which the number for the coming year begins to be felt. This marks an overlapping period in which the old year's influence is waning, while the new year's influence is ascending.

To clear up a lingering question, some numerologists maintain that the Personal Year begins around your birth date. However, the Personal Year is rooted in the Universal Year, and consequently determines the rhythm of the cycle, to unfold in synchronicity with the Universal Year.

For an example of how to record your Personal Year number see the Progressive Chart (Figure 6.2 on page 230).

1   Personal Year Number

Be ready for major changes. You will be inspired to start new projects or enterprises. You will feel a strong forward push toward new goals.

This is a time for vision and planning. Share you dream with others; make plans; get the necessary support; but, above all, rely on yourself as the driving force. Be decisive!

You are starting a new nine-year epicycle. Everything you do now will affect your future. Do not hold back the inner force of creation. Be direct, daring, and bold.

You will have more confidence and determination this year, particularly in comparison with last year, which was a time of letting go. This year represents a time of birth.

It's a time to take charge, and to apply yourself to your dream.

This is also a good time to make the personal changes you have long wanted to make: start a diet, or an exercise program, or begin a new course of study.

There may be some emotional turmoil, especially in the first two or three months. It takes a while to get the ball rolling. There are many changes you must make, and much work to be done.

Be open-minded, organized, and focused. Avoid distractions and procrastination.

You are at a crossroads. You will need courage and a clear head to stay on the right track.

This is a year of opportunities.

The key months in your year ahead include March, April, July, August, and October. In March, you are able to lay the foundation to your plans. In April, changes take place, such as a change of residence or career. July and August mark a time in which you will see the fruits of your labors begin to take place. October represents a major turn in events, often fraught with emotional turmoil; and the fall marks a coalescing of your plans into a more concrete form.

2   Personal Year Number

This is a year to carefully protect and nurture your plans. You will be like a mother watching over her children, conscious of every threat, real or imagined.

You need tact and cooperation to keep yourself moving forward. There will likely be confrontations with others, requiring a subtle and gentle approach. You will have to stay focused on your goals, yet use intelligent persuasion. Being forceful may work against you; compromises will work in your favor.

You will be unusually sensitive, and you may wonder at times what happened to the drive and momentum you felt last year. This year requires something else from you: a delicate sense of balance, and a willingness to go around obstacles, without losing sight of your goal.

You may experience some emotional depressions and frustrations. The year is marked by struggle, but there are many opportunities to advance your plans.

This is a year of slow growth, which requires patience. Be discriminating in your associations; don't talk to much about your ideas; be a bit secretive; and guard yourself and your ideas. You are somewhat vulnerable now.

This is a good year to improve yourself through reading and research. Your growing awareness of the less visible and less obvious aspects of life will make you much stronger and better prepared for the future.

You must be wise in all of your relationships and associations this year. You are far more capable of establishing close, even lifelong relationships now.

Because sensitivity and openness are heightened, many people find their soul mate in a 2 year.

May is the pivotal month in the year. You are extremely intuitive and sensitive. You are also self-reflecting, and better able to influence your peers and situations through spiritual awareness. July brings a culmination of plans and a distinct step forward. August sees things become more concrete and brings a new beginning. September is emotional, requiring adjustments, tact, and inner resolve. The 2 year is one of growth and advancement, but through gentle means, and the indirect use of your personal power.

3   Personal Year Number

This is a year of expansion and personal growth. It is a time of heightened personal expression. Creativity and artistic talent come to the forefront. You are lighthearted, and you are drawn to all kinds of social events.

More than during most other years, you will entertain and be entertained. You meet new and exciting people. It is a time to appreciate all that you have.

You are highly dynamic and charismatic. Your challenge is to avoid scattering your energies. You have a rare opportunity to bring forth new and creative ideas. But that requires discipline and focus.

It is easy to be optimistic and enthusiastic this year, and this may result in speeding up your projects. Yet there will be delays and disappointments unless your enthusiasm is based upon the reality of work and concentration.

This is a pleasant time in which friendship is enjoyed, and love is easily shared.

This is often a good financial year, particularly if your creativity is well-directed. Surround yourself with upbeat and positive people.

You may travel more than usual, which in all likelihood will be an experience filled with exciting people and pleasure.

Control this year's tendencies toward glamour and extravagance, yet allow yourself more room to enjoy and to celebrate.

You communicate well this year, and you are more capable of getting your ideas across.

Love is in the air.

February brings changes; June sees the completion of a project; and July signals a new beginning. August can be emotional, as can November.

4 Personal Year Number

This is a year to be organized and practical. Take care of details. Commit yourself entirely to your goals. Your concentration and ability to focus will be much improved over last year. You will have an attitude of realism and determination.

There can be a sense of limitation and some frustration this year. However, it is a time of important opportunities that must be seized. There can be considerable work-related travel.

You must be flexible this year to make full use of the opportunities that present themselves. It will require a combination of perseverance, hard work, and versatility. You will receive recognition for your efforts and support from your friends and family.

It is a good year to buy real estate or to remodel your home. It is also a good time to take care of projects that have been postponed for too long.

Fulfill your obligations, and do not be afraid to spend some of that hard-earned money. Selling and trading during this year are usually quite successful endeavors.

This is the year to work on your foundation and prepare yourself for the many changes that will undoubtedly come next year.

As a result of your hard work, there will be much satisfaction and a feeling of accomplishment.

January and February will bring some important change; a new opportunity perhaps. March requires self-reflection and reshaping of your plans. It is a good time to meditate on what lies ahead. June brings a new and important step, a breakthrough, perhaps, in your work. October brings changes and a sense of chaos. You may feel threatened by the changes that are on the horizon. But November brings assistance in the form of a promotion or additional financial support.

5 Personal Year Number

This is a year of dynamic change. Many surprises will come your way. Be open and ready to embrace new opportunities. Do not be overly careful this year. This is a year in which a major step forward can take place if you are willing to take some calculated risks and do a little gambling.

Wisdom and prudence are the keys, but you will definitely be faced with choices that require fast action, and a willingness to act before all the facts are in.

This is an exciting year in which you will be required to promote yourself in order to take full advantage of the opportunities that await you.

There will be increased opportunity to travel, and possibly a change of residence.

You may be tempted by the desires of the flesh: too much food, alcohol, sex, and drugs. Be careful and discriminatory. You could make mistakes in these areas.

You will have some unexpected adventures and lucky breaks this year.

This can be an unsettling year if you try to cling to outmoded methods or characteristics. Throw off the old, and adopt the new. It is a year of rebirth and release after last year's struggle.

This is a year in which change takes place consistently, and particularly so in April and May. July is a breakthrough, a time to enjoy life. September can be intense, while October requires tact and balance in relationships.

6   Personal Year Number

This is a year of progress and financial advancement. Major career opportunities present themselves. It is a challenging year in which personal growth is joined with new responsibilities and challenges.

This is a year of domestic responsibility and attention to the needs of family and friends. It is a time of heartfelt emotions and some sacrifice, and of comforting and caring.

You realize the importance of your place within the community. You will be called upon to help others bear their burdens. You are the proverbial friend in need. You must work to create an atmosphere of harmony and balance. It is often a time when marital issues surface and need attention. However, you possess the understanding to deal with such issues effectively if you apply yourself with love and flexibility.

These deep feelings bring renewal to relationships, and often a birth in the family.

May is an emotional month filled with the promise and the stress of imminent changes. June is a breakthrough and a relief. September brings advancement; October brings self-reflection and readjustments; and December brings a sense of completion and fulfillment.

7   Personal Year Number

You will experience a strong tendency to spend more time alone, to delve inside and find some answers, and to reach a better understanding of yourself. This is not a year for social activities, nor is it a year to try to reach goals on a material level.

You will find that the necessities of daily life seem to be taken care of by themselves. Do not worry about your physical and material needs without of course slacking on your daily duties and responsibilities; instead give yourself more attention. It is your spiritual and mental presence that requires attention.

Improve the quality of your life, read, contemplate, and gain personal insight. You are important now. Rest and attend to your health.

It is during this year that you strengthen the foundation of your life. After all, your success in all matters rests upon the strength of your inner self. There will be many strange and unusual events inspiring you to take a closer look at life. An opportunity is there to experience the joy and beauty of life without any artificial or exterior involvement, but purely the growing awareness of yourself.

Too much concern and desire for material rewards will turn this period of your life into a very bad experience indeed, while a "let go and let God" attitude will make this such a fruitful and pleasant year that you may find yourself wondering what you did to deserve it.

8   Personal Year Number

After last year's constant involvement with yourself, and very possible occasional doubts about the state of your business or career, you will find this year to be a relief. Things finally work out. Long postponed checks and promotions come through. You see the light at the end of your financial tunnel, and an inner strength and confidence is breaking through.

This is your year of harvest, and, depending upon the effort you put out in the past seven years, your reward will be equally large.

There is a beauty in these cycles that we can recognize and understand, and in doing so we find ourselves in the flow, and there is no more need to try to struggle upstream.

So this year you will have an opportunity to involve yourself fully in work and material growth, and to bring home the rewards. At the same time, a certain detachment is also necessary for you and for the experience you have, because it is not the reward that brings you happiness, but your experience of life. This is why before the rewarding 8 year you have had such opportunity for growth during the soul-searching of a 7 year.

Give in to your ambitions; you will find yourself more clear-headed, better focused, and better able to pursue and reach your goals.

Your power is visible and strong; mental creativity is high; vision and intuition will guide you; and at the same time you are more efficient and focused. There can be a loss, a serious loss like bankruptcy and failure, because the rewards are always directly proportionate to your effort and motivation. However, you know the effort you put out and you know your motivations, so there must be no room for fear and doubt, only for success and winning. This year will undoubtedly turn out to be a very satisfying one.

9 Personal Year Number

This is your year to finish up all unfinished business, to clean house, and to make room for new things.

On a material level, this is a good time to get rid of unnecessary weight, to give away or sell what you do not need anymore, and to pay off old debts.

On a spiritual level, you will experience a different mode altogether. Your attention should turn to others and their needs. Find ways to be of help, and give time and energy to worthwhile causes. You must lighten your burden of questions and doubts, and the best way to do so is by focusing your attention in another direction, away from yourself. You will find yourself becoming lighter and more in touch with yourself.

This is a time of completion. Problems can be solved and ended. Strained relations relax or disappear. The sources of stress in work or business can be better understood and dealt with.

Be social and communicative, and enjoy music and other arts. Your creativity is higher than usual.

There can be some difficulties this year due to your desire to face obstacles and overcome them; decisions have to be made; and your courage and strength may be severely tested several times. This is not going to be an easy year all of the time, but you will feel relieved and on the brink of a positive break-through by the end of this year.

This is the end of a nine-year epicycle, and many times you will feel the excitement of a new and promising era when optimism is your friend, but you will also experience the fear of letting go. However, the more you let go, the more room there is to be filled during the next epicycle.

The influence of the Personal Year Cycle is felt strongly, perhaps stronger than any other cycle. There are a number of cycles that influence you at any given time, but each of them influences you in a different way. The influences of cycles that are based on your date of birth tend to feel as if they come "from outside." Events and circumstances seemingly caused by forces other than your own bring changes or redirect your energy. On the other hand, cycles that are based on the letters in your name (and we will discuss those shortly) seem to come "from inside." The effects of these cycles come from forces inside of you; they are changes you want to make, or feel ready to make. You can look at your Personal Year Cycles as the different stages you are required to pass through, like the grades of a school. Hence the order in which they follow each other; 1, 2, 3, and so on, to 9, at which time they start over. The Personal Year Cycle is the only cycle that follows this simple pattern. All other cycles follow a rhythm that is tied to your personal chart; your name and your date of birth. For that reason, the Master numbers do not apply in Personal Year Cycles.

THE PERSONAL MONTH AND THE PERSONAL DAY NUMBER

Just as we evolve through a nine-year cycle, so, too, do we experience nine-month and nine-day cycles, even though their impact is subtle compared to the Personal Year Cycle. The Personal Month and Personal Day Cycles proceed according to the same pattern—1 through 9—that the Personal Year Cycle does. The numbers within the monthly and daily cycles have a similar, though less pronounced, impact on us than the yearly cycle has.

We can think of the yearly, monthly, and daily cycles as spirals within spirals, all interconnected. In any case, the patterns are essentially the same. They widen and encompass greater sweeps of time—daily, monthly, and yearly patterns—thus becoming more profound and powerful as they grow.

How to Find Your Personal Month and Personal Day Number

To find your Personal Month, add the single-digit value of the month to your Personal Year number. For example, someone with a 5 Personal Year who wants to know his Personal Month for July should add the 5 (for the Personal Year) to the 7 (for July) and arrive at 12, which is reduced to 3. July is a 3 Personal Month for someone in the 5 Personal Year.

To find your Personal Day, add the number of the day to your Personal Month number, and reduce that to a single digit. Using the above example, a person in a 3 Personal Month finds his Personal Day for July 17 by adding a 3 (Personal Month) and 8 (for the seventeenth day) and arrives at 11, which is reduced to 2. (For Personal Years, Personal Months, and Personal Days, always reduce Master numbers.)

For example, in 1991, a person with a birthday of May 15 is in a 4 Personal Year, which is arrived at by adding 5 (for May) plus 6 (for the fifteenth day) plus 2 (for $1 + 9 + 9 + 1 = 20$, which is 2), which equals 13, which is reduced to 4. His Personal Year for 1991 is 4.

To find his Personal Month for august of 1991, we would add 8 (for August) plus 4 (Personal Year), which equals 12, which is reduced to 3. His Personal Month number for August is 3.

To find his Personal Day for August 23, 1991, we would add 5 (for 23) plus 3 (for the Personal Month), which equals 8. His Personal Day number for August 23, 1991 is an 8.

Perhaps an easier way to understand this formula is as follows. Let's find the Personal Year, Month, and Day numbers for October 8, 1993, for someone born on the twelfth day of February.

February is the second month =	2
the twelfth day = $12 = 1 + 2 =$	3
$1993 = 1 + 9 + 9 + 3 = 22 = 2 + 2 =$	4
The Personal Year number is	9
October is the tenth month = $1 + 0 =$	1
The Personal Month number is $10 = 1 + 0 =$	1
the eighth day is	8

The Personal Day number for this person for October 8, 1993 is 9.

The Personal Months and Days are as follows.

For an example of how to record your Personal Month and Personal Day numbers see the Progressive Chart (Figure 6.2 on page 230).

1 Personal Month and Day

This means new beginnings, new people, new ideas, high energy, willpower, courage, ambition, independence, leadership, decisiveness, inventiveness, and initiative.

The negative side is that you are impulsive, opinionated, chauvinistic, confrontational, impatient, and cynical.

You should wear red, orange, copper, or lilac.

2 Personal Month and Day

You are sensitive, tactful, diplomatic, cooperative, persuasive, modest, resilient, outgoing, friendly, romantic, healing, and comforting.

The negatives are self-consciousness, timidity, discordance, deceitfulness, melodrama, and cowardice.

You should wear gold, white, black, yellow, or salmon.

3 Personal Month and Day

You are creative, imaginative, inspiring, motivating, optimistic, self-expressive, dynamic, happy, lucky, attractive, loving, and prophetic.

The negatives are egotism, scattered energy, moodiness, gossipiness, extravagance, and criticalness.

You should wear amber, wine red, forest green, or rose.

4 Personal Month and Day

The 4 is a good manager, hard working, opportunistic, detail-oriented, dependable, punctual, practical, methodical, constructive, determined, and perseverant. The 4 also has good concentration.

However, the 4 is also limited, frustrated, chaotic, slow, rigid, and angry.

You should wear green, turquoise, blue, grey, or light brown.

5 Personal Month and Day

You are dynamic, promotive, progressive, verbal, sociable, original, quick-witted, flexible, adaptable, resourceful, versatile, freedom-loving, tolerant, romantic, adventurous, and travel-loving.

The negatives are that you lack focus, and you are unreliable, temperamental, and discontented.

You should wear red, turquoise, pink, black, or blue.

6 Personal Month and Day

You are domestic, committal, helpful, self-sacrificing, harmonious, loving, caring, compassionate, counseling, balanced, contented, receptive, romantic, artistic, and skilled with legal affairs.

The negatives are guilt, selfishness, loss, and instability.

You should wear bright red, yellow, mustard, navy blue, or silver.

7 Personal Month and Day

You are spiritual, meditative, contemplative, self-aware, insightful, relaxing, perfectionistic, observant, charming, and a reader, studier, problem-solver, and a researcher.

You are also withdrawn, irritable, suspicious, and possessive.

You should wear violet, purple, magenta, or turqoise

8 Personal Month and Day

You are businesslike, efficient, strong, rewarding, respectful, recognizable, generous, powerful, authoritative, a visionary, a planner, and you are good with contracts, sales, money, and you are a good judge of people.

The negatives are greed, dishonesty, money problems, conspicuousness, and aggressiveness.

You should wear beige, tan, gold, blue-grey, or lime-green.

9 Personal Month and Day

You are complete, detached, instructional, healing, artistic, serviceable, humane, broad-minded, compassionate, sociable, just, forgiving, idealistic, opportunistic, and charitable.

The negatives are aloofness, indifference, narcissism, and self-pity.

You should wear lavender, gold, green, red, white, or olive.

It is interesting to note that the rhythm of your Personal Year, Month, and Day Cycles has a certain logic built in, which I will attempt to explain.

You begin your life, and live the number of years allowed to you, following the direction represented by your Life Path number. Your Life Path can be seen as a cycle; one Life Path for one life.

Your Life Path number is always the same as your first Personal Year number. Your Personal Years then follow each other in nine-year epicycles. However, the first and last nine-year cycles are incomplete (except if one would be born at the start of a 1 Personal Year, and die at the end of a 9 Personal Year).

These nine-year epicycles are divided into nine-month cycles. However, most years neither begin, nor end, with complete nine-month cycles. Below is a chart showing the rhythm in which your nine-month cycles fill a nine-year epicycle.

Personal Year	Personal Months
1	2, 3, 4, 5, 6, 7, 8, 9, 1, 2, 3, 4
2	3, 4, 5, 6, 7, 8, 9, 1, 2, 3, 4, 5
3	4, 5, 6, 7, 8, 9, 1, 2, 3, 4, 5, 6
4	5, 6, 7, 8, 9, 1, 2, 3, 4, 5, 6, 7
5	6, 7, 8, 9, 1, 2, 3, 4, 5, 6, 7, 8
6	7, 8, 9, 1, 2, 3, 4, 5, 6, 7, 8, 9
7	8, 9, 1, 2, 3, 4, 5, 6, 7, 8, 9, 1
8	9, 1, 2, 3, 4, 5, 6, 7, 8, 9, 1, 2
9	1, 2, 3, 4, 5, 6, 7, 8, 9, 1, 2, 3

(Notice that only the last four years of your nine-year cycle contain a complete nine-month cycle.)

A similar rhythm can be found in the Personal Day Cycles, whereby only the Personal Months 6, 7, 8, and 9 contain three complete nine-day cycles. All other months have only two complete nine-day cycles. The 5 Personal Month contains three complete nine-day cycles if the month has thirty-one days.

THE TRANSIT LETTERS

The Transits are found among the individual letters of your name, and are used in conjunction with the Essence Chart to provide additional information about your year ahead.

Your name can be viewed as a piece of music that vibrates in time. Your life, therefore, can be visualized as a musical score, with the individual letters making specific contributions at given points, just as notes in a musical piece are played at specific moments to give a piece of music its rhythm, character, and nuance. Each note or letter has a specific duration and influence over your life during a specific period of time.

How to Find Your Transits

The Transits are derived from the letters of your first, middle, and last names. Each name provides information on a particular level of your consciousness: the physical, mental, and spiritual. The Physical Transit is derived from your first name; the Mental Transit from your middle name; and the Spiritual Transit from your last name. For those who do not have a middle name, the last name provides the Transit information for both the Mental and the Spiritual. For those who have more than one middle name, the middle names should be strung together into one long name. If you received more than one last name, string the last names together into one long last name.

Let's take Thomas John Hancock's name again as an example. His first name, Thomas, is used to find his Physical Transits. Starting at birth, the T in Thomas's name has a value of 2, and therefore lasts for two years. The H follows that two-year period with a numerological influence of 8, which will last for eight years. Each letter has a duration equal to its numerical value.

When you add the numerical value of each of the letters in the name Thomas, you find that Thomas has a full numerological value of 22, and therefore lasts for twenty-two years, at which time the name's influence will return to the T and go through the letters again.

For the Mental Transit, we use the middle name John, which begins with the letter J, with a value of 1, and lasts for one year. The letter O has a value of 6 and lasts for six years. The letters of the name John have a full duration of twenty years, at which time the cycle starts again with the letter J.

For the Spiritual Transit, we use the name Hancock, which begins with the letter H, with a numerological value of 8 that lasts for eight years. The A follows, which has a value of 1 and lasts one year. The N has a value of 5, and lasts for five years. The full name of Hancock has a value of 28, and lasts for twenty-eight years before the cycle starts over again.

Below is a description of the meaning of the Transits for the Physical, Mental, and Spiritual levels. Understand that a Transit has to be read in relation to the level on which it is found. For an example of how to record your Transit numbers see the Progressive Chart (Figure 6.2 on page 230).

A Transit Letter

You have a mental approach to practical matters. This is a period of change, activity, progress, and creativity. The letter A adds independence and leadership to your personality. There can be quite a bit of travel, and possibly a change of residence. You can expect promotion and opportunities. There may also be a real breakthrough in your awareness and perspective of life.

B Transit Letter

You may be more emotional and shy than usual. You have a strong need for love, and you can fall prey to emotional love affairs. You have to watch for problems with health, especially those related to your nervous system. You need plenty of rest. Be receptive, and listen to the advice of others. There will be improvement in your career due to your sensitivity and diplomacy. Others are attracted to you and want to help you in your endeavors.

C   Transit Letter

You will be better able to express yourself. You are more creative and original. You will be intuitive, and you may experience premonitions or other psychic experiences. You feel more adventurous, and you make several new friends. There will be an increase in social events. You are capable of self-promotion. This is a good time for business, especially sales.

D   Transit Letter

You have to keep an eye on your health, and you may want to reevaluate your diet and exercise habits. Preventive health measures go a long way.

You will have to work at expressing your feelings this year, and you may want a loving shoulder to cry on. Your love relationships may be somewhat strained, but it will be easier if you are able to share your feelings. There is opportunity for growth, and an increase in self-confidence. There will be travel.

E   Transit Letter

You will feel inspired and helpful. There can be change in career, travel, and possibly another residence. You are attracted to new and adventurous experiences, including love affairs. There can also be marriage. Although this is a good letter for finances, there may be a lack of focus and a more frivolous attitude, which will adversely affect your chances of real material progress. You feel attracted to new religions and philosophical ideas.

F   Transit Letter

This is a period of much soul-searching and spiritual growth. There will be plenty of hard work and responsibility, both at home and on the job. During this year you are intuitive and sensitive, but less clear about what you want out of life. You will need to turn inward, to contemplate and to meditate. You may have a tendency to play the martyr during this time; you may sacrifice too much. However, this is likely an avoidance of responsibility other than an act of genuine selfless love. There will be more than enough opportunity to help and to give comfort, however, because many people will come to you for guidance and a shoulder to cry on.

 Transit Letter

This is a time of contradicting forces. There is a promise of financial gain, yet there is also a warning not to seek reward for yourself. The G is both mental and spiritual. There can be success and happiness—if it is not sought after. You will feel alone and lonely many times during this year, and you will spend time in meditation and contemplation. There is also a strong tendency to spend much time brooding. Your self-expression is high, but you tend to stay on the surface. You act secretive and self-contained. You will be impulsive more than usual, particularly in emotional matters.

 Transit Letter

Your mind will be very active during this year. Your thoughts are surprisingly unconventional. You come up with original, even inventive, ideas. This is an ambitious time, and self-promotion will pay off. Advancement and success are possible. You have self-discipline and a clear understanding of what you want. Emotionally you are a little vulnerable and in need of love and attention.

I **Transit Letter**

This is a very emotional time with many ups and downs. You are high-strung and vulnerable to stress. You are somewhat accident-prone. You need to develop calmness, centeredness, and an acceptance of life. You must control your moods and not slip into feelings of self-pity and insecurity. At the same time, you are very competitive and have the opportunity to achieve success and financial rewards.

J **Transit Letter**

You will have more initiative during this period, and you may change career direction. There will be opportunities to increase your earnings; however, you will have to research all the details and possible consequences of your actions. Avoid any shortcuts. New responsibilities come into your life. There may be a change of residence. After an initial period of emotional ups and downs, you will experience a form of rebirth and realization, giving you renewed confidence.

K   Transit Letter

You will be extremely intuitive during this period. Revelations and spiritual breakthroughs are far more possible. You will associate yourself with new people, and new business endeavors. Your creativity and inner drive are stronger than usual. You will need to cooperate more, and to share responsibilities with others. You will experience many strange and unusual events and situations. This may take a toll on your nerves, especially because you are so sensitive. The letter K in the Transit is often associated with fame and fortune. You must guard against dishonesty, indiscretion, and exaggeration.

L   Transit Letter

This is not a time to hurry. You want to carefully and thoroughly consider your path, plans, and future. This is a mental time, a time to think and to look for the deeper meaning of your desires and expectations. Try to take all available opportunities to travel. Involvement with the arts, and expressing your own creativity are highly rewarding during this time. You will make new friends easily. This is also a favorable time for marriage. However, thoughtlessness and careless action may cause you to lose friends and resources.

M   Transit Letter

This is a time for hard work and a practical approach. You may appear reticent, which can create distance between you and those who are close to you. Make an effort to express your feelings to them. Relationships may be demanding and require more sacrifice. Think carefully before making important decisions. Do not be impulsive, and don't let your mood changes influence your direction. Take your time!

N Transit Letter

You will have opportunities to expand your horizons. There will be adventurous experiences and travel. A change of residence is very possible. This is a dynamic time with many new activities. You will make some important social contacts. You search for love and fulfillment. Sacrifice, adaptability, and flexibility are called for. You will also be concerned with finances, and you may worry too much about these matters. You tend to be forgetful during this time. You will also feel more sensual than usual. Physical exercise is important during this period.

O Transit Letter

This is a time of strong emotional experiences, which can affect your health if you let it. You may find yourself worrying unduly. There is much responsibility placed on your shoulders, and there are sensitive emotional issues involved. You will find yourself more interested in religious and physical studies. Your leadership abilities are enhanced during this time.

P Transit Letter

Many unexpected events take place during this period. It is a time in which you feel less in control. Do not take any unnecessary risks. Your reflexes are not as fast as usual. You may experience confusion and disappointment in relationships. You have difficulty expressing yourself now. This is a time to focus on spiritual development. There will be recognition for your skills and talents, possibly resulting in a promotion or business success. But this is more a time for spiritual growth than financial growth.

 Q Transit Letter

Your intuition and intelligence are greatly enhanced under the influence of the Q. You will have many original ideas, and may even invent something. Your problem-solving skills are excellent at this time. However, you are more unstable and erratic now. You will attract some highly unusual and eccentric people, and you will have to guard against impulsive actions. This is a good time for financial growth. You have a strong need for recognition and power. You may experience a major change in your work environment.

R   Transit Letter

You have much understanding and insight now, a time during which you have to deal with money, power, and authority. You have an opportunity to elevate your financial status and personal growth. You will meet the best and the worst. You have to exercise caution in everything you do, and in every decision you make. Be aware of your surroundings.

S   Transit Letter

Your feelings run deep, and your awareness is higher than usual. It is a period of rebirth and awakening, especially of hidden aspects of your personality. Freedom in a very real and lasting sense can be your reward. You will experience sudden changes in all aspects of your life, accompanied with spiritual and mystical revelations. Your dreams may be rather intense, and they should be looked into for messages and an understanding of your subconscious. There will be confrontations with strong-willed people to test the strength of your convictions. This is an exciting time full of surprises and extraordinary events.

T   Transit Letter

This is a time of strain and high-strung emotions. You are willing to sacrifice and to carry your burdens heroically, but you will have to guard against self-pity. You will benefit from solitude and meditation. You are looking for new activities and are eager to learn. You have a strong desire for knowledge. This is a good and rewarding time for business and new partnerships, but you have to guard your territory against those seeking to interfere in your work. There will be opportunities to travel and see the world.

U   Transit Letter

This is an intuitive and sensitive time in which you may find yourself unwilling to put forth much effort. You lack motivation and initiative. A lot of old and long-forgotten emotional issues may surface. People you have not heard from in a long time will call upon you. Relatives and family may require effort and attention. You have much creativity and enhanced self-expression. Use it and promote yourself.

V   Transit Letter

The letter V is the most mystical and spiritually powerful. You will be very intuitive, experiencing revelations and moments of deep religious understanding. You will be very inspired, but you will need time alone to contemplate your thoughts. Financially this is also a good time. You will have opportunities to invest in promising enterprises. You pay off old debts, and you experience increased prosperity. You will have to keep a tight control over your projects, and listen carefully to your intuition.

 W   Transit Letter

This is a time to let go of the past and to accept change with open arms. The letter W introduces many new activities and exciting events. You will find yourself behaving erratically at times, and being totally unpredictable. You will have to control this tendency in order to prevent chaos and unpleasant results. This can be a time of explosive growth, but self-discipline is absolutely necessary. You may find yourself involved in legal matters, and in all probability on the winning end. Your health needs special attention during this period.

 X   Transit Letter

You may feel more vulnerable under the influence of this letter. Your emotions are prone to turmoil. Avoid unconventional groups or ideas for the time being. Wait until your judgment is better. Adjustments are necessary in all areas of your life, but will be felt mostly in the areas of love and sexuality. You may find yourself involved in a secret liaison, which can cause you much trouble. The positive aspects of the X Transit are the opportunities for purification and sacrifice. You may receive public attention, and you may gain a certain amount of respect for your unselfish actions. You are aware of your need for guidance in spiritual matters. You have the ability to move fast, and to decide quickly. There can be much progress on the material level, and considerable financial gain.

Y   Transit Letter

This is a time of spiritual growth and perception of higher realms. You are very intuitive, and psychic perceptions will take place. Soul-searching and meditation are extremely beneficial to you during this time.

Your sense of direction is somewhat clouded, inspiring serious self-examination. You are in search of new friends and contacts with others of similar intellectual needs. There may be some minor health problems. You should avoid stimulants and spicy foods.

 **Transit Letter**

This is an inspiring time. You can overcome limitations, and you can see enormous progress in your life. Financially this is a good time, as long as you put your faith in hard work and avoid schemes. You are able to make accurate judgments based on sound intuition. A new and unusual relationship will cause many changes in your life, which may include a change of residence.

Your Transit Cycles can last from one to nine years and run from birthday to birthday. The purpose of the Transits is to help you to take advantage of the talents and abilities as they are represented in the letters of your name. Each letter in your name represents a certain strength or resource. For the period that this letter is also a Transit in your chart, you find yourself having to bring forth all the characteristics that are unique to this letter. It is a learning process.

Let's say that your name is Mary. You have come to this world with the specific strengths implicit in the name Mary, and from the day you are born, you learn to take advantage of these strengths. The first four years of your life, you work with the aspects of the letter M, followed by one year dedicated to the letter A. This is followed by a nine-year period covered by the R, and seven years for the letter Y. After this twenty-one year period that takes you through the name Mary, you start over, in order to learn more of the qualities contained in this name.

A study of the three Transits that together influence you in any particular year can tell you much about the kind of events and experiences you can expect for that year.

THE ESSENCE NUMBER

The Transits are the individual letters and individual influences. The Essence number is the combined total of the Physical, Mental, and Spiritual Transits that are influencing you during a particular year of your life.

There are some important differences between Personal Year and Essence

Cycles. The Personal Year Cycles represent a regular and repetitive cyclic system beginning at a 1 Personal Year and ending at a 9 Personal Year, at which point the cycle starts again. Although we do not all go through the same Personal Year Cycle at the same time, this pattern is the same for everyone. However, the Essence Cycles are neither regular nor repetitive. Some Essence Cycles last as long as nine years, while others last only one. In addition, the Essence Cycles can change from any one number to another. For example, you may have a 6 Essence this year and move into a 1 Essence next year. Or you may have an 8 Essence this year and the next three years, after which it may change to a 5 Essence for the duration of two years.

Another important difference is that the Personal Year, which is closely tied to the Universal Year, starts at the beginning of the year; whereas the Essence, which is tied to the name you received at birth, starts around your birthday.

There is a subtle but significant difference in the way the Essence number is experienced as opposed to the Personal Year number. Your Personal Year implies what kind of opportunities and challenges will come your way, but your Essence reveals what you are ready to attract and integrate into your life. You can almost say that the Essence number seems to be felt from the inside out, whereas the Personal Year number tends to be felt more from the outside in. Your Essence number represents a stage in your personal growth. For that reason, the Master numbers 11 and 22 are not reduced, and the Karmic Debt numbers 16 and 19 are more important here than in almost any other area of the chart. Both the Master numbers and the Karmic Debt numbers deserve extra attention.

How to Find Your Essence Number

At Thomas's birth, the letters T, J, and H, are the first Transits for the Physical, Mental, and Spiritual Planes. Their values are 2, 1, and 8, respectively, which totals 11. Hancock's first Essence at birth is an 11.

Since the influence of the letter J lasts only one year, Hancock's Essence will change during the second year, when the O from John takes over, while the T and the H are still influencing him on the Physical and Spiritual levels respectively. Beginning in his second year, therefore, his Essence number will be derived from the T (2), the O (6), and the H (8), giving him an essence of 16, which reduces to 7.

When arriving at the Essence number, it is particularly important to look for Karmic Debt numbers (such as the 16 in our example above) and Master numbers.

Note that your Essence number for the year of your birth is the same as your Balance number.

To illustrate what I have just explained, see an example of Thomas John Hancock's Transits and Essence Chart, from birth to age 19, below.

For an example of how to record your Essence numbers see the Progressive Chart (Figure 6.2 on page 230).

Age:
0 1 2 3 4 5 6 7 8 9 10 11 12 13 14 15 16 17 18 19
Physical Transit:
T T h h h h h h h h o o o o o o m m m m
Mental Transit:
J o o o o o o h h h h h h h h h n n n n
Spiritual Transit:
H H H H H H H H a n n n n n c c c o o o
Essence Number:
2 16 22 22 22 22 22 6 8 3 19 19 19 19 8 14 3 6 6 6
   7   1 1 1 1   5

1 Essence Number

You will now start an entirely new phase of your life. You are on the threshold of a new beginning. Not only will you have fresh ideas, but you will also accept and even embrace them. It is a time of radical change, and in all likelihood you are ready for it. Now is the time to advance the new, and let go of the old. All inefficient methods will have to be eliminated from your life. In the same way, you must let go of relationships that no longer service your future. Discard habits and liabilities that you have been holding on to. A new identity is emerging, one that is efficient, innovative, highly creative, and courageous.

Your leadership qualities will rush to the surface. Your environment will demand that you stand up to challenges and face difficulties head on. You can no longer hide from the truths of your life. The facts are now blatantly clear. You must take a stand. Change is a given. You possess the power to make those changes. All you need is the will and the energy to enact your plan. This is a period of struggle and great reward. You have the chance to achieve independence. But it will not be handed to you. You must wrest from old habits and inertia of the past.

As with all beginnings, this one will be marked by false starts and blind alleys. You will be forced to start again and again. You are like a baby learning to walk. There will be falls. You will have to persevere. This is a period in which your willpower will be tested. You are, in fact, forging your own determination. You must not give up. But the rewards are great. The general influences are raising you to new heights of independence, courage, and self-esteem. At the conclusion of this 1 Essence, your knowledge and self-respect will be greatly increased, as will your capacity to stand on your own two feet.

2 Essence Number

You must learn to cooperate with others in order to accomplish some greater good. This is not a time to lead, but to follow. You must be content to draw your guidance from the environment and those in positions of greater power. You must maintain your own center, but avoid arrogance, rigidity, and stubbornness. The more you insist on your own priorities, the more resistance you will meet. This is a period of partnerships. Your success depends on your ability to work with others.

You will be extremely sensitive and intuitive. Your powers of understanding will be at an all-time high. These abilities will give you the insight you need to perceive subtle changes in people and situations. Therefore, you will be better able to adapt to changing circumstances.

Your intuition makes it possible to accomplish great tasks, even though you may not be in a leadership role. The reason: You instinctively know how to react to change, and to gently advise people to go in the right directions.

Your role as an advisor or confidant is the key to your success during this period. You are learning the lesson of interdependence. You will also come to know how valuable you can be in a more passive role. It is a period to serve; to be the helper; to be the assistant. Your ability and willingness to work with others will be tested and rewarded. It is essential that you listen. Be shrewd in your evaluations of others and of situations, but do not enforce your judgments directly on people.

Your sensitivity will make it necessary for you to seek out harmonious and peaceful environments. Be careful of the health of your nervous system. You can become anxious more easily during this period. Therefore, seek out people you trust; share your deeper feelings; and allow yourself to be supported by friends and loved ones. Keep your spirits high, and avoid depression.

Music plays an important role during this period. Any musical talent you possess will be enhanced. You even have a certain physical grace that can emerge in dancing, athletics, or simply walking down the street.

In your passive, centered way, you will be charismatic and attractive to others. People will sense your fine intuition and sensitivity, and seek you out for private talks. Be loyal to friends and partners.

Remain strong inwardly, and flexible without. In this way, you will avoid the obvious difficulties and remain on your path to success. This is a period of accomplishment through gentle persuasion.

3   Essence Number

Your ability to express yourself will reach an all-time high. Any talent you possess in the arts—especially in writing, acting, or other performing arts— will be greatly enhanced. This is a period of success through personal creativity. You have much opportunity to advance yourself and your career through your own personal expression, charm, and creative talent.

This is a social time, filled with much fun and friendship. You will feel lighter, fresher, and more alive than in previous years. It is as if life has relieved you of a burden, allowing the more creative, upward, and joyful energies to flow more freely. People are naturally attracted to you. They sense your joie de vivre, your spirit, and creativity.

Your challenge is to focus your heightened creativity on a worthwhile task. Discipline is essential. Choose a goal worth reaching. Pour your energies into something that will last. In this way, you will emerge from this period having accomplished something worthwhile, and you will have learned to harness your creative abilities. If you fail to focus, you will likely spend your opportunity and creative urges on loose talk, superficiality, and socializing.

This is an emotional period. The upward, heart-centered energies are peaking, bringing with them many old emotional issues. You can easily exaggerate the importance of an unkind word, or react too emotionally to a troubling situation. In short, you need perspective now. You are in a very volatile period, making you highly creative, sensitive, and given to emotional mood swings. You are very romantic and likely to fantasize. There can be many wonderfully romantic times; however, it is important to avoid being swept away by your fantasies. Do not fail to see people for what they are.

This is a time when you will learn the value of your personal expression, and your own uniqueness. It is also a time of personal accomplishment and advancement.

4   Essence Number

This is a period of much work, attention to detail, and career advancement. Your rewards will be directly proportionate to your effort. Much will be demanded of you, but you now have the opportunity to lay a sound foundation for your life. You must be orderly and disciplined. Attention to detail in all areas—especially in personal finances and business—is a necessity. Your workload will likely increase. Only through the correct management of time and resources will you be able to apportion your energies correctly to meet the increased demands made of you.

You are now being trained in the ways of the world, and only sound practical management will bring you the results you desire. Any flimsy or unsound business practices will likely bring trouble and increased work for you. Only by dealing with reality—that is, by facing situations exactly as they are, and not by how you might like them to be—will you be able to find the correct path to success. Avoid feelings of restriction or limitation. Be economical in all of your expenditures. Be sure to care for your health. Maintain a healthy diet, and follow a sound exercise routine. Pay attention to preventive health methods, and get the rest you need, and know when to allow yourself some breathing room. Be moderate in all things, including moderation. Balance is the key to this period.

In-laws and family members can be demanding now. People see you as a rock of stability, and are naturally attracted to you for support. Be helpful without allowing yourself to be used.

You are being called upon to work hard, and to establish a firm foundation upon which your life will rest for many years to come.

5 Essence Number

This is an important time of progress and advancement along the lines of your talents. You will experience a relief from burden and increased personal freedom. Any talent you possess in writing, public relations, and the arts will be greatly enhanced. At the same time, business matters flow quickly, and new opportunities for expansion seem to arise out of nowhere.

People are attracted to you, and seek to help you to achieve your goals. You possess an almost magical ability to promote yourself. Your fluency with words is greatly increased. You are more charming and attractive, which opens many new doors. This is a period of travel and much learning. Opportunities to visit distant lands, encounter foreign cultures and peoples, and learn about life will come to you. Your personal growth will speed up considerably. As such, many old habits and outdated methods will fade from your life. It is as if you are being catapulted from an old and outworn, into a new and fast-paced period of personal growth and development.

Your desire to satisfy your senses will also increase dramatically. You must be careful not to overindulge in food, alcohol, sex, and drugs.

Sudden events and chance occurrences will be encountered. You must be alert to your opportunities. This is not a period of sitting back and waiting, but a time to move ahead rapidly.

Your challenge is to remain focused on your more long-term goals. Be disciplined in your work. Don't have too many irons in the fire. Sort out the important projects and endeavors, and see them through from start to finish. Focus, discipline, and completion are the keys to your success.

6   Essence Number

This is a time of responsibility, duty, family matters, and high ideals. You will be called upon to support others, and to maintain high standards in all areas of life while you do it. Others look to you as an inspiration and a source of guidance. There is an element of self-sacrifice present in you that you must serve those closest to you. Unselfishness and a willingness to be of help to others are the keys to your success.

You will likely experience advancement in business, career, and financial matters. Progress comes more easily during this period as new opportunities open up to you. At the same time, your achievements bring added responsibility and new demands. You will have to devote yourself entirely to the task at hand to realize your goals.

This can be an emotional period, as family members may be demanding. The whole issue of love comes to the forefront. Your ability to love and to be loved will become absolutely clear. This is an Essence during which many marriages and divorces take place. People discover how much they truly love their partner, or how little love they have in their lives. Protect your family relationships. Work to maintain harmony in your home. Stay especially focused on the needs of children.

There can be a domineering figure in your life who can oppress you during this time. The key is to be balanced and centered when dealing with all authority figures. Refuse to act harshly or emotionally. Remain focused and in harmony with your long-term goals. If you keep a stronghold on your ideals, you will gain many supporters and admirers. This brings many great rewards and much appreciation. New and lasting friends come into your life now, and many seek to advance you along the lines of your abilities.

There is a strong artistic urge present. Those with artistic talent, or who are already working in the arts, will find their abilities greatly enhanced, with many new and rewarding challenges for advancement.

Most people under the 6 Essence will improve their lives, and will experience growth in their career goals.

7   Essence Number

This is a period of much self-reflection, analysis, and inner growth. The journey now is inward. You will feel a need to spend more time alone to contemplate your life and those close to you. The questions that pursue you are the fundamental ones of life: Who am I? What am I doing? Why am I doing it?

Your environment or milieu will seem more aggressive than during previous years. This is a function of your heightened sensitivity and intuition. This will naturally drive you deeper within yourself, causing you to ferret out the important issues that have directed your life to this point.

In order to deal effectively with those around you, especially family members and co-workers, you will have to refine your expression in all respects. Don't push people too hard, lest you damage close friendships unnecessarily.

This is not a time for being extroverted or aggressive. This is a time of introversion and deeper self-understanding. Be gentle with yourself and those around you. Think carefully before making important decisions. Be cautious when making major changes.

It is a wonderful time to study and to specialize in one particular field. Your ability to think deeply and clearly is at an all-time high. Indeed, your mind is your best tool. You are attracted to the great books, new realms of study, and higher learning. You have the ability to focus and to concentrate. You can penetrate below the surface of subjects to see the inner workings of yourself, others, and life around you.

Avoid becoming cynical and skeptical. Don't be too intellectual, lest you leave your heart behind. This is a time of deep spiritual and psychological integration. The head and the heart should be working together, not opposing each other.

You will likely discover what you most enjoy doing now. Follow these urges; study areas that you have long neglected, but have wanted to pursue. The inner self guides you during this time. Listen carefully to its advice.

8   Essence Number

This is a period when business and career affairs dominate your agenda. A major new opportunity will unfold to you and you will have to give yourself to it entirely to make it work. It is a time of progress and much personal power, but the demands of the time are equally large, thus requiring careful planning and attention to detail. All business matters—including personal economies—will come under sharp scrutiny. You will likely have more money than during previous years, but, conversely, you must be more careful with it.

A new start can be made. You sense the need to grasp it. But you are also aware that it must be treated with great care. Therefore, be astute in all your business dealings. Major mistakes can be made if you are not careful. These mistakes can affect you for some years to come.

It is a time of cautious use of power. You are being asked to develop wisdom in all your dealings. Balance in areas from your mundane affairs to your eminently important relationships is the key to your success. Keep a tight control on your bookkeeping, while providing strong leadership and gentle guidance to your family or close associates.

It is also a time when old issues, especially debts from the past, surface with a vengeance, making it necessary to pay the piper before further progress can be made. The irony is that while you have greater resources, there are often equally large demands made of you. This is a time, too, when you will realize that you are a survivor. No matter what difficulties you have experienced in the past, this is a period when you can regain a sense of progress in career matters. You will feel that you are doing important work, and you will be richly rewarded for it.

9 Essence Number

This is a period during which your ideals will be tested and forged anew. You will be broadened in ways that you would never have dreamed possible. You will likely experience a dramatic psychological and spiritual expansion. Old relationships that no longer have a place in your life will be let go of. Even old habits or characteristics that you believed were fundamental to your identity seem to evaporate.

There is a need to forgive those in your past and to let them get on with their lives, as you must with yours. Hanging on to negative attachments, either out of anger or a sense that justice has not yet been done, will bring you much misery, and, if the courts are involved, protracted lawsuits.

You now have the ability to reach out to the masses. This is a time that requires much self-sacrifice and service to others. You are deeply affected by the pain and sufferings of others, and you will feel a need to change your milieu or society for the better.

Those in the arts, especially actors, writers, and other performers, will see an enhancement of their talents, and the opening of many new opportunities for advancement. Your focus is mostly outward. Teach, perform, and advance society in your own way. Dedicate yourself to a higher cause. These are the areas that will meet with much success.

Conversely, selfishness, negativity, and pettiness will blow up in your face. The time demands a broad view of life. You are now the visionary who must see the greater trends in humanity. Out of this will come much compassion for all. This is the lesson of the period: As you work for the greater good of society, you will be personally rewarded, so much so that your cup will runneth over.

11   Essence Number

This is a time of enormous sensitivity and equally enormous change. Your intuition is galvanized. You are capable of even psychic experiences. But your awareness of the higher realms serves to throw a light upon all that is low and enlightened in your own life. The contrast can be shocking.

You are very aware of your shortcomings as a human being. This can drive you more deeply inward. You are extremely self-conscious. There may be feelings of failure and self-recrimination. These must be kept under control. All of this stems from an element of shock present in your life. The very ground upon which your personality is based seems to have experienced an upheaval. This psychic quake can often be replicated by some event in your life. Consequently, your identity is shaken.

It is time for self-examination. Are you happy with what you are doing? Is your work directly in line with your higher values and talents? During this period of self-review, you will have a great opportunity to set your life upon a more deeply spiritual and lasting foundation. Consequently, you can make much progress, and experience a great deal of future happiness as a result of this period. There is a realignment occurring that is putting you in touch with your deeper nature. The inner and the outer are now becoming one. It is a period of quickened psychological and spiritual growth.

Your intuition will now guide you safely from the storm. While your emotional life may be turbulent, your intuition gives you a sense that you are on the right track. In fact, you have not lost direction, but have taken a quantum leap along your path. It can be a bit jarring, but it is altogether positive.

Meditate, pray, seek out harmonious settings, take walks in the woods, and be close to nature. Let your inner self guide you to a greater happiness.

There can be many wonderful inner, and even psychic experiences, that reassure you of the love and support coming to you from the universe itself.

It is a time of illumination on all levels. Make the most of it. Allow the higher forces to guide your rapid growth.

16 Essence Number

There are structures of thought and behavior patterns that keep us from experiencing our true natures and the deeper happiness within. By some great benevolence of the universe, these structures collapse from time to time. You are now in one of those benevolent periods.

This is the proverbial dark night of the soul. You will find many things not working out as you had planned. There can be unexpected, turbulent, and shocking events. There are debts to be paid that may seem unduly harsh or imbalanced. The time is confusing, and you may feel that you have lost direction entirely.

Your challenge is to surrender to the larger forces that now seem so threatening. Let the transformative powers redirect you. This is the surest path out of the confusion that now dominates your life.

The 16 Essence is very like a storm that seems, on the surface, to be knocking down buildings, but it is in fact rearranging your life so that you emerge healthier and happier than before.

The 16 Essence usually does not last long. You will find yourself on much sounder footing, and in much better circumstances, once it passes. You are experiencing the night that will surely bring the dawn. With it will come a new life.

Part of the lesson you are learning is gratitude. Take time to truly examine everything that has been given to you. You are overlooking the love in your life, the talents you have been given, and the good things that have been added to your life without your acknowledgment. There is something of a blind spot in you that has brought about the current period of confusion. Now is a time to self-reflect, and to truly take stock of your life. Gratitude is one of the keys to a healthy transformation. Offer thanks to the universe for all that has been provided to you. This is an act of true magnanimity, because you likely feel that you have been treated unjustly by the greater forces. But such thinking is a delusion that has blinded you to your true nature and destiny. Open your heart. Accept that your vision is not of the infinite, but of the relative world. Accept that the infinite is guiding you lovingly toward higher planes of consciousness.

Surrender to the greater forces. This will cause you to open up to the higher planes and allow them to guide you. Now is a time to develop faith. The power of faith can help you feel secure in the midst of change. Faith allows you to feel that you are heading in a good direction, even when you do not know what that direction is. It is also the key to your happiness now.

Meditate, pray, and do regular spiritual practices. Take care of your health with sound diet and exercise programs. Try to eliminate all unhealthy attitudes and practices. Live a more enlightened inner life. Learn to trust.

19 Essence Number

You are in a struggle for independence, and you are possessed by personal ambition. You will feel the need to work hard to establish yourself and your foundation. You are forward looking and even visionary, but this is for personal gain.

This is a period of struggle. It is a time when you may feel torn between your personal desires and your concerns for others. It can be a time marked by stubbornness and rigidity, characteristics you will have to keep in check. This duality between the lower desires and the higher realms of love can cause you much internal conflict.

Secretly, you may feel torn between a desire to serve some greater good, and your ambition for personal accomplishment. You are aware of the needs of others. At the same time, you are skeptical of ideals and idealists. You may tell yourself now that you must be realistic in your dealings with the world. But you must avoid shutting out the voice of your higher nature. Do not let your higher ideals go, lest you be guided exclusively by materialism and greed.

All too often, those in the 19 Essence finally resolve this conflict by conceding to personal ambition and selfishness. This can lead you to much trouble. People may perceive you as greedy and self-centered. Because you are driven by ambition, you may be attracted to people who have no other priority but personal gain. For some, this will lead to shady business practices, and even to brushes with the law.

This can be a time when you feel a need to pull back from others, and to become less social than during previous years. But this can lead to isolation. You may also feel frustrated, because your ambitions want instant gratification, which the time does not allow.

The challenge during this time is to strike a balance between your worldly needs and your inner spiritual nature. The time requires much soul-searching, and a willingness to accept the perspective of others. Don't shut yourself off, or become jaundiced to your more idealistic brethren. At the conclusion of the 19 Essence, you are often better off materially, and far more independent, but there may also be a sense of disconnectedness from friends and loved ones. Therefore, it is important to work at maintaining close ties. Be open to others, and recognize that "man does not live by bread alone."

 **Essence Number**

This is a period of enormous demands, and, consequently, it is the chance to achieve greatness. You will find yourself at the center of some larger movement or social cause. Power has come to you, but you will need every ounce of strength to accomplish the task that lies before you.

You now serve some greater social good. Selfishness, pettiness, and timidity will cause you much trouble, as they are antagonistic to everything that you have set your sights on.

Now is a time to build some great and lasting structure. That structure may be physical, like a building or a business, for example, or it may be social, as in advancing a truly worthy social cause. Whatever it is, it has come to you from a higher plane, or what might be termed the archetypal world. You will see this truth everywhere you look. Practically speaking, your well-being, your livelihood or general attitude, rests in a large measure with what you do. People naturally look to you for leadership and inspiration. Your vision is truly wide and distant in scope. Your actions have dramatic effects. Therefore, you are more cautious and responsible with what you do.

This can be a sensitive period. You are being asked to live according to higher ideals. Your values must be above reproach. Avoid disagreements; be magnanimous and patient with others. Take the slower, sure path toward problem solving. Get sufficient rest, and take care of your own personal needs. Be balanced in your activities. Avoid excessive work.

Pay attention to details without losing your vision of your long-term priorities. You are now building a foundation for something that will serve a greater social good. Think big, and take practical steps to ensure that your dreams become reality.

The Essence Cycle and the Personal Year Cycle are the strongest-felt, short- or medium-term Cycles in your chart. Your Personal Year Cycle appears to come "from the outside," and represents changes and influences that come your way. The Essence Cycle seems to come "from the inside" and represents your personal stage of development. The Essence number reveals your needs and desires, your priorities and your perspective, during that year.

For this reason, it is important to look at the Personal Year number and the Essence number together.

Note: When the Personal Year number is the same as the Essence number, this is called a duality, and almost always represents a time of great difficulties and obstacles, especially during the period between the date of birth and the end of the year.

THE PERIOD CYCLE NUMBER

Like most stories, there are three great divisions of our lives. The First, or opening period, finds us groping to find our true nature. At the same time, we are trying to cope with the powerful forces that are present in our environment, our parents, and the socioeconomic conditions of our family, for example.

The Second Cycle, or middle period of our lives, brings about the gradual emergence of our individual and creative talents. The initial part of this cycle, the early and mid thirties, represents a struggle to find our place in the world, while the late thirties, forties, and early fifties see us with a greater degree of self-mastery and influence over the environment.

The Third, or final, Cycle represents a flowering of our inner being. Our true nature has come to fruition. It is during this period that one has the greatest degree of self-expression and personal power.

Your Period Cycles are based on the date of your birth. Each Period Cycle lasts approximately twenty-seven years, or three complete epicycles of nine years each. The exact age you make the transition from one Period Cycle to the next is determined by your Life Path, and is listed in the chart below.

Life Path number	End of First, start of Second Cycle	End of Second, start of Third Cycle
1	26–27	53–54
2 and 11	25–26	52–53
3	33–34	60–61
4 and 22	32–33	59–60
5	31–32	58–59
6	30–31	57–58
7	29–30	56–57
8	28–29	55–56
9	27–28	54–55

Your First Period Cycle starts at birth. Your Second Period Cycle starts in your 1 Personal Year closest to your twenty-ninth birthday. The Third Period Cycle starts twenty-seven years later.

How to Find Your Period Cycle Number

The number used to interpret your First Period Cycle is derived from the month you were born. (If the Birth month is October or December, reduce it to a single digit; November, the eleventh month, remains an 11, since it is a Master number.) The person born on May 15, 1949 would have a First Period Cycle of 5 (for May, the fifth month).

Your Second Period Cycle is based on the day of your birth, which, again, should be reduced to a single digit, except in the case of a Master number (11 and 22; 29 is reduced to an 11, and not reduced further). In our example, the person was born on the fifteenth day of the month; the Second Period Cycle is 6 (1 + 5).

Your Third and last Period Cycle is derived from the year of your birth, which is reduced to a single-digit number, except in the case of a Master number. The birth year of 1949 gives a Third Period Cycle of 5, since 1949 reduces to 5.

For an example of how to record your Period Cycle numbers see the Progressive Chart (Figure 6.2 on page 230).

 Period Cycle Number

This is a Period of much intensity. It requires fortitude, courage, and flexibility. You will be forced to use every one of your talents in order to achieve your own personal individuality and independence. It is also a Period of integration, and of focusing on your life's dream. Your grip on your direction will be tested, but somehow the resources are available to overcome any obstacle, and to emerge from this time as a stronger person. It is a time that requires independence, resilience, and strength, but these characteristics become an integral part of your personality. This cycle marks a time of progress.

2 **Period Cycle Number**

This is a period of slow and patient development. You are acutely sensitive to your surroundings, and you are highly intuitive. You possess a gift as a peacemaker, and you have tremendous power through gentle persuasion. Cultivate the talents of tact and diplomacy. Cooperate with others.

Musical and other artistic talents come to fruition. Partnerships are important, requiring understanding and compromise. You need patience and flexibility, but you are under a gentle and benevolent influence which makes others happy to support you. Seek out beauty and harmonious environments, spend time in nature, and enjoy the peace of close companionship. This is a period of slow, but steady progress.

3 Period Cycle Number

This is a time of heightened self-expression, and of much social support. Any ability you possess in the arts, especially in writing, acting, or dance, will be brought to new heights, and will meet with much reward. You are socially active as never before. You will appear to others as charming, attractive, and even charismatic. However, be careful not to waste your energies on too many superficial projects or relationships. The cycle requires discipline and focus in order to make the most of the great upward energy that is filling your life.

4 Period Cycle Number

This cycle is a time of hard work and all the rewards it can bring. This is a Period in which you are very concerned chiefly with the practical things of life: work and career, sound family, and a solid community. You are not given to flights of fancy or idealisms, but want to place your life on sound financial footing. You can be overly concerned with details and thus can find yourself in ruts that will have to be broken free of. Find work you love, and do it to your heart's content, but do not neglect the rest of your humanity, or that of others close to you. This is a time requiring discipline, order, and self-motivation. Work is the order of the day. But through these characteristics, you will be seen as the foundation of your family, your job, and even your community.

5 Period Cycle Number

A period of rapid progress and much change characterizes the 5 Cycle. You are learning the lesson of freedom. You will travel, move your residence many times, and change jobs. You are footloose. It is a time when you will be free of the burdens of responsibility. You will have a flair for successfully promoting yourself. Your abilities with words will be greatly enhanced. You can learn foreign languages, write, and edit. You will meet many exciting people, visit foreign lands, and encounter many new ideas. Identify yourself with all that is progressive and farsighted in your field. Seek change, and take hold of new opportunities.

6   Period Cycle Number

This is a time of family, responsibility, and duty. The issues of commitment, marriage, and family all come into sharp focus. When the commitments are made, and one responds lovingly and with acceptance, this is a period of much harmony and support. You are greatly needed by those around you. You will be loved and appreciated. This is the best cycle for marriage. In the same way, partnerships go well, and much progress is made from joint activities.

Conversely, if commitments are not deeply made or are broken, separation and divorce often occur. Any artistic talent you possess will surface, and new opportunities for self-expression will present themselves. You are also under very supportive influences for starting a business. This is a time of progress through flexibility, cooperation, and compromise.

7   Period Cycle Number

This is a time to specialize, think deeply, and contemplate the deeper questions of life. Study a subject you enjoy in depth. You are attracted to the fields of science, technology, philosophy, and metaphysics. Become an expert in a specific area. You have excellent intuition, and a mind that can penetrate beneath the surface of any subject you commit to. Focus your energies and thoughts. The 7 is a Period of inner development. Meditation, contemplation, and self-reflection are means of inner enrichment. Develop wisdom. Relationships may seem burdensome at times, because of your desire to spend time alone. There is some resistance to sharing your deeper feelings with others. The inner life is so compelling that you will want to immerse yourself in it. Share the knowledge you accumulate by teaching, counseling, or simply talking to others.

8   Period Cycle Number

You are under an extremely benevolent Period for work, career, and financial reward. The keys are hard work and the willingness to rededicate yourself after setbacks or difficulties. You will have greatly enhanced abilities as a manager, organizer, and financial planner. You have a gift for seeing the broad picture, and for carrying out bold plans. You can gain financial freedom during this period. Business and career activities go well, but require much attention and commitment. You are being pushed to take control of your career or enterprise and bring it to new heights. It is a time when power falls to you, but it must be used wisely and with purpose.

9 Period Cycle Number

This is a Period in which a broad view of humanity, and a sincere concern for the well-being of others will be developed. Tolerance, acceptance, and universal love are the goals of the 9 Cycle, and while such perfection will not be fully achieved, the person under this influence will grow toward these ideals. Humanitarian principles and social service are the keys to personal happiness. All work directed toward the improvement of the general welfare will bring great personal rewards as well. Hard work directed toward higher ideals is rewarded. Creative talent is also enhanced, especially when it is joined with some larger social purpose or message. There is an element of sacrifice or letting go, as one is asked to forgive past grievances and let go of negative attachments. The person is being asked to live according to a higher ethical standard, with much spiritual and personal enrichment as his reward.

11 Period Cycle Number

The 11 Period Cycle is a time of spiritual expansion, and even illumination. You will grow in understanding and wisdom. It is not a time to pursue material goals for themselves, but to seek the higher human ideals. There is a temptation, however, to chase after the infinite without grounding yourself in the practical. That must be avoided. Focus your studies, and deepen your understanding to the point that your knowledge can be conveyed to others in simple and acceptable terms. You possess a message or an ability that should be shared with your community, but only through deep personal transformation and improvement of self-expression can this gift be given. The more willing you are to work on yourself, the more good you will do for the world at large.

For those who accept and embrace this path, there is much reward, including ample financial support, and even fame. There is also the deeper satisfaction of knowing that one has made a contribution to the advancement of others.

22 Period Cycle Number

The 22 Cycle is a time of enormous potential for establishing some lasting institution or teaching that will greatly benefit others. You have the ability to perceive something in the archetypal world and make it manifest on the earth. Your abilities as a builder, organizer, and visionary are at a peak. You are able to perceive a deep need in people, and to create a constructive and practical plan to fulfill that need. You will be forced to commit yourself entirely to the work at hand. For many, this dream will last a lifetime, and require every ounce of energy, and every bit of talent. It is an all-consuming role that beckons, but one that will provide the greatest sense of personal accomplishment and reward. You are able to make a lasting contribution to the well-being of humanity.

Your Period Cycle numbers reflect your state of being during your travel along the path that begins at birth and ends at death. They give insight to your state of mind, your attitude, and your approach to life. They reflect the tone and intensity with which you experience the events and circumstances you encounter. They are subtle and not easily recognized. However, when you do a little soul-searching, you realize that they are true indicators of a deep, underlying experience.

THE PINNACLE CYCLE NUMBERS

The Pinnacles are four long-term cycles on our Life Path. They represent specific attributes that must be assimilated into your being. This process occurs by having to measure up to the demands and opportunities the Pinnacle presents to you. It forces you to deal with the qualities of that Pinnacle number. In the process, the Pinnacle shapes you.

The First Pinnacle lasts from birth until age thirty-six, minus your Life Path number. Each of the next two Pinnacles last nine years. The Fourth and last Pinnacle lasts for the remainder of your life.

A Pinnacle change always takes place during the 9 and the 1 Personal Years, which signify the end and the beginning of long-term cycles. While we go through numerous nine-year cycles, each one of which causes changes in the beginning and the end, the Pinnacle changes mark intense episodes of transformation in our personal lives. Because we start out in one Pinnacle, everyone experiences only three Pinnacle changes during the course of a lifetime.

You can prepare yourself for the times ahead by knowing your approaching Pinnacle number, and the time these changes occur.

How to Find Your Pinnacle Numbers

To find your First Pinnacle, add the numbers for your month and day of birth, arriving at a single-digit number. For example, if you were born on May 15,

1949, your First Pinnacle would be found by adding the 5 (for May) and the 6 (for the fifteenth) to arrive at 11. Master numbers encountered during the Pinnacle calculations are not reduced. Someone born on November 5 would add 11 (for November) and the 5 (the fifth day) to get 16, which is 7.

To find your Second Pinnacle, add the day you were born to the year of your birth. Using May 15, 1949 again, add the 6 (for the fifteenth day) and the birth year 5 (for 1949), and arrive at another 11.

To find your Third Pinnacle, add the sum of the first and the second Pinnacles—in this case, 11 plus 11—and arrive at 22. The 22 is a Master number, and is therefore not reduced.

To find your Fourth and last Pinnacle, add your month and year of birth. Using the example, add 5 (for May) and 5 (for 1949) to arrive at 10, which reduces to 1.

The year at which the First Pinnacle change takes place can be found by subtracting the Life Path number from age 36. In the case of the person whose birth date is May 15, 1949, subtract the 7 Life Path from 36 to arrive at 29. This person's First Pinnacle concludes at age 29. (Note that the Life Path number is always the same as the first Personal Year number at birth. We complete the nine-year cycle during which we are born, and follow it with three complete nine-year cycles before our first Pinnacle change.)

The Second and Third Pinnacles each last nine years. Using the example once again, the end of this person's Second Pinnacle would occur at age 38; the Third Pinnacle would end at 47, at which time his Fourth and final Pinnacle would begin.

First Pinnacle	= month of birth	+	day of birth
Second Pinnacle	= day of birth	+	year of birth
Third Pinnacle	= First Pinnacle	+	Second Pinnacle
Fourth Pinnacle	= month of birth	+	year of birth

Figure 6.1, shown on page 220, illustrates how the Pinnacles are charted in combination with the date of birth, the Challenge numbers, the Birth Day number, and the Life Path number. Figure 6.2, shown on page 230, is an example of how Pinnacles are charted on the Progressive Chart.

1 Pinnacle Number

This is a period that requires much independence, courage, resilience, and initiative. You must bounce back after many difficult experiences. The challenge of this Pinnacle is to gain willpower.

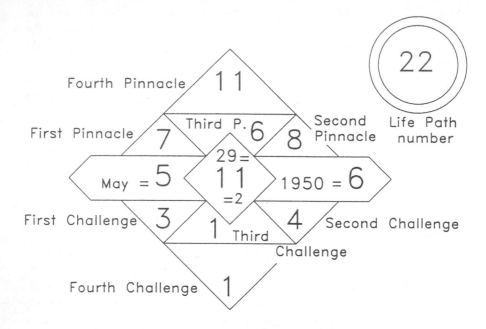

Figure 6.1 The Birth Day Chart with Pinnacles

There is not a lot of support from others or from family. You must draw on your own strength. You will have to guard against self-pity.

Keep focused on your dreams. This Pinnacle will require an iron will to keep hold of your goals, and also the flexibility to maneuver around difficulties, and to bend with the winds of adversity.

This is a period of rapid self-improvement and growth. You will be forced to use every talent and capability you possess. You will need to be resourceful. You must continually put out effort, but with it comes great reward. Without effort, there is no accomplishment or satisfaction, only a negative attitude toward life. Be careful not to become too self-centered, headstrong, or self-important. Be strong but flexible. Be open to the counsel of others, but make up your own mind.

The benefit of this Pinnacle number is a strong sense of your individuality and strength. You will know what you are made of. There are many hidden gifts in this period, perhaps the greatest of which is faith.

Your Pinnacle provides you with the characteristics of leadership, boldness, and daring. You will have many unconventional ideas, and the skill and courage to make them a reality. Your abilities to manage and organize people and institutions are greatly enhanced. You have confidence in the worth of your dreams.

These characteristics provide a great opportunity for success and major accomplishments.

2   Pinnacle Number

This Pinnacle causes you to be extremely sensitive, intuitive, and full of insight. It is a period that requires patience, and the development of inner awareness. You are being asked to use gentle power and persuasion to obtain your desired goals. Direct approaches, forceful displays, and confrontations will likely work against you. You will find the most satisfactory roles to be supportive. You are now a gifted advisor, a diplomat, and a peacemaker. Your insight into other people's feelings and motivations is so acute that you seem to be able to see right to the core of things. But rather than use these gifts to create differences between people, you must use them to create peace, to mend rifts, and to harmonize.

Your challenge during this period is to bring balance to duality in every form, and at every level. You will recognize the value of both sides of an argument, and you will be able to see the middle ground where peace can be made. You can create the atmosphere in which both sides can compromise and work harmoniously. You are the glue that keeps people and important projects together.

Sensitivity is the weakness you must face and overcome. You may be tempted to indulge your feelings, and to be too easily hurt. You may lack self-confidence, especially at the beginning of the Pinnacle when your heightened sensitivity and awareness make you conscious of your own shortcomings. You may succumb to fear and hesitation. All of this can lead to emotional turmoil. You need courage and the willingness to reach out for support.

Your sensitivity will make you acutely appreciative of beauty and harmonious environments. At the same time, you need beauty and harmony around you.

You have an increased appetite for music and the arts in general. You may find your musical talents coming to the surface. If you do not already play an instrument, give in to any inclination to take one up.

A person in a 2 Pinnacle who uses his or her sensitivity, understanding, and insight is very appreciated by others. You may not fully realize just how much others appreciate and respect you. This may cause you to feel undervalued, or to feel that you are not getting the recognition you deserve.

You appear shy and humble, particularly if this is your first Pinnacle, but inside there is much pride that must be kept in check.

You may want to hide from the tumult of life, or from difficult situations. This may tempt you to color the facts in order to protect harmony. Be careful of this tendency, because it often backfires.

You have an eye for precision and detail. Your taste in all aspects of life is enhanced, and you possess a certain class that others admire. If you make the most of these qualities, your appearance is considerably improved, making you both attractive and graceful.

The world depends on those who maintain harmony and balance.

3   Pinnacle Number

This is a highly creative period. Your self-expression is greatly enhanced. Your creative and artistic talents will peak. You should do everything possible to refine these abilities and make the most of them. Many under the 3 Pinnacle are drawn to writing, theater, singing, and dance. Your chances of success are also heightened. Hard work in any artistic field that one has a talent for can result in much reward.

This is also a highly social and emotional time. You attract friends and admirers with your charm and gregarious nature.

You have the ability to inspire and motivate people. Your upbeat energy causes people to want to work with and for you. This is a lucky period, as well. You can overcome problems with considerably less effort than in the past.

All of this can lead to self-indulgence and lack of productivity. Life is a little easier, which can make you less vigilant. You need focus and discipline. Under the influence of this Pinnacle, hard work is the key and the challenge to making the most of your opportunities. Be careful of impulsive behavior or doing things on a lark. You must know your limits during this period. Watch your money; balance your accounts. Guard against disorderly thinking and behavior. Otherwise, you may do things you regret, or you may simply squander away many opportunities.

Children born under this Pinnacle must be disciplined and kept from being spoiled. An early education in the arts will inspire the child to make the most of his or her artistic talent.

4   Pinnacle Number

This is a Pinnacle of hard work and many rewards. You have the opportunity to build a foundation that will last. Your abilities as an organizer, manager, or simply the rock of any institution are greatly increased. You are dependable and reliable. Your ability to fulfill responsibilities is likewise enhanced.

As a result of your industry and perseverance, success is well within your reach. It is a step-by-step process in which you build something by small bricks laid one after another.

You will find yourself caring for others in a very material way. Family and in-laws can be burdensome, since you are seen as the cornerstone of the foundation.

Your life is preoccupied with details and responsibilities that must be taken care of. You have set in motion projects, that are your children, demanding your constant attention. While there are many rewards, there are also many frustrations. Your sense of your own limits, and the consuming nature of details, may at times seem overwhelming. You must remember that things that last require slow growth. You may mistakenly believe that your progress should be faster, or should happen with greater ease.

The need for efficiency, orderliness, and methodical systems limit your creativity.

Your challenge is to be flexible and adaptable. Learn to play more, and to allow yourself to be more spontaneous.

Children born under this Pinnacle will tend to be serious and affected by the financial limitations of their parents. The child may feel the need to leave home early and start a family of his or her own. He or she must be encouraged to be more farsighted and flexible. The child should avoid jumping into the harsh realities of life too soon.

5 Pinnacle Number

This is a period that will teach the realities of freedom and expansion. You will travel great distances, meet many new and interesting people, experience many adventures, and essentially come to know the world. You are in a period of accelerated experimentation and learning. Experience is your teacher.

Your ability with words is greatly increased. You can write and speak with ease. You are also able to successfully promote yourself. In fact, this is the source of much adventure. New opportunities for work, travel, and exotic experiences present themselves with regularity.

Your challenge is to prevent yourself from becoming a rolling stone. You need to ground yourself in a particular discipline, career, or relationship. This will not limit your freedoms so much as give you a base for operation. Otherwise, you may find yourself skipping from one meaningless job to the next, or to one superficial relationship after another. You can also fall victim to the abuse of food, alcohol, sex, and drugs.

You may fear being anchored or tied down, which can cause you to skim the surface of a pursuit you enjoy; or you may fear important relationships.

You must come to know the true meaning of freedom, which is unconditional love. You give your love and energy without the condition of holding on to a place, a person, or an occupation; and you expect the same in return: to be loved for what you are, rather than as someone who belongs to another. There is a highly spiritual path offering itself that requires detachment without loss of love.

Many turn away from this, and instead choose to maintain a superficial relationship with the world, or with other people.

You must cultivate your talents, especially your verbal and writing abilities. You are likely a gifted salesperson or promoter.

You must accept limitations as a necessary base for your freedom. Freedom cannot exist without limitations, otherwise you would be without identity, and without existence.

6 Pinnacle Number

Under this Pinnacle, you will be very involved with your family, friends, and community. You will face an increase in responsibilities and duties, but you will have a greatly enhanced sense of balance and perspective that allows you to handle emotional issues well.

Your family demands much of your attention. Matters involving spouse and children require much security, love, and sacrifice. You are the centerpiece of your family, the one people come to for solace and understanding. You may feel an increased burden, as you carry the cares of many. You will experience a deep sense of being needed. This Pinnacle is full of love, closeness, and warmth, but you must rise to the challenges that close relationships bring. You must settle and bring harmony to personal conflicts between others. You are often the only one with perspective in a conflict. It is as if you are the keeper of justice, bringing understanding and compromise to situations that are polarized.

Under the influences of this Pinnacle, especially at its outset, people are often married or start families. In-laws come into your life, and children are born. You are the nucleus of a little world.

You must maintain your dignity. This is a period that makes it easier to sacrifice, but you can overdo it, becoming a doormat for others to step on, simply to maintain a degree of peace. Know your limits and maintain healthy relationships.

This is a fine period for growth in business and financial matters. You attract people with resources who can help to further your personal goals. Moreover, you are balanced in your approach to business affairs. This can bring many rewards.

Your heightened sense of harmony and your genuine compassion make you an excellent counselor and healer, especially if you already have a native talent in any of these areas. Personal health matters can also surface, causing you to reflect on diet, exercise, and other health habits.

Your desire to help others is also increased. But this can lead you to put yourself into situations where you do not belong, or delve too deeply into other people's personal affairs. Be careful not to meddle or to interfere.

The 6 Pinnacle is a time of progress and growth as a full human being. You are capable of developing yourself in many different directions, as a loving mate and parent, as a sound business person, and as a pillar of your community. This Pinnacle requires the balance you possess, since you can easily stretch yourself in too many directions, and ultimately feel burned out by the demands in your milieu.

7 Pinnacle Number

This is a period of inner development and soul-searching. You will deal with the deeply important questions of personal existence, and the meaning of life.

You will need time to be alone to contemplate your inner world. This is a time of spiritual growth. You will experience a heightened sense of faith. The power of the universe will be the force that carries you along. You have an enhanced appreciation of poetry and nature. Walks in nature provide great therapeutic value and spiritual nourishment.

This is a time of specialization. You will pursue some course of development with fervor and focus. Your ability to concentrate will be greatly increased. Your desire to study in all forms, reading, self-reflection, and contemplation, will reach an all-time high. Your intuition is much more sensitive, making your path a little easier and more direct, since you intuitively know the appropriate next step.

Under this Pinnacle, you will become an expert in one particular field. Your capacity to penetrate the depths of a subject area is enormous. You will look below the surface in virtually everything you encounter. It is very possible that you will find yourself in a teaching role. You must consciously work on your closer relationships, especially with your spouse and children. You must explain that your desire to turn inward is not an escape or an avoidance of those you love, but a deep need for knowledge.

During this 7 Pinnacle, spiritual growth, increased knowledge, and wisdom are the big rewards. The 7 Pinnacle provides the basis for contentment in older age, because you now begin to understand life more deeply.

Your challenge is to avoid becoming critical or cynical of others. You can become so withdrawn from society that you look down on others. You may forget that you, too, are part of the imperfect human race. Sarcasm is the lowest form of communication, and a trap you could fall victim to.

Your desire to attain some high degree of perfection is sincere. But that pursuit can make you miserable if you lose perspective and fail to realize the relativity of human existence. Perfection is a Utopian goal, but an unrealistic ambition. It can cause you to be dissatisfied with yourself and others.

The 7 provides the possibility of true refinement, insight, and a high degree of wisdom. This deep understanding is the basis for self-love and true happiness.

8   Pinnacle Number

Under the influences of this Pinnacle, you will have greatly enhanced talent for dealing successfully with business and finances. This is a time of material growth, and a time of expansion and reward. It is the cycle of harvest.

An 8 Pinnacle also increases your personal power. You have sound judgment and vision. In fact, this is the basis of your financial success. People sense your power and effectiveness. They defer to you much more easily, and look to you for answers. This makes it easier for you to use power without having to be a bully or force your way through situations. They perceive your ableness and want to join you in your vision. Others have faith in you.

You will be able to organize large enterprises. Problems do not threaten you so much as provide you with a challenge. You sense your enhanced personal powers yourself, and feel a growing sense of stability and centeredness. You will be capable of influencing matter in an almost magical way. As a result, you are extremely goal-oriented, moving toward the realization of your dreams with confidence and clarity. Your challenge during this period is to maintain a hold on your human and spiritual values. You must remain balanced between heaven and earth. There will be enormous temptations to make money and status your only priorities, excluding the more human or immaterial matters entirely. This will undoubtedly lead to losses. You are being tested and instructed in the real value of money, or its natural place in life. If money is placed on a high altar, overshadowing all other facets of life, you will become its slave.

If you are balanced in your approach to money, and you have proper perspective, this can be a truly rewarding period, both materially and spiritually. That is the true promise of the 8.

The number 8 symbolizes the balance between the finite and infinite, matter and spirit. It offers a great opportunity to grow.

9   Pinnacle Number

This is a period in which you must identify with some larger project or goal that is bigger than you. Your greatest satisfaction will be in providing for others, as well as for yourself. Those in business will draw much personal gratification in knowing that they are helping their employees support their families. Those involved in social activism—a particularly appealing choice of careers during the 9 Pinnacle—will feel themselves strengthened by the knowledge that they are advancing the safety and well-being of society. The 9 Pinnacle is a time in which you apply your energies to the good of the larger community.

As a result, there is an element of self-sacrifice present. To some degree, you must subordinate your personal priorities to those of a larger cause. I am not suggesting martyrdom, but making a conscious effort on your part to strike a balance between the good of your milieu and your own personal desires.

This is a good time for financial growth and progress in business affairs. It is a period in which you face a large challenge, and you must give yourself entirely to it.

The 9 Pinnacle also promises much reward in drama, writing, and art. You have a heightened aesthetic sense, and any latent artistic talent you already possess will be enhanced and brought to the surface. If you have been in business, you may suddenly be drawn to the arts as a benefactor or patron, supplying support for theater productions or artists.

You will feel an increased sense of social responsibility and compassion for the many. You will want to help those less fortunate than yourself, and you will likely apply yourself to some social cause or philanthropy. This is a period in which you feel a greater love for the good of your community, country, and the world.

Interestingly, you are not restricted by prejudice or boundaries of class or country. You see humanity as a whole. However, your love is not personal, but for the many.

Many under the 9 Pinnacle are drawn to religion or philosophy, and have the capacity to spread some doctrine or teaching.

In short, you are highly idealistic. You will likely travel extensively during this period and meet people from many walks of life.

No matter what your area of expertise, you have a chance not only for success, but also for fame.

11   Pinnacle Number

This is a challenging period in which you are at a high point of sensitivity and intuition. There is so much going on in your psyche that you can suffer much confusion over direction and identity. On the other hand, there is a wide open channel between the personal consciousness and the higher realms of the unconscious. You are constantly being inspired and even assaulted by information and insight. Because of the intensity of these revelations, you must learn to ground your life in faith and a practical vocation that keeps your feet on the ground every day.

This is a period of enormous spiritual and personal growth. You will come out of it with a highly uncommon clarity and understanding of life. At the same time, it is a period of enormous demands, emotionally and spiritually.

Any attachment you might have to specific identity traits, who you think you are why you are here, for example, is constantly challenged.

There is a desire to settle into some field or way of life to attain stability, but the energy of this Pinnacle does not allow it. It is as if there is a destination to which you are being driven. You do not feel in control of this process. Instead, you are acutely aware of the forces that are shaping your life. You must surrender to them.

Meanwhile, you experience the emotional turmoil that can come with this highly charged period.

There is a definite, even compelling sense of being different. You are aware of a feeling of receiving special attention from spiritual forces. Your perception of life is somehow more acute than others; you see more clearly and more spiritually due to your high degree of sensitivity. It is as if you have a perfectly accurate peripheral vision, in which everything stands out in sharp relief. At times, you may feel that you can see into the souls of things.

At the same time, you may feel like a foreigner to the earth. You are completely impractical. Sometimes you may feel that you do not understand the workings of the physical world. Practical things escape you. You feel awkward and clumsy at times, and are aware, perhaps, how fluidly other lives are going. This increases your sense of being an outsider.

More important than all the awkwardness and feelings of being different is the overwhelming sense of having a purpose or a message to reveal that will make other people's lives happier, healthier, and more at peace. You want desperately to bring this out.

The challenge of the 11 Pinnacle is to remain grounded and attached to this dream. You must find practical and useful ways to be of service to others, at the same time developing yourself so that one day you may be able to bring forth that which is within you.

The influences of this period make you highly creative, innovative, and inventive. You have a completely unconventional approach to problems. Trust your intuition, seek harmonious settings to restore your sense of inner peace, and work hard to keep your feet on the ground. This period will bring great rewards on all levels, and with perseverance, you will find your rightful place.

22 Pinnacle Number

This is a demanding time in which all your personal power comes to the surface and is made available to you. At the same time, you face an enormous challenge in which all that power is needed. This challenge is both physical and spiritual. The physical side is obvious in some large enterprise or dream that you are struggling to make manifest. The spiritual side is more hidden, but just as important, in that one must deliver the full wealth of his spiritual understanding and vision to create something great and lasting for the general well-being of society. Your mental powers are greatly enhanced. At the same time, your determination and efficiency are proportionately increased, making you the Master Builder. The 22 is a Master number, which means that you must perceive something large in the archetypal world, and materialize it. Everything you focus on is large: Your plans are big and cover long periods of time; and you envision making an enormous and lasting impact on the world. At the same time, your problems and challenges are equally large. You will have to devote yourself entirely to this dream. Without a full commitment to your largest ambitions, you will slip into frustrations and the world of broken dreams.

Nothing less than everything you have is necessary to bring forth your full potential and the gift you must give to the world. This is why the 22 Pinnacle is so demanding. This is a Pinnacle of extremes.

However, you are not alone in your struggle. There is much spiritual and material support to help you realize your plans. People are attracted to you who intuitively understand your larger purpose. You gain a close following of friends and supporters who feel enriched by participating in the dream you have articulated.

Courage is essential. You need confidence and faith to help you endure the challenges of the period, and overcome the many obstacles in your path.

You are eminently practical during this period. Your approach to problems

AGE																			
PHYSICAL TRANSIT																			
MENTAL TRANSIT																			
SPIRITUAL TRANSIT																			
ESSENCE																			
KARMIC DEBT NUMBERS																			
PINNACLE																			
PERSONAL YEAR																			
PERIOD CYCLE																			
YEAR																			

Figure 6.2 The Progressive Chart

The Progressive Chart covers 49 years and may begin at birth, or any later age.

is methodical but bold. You are careful about details, yet courageous in your attack on the problems at hand. It is a period during which you must dive in, never hesitating over the possible consequences. Your personal life will likely take a back seat to the excitement of the dream.

This is a Pinnacle of enormous potential that requires much effort. Your day has arrived. Now you must make the most of it.

The influence of the Pinnacle Cycles is generally stronger felt than that of the Period Cycles. The Pinnacle Cycles depict more specific events and experiences, while the Period Cycles are subtle and indicate a somewhat hidden, underlying current.

The transformation from one Pinnacle Cycle into another is much more dramatic than that between Period Cycles. During the course of one lifetime, you will experience three Pinnacle changes. You can be sure that the impact of each of these changes leaves a lasting impression.

The Personal Year, Month, and Day Cycles, the Transit Cycles, the Essence Cycles, the Pinnacle Cycles, and the Period Cycles, together form the progressive chart. As is the case with the personality chart, the greatest challenge in delineating the progressive chart lies in the need for a clear separation of where and how these cycles influence a person, as well as how they influence each other.

Perhaps it helps us to compare the whole process to a walk in nature. The long-term cycles reveal the general environment. For example, you might say that your current Period Cycle indicates a mountainous terrain. Your Pinnacle Cycle tells you that this terrain is heavily forested. Your Essence Cycle shows that at this time in your life you are full of energy and playfulness, or maybe somewhat tired and emotional. Your Transits imply something about your health or state of mind, or if you are passing through a valley or climbing a hill. The Personal Year, Month, and Day Cycles show that it is raining, or that you are approaching a pond from which to quench your thirst.

Mastering the art of numerology relies heavily on your ability to analyze and deduce, as well as on your imagination. One has to be perceptive in order to recognize how a particular Personal Year number may influence a certain Essence number. These are things one learns only through practice. However, it is helpful to look at your own chart, and to go back all the way to the beginning to see if you can recognize the reasons why you made certain choices or had certain experiences, and how they relate to the cycles you were passing through at the time. Taking it one year at a time, you will be surprised how revealing the numbers that represent the cycles can be.

Chapter 7

Other Uses
for Numerology

De omnibus rebus et quibusdam aliis.
(Concerning all things and several others.)

—Anonymous

Numbers are all around us on a daily basis. We use them to dial our telephones, and to identify our houses, cars, and bank accounts. In fact, there is little about your life that is not associated with a number. All of these numbers reveal something about your relationship with that thing that is numbered. The number will tell you something about the nature of this "object," or how it will influence your life. Understanding the meaning of these numbers may give you insight and guidance on how to act in certain situations; whether or not to change times and dates; and how to change the numbers in your life to your advantage.

The following pages describe some of the more common, and more important, numbers that turn up in our lives, such as house and telephone numbers, and how your ancestors travelled similar life courses. I will also discuss how you can find lost objects with the help of numbers, and the general meaning of double-digit numbers. By understanding this information, you will be able to apply the underlying principles to the numbers elsewhere in your life.

ANCESTRAL INFLUENCES

For most people, the family name has been carried on through many generations, usually on the father's side. Your last name represents a strong connection you have with your ancestors, as well as a similar spiritual path. As you learned in Chapter Six, your Spiritual Transit is taken from your last name. In other words, when you have your last name in common with others, your spiritual path also develops along similar lines.

However, the level and intensity of spiritual experiences is very personal, and it cannot possibly be compared with that of someone else.

For example, our friend Thomas John Hancock and his father, grandfather, great-grandfather, and so on, all are identified by the name Hancock. Each one of them had an O Spiritual Transit from age seventeen through twenty-two, forty-five through fifty, and seventy-three through seventy-eight. During these times in their lives, they experienced their spiritual evolvement in an emotional way; they were connected to the recognition of beauty, and to the responsibility towards family and community; they had a desire to paint or to otherwise express their feelings; and they had warm, nurturing human relationships. There is confidence, yet also melancholy and emotional prayer during the O Spiritual Transit.

How strong and intensely each of them experienced this probably varied widely, and, even to the close observer, might have made the similarities totally unrecognizable.

Your last name reveals many other generic aspects. Contemplate and study your last name closely. Does the name have a certain letter or number represented more than once? How does the name read if you look at each number?

The name Hancock reads as follows: An 8, 1, 5, 3, 6, 3, and 2, which total 28, reduce to 10, and further reduce to 1.

The family line on the father's side will likely show a number of financially capable (8 Cornerstone) people, many of whom own their own businesses (1 and 8, as well as two 3s), probably promoting or selling something, and relying heavily on their verbal abilities and sense of humor (3 and 5). Family and responsibility (6 as a second vowel) were also a priority. They were often quite aware of the needs and emotional states of others (2, actually an 11, since the K is the eleventh letter of the alphabet).

Among his ancestors, Tom Hancock may discover some pirates, or otherwise social outcasts, as well, because the name reveals a considerable amount of adventurism (1 and 5), and a lack of conventionality (1, 5 and 3).

One thing almost all of them had in common was the desire to do their own thing (the sum of 1, and the letters with values of 8, 3, 5, and 1).

Once you have a good understanding of the numbers, you will enjoy meditating on the name(s) that identified, in different times through history, your ancestors.

HOUSE AND TELEPHONE NUMBERS

The numbers in your environment give indications that should not be ignored. Understanding their meaning and their purpose can help you to move along the path of life smoothly, and with less anxiety.

One of the most important and telling numbers is your house number. It foretells the kind of events and experiences, both positive and negative, that you will likely encounter during your stay in that house. As I explained earlier in the book, all numbers have a front and a back, a light side and a dark side. No one number is better than another, although you may want to avoid house numbers that reduce to a Karmic Debt number, such as 13, 14, and particularly 16 and 19. A house with a Karmic Debt number will undoubtedly attract the attributes of that number to the people who inhabit it. You would welcome a house that carries a Karmic Debt only if: you are consciously and willingly looking for a breakdown of the old you; are aspiring to a path of deep soul-searching (16); or you feel you need to be alone and learn to find the strength inside of you to deal with life's challenges without the help and support of others (19).

You should judge a number to be desirable only in relation to your personal needs and hopes.

The house number is much more important than the street name, the influence of which is felt by all the individuals living in that street, and is therefore not as personal.

Similarly, your telephone number gives an indication of the contacts and communications that are channeled through this number. The area code and the first three digits are negligible for the same reason a street name is unimportant. Too many people share this combination of numbers. However, the last four digits of your telephone number are yours, and yours alone. You are not sharing any common denominators with your neighbors or anyone else in the neighborhood through either your house, or your telephone number.

Understanding Your House or Telephone Number

To understand your house or telephone number, you have to have a good understanding of the nine single-digit numbers, and to use this insight to analyze multiple-digit numbers in your environment in the following manner.

First, you add the digits together and reduce them to a single-digit number. You want to pay special attention to possible Master numbers and Karmic Debts.

For example, a house number 3417 is $3 + 4 + 1 + 7 = 15, 1 + 5 = 6$. The 6 in this case is the singular most important number, and would, taken by itself, be a good number for a house occupied by a family with children, because it is a family-oriented, domestic number.

There are three layers of information to be found in this delineation. First, contemplate the number 6, which is the sum of the individual digits. Next, look at the double-digit number of 15. This reveals that, in this case, 6 gives high marks to individualism and personal freedom (1 and 5). Finally, consider the individual numbers.

When you consider moving into a house that is very much to your liking, I would not recommend passing it up just because the numbers do not add up to your personal favorites. If, however, the house number is unacceptable to you, it may be possible to have a different number assigned to the house.

You are more in control with telephone numbers. In my experience, the employee from the telephone company who assigns you your number is usually very helpful, and will allow you to choose an alternative number. I recommend taking advantage of that.

FINDING LOST OBJECTS WITH THE HELP OF NUMBERS

Every action you take, and every observation you make, whether consciously, or distractedly, is permanently stored somewhere in your subconsciousness.

When a car passes by while you are talking to someone, the car may take up no more than a blur in your peripheral vision. Yet, it is recorded and stored permanently. It happened, your eye caught it and sent the information to the brain, and there it leaves an imprint. This is the case whether you have a good memory or not. Your ability to retrieve such information is another matter entirely.

In theory, it is possible to remember at a much later date, the license-plate number of the aforementioned car. In fact, this kind of thing is commonly achieved with the help of hypnosis.

Numerology can help you to take advantage of the vast storage room of information your subconscious contains by offering you a unique retrieval system.

Let's say, you have lost a ring. The only thing you know for sure is that you were there when you last had the ring in your possession.

Perhaps it fell out of your pocket, which caused a barely noticeable decrease in weight, or made a quiet "ploink" when it hit the carpet and rolled under the couch. Or you put it somewhere and forgot it. Whatever happened, you do not discover the loss of your ring until several days later.

The moment you lost the ring, however, is stored in your subconscious. The way to tap into that source is by exercising your subconscious.

How to Find Your Lost Object Number

Concentrate on the lost object, then scribble a nine-digit number on a piece of paper. Add the nine digits together, but do not reduce them to a single digit. Next, look for that number in the listing below.

For example, if you scribbled down the number 934710138, which totals to 36, look under 36 to learn where to look for the object. Note that the highest possible total is 81, and the lowest is 6.

Look below for directions in locating lost objects:

6 Lost Object Number

It is near cleaning materials or footgear. Be careful not to blame someone else.

7 Lost Object Number

It is near items of clothing.

8 Lost Object Number

Someone you dislike will deliver it to you.

9 Lost Object Number

It is in the possession of a young person, but this person is not aware of that. It will be presented to you innocently as a gift.

10 Lost Object Number

Look for it in the room you occupy most during your waking hours; not necessarily in your own house.

11 Lost Object Number

The object is close to a large body of water, such as a lake, pond, or ocean.

12 Lost Object Number

It is in a safe place, and you will find it while looking for something else. It is better not to look for it.

13 Lost Object Number

It is in your clothes closet, possibly in a box containing shoes or a hat.

14 Lost Object Number

It is under water. You may need a plumber to recover it. If the object is made of cloth, look among your umbrellas, coats, and head or neckgear.

15 Lost Object Number

It is near animals or items kept for animals. A child will be involved with the recovery of this object.

16 Lost Object Number

Without being consciously aware of it, you desired to lose it—permanently.

17 Lost Object Number

It is close to expensive items stored in a small place.

18 Lost Object Number

It is near soft objects, pillows, clothing, towels, or blankets. You will find it and lose it again. You will not retrieve it the second time.

19 Lost Object Number

It is near your house, but not near water. Look around dry dirt or sand.

20 Lost Object Number

It is close to water inside the house. Look near the sink, in the bathroom, or around the water heater.

21 Lost Object Number

You will find it in a small storage area, possibly a file cabinet. Also look in your briefcase or purse.

22 Lost Object Number

You will find it shortly, possibly through a dream.

23 Lost Object Number

It is not far from where you are at this time. Look under or inside furniture.

24 Lost Object Number

Look in places where you used to store it in the past. Also, ask other members of the household to look for it; they have a better chance of retrieving it.

25 Lost Object Number

It is surrounded by something white, or a source of light. It is not far away from you.

26 Lost Object Number

An older man, probably a relative, knows where to find it, but is not aware that you are looking for it.

27 Lost Object Number

It's in the garage, possibly inside a car. It is damaged.

28 Lost Object Number

Someone else has found it and is unwilling to surrender it to the rightful owner. This is a Karmic Lesson in detachment.

29 Lost Object Number

Someone close to you will return it to you. This person is either much older than you are, or is a very young child.

30 Lost Object Number

You lost the object while you were enjoying yourself in the company of children, probably during a creative endeavor. Look among toys or art materials.

31 Lost Object Number

It is near moving water, not far from the house. You will find it.

32 Lost Object Number

It is in a high place, probably outside the house or on a window ledge.

33 Lost Object Number

It is near a religious artifact that has been stored. Also look where you store Christmas decorations.

34 Lost Object Number

It is near a light or heat source in your house or in your place of work.

35 Lost Object Number

It is near running water inside the house. It is not visible without moving other items.

36 Lost Object Number

It is in the possession of someone close to you. Look in the closets and storage places of other members of your household.

37 Lost Object Number

Look near a religious artifact, in your house or in the house to the east of you.

38 Lost Object Number

It was lost on your way to a place you visit regularly, such as a grocery store, a friend's home in the neighborhood, or your place of work. It is visible and in the open.

39 Lost Object Number

It is in a high place. The items surrounding it are related to play or creative activities.

40 Lost Object Number

It is surrounded by soft material, possibly as a form of safekeeping and protection.

41 Lost Object Number

It is low in a closet or near footgear.

42 Lost Object Number

It is in a place where cooking is done, probably not your own house. Call restaurants or other places you visited.

43 Lost Object Number

It is near a place of rest, a bed or a lounge. It may also be between folded sheets or blankets.

44 Lost Object Number

The object is in a dirty place, or in a part of the house that is being remodeled, and it will be found by a worker.

45 Lost Object Number

You pass it closely every day. Keep your eyes open.

46 Lost Object Number

Ask a co-worker, in particular the one you feel close to. Wait a few days from now before asking.

47 Lost Object Number

More than one person is aware of the location of the object. One is a liar. Question your subordinates.

48 Lost Object Number

It is close to water or cooking utensils. Also look in any place you store alcoholic beverages.

49 Lost Object Number

Don't bother looking for it. The chances of finding it are remote, and it has already been badly damaged.

50 Lost Object Number

It has been moved since you lost it. Look inside carrying cases or vehicles of transportation.

51 Lost Object Number

It is in a church or another place of worship. It may also be in a place of healing, such as a hospital.

52 Lost Object Number

At least one person has handled the object since you lost it, probably someone you have never met, but who is close to someone you know well.

53 Lost Object Number

You are going on a trip, and you will receive it upon your return. It will be found during your absence.

54 Lost Object Number

It is carried around, or otherwise being transferred from one place to another. Recovery is certain, but it will take some time.

55 Lost Object Number

It was displaced by the movement of water or wind. You will find it when you least expect it.

56 Lost Object Number

Retrace your steps now. Even when you lost it several days ago, you passed by it a short while later. Water is nearby.

57 Lost Object Number

You lost it, and you will find it during sporting activities. In particular, look in the pants pockets of sportsgear.

58 Lost Object Number

You are the victim of someone's greed or anger. Your chances of getting it back are slim.

59 Lost Object Number

It is in a dry and dark place, probably a small cabinet. Look around food or eating utensils.

60 Lost Object Number

There is no chance of recovery.

61 Lost Object Number

Look in the cellar or in some other place underneath the house. It is exposed to the elements.

62 Lost Object Number

You lost it a considerable distance from the house, and you will not recover it.

63 Lost Object Number

The object is in a forgotten place of storage, surrounded by items you have not laid eyes on in some time.

64 Lost Object Number

There is no need to look for it. You will find it when you clean or reorganize your house.

65 Lost Object Number

You will pass by it in the next few hours. Your chances of finding it, however, are not good.

66 Lost Object Number

Thievery is the cause of your loss. The person who took it has a physical problem; either the hand or the foot is damaged.

67 Lost Object Number

A younger family member, probably female, will find it, and return it.

68 Lost Object Number

It was lost twice. Someone has retrieved it, and lost it before returning it to you. That someone will not admit to this. A third person will find it and return it.

69 Lost Object Number

It is a considerable distance from your house. Call friends or relatives you visited not too long ago. It was found, but the honest finder does not know that it is yours.

70 Lost Object Number

You did not lose it. It is simply mislaid. Look near study materials. Think.

71 Lost Object Number

The object is close by. You will find it when you relax. It is near printed material.

72 Lost Object Number

Look in vases, bowls, or other containers that have an open top.

73 Lost Object Number

You should involve the police or another official. It was most likely taken from you.

74 Lost Object Number

It will be returned to you by someone whom you have not respected, or whom you have treated with some injustice.

75 Lost Object Number

It will be returned to you, but it will be damaged.

76 Lost Object Number

It is in the kitchen or pantry. Look near flour products.

77 Lost Object Number

Don't spend too much time search-ing. It will be found and returned to you only after you do the potential finder a favor.

78 Lost Object Number

It is near animals. It is damaged, and the chances of recovery are not good.

79 Lost Object Number

It is in a tin can or other metal con-tainer.

80 Lost Object Number

It was locked away with other items, and it is now in a container inside another container. You will find it when you are not looking.

81 Lost Object Number

It went out with the garbage; you will not be able to retrieve it. It's covered by dirt, and it will soon disintegrate.

Finding lost objects with the help of numbers is an old and proven method of tapping into your subconscious. As with other aspects of life where the relationship between cause and effect is obscured, doubts have no effect on the reality of what takes place. Hence, if you find it difficult to create a nine-digit number, perhaps because you feel too self-conscious, changing your mind ten times in the process, remember that no matter how you reach the final number, it is the number that tells all. Period.

THE DOUBLE-DIGIT NUMBERS

So far, we have worked only with single-digit numbers in your chart, with the exception of the Master numbers and the Karmic Debt numbers. Now, let's look at the numbers 10 and up.

Every one of the cardinal numbers can be based on several different compound numbers. The 7, for instance, can be based on 16, 25, 34, 43, 52, 61, or 70. (It cannot be based on 79 or 88 except indirectly, because 79 and 88 are 16.) When a 7 is based on 25, it is slightly different from a 7 based on 34 or 61. For this reason, I have made it a habit to include the double-digit numbers in the chart. I write a 7 based on 25 in this manner: 25/7; and a 7 based on 34 like this: 34/7.

Now that you have come this far in the book, your understanding of the meaning of numbers is sufficient to analyze the double-digit numbers.

A double-digit number's characteristics are dominated by that of the single digit it represents. First and foremost, it is that cardinal number.

The double-digit number highlights certain aspects, and diminishes others, but it never eliminates any aspect completely. You may want to study the double-digit numbers in your personal chart to see if you can gain additional insight or clarity.

For example, a 7 based on a 25 is not as withdrawn as a 7 based on a 16. A 7 based on a 34 is more creative than the 7 based on a 25.

The already considerable leadership ability of a 1 is enhanced in the 10. As a rule, numbers that are dividable by 10 strengthen the characteristics of the single-digit number across the board. A 10 is a high octave 1, a 40 is a high octave 4, and a 70 is a high octave 7.

Below is a short description of double-digit numbers 10 through 99. As an exercise, you may want to contemplate a few double-digit numbers, then see if you picked the same main points as those described below. To find your double-digit number, take the total of the letters in your full name BEFORE you reduce them to a single digit.

10 Double-Digit Number

It enhances all the qualities of the 1. It is a powerful leader, sharply focused, and streamlined for success. It can be ruthless in the pursuit of its goals. It can become a dominating tyrant.

11 Double-Digit Number

See "The Master Numbers" in Chapter 1.

12 Double-Digit Number

It is highly creative, individualistic, and unconventional. It represents the interests of the self versus those of the group.

13 Double-Digit Number

See "The Karmic Debt Numbers" in Chapter 1.

14 Double-Digit Number

See "The Karmic Debt Numbers" in Chapter 1.

15 Double-Digit Number

It is loving, forgiving, and extremely tolerant. It is responsible, successful, dynamic, and strong. It represents travel, adventure, and experimentation. This number can bring self-indulgence.

16 Double-Digit Number

See "The Karmic Debt Numbers" in Chapter 1.

17 Double-Digit Number

It is spiritual growth, faith, and balance. It is also wealth or bankruptcy. It is an inner struggle to remain true to spiritual and moral values.

18 Double-Digit Number

It is involved with business on an international scale, and it is a discordance between idealism and selfishness. There is a lack of conscious spiritual effort.

19 Double-Digit Number

See "The Karmic Debt Numbers" in Chapter 1.

20 Double-Digit Number

It is overly sensitive, intuitive, and vulnerable to criticism. It has emotional problems. It can show weakness and cowardice in the face of challenges.

21 Double-Digit Number

It is similar to 12, but much more intuitive. It tends to procrastinate.

22 Double-Digit Number

See "The Master Numbers" in Chapter 1.

23 Double-Digit Number

It loves people and is a freedom fighter, a promoter of causes, a quitter, and unrealistic.

24 Double-Digit Number

It counsels and comforts others. It likes music, particularly rhythm. It represents domestic struggles and divorce.

25 Double-Digit Number

It is spiritual leadership. It likes group endeavors. It can be too serious. It has great difficulty sharing feelings.

26 Double-Digit Number

It is excellent in business and management. It is a good strategist, a workaholic, and is often disorganized in personal affairs.

27 Double-Digit Number

It is a counselor, a volunteer, and an artist, and is often successful. It represents inheritance. It is sometimes rigid and narrow-minded.

28 Double-Digit Number

It is a 10, but with more compassion and tolerance.

29 Double-Digit Number

It is the same as 11. See "The Master Numbers" in Chapter 1.

30 Double-Digit Number

It is communication and creativity. It is a high octave 3. It has a great sense of humor, and while jovial, can be superficial.

31 Double-Digit Number

It is more extrovert and fun-loving than other 4s. It is also more creative. It can be unfaithful.

32 Double-Digit Number

See 23. It is more sensitive, and has emotional ups and downs, and is moody.

33 Double-Digit Number

Some numerologists consider this a Master number. Its ultimate potential is in teaching. It is called the Christ number. It comforts others. It represents self-sacrifice and beliefs in Utopia. It is often co-dependent, and is sometimes a compulsive liar.

34 Double-Digit Number

It is very intelligent. It is spiritual purity through effort. It shares with others, and is a warrior.

35 Double-Digit Number

It is creative in business. It is an inventor, gadget-designer, or business adviser. It is social, but does not work well with others. It should freelance.

36 Double-Digit Number

It is very creative. It is sometimes a genius. It is also self-conscious, inhibited, and aloof.

37 Double-Digit Number

It is very individualistic, a scholar, a voracious reader, has an excellent imagination, and is often disorganized.

38 Double-Digit Number

See 11 in "The Master Numbers" section (page 14). It is more realistic. It is very intuitive, but will not easily admit that. It often earns money in the sale of art or antiques. It has phobias.

39 Double-Digit Number

It likes functional art. It is often in acting and dancing. It has difficulties with rejection and separation.

40 Double-Digit Number

It is a high octave 4. It is extremely organized, systematic, and methodical. It is critical of others, intolerant, and sometimes prejudicial.

41 Double-Digit Number

See 14. It is capable of directing energies to many different projects successfully. It is selfish, has a lack of humor, and is sometimes a criminal.

42 Double-Digit Number

See 24. It has political aspirations. It can be an administrator, often in government institutions. It can be insensitive.

43 Double-Digit Number

See 34. It represents concentration, perfectionism, sometimes frustrations, and feelings of inferiority.

44 Double-Digit Number

It is an excellent number for business, and it is also good for a military career. It is a visionary and a doer. It has great potential.

45 Double-Digit Number

It is often involved in banking, or international institutions. It struggles to be comfortable with itself. It can be cynical.

46 Double-Digit Number

It represents leadership (see 10), and is often tactless. It is always well-prepared, and confident.

47 Double-Digit Number

See 11 in "The Master Numbers" section (page 14). There is an inner struggle between practical, down-to-earth 4, and spiritual 7. Once balance has been achieved, it is a prophet and counselor extraordinaire, .

48 Double-Digit Number

It is a visionary and a planner. It is sometimes lost in unrealistic dreams.

49 Double-Digit Number

See 13. It is a caretaker that makes effort for others. It is a problem-solver. It wants to be a hero and friend to everyone.

50 Double-Digit Number

It is a high octave 5. It is extremely freedom-loving and versatile. It is open to new ideas, and is willing to take a chance. It sometimes has sexual hang-ups.

51 Double-Digit Number

See 15. It is more independent and aggressive.

52 Double-Digit Number

See 25. It is more sensitive, intuitive, and creative.

53 Double-Digit Number

See 35. It is more verbal, creative, and business-oriented.

54 Double-Digit Number

See 45. It is less organized and disciplined. It has a difficult time finishing projects. It tends to be a dreamer. It is very idealistic.

55 Double-Digit Number

It is extremely freedom-loving, and likes to travel. It is social, but can also be selfish and lonely. It represents success for anyone in sales.

56 Double-Digit Number

This is a difficult combination that represents extreme sensitivity and the need to balance a desire for freedom with an equally strong desire to be part of a family. Also see 11 in "The Master Numbers" section (page 14).

57 Double-Digit Number

It represents intelligence and inventiveness. It brings wisdom in the later part of life. It is very creative and unconventional.

58 Double-Digit Number

This number shows a willingness to work hard and is usually successful. It recognizes opportunities and can make quick decisions. It is somewhat dogmatic and opinionated.

59 Double-Digit Number

It is very persuasive and convincing. It is often found in the charts of successful lawyers and fundraisers. It brings an uncanny ability to be comfortable with people of all walks of life and diverse cultures.

60 Double-Digit Number

It is loving, caring, and responsible. It sometimes brings subservience.

61 Double-Digit Number

This is a number that represents difficulties in love relationships. However, the need for family and friends is strong. It is demanding and secretive; an excellent number for researchers, law officers, and people in the Secret Service.

62 Double-Digit Number

See 26. This number is less sensitive.

It is an excellent caretaker. A good number for people with careers in the medical field.

63 Double-Digit Number

See 36. It is less outgoing. However, it can be sexually promiscuous.

64 Double-Digit Number

See 46. It is less organized and more creative.

65 Double-Digit Number

See 56. The need to balance freedom and domestic affairs is even more important here. This number sometimes brings a criminal tendency.

66 Double-Digit Number

Generous to a fault, this number brings financial ups and downs. It is extremely loyal and loving.

67 Double-Digit Number

This number merges analytical intelligence and creativity. Inventors and mathematicians often have this number prominent in their chart, often behind a core number.

68 Double-Digit Number

It is good for business. It has a tendency to be insensitive, but it is also very loyal. It has a great sense of humor.

69 Double-Digit Number

Few numbers are as responsible and self-sacrificing as the number 69. Political activists and environmentalists often have this number, as do doctors, nurses, and teachers. It is also extremely creative.

70 Double-Digit Number

This is the hermit's number. It is a loner and a seeker of truth who can get caught up in the act of seeking knowledge to such an extent that it loses touch with the material world. It has high intelligence and originality. It is eccentric.

71 Double-Digit Number

See 17. It is less authoritative and is often a loner.

72 Double-Digit Number

See 27. It tends to be an excellent conversationalist and it is usually a voracious reader.

73 Double-Digit Number

See 37. It is independent and likes to work alone. It is demanding in relationships.

74 Double-Digit Number

See 47. It brings premonitions and intense dreams. This number can bring eating disorders.

75 Double-Digit Number

See 57. It is more analytical and less creative.

76 Double-Digit Number

See 67. This is an excellent number for anyone involved in management or organization. It can turn ideas into reality. Sometimes this number brings dogmatism and religious fanaticism.

77 Double-Digit Number

This is perhaps the most intelligent and inventive of all numbers. It also represents spiritual wisdom.

78 Double-Digit Number

This number brings struggle between the spiritual and the material. People with this number prominent in their charts make and lose fortunes.

79 Double-Digit Number

Political and spiritual leaders often have this number. It brings concern for mankind, but it can also be ruthless and self-righteous.

80 Double-Digit Number

This is a good number for business. However, it is found more often among people in top management and the military, than among entrepreneurs, due to a lack of independence. It is an extrovert number.

81 Double-Digit Number

See 18. It is more money-oriented. It often lacks spiritual understanding. Sometimes this number brings violence.

82 Double-Digit Number

See 28. This is a number that brings strong leadership and courage. It is the survivor. This number can bring a lack of stability in marriage. Many people with this number prominent in the chart either never get married, or get married many times.

83 Double-Digit Number

See 38. It is more business-oriented and less sensitive and vulnerable.

84 Double-Digit Number

See 48. It is more the visionary and less the organizer.

85 Double-Digit Number

See 58. It is more masculine, and it can be bullish.

86 Double-Digit Number

See 68. This number is more self-oriented. It is also somewhat irresponsible and self-indulgent.

87 Double-Digit Number

See 78. This number is somewhat more practical and handles money better, but the struggle between the spiritual and the material is just as intense.

88 Double-Digit Number

This number is full of contradictions. It is excellent for business, but it is not good for relationships. It is insensitive.

89 Double-Digit Number

This number represents the aristocrat and the man or woman of the world. It brings much travel. This number can make it difficult for a person to be alone, even for short periods of time.

90 Double-Digit Number

It is self-sacrificing and humble. This number often brings religious fervor, but almost always of a positive and inspiring nature. People with this number prominent in the chart tend to be aloof, yet loved and respected by many.

91 Double-Digit Number

This is a combination that brings success in career, particularly in the creative fields, but it is unable to handle money. It is eccentric and opinionated.

92 Double-Digit Number

See 11 in "The Master Numbers" section (page 14). This number brings great concern for mankind.

93 Double-Digit Number

See 39. It is creative, particularly in architecture, and landscaping. It has difficulties with commitment.

94 Double-Digit Number

See 49. It is the practical humanitarian. It is not comfortable with travel, and dislikes changes.

95 Double-Digit Number

See 59. It is the humanitarian, but it is impractical, a dreamer. It loves travel and change.

96 Double-Digit Number

See 69. Its self-sacrificing and loving nature is more focused on family, friends, and the community.

97 Double-Digit Number

See 79. It is more sensitive. It is a quiet worker and loves to read.

98 Double-Digit Number

See 89. It is an idealist, but comes across as indifferent. It has a hard time showing emotions. A person with this number prominent in his or her chart is not easily understood by others.

99 Double-Digit Number

It represents artistic genius. A person with this number is often misunderstood, and is frequently the victim of gossip. It can bring jealousy and possessiveness to relationships.

Numbers, as we discussed earlier in this book, have personalities, much like people do. Once you have a good grip on the individual personalities of the cardinal numbers, you are able to understand a multiple-digit number by contemplating the combination of personalities represented. Keep in mind that a multiple-digit number is dominated by the single-digit number to which it is reduced. Then, read the separate digits in such a way that each digit has to work its influence through the digit in front of it.

For example, the number 324 has first and foremost the characteristics of the single-digit number 9, to which it can be reduced. However, the number 3 influences the way this number 9 is expressed. The numbers 2 and 4 are also represented, but are less important.

PLAYING WITH NUMBERS

If you were to encounter an extraterrestrial being, it would be unlikely that the two of you would have any other form of communication other than the language of numbers. The shape of the numbers might not be useful, but if the two of you sat down with a pocketful of pebbles, you'd be able to demonstrate a certain amount of intelligence, and even to share information. The point is that numbers are a universal means of understanding and communication. Numbers transcend the limits of our world.

On one hand, numbers are free of subjective realities, such as emotions and personal preferences. In their purest sense, numbers possess objectivity, which is why they are the language of science. They are the most reliable means of communicating abstract ideas, and of quantifying physical realities.

On the other hand, numbers can be used to reveal the "soul" of words. Words evolve with an underlying feeling for the objects they describe. Each word has specific definition, as well as a connecting emotional and spiritual feeling. Numerology can be used to reveal that underlying feeling or spirit.

We will now look at some important words to see how numerology reveals their deeper meaning.

Love

Let's begin with the word love.

When you do the numerology on love, you find that the Expression number is a 9, suggesting the humanitarian and universal nature of love. It's generous, giving, self-sacrificing, and concerned for others. It's the great healer and teacher. It gives of itself unconditionally.

The Heart's Desire number of the word love is 11, which reveals its sensitivity, intuitive nature, need for harmony, and connection with the highest power. The 11 is called the Channel, or the Illuminator.

Love's 7 Personality number indicates the need for careful self-reflection and the implicit wisdom inherent in love.

Hate

Now, let's look at love's opposite: hate.

Hate's Expression number is 16/7, a Karmic Debt number, indicating a self-destructive nature. (See Karmic Debts in Chapter 1.) The 16/7 reveals its isolation. The reason it is isolated is because it is cold, clinical, and self-contained. It is highly mental, and, as a result, it is often lacking in compassion for matters of the heart.

The 6 Heart's Desire in the word hate reveals its powerful emotional connection to the subject of its hatred. The dark side of the 6 is its need to control. It cannot let go. It smothers the object of its hatred with excessive attention.

Hate's Personality number is 1, suggesting the negative attributes of the

1: bullishness and insensitivity; and its inability to share itself with others, thus creating aloneness and loneliness. The stubborn side of the 1 prevents it from being receptive to the positive attributes of the hated person.

Light and Dark

Now, compare the words light and dark and see how they reveal our association with each word, especially in their relationship to love and hate. The core numbers for the word light are very similar to those of love. Light has an 11 Expression number, a 9 Heart's Desire, and a 2 Personality. (As stated previously, love has an 11 Heart's Desire, a 9 Expression, and a 7 Personality.) The 11 stands for illumination and insight. It exposes the true nature of whatever it touches. The 9 Heart's Desire obviously indicates its need to reach the farthest concerns. It is available to all; it is an indiscriminate gift to everyone and everything. The 2 Personality reveals its inherent gentleness.

The word dark has a 16/7 Expression, a 1 Heart's Desire, and a 6 Personality. Its only difference with the word hate is that the Heart's Desire and Personality numbers have switched places. (Note that although the words dark and hate have only one letter in common, they have the same core numbers.) Again, the core numbers represent self-destruction, isolation, and loneliness. The 6 Personality number suggests the illusion of protection offered by darkness.

Dog and Cat

Let's look at the words for our animal friends, dog and cat, which, as we all know, have very different natures.

Dog has an 8 Expression, suggesting its innate power and ability to protect; a 6 Heart's Desire, revealing its desire for a domestic environment and for love and attention; and a Personality number of 11, showing its sensitivity and intuitiveness to the mood of the owner.

A cat, on the other hand, has a 6 Expression, revealing its domestic nature, but a 1 Heart's Desire, which shows its independence and often stubborn character. It has a 5 Personality, which reinforces the independence and the need for freedom. You cannot control a cat.

Interestingly, both the dog and the cat have 6s in their core numbers, but the dog has a 6 Heart's Desire—the desire for love, attention, and domestic harmony—while a cat, with a 6 Expression, is perfectly suited for the domestic environment, but its 1 Heart's Desire gives it a need for independence. A cat, by nature, is not obedient; a dog is.

Food and Roof

Keeping with the domestic theme, let's look at two words that go directly to our basic needs: food and roof. Each word has three 6s! The 6 stands for all that is protective, comforting, mothering, domestic, and nurturing. In addition, food has a 22 Expression, indicating its link to the very foundation of life: the transformation of matter to energy (metabolism), and its opposite, energy to matter (the growth of organisms). As you know, the number 22 is called the Master Builder, and here it is demonstrated at its finest.

Roof has a 9 Expression coupled with a 6 Personality, revealing its clear purpose of protecting the domestic environment.

River and Tree

Let's look at the words river and tree. River has a Heart's Desire of 5, meaning movement, freedom, dynamism, and change. Its Personality number is 22, revealing that it is one of the most powerful forces in nature. It slices through all obstacles. The 9 Expression means that it gives of itself for the well-being of all.

Tree provides a wonderful array of numbers, beginning with its 1 Heart's Desire, suggesting its independence and its strong will to survive. A tree's upright form itself suggests the 1. Its Personality number is 11, showing its spiritual nature: its reaching up toward heaven and its inspirational influence to all. Its 3 Expression symbolizes the ability to communicate both its spiritual power and beauty.

Work

Finally, let's examine the word work. Work has a 22 Expression, showing that it is the means for bringing the ideal into the material world, again apropos of the Master Builder. It also reflects its potential power: We build our lives and gain our rewards from our work. Work has a 16/7 Personality. The 7 reveals its concentration, focus, and search for perfection. The 16 Karmic Debt shows that work can become self-destructive if it is allowed to be your master, or the only thing that motivates your life. This is the workaholic, whose obsessive nature destroys all of life's other rewards.

One of the best ways to learn numerology is simply by practicing on common words, names of cities and states, and, of course, people.

The following list of words offers excellent exercises in the art of numerology.

Sun is the "happy go lucky" 3, which is located smack in the middle of the word, and is also the Heart's Desire number. It has a 6 Personality and a 9 Expression. Could this possibly be a coincidence?

Lake has an 11 Expression, suggesting the connection between the subconscious and the conscious; a 6 Heart's Desire, pointing to stability; and a 5 Personality, suggesting movement.

Compare sea with the word lake!

Flower has an 11 Heart's Desire, a 6 Cornerstone, a 7 Expression, and a 5 Personality, as opposed to plant, which has a 1 Heart's Desire, an 8 Personality, and a 9 Expression.

Or try these: man, woman, tool, hammer, car, box, war, needle, wool, baby, friend, sister, and brother.

Animal names also offer great opportunities. First do tiger, lion, wolf, bear, eagle, and shark. Then do lamb, sheep, dove, dolphin, and whale.

President Bill Clinton's Chart

Let's turn now to an example of how numerology can give us insights into a public figure who will have a major impact on the world. That person is President Bill Clinton.

President Bill Clinton's birth name is William Jefferson Blythe. He was born on August 19, 1946. From these facts, we derive the following core numbers: Life Path, 11/2; Expression, 6; Heart's Desire, 11/2; Personality, 13/4; and Birth Day, 19/1.

From the perspective of numerology, President Clinton offers America an array of powerful and inspiring characteristics, as well as an unusual set of contradictions. This latter quality is due in part because he has two very different names, a birth name and a name given to him by virtue of adoption. As I mentioned in Chapter 3, the addition of a second name can focus, and even heighten, certain inherent abilities. And certainly, the name Bill Clinton does that for William Jefferson Blythe. Let's begin by looking at the numbers derived from his date of birth, that is, the Life Path, 11/2, and Birth Day number, 19/1.

The 11/2 Life Path number gives President Clinton a highly sensitive and accurate intuition. He can perceive the thoughts and feelings of others, as well as trends in society. He often responds to another person or large group of people with just the right tone, a perfect balance between understanding, compliance, and persuasion. He radiates sincerity, which can mask his intuitive awareness of what people want, and of what they want to hear. These characteristics have gotten President out of a lot of tight spots, as evidenced by his ability to overcome the difficulties that emerged when reports of infidelity and marijuana use surfaced early in his campaign for President.

The 11/2 also provides President Clinton with an open channel to his intuition, a kind of clear window into perceptions that are constantly flowing from his subconscious or intuitive self. He possesses highly developed intuitive reflexes that perform without conscious effort.

His Life Path also gives him a strong desire to work cooperatively with others, to maintain harmony, and to serve as a peacemaker. He wants to be liked by others, and, consequently, tends to be sensitive to criticism.

All of these qualities are reinforced by his 11/2 Heart's Desire, and give him a well-defined vision for America.

Something that is not reported in the popular press much, nor is it obvious to most people, is that President Bill Clinton possesses a strong and well-developed spiritual understanding. President Clinton is not much of a church-goer, and consequently this part of his nature remains a private part of his being, but his understanding of spirit is well-developed and sophisticated. Consequently, he is strongly motivated by spiritual ideals.

Balancing all this sensitivity and desire for harmony is his 19/1 Birth Day, which reveals an iron will, determination, and leadership. The 19/1 is stubborn and tends to carry great weight by itself. It sees, and sometimes even seeks out, the struggle of life, the place where it can feel its own mettle. As with his two names, the combination of 11s and 19/1 reveal President Bill Clinton's duality: sensitive, aware, subtle, and intuitive, yet strong, hard-headed, driven, and willing to stand in the face of conflict.

Sticking with William Jefferson Blythe, we see that President Clinton's Expression number is 6, showing him to be responsible, caring, service-oriented, and loyal.

The 6 and 11 like center stage, and consequently do not enjoy being outshined by other members of the cast. Add to this the influence of the 19/1, which likes to take burdens upon its own shoulders, and you have a person who is motivated by both his own sense of responsibility, as well as a powerful desire to be king of the mountain.

Moving to the 13/4, the Personality number derived from William Jefferson Blythe, we find another set of characteristics that President Clinton is widely recognized for: his attention to detail and ability to work long, hard hours. This is a hands-on President. He loves the challenges in the numbers, and the details of so many plans. The shadow of the 13/4—the Karmic Debt—is its discomfort with relaxation, peace, and vacationing. There is a strong tendency to workaholism, which gives the person with a 13/4 the security of knowing that he is being responsible and productive.

The 13/4 draws President Clinton to the small, and sometimes insignificant, details, which could have prevented him from becoming President. However, he was rescued from the petty by the name he has become identified by: Bill Clinton. That name conveys the 8 Personality, which is the visionary, the grand-scale planner, the person who transcends the details to become involved in broad and even worldwide affairs.

President Bill Clinton has the 6 Minor Heart's Desire, enhancing the already strong urge for responsibility; and the 5 Minor Expression, making him more flexible and adaptable to changing conditions. All in all, the name Bill Clinton enlarges his personality, making him a more impressive person.

Finally, William Jefferson Blythe contains all 9 numbers in his name, revealing President Clinton as a very able person. He's a people person, a musician, a lawyer, and a politician, and he possesses a vision for the country. He has the confidence and poise that arise from having a wide array of talents and abilities to draw from in virtually any situation.

Let's turn now to President Bill Clinton's progressive chart. The first thing you notice is the repetition of the 16s and 22s in his Essence Cycles. This denotes periods of isolation and uncertainty (as indicated by the Karmic Debt of 16) balanced by the powerful and very public Master number, 22. Obviously difficult periods for President Bill Clinton were ages 18 and 19, 30 and 31, and 39 and 40. Years marked by strength, personal power, and enormous influence were 20 and 21, 41, 42, and 43, 45, 46 (1992–93, when he was elected), and 47 (1993–94). However, the conclusion of 1994 marks a time of deep soul-searching, and perhaps inner doubt, for President Bill Clinton, as revealed by the return of a 16/7 Essence. Since people participate vicariously in a leader's personal drama, and vice versa, the latter part of 1994 will be a time in which America and President Bill Clinton experience some inner searching, turmoil, and doubt as to their direction and the role they play in the world. President Clinton's chart, and stretch of 22 Essences, reveal America's power and confidence on the world stage. We are the last superpower, but we also recognize that there are inherent weaknesses in our system that must eventually be dealt with. Those weaknesses will begin to emerge in more obvious ways, beginning the later months of 1994, when President Clinton and America must dig deeper for answers to our growing problems.

The single year of 16/7 Essence is followed by the 13/4 Essence, suggesting hard work and a willingness to address fundamental problems. It is a time to strengthen and rebuild the foundation. President Bill Clinton's chart reveals a highly talented and highly motivated person capable of meeting the demands of time.

In order to determine whether President Clinton will be reelected, the chart of his opponent would have to be available, which at the time of this writing, it is not. Therefore, no prediction can be made at this point. However, President Clinton's numbers suggest many years of leadership and influence ahead, indicating that his chances of reelection are quite good.

Now, meet a few of our past presidents. Richard Milhous Nixon was born January 9, 1913. A 16/7 Heart's Desire and a 19/1 Personality spell disaster for anyone in high political office. Check his cycles, and you will see that his timing was very bad. On the other hand, even those of us who are the least likely to forgive him, grudgingly admit that he seems to have attained some wisdom and respect. This man fell from grace faster and harder than any other American president. Yet now, his ideas and opinions are sought by many, and he appears regularly in the media. That is the rebirth of the 16 in all its glory.

James Earl Carter, born October 1, 1924, has two 9s among the four core numbers, and was by far the most humanitarian president in recent history. The two 5s, which are his Expression and Personality numbers (one of which carries the Karmic Debt number 14), made him too impulsive to be very effective. In addition, his 3 Karmic Lessons made him weak in domestic affairs (6), spiritual matters (7), and business/power/negotiation (8). When it comes to moral strength and genuine concern for the well-being of people (9 Life Path, 9 Heart's Desire), he was a champion among presidents. By the way, Jimmy Carter, like Bill Clinton, introduces himself with a first name that is terribly wrong in relation to the ambitions of the person.

Ronald Reagan, born February 6, 1911, with the middle name Wilson, has an 11 Life Path, 11 Personality, 2 Heart's Desire, and a 13/4 Expression. With three 11/2s among his four core numbers, the teflon label suits him to a T. The 13 Karmic Debt is common for people who continue to be extremely active and ambitious into old age, but it makes me wonder how much Ronnie enjoyed his time in the White House. The 13 is a number that pushes the person, often allowing little room for peace and quiet.

The most obvious aspect of George Herbert Walker Bush's chart is the 2 Personality. In this case, this 2 clearly explains the "wimp" factor that Bush has had to cope with. The 2 is diplomatic, tactful, and feminine. It is the power behind the throne, the silent manipulator, the peacemaker, and the one who holds back. The other core numbers, the 8 Heart's Desire and the 1 Expression, are very masculine numbers representing a hard core and an enormous drive. The 8 is business association with others, a powerful will, and a strong desire for reward. The 1 is leadership, the ability to make things happen, and a need to be on top, to be the best, to be king. In addition, George Bush has a 16/7 Life Path, and so we recognize the analytical and methodical thinker who learned to hide his emotions early in life, and to deal with facts and facts only. Of great help to Bush is his 5 Hidden Passion, which gives him the ability to change and to adapt ("read my lips"), and to be versatile and energetic.

In a nutshell, George Bush is a goal-oriented, capable, power-hungry, strong-willed person, wrapped up in a diplomat's jacket. In an article I wrote for *East-West Journal* in the spring of 1989, I predicted that George Bush would become a controversial president. This prediction was mainly based on the contradictions between his 1 Expression number and his 2 Personality number.

PROFESSIONAL NUMEROLOGY

For most readers, numerology will remain a hobby and a beneficial source of information. However, if you aspire to become a professional numerologist, you will want to practice extensively on friends, family members, co-workers, neighbors, and anyone else you can find. But keep in mind that there are responsibilities to this profession that should be taken seriously.

First and foremost, you have to accept the fact that numerology is not an exact science. It is one that is based on some 5,000 years of experience and limited research, but human beings are incredibly complex and numerology is no more than an attempt to identify and label some of the more visible aspects. There are countless variables that are too subtle and too hidden to be recognized. Therefore, it is simply not possible for a numerologist to be right 100 percent of the time. For that reason, you will have to be careful with what you say, in order to avoid harming the person who comes to you in good faith, and who may well take your words more literally than you realize. This is particularly important when you wish to explain weaknesses or shortcomings represented in a person's chart. For example, let's say that your client's chart reveals a lack of self-confidence, and that he or she compensates for that with self-indulgence, such as alcohol abuse. Instead of saying, "You lack self-confidence and you are an alcoholic," which will probably only increase your client's insecurity, and inspire him or her to reach for the bottle, you may want to point out some of the client's talents and positive characteristics. You want to motivate your client to take advantage of these talents. You want to enhance your client's confidence, and you may well decide that it would be unwise, even harmful, to mention his or her lack of confidence, saying instead: "You have much going for yourself, but you do not give yourself the credit you deserve."

Your job as a professional numerologist is to motivate, inspire, and elevate your client, as well as to offer your client insight into his or her make-up.

I believe that a numerologist's strongest asset is a true and indiscriminating love for the client. The client almost always is a person in need of guidance and support. Someone who is happy and content is much less likely to visit a numerologist as a person who is going through a difficult time. Often, the client who comes to you, and is willing to pay for a consultation, experiences pain and confusion; is perhaps even desperate. He or she is reaching out to a professional in the hope that a person with training and experience will shed some light on his or her confusion, will help them to cope, and perhaps start the healing process. You may be a stranger to the client, but you will hear intimacies that are in many cases not shared with friends or relatives. You are in a position to help and comfort. You are asked for insight and wisdom, and perhaps you will be able to offer some. But more important is the opportunity to spiritually embrace the person, to touch the heart, to replace desperation with hope, and to inspire faith where there was little left.

Numerology is a difficult, but intensely rewarding profession.

There are many areas in your life in which numerology can be beneficial. It gives you insight into your own make-up or that of someone else. It can help couples to understand each other better, which in turn stimulates tolerance for each others' peculiarities. It is an excellent guide when it's time for a career or business decision. It alerts you to turbulent times and helps you to take advantage of coming opportunities.

You will find that once you make it a habit to do the numbers on people you meet, famous people in politics or the arts, special words you encounter, names of cities, states, and countries, fictional characters in books and movies, telephone numbers, and so on, you will quickly become confident and comfortable with numerology.

The insight you can gain from numerology is relative only to your understanding of this art.

Glossary

Balance number: The balance number is the sum of the numerical value of the initials of the full name as it was given at birth.

Birth Day number: The Birth Day number represents the day of birth. This number is reduced to a single digit only when it is part of a calculation to find other numbers.

Bridge numbers: The Bridge numbers are found by subtracting one core number from another. The Bridge numbers represent the relationship between the individual core numbers.

Capstone: The Capstone is the last letter of the first name as it was given at birth.

Cardinal number: Any of the numbers 1 through 9.

Challenge numbers: The Challenge numbers are derived from the date of birth through subtraction.

Core numbers: The core numbers are the most important numbers in a numerology chart. They consist of the Life Path number, the Expression number, the Heart's Desire number, the Personality number, and, after age thirty-five, the Maturity number.

Cornerstone: The Cornerstone is the first letter of the first name as it was given at birth.

Current name (also called the short name): The current name is the name one uses to introduce oneself, including the last name. (Middle initial, titles, or extensions such as Jr. or the III are not used.)

Destiny: See Life Path.

Essence Cycle: The Essence Cycle can last from one to nine years, and is based on the combination of Transits that are in place during any given year. (*See also* Transits.)

Expression number: The Expression number is the sum of the numerical value of all the letters in the full name as it was given at birth.

First Challenge: The First Challenge is the difference between the single-digit numbers that represent the month and the day of birth.

Fourth Challenge: The Fourth Challenge is the difference between the single-digit numbers that represent the month and the year of birth.

Heart's Desire number: The Heart's Desire number, sometimes called the Soul Urge number, is the sum of the numerical value of all of the vowels in the full name as it was given at birth.

Hidden Passion number: The Hidden Passion number is the number that is represented more often than any other number in the full name, as it was given at birth. A name may reveal more than one Hidden Passion number.

Karmic Debt numbers: The Karmic Debt numbers are the numbers 13, 14, 16, and 19.

Karmic Lesson number: A Karmic Lesson number is a number that is not represented anywhere in the full name as it was given at birth. A name may reveal more than one Karmic Lesson number.

Life Path number: The Life Path number is the most important number in the chart and is based on the sum of all the digits in the date of birth.

Main Challenge: The Main Challenge is the difference between the numbers that represent the First and Second Challenge.

Master numbers: The Master numbers are the numbers 11, 22, and, in extremely rare cases, the number 33. (Note: Some numerologists believe that the numbers 44, 55, 66, 77, 88, and 99 are also Master numbers. However, the Master numbers 11, 22, and 33 form a triangle that represents potential mastery. The number 33 in the top depicts enlightenment. The numbers 44 and up have no place in this triangle, and should be reduced to single digits.)

Maturity number: The Maturity number is found by adding the Expression number to the Life Path number, and by reducing the number found to a single digit. The Maturity number comes in later in life, around age thirty-five.

Mental Transit: The Mental Transit is based on the middle name as it was given at birth, or, in case no middle name was given, on the last name as it was given at birth. *See also* Transits.

Minor Expression number: The Minor Expression number is the sum of the numerical value of all the letters in the current name, including the last name.

Minor Heart's Desire number: The Minor Heart's Desire number is the sum of the numerical value of all the vowels in the current name.

Minor Personality number: The Minor Personality number is found by adding the numerical value of all the consonants of the current name, including the last name.

Period Cycles: The Period Cycle is a long-term cycle and is based on the date of birth.

Personal Day number: The Personal Day number lasts one day. The Personal Day number is found by adding the current day to the Personal Month number.

Personal Month number: The Personal Month number lasts one month. The Personal Month number is found by adding the current month to the Personal Year number.

Personal Year number: The Personal Year number lasts one year. The Personal Year number is found by adding the month and the day of birth to the current year.

Personality number: The Personality number is found by adding the numerical value of all the consonants of the full name as it was given at birth.

Physical Transit: The Physical Transit is based on the first name as it was given at birth. *See also* Transits.

Pinnacle Cycles: The Pinnacle Cycle is a long-term cycle and is based on the date of birth.

Planes of Expression: The Planes of Expression reflect the proportions of physical, mental, emotional, and intuitive letters in the full name, as it was given at birth.

Rational Thought number: The Rational Thought number is based on the day of birth, plus the sum of the numerical value of all the letters in the first name as it was given at birth.

Second Challenge: The Second Challenge is the difference between the single digits that represent the day and the year of birth.

Short name: See Current name.

Single-digit number: (Same as Cardinal number.) Any of the numbers 1 through 9.

Soul Urge number: See Heart's Desire number.

Spiritual Transit: The Spiritual Transit is based on the last name as it was given at birth. *See also* Transits.

Subconscious Self number: The Subconscious Self number shows how many numbers are represented by the letters in the full name as it was given at birth. Or the Subconscious Self number is 9 minus the number of Karmic Lessons found in the name.

Third Challenge: See Main Challenge.

Transits: The Transits are one- to nine-year cycles based on the letters of your name.

Universal Year number: The Universal Year starts in January and ends in December. The Universal Year number is found by adding the four digits of a particular year, and then reducing to a single digit.

Master Number Guide

Master numbers are not reduced in:

- The Life Path number
- The Birth Day number
- The Expression number
- The Minor Expression number
- The Heart's Desire number
- The Minor Heart's Desire number
- The Personality number
- The Minor Personality number
- The Planes of Expression
    (Except in the Planes of Expression Emotional and Intuitive,
in which the 11 is not reduced, but the 22 is.)
- The Maturity number
- The Rational Thought number
- The Essence number
- The Period Cycles
- The Pinnacle Cycles

Master numbers are reduced (or not applicable) in:

- The Challenge numbers
- The Karmic Lessons

- The Hidden Passion number(s)
- The Subconscious Self number
- The Balance number
- The Planes of Expression Emotional 22
- The Planes of Expression Intuitive 22
- The Bridge numbers
- The Personal Year, Month, and Day numbers

About the Authors

Hans Decoz was born in Amsterdam, the Netherlands, in 1949. He attended the Academy of Fine Arts, majoring in advertising and industrial design. He traveled extensively throughout Europe, the Middle East, and Asia, and came to the United States in 1978.

Decoz has been studying numerology for over two decades. In 1988, he started Decoz Corporation, which offers computer-generated, personalized numerology charts, readings, and forecasts, which he designed and developed. Decoz Corporation has sold 20,000 numerology products to clients throughout the United States, Canada, Europe, the Middle East, Japan, Australia, and South Africa. His charts and readings can now be purchased via Decoz Corporation by dialing (713) 529-9103.

Decoz has contributed articles on numerology to numerous magazines and newspapers, including *East West Journal,* and has appeared on radio and television interview shows. He has conducted numerous workshops and lectures, and he continues to be in demand as a speaker at conventions and expositions nationwide.

Tom Monte has written eight books. He specializes in the areas of health and the environment. He is the author of *The Way of Hope,* published by Warner Books in September 1989 and co-author of two books with Dr. Anthony Sattilaro, the first entitled *Recalled By Life: The Story of My Recovery from Cancer* and the second called *Living Well Naturally,* both published by Houghton Mifflin, Inc. (1982 and 1984, respectively). *Recalled By Life* became a bestseller in hardback, and is now available in paperback from Avon

Books. After selling nearly 50,000 copies in hardback, *Living Well Naturally* was republished as a quality paperback by Houghton Mifflin.

Other books by Tom Monte include *Reading the Body* (Viking Press, 1991), with Waturo Ohashi; *Pritikin: The Man Who Healed America's Heart* (Rodale Press, 1987) with Nathan Pritikin's widow, Ilene; *Fighting Radiation and Chemical Pollutants With Food, Herbs, and Vitamins* (East West Health Books, 1987), written with Stephen Schechter; *30 Days: A Program to Achieve Optimal Weight Loss, Lower Cholesterol, and Prevent Serious Illness* (Japan Publications, 1991); and *Set Free: A Woman's Victory Over Eating Disorders* (Japan Publications, 1991), with Linda McGrath.

Monte's work has been published throughout the United States and Europe, including *Life* magazine, *The Saturday Evening Post, The Chicago Tribune, Runner's World, East West Journal, Paris Match,* and *London's Sunday People.*

Index